Tracks of Change

Railways and Everyday Life in Colonial India

Ritika Prasad

CAMBRIDGE
UNIVERSITY PRESS

CAMBRIDGE
UNIVERSITY PRESS

314 to 321, 3rd Floor, Plot 3, Splendor Forum, Jasola District Centre, New Delhi 110025, India

Cambridge University Press is part of the University of Cambridge.

It furthers the University's mission by disseminating knowledge in the pursuit of education, learning and research at the highest international levels of excellence.

www.cambridge.org
Information on this title: www.cambridge.org/9781107084216

First published 2015
Reprint 2016, 2022
Printed in India by Avantika Printers Pvt. Ltd.

A catalogue record for this publication is available from the British Library

Library of Congress Cataloging-in-Publication Data
Prasad, Ritika, 1975-
Tracks of change : railways and everyday life in colonial India / Ritika Prasad.
pages cm
Summary: "Discusses how railway technology, travel, and infrastructure became increasingly and inextricably woven with everyday life in colonial South Asia, how people negotiated this increasing presence of railways in their lives, and how the ensuing processes has materially shaped South Asia's present"-- Provided by publisher.
Includes bibliographical references and index.
ISBN 978-1-107-08421-6 (hardback)
1. Railroads--Social aspects--India--History. 2. Railroad travel--Social aspects--India--History. 3. Social change--India--History. 4. India--Social life and customs. 5. India--Social conditions. 6. India--History--British occupation, 1765-1947. I. Title.
HE3298.P73 2015
385.0954'09034--dc23
2014044740

ISBN 978-1-107-08421-6 Hardback

For my grandparents

Kanti Prasad, Kumar Nandan Prasad,
Rajeshwari Prasad, and Sumitra Prasad

who lived many of the experiences that I write of here.

Contents

List of Tables and Figures

Tables

Figures

Acknowledgements

It is impossible for me to adequately thank either Vinay Lal or David Warren Sabean. Listening to Vinay's vivid description of the relationship between the growth of railways and the spread of hill stations was what first piqued my interest in the subject. Since then, as the project has grown and changed, he has patiently read (and re-read) innumerable drafts, his uncompromising eye catching every misplaced comma no less than every unwieldy argument. Right from the start, David understood my project much better than I did. Answering his many questions (increasingly difficult!) was critical to my understanding what it means to be a historian and to developing much of the intellectual spine of this book. Both Vinay and David have challenged me unceasingly, while being generous to a fault—I am singularly privileged to be able to learn from them.

Over the years, many have enriched this project. I have long and abiding debts to David Baker and Laurence Brockliss, who first taught me what it is to think historically. At UCLA, where I started my research, Michael Salman and Aamir Mufti were vital to my developing a jumble of ideas into a coherent research project. Ever since a serendipitous meeting in the India Office reading room, Ian Kerr has kindly shared with me his wealth of knowledge about India's railway history. John David Smith and Jerry Davila have patiently smoothed over for me the endless anxieties that accompany a first book, never balking at the demands that I made on their time. Lisa Mitchell, Leo Coleman, and David Johnson have offered me much by way of ideas and critique, as well as by sharing their own research with me. Geraldine Forbes has pointed me towards vital questions and resources, David Gilmartin has generously made time to comment on large parts of the manuscript, and Thomas Rogers' incisive critique has alerted me to many a problem and possibility. John Cox, Gabriel Piterberg, and Jurgen Buchenau read and commented on several versions of the Introduction. I am equally grateful to the four reviewers for Cambridge University Press, whose critiques and suggestions have helped me hone in on vital threads in the manuscript.

I have been lucky to have had sustained institutional support. The History Department at UCLA provided me a host of opportunities for exacting discussion as well as funding for several years of research. At UNC Charlotte I am surrounded by colleagues who provide as much conviviality as they do encouragement and intellectual engagement. The colloquiums and research forums at both places have been vital to the critical feedback that I have received. I am most grateful to UNC Charlotte for a Faculty Research Grant and a research leave in 2011–12: together, these provided me with crucial time and funding to complete research and writing for this manuscript. I am also grateful to the incredibly knowledgeable archivists and staff at the National Archives (Delhi), the Railway Museum Archive (Delhi), the Nehru Memorial Museum and Library (Delhi), and the India Office Records Room in the British Library (London) for helping me navigate each of these archives.

Many of my friends have been drawn into this manuscript. Yogesh Patel practically handed over to me his flat in London, allowing me the luxury of months of uninterrupted research there. Jillian Tullis, Amanda Pipkin, David Mozina, Oscar Lansen, Bill Jeffers, Karen Cox, and Devika Bordia have read draft after draft, never complaining about having had to learn so much more about railways than they could possibly want to know. Without Ayesha Seth, the sketches that accompany Chapter 3 would most likely have remained incomprehensible squiggles. Their affection and humour has kept me sane during intense stretches of writing and revising, as has their insistence that the manuscript would not vapourize if I left it alone for a few hours.

My largest debts are to my family. As much as he has gamely dug up obscure case references for me, my brother Anoopam Prasad took it upon himself to remind me that there was so much more to Delhi than the archives. Buddy's insistence on walks, belly rubs, and tug-of-war never failed to put things in their proper perspective. From shuttling me to archives to shielding me from the fallout of various misadventures, my parents Mukesh and Purnima Prasad remain a bulwark—this book is as much theirs as it is mine.

List of Abbreviations

BBCI	Bombay, Baroda, and Central Indian Railway
BLR	Barsi Light Railway
BNR	Bengal–Nagpur Railway
BNWR	Bengal and North-Western Railway
BR	Burma Railway
D-U-K	Delhi-Umballa-Kalka Railway
EBR	Eastern Bengal Railway
EBSR	Eastern Bengal State Railway
EIR	East Indian Railway
GIPR	Great Indian Peninsular Railway
IMR	Indian Midland Railway
MR	Madras Railway
MSMR	Madras and Southern Mahratta Railway
NGSR	Nizam's Guaranteed State Railway
NWR	North-Western Railway
O&RR	Oudh & Rohilkund Railway
PNR	Punjab Northern Railway
R&K	Rohilkund & Kumaon Railway
RMR	Rajputana–Malwa Railway
SIR	South Indian Railway
SPDR	Sind, Punjab, and Delhi Railway
SMR	Southern Mahratta Railway

Introduction

On 18 June 1920, cultivators in the Chai and Fakria areas of Bhagalpur congregated in vast numbers at Jhanjhara. Aggrieved and desperate, they stressed how in the last few years the high and poorly drained embankments of the Bengal and North-Western Railway had converted the regular and seasonable floods that occurred in the area into catastrophic ones. In 1917, the Ganges flood had breached the railway line at Mansi and Mahadeopur Ghat stations and left several villages submerged in six to nine feet of water. As a result, 'hundreds of lives' were lost, cattle died, and property was destroyed. Despite repeated appeals, little had been done to increase the inadequate waterways provided in railway embankments.[1]

Roughly at the same time but hundreds of miles west, a shopkeeper in Gujranwala was hoping that railway timetables would help alibi him against charges of treason.[2] Under section 121 of the Indian Penal Code, a martial law tribunal had accused Jagannath of fomenting agitation and inciting violence in the town between 12 and 14 April 1919. In his defence, Jagannath pointed out that it was impossible for him to have committed the crimes that he was being accused of for he had left Gujranwala on 12 April by the 5 p.m. train

---

[1] Chai and Fakria Parganas Combined Tenants' Conference, 18 June 1920, no. IP-3 of 1919, PWD: Railway: A, Bihar and Orissa Prog., IOR.P/10744, British Library (BL), London.

[2] M.K. Gandhi, 'Jagannath's Case,' *Young India*, 30 July 1919, reproduced in M.K. Gandhi, *Law and the Lawyers*, compiled and edited by S.B. Kher (Ahmedabad: Navjivan, 1962), 170–74.

en route to Kathiawar. Further, railway timetables unequivocally proved that he could not have been physically present in Gujranwala after 6 p.m. on 13 April. The *foujdar* of Dhoraji could testify to his being present there on 16 April and even the fastest train from Delhi took 44 hours to reach Dhoraji.

At first glance, much distinguishes these two accounts from each other. One details the distress engendered by unseasonable flooding in Bhagalpur while the other recounts the legal travails of a shopkeeper from Gujranwala. Yet these two experiences are, in fact, part of the same historical story: one that explores how railway travel, technology, and infrastructure became palpably present in the everyday lives of Indians. Of course, neither Bhagalpur's peasants nor Jagannath were the first in colonial India to experience the increasing presence of railways in their lives; by the time we encounter them railways had become quite ubiquitous. Figures for 1919–20 show that in that single assessment year alone, 520 million passengers travelled across a railway network stretching to more than 36,000 miles.[3] The significance of these numbers is heightened by the fact that the 1921 census estimated India's population at 318 million.[4] It is equally true that neither railways nor railway travel spread either instantly or evenly across the country. In 1854, the first year that railways were open to passengers, only 0.5 million people travelled on the limited 35 miles of track open, all of it concentrated in Bombay Presidency.[5] However, both the number of railway passengers and the extent of country covered by railways grew continuously in the 1860s and, from the 1870s onwards, quite remarkably. By 1875, the length of track had expanded to over 6,500 miles and the annual number of passengers had increased to 26 million.[6] By 1900, these same numbers had increased exponentially to around 25,000 miles and 175 million passengers, respectively.[7]

These figures suggest that from the mid- to late-nineteenth century onwards, increasing numbers of Indians felt the ever-increasing presence of

---

[3] *Statistical Abstract Relating to British India from 1910–11 to 1919–20* (London: HMSO, 1922), 138–44.

[4] Ibid., 252 (Appendix D—Population Census of 1921).

[5] *Statistical Abstract Relating to British India from 1840 to 1865* (London: HMSO, 1867), 58.

[6] *Statistical Abstract Relating to British India from 1867/8 to 1876/7* (London: HMSO, 1878), 88–90.

[7] *Statistical Abstract Relating to British India from 1894–95 to 1903–04* (London: HMSO, 1905), 138–40.

railways in their lives. Further, that like millions of people across the globe, they were gradually but inexorably compelled to negotiate the substantial transformations being wrought by this new technology. Passengers were the most immediately and visibly affected but they were not the only ones. Even at a glance, railway tracks, embankments, and crossings reshaped familiar landscapes; railway construction was increasingly correlated with miasma and ill-health; towns and villages alongside well-frequented railway lines began to be seen as particularly susceptible to epidemic contagion; train timetables announced new formats of organizing and comprehending both railway and civil time; and railway stations became the foci of popular politics and dissent as much as spaces for commerce and exchange.

In this context, this book asks how railway technology, travel, and infrastructure became increasingly and inextricably woven with everyday life in colonial India, how people negotiated this increasing presence of railways in their lives, and how the ensuing processes of adaptation, contestation, and accommodation have materially shaped India's history. In colonial India, railways became integral to how inordinate numbers concretely experienced many of the historical abstractions shaping their contemporary world, specifically the intrusion of a new and alien technology structured through the demands of capitalist expansion and imperial dominance. However, even as millions found it impossible to ignore the increasing presence of railways, they also sought to inhabit the ensuing changes in ways that accommodated their specific needs. This was as true of a cultivator who destroyed a railway embankment that trapped rainwater and flooded crops, as of the shopkeeper who tried to used railway timetables to establish a legal alibi; as true of the passenger avoiding medical inspection by alighting a few miles ahead of her destination, as of the one who gained access to a racially exclusive retiring room by donning a hat and changing his name from Jnanamuttu to John Matthew. Consequently, everyday life became a space of daily and continuous negotiation between people and the new technology that permeated their lives. It was where popular needs, actions, and experiences engaged with the structural power of technology and where colonial society shaped its historical present, both individually and collectively.

In arguing for the importance of railways in people's lives, questions of continuity and change are important. First, imperial claims notwithstanding, railways did not introduce travel in India. A range of scholarship has established that varied networks of mobility and patterns of circulation existed in precolonial India, not only before railways but also well before any of the massive communication projects undertaken by the colonial state.[8] Second, scholars looking at the nineteenth century have emphasized how railways should be situated 'amidst the existing patterns and networks of circulation in which the role of roads and ferries was crucial.'[9] Some emphasize the complementarity of multiple modes of travel and transport—often in the same journey—while others stress the competition among these. Thus, in his study of nineteenth-century Awadh, Robert Varady demonstrates the competition that roads posed to the railway line that opened in 1867, not only in relation to passengers but also merchandise and livestock; in contrast, Ravi Ahuja describes how the 'transport revolution' of railways and steamships 'superimposed itself upon older patterns of land and water transport, rather than superseding them altogether,' while Nitin Sinha shows the intertwining of travel mechanisms when discussing how colonial-administrative practices of touring 'used a variety of means of transport—horses, palanquins, boats, steamships and not least railways.'[10]

Recognizing such continuities is important to historicizing communication patterns in colonial India: as scholars have cautioned, the history of transport in the nineteenth century is not simply the history of railways.[11] In many areas, railway links were only completed in the closing decades of the century; even where railways were built earlier, they became part of existing networks of

---

[8] Kumkum Chatterjee writes that while the 'Bengali middle-class' travelled for multiple reasons, 'pilgrimage was probably the motive for long-distance, cross regional travel inside India.' 'Discovering India: Travel, History and Identity in Late-Nineteenth and Early Twentieth Century India,' in Daud Ali, ed., *Invoking the Past: The Uses of History in South Asia* (Delhi: Oxford University Press, 1999), 197. In contrast, discussing eastern India, Nitin Sinha argues that the Company-state was 'well aware of' a diverse group of mobile people and groups who were not travelling for purposes of pilgrimage. *Communication and Colonialism in Eastern India, Bihar: 1760s–1880s* (London and New York: Anthem, 2012). For a discussion of circulation networks between 1750 and 1950 see Claude Markovitz, Jacques Pouchepadass, and Sanjay Subrahmanyam, eds., *Society and Circulation: Mobile People and Itinerant Cultures in South Asia, 1750–1950* (Delhi: Permanent Black, 2003). Ravi Ahuja discusses conceptual differences between mobility and circulation in his *Pathways of Empire: Circulation, Public Works and Social Space in Colonial Orissa, c. 1780–1914* (Hyderabad: Orient BlackSwan, 2009), 69–74.

[9] Ahuja, *Pathways of Empire*, 5, 39; Sinha, *Communication and Colonialism*, xx–xxi.

[10] Robert Varady, Rail and Road Transport in Nineteenth Century Awadh: Competition in a North Indian Province, unpublished PhD. dissertation, University of Arizona, 1981, quotes on 73–75; Ahuja, *Pathways of Empire*, 39; Sinha, *Communication and Colonialism*, xx–xxi, xxx, Chapter 3.

[11] Ahuja, *Pathways of Empire*, 6.

communication. At the same time, it is equally vital to delineate the increasing importance of railways both in and to people's lives. Thus, even as he describes how roads competed with railways in Awadh, Varady also documents that in the 20 years after the railway line opened, its earnings increased 'roughly thirty-fold from £22,000 to nearly £665,000.'[12] Similarly, discussing eastern India, Sinha recognizes that: 'Undeniably, from the 1860s a stable and clear policy was evolving that kept railways in the centre of the emerging communications grid, followed by four types or categories of roads, devised to connect the "interiors" with the nodes of railway communication.'[13] The disproportionate focus on developing railways is also documented in Ahuja's study of colonial Orissa, where he points out that while government expenditure on roads was estimated at £1.5 million per year in the three decades before 1889, the capital expenditure on railways 'amounted to an annual average of almost £4 million between 1849–50 and 1878-79.'[14] Even as they document the colonial state's increasing interest in railway infrastructure, the figures also suggest the growing *material* presence of railways in colonial India and in the lives of its population.

Railways and the everyday

As Indians embraced the speed of railway transport in numbers far beyond what colonial authorities had expected, the daily details and routines of being passengers became integral to simultaneously homogenizing and stratifying social relations in colonial society. Nearly 90 per cent of Indians could afford only the third or lowest class of travel, whose discomforts and indignities exposed them collectively to the intertwined structures of capitalist profit, colonial control, and state paternalism that determined the concrete shape of technological change on the ground. Passenger experiences certainly differed, for railway companies varied in size, capital outlay, the combination of private and state ownership through which each was controlled, and the local conditions under which lines operated. However, railway policy and law were centrally constituted and, differences notwithstanding, significant aspects of third-class travel remain comparable.

---

[12] Varady, Rail and Road Transport in Nineteenth Century Awadh, 73–75.

[13] Sinha, *Communication and Colonialism*, xxxiv.

[14] Ahuja, *Pathways of Empire*, 96–97. Further that between 1880–81 and 1897–98, investment in railways was Rs 1,925 million, 'as opposed to the Rs 988 million in roads and building' (97).

Chapter 1 explores those conditions that defined everyday travel for ordinary Indians across region and railway line: the limited sitting space and rampant overcrowding that characterized third-class travel; the discomfort generated by the fact that, until the early 1900s, hardly any third-class carriages were provided with lavatories; the inability of third-class passengers to leave their carriages at intervening stops, whether to use the facilities or to procure food and water; and the use of insanitary goods wagons to transport people, many of whom had paid for third-class tickets. Such routine discomforts and indignities, especially when shared across regions and continuing across decades, meant that for large numbers of Indians negotiating technological change and negotiating colonialism often resided in the *same* experience of third-class travel. Railway and state officials were adamant that such discomfort did not result from any structural paucity of amenities but instead that it was caused by the physiological and psychological 'peculiarities' of third-class passengers themselves. Thus, despite repeated complaints and appeals, many of these conditions persisted. At the same time, the collective demographic strength of third-class passengers made them a critical political constituency whom neither the colonial state nor the emerging nationalist one could afford to ignore.

While shared conditions—and difficulties—created a distinct affinity among third-class passengers, the aggregation of people in railway space generated unprecedented opportunities for proximity and contact. Chapter 2 examines how anxiety about unregulated proximity, whether in railway compartments and carriages or in retiring and refreshment rooms, generated minute conversations about inclusion and exclusion: who could or could not sit next to whom; whose bodies were not permitted to come into contact with whose; which railway spaces would be reserved for which groups of people; who would eat where, who would serve them, and what food would they be served. Such conversations sparked demands for exclusive reserved spaces that were justified through a mobile and layered set of arguments: combining social and religious proscriptions on physical contact with narratives of hygiene and sanitation as well as with claims of privilege premised on wealth and status. Colonial officials and railway functionaries were quite sympathetic to demands that food, water, and spaces of commensality be organized around caste and religious difference. However, they were less amenable to demands that railway carriages be similarly differentiated, dismissing this as being logistically unviable (while using the very fact that such demands existed to justify racially-based privilege in railway spaces). Irrespective of whether exclusionary demands were aimed at maintaining a privileged position in colonial society or at securing creature comforts during railway travel, the fractious public conversations and legal confrontations that ensued from them compelled millions of railway passengers—and hence colonial society at large—to grapple with fundamental questions about inclusion and exclusion on a daily basis.

After exploring how daily routines of railway travel affected people, the next three chapters examine how the process of building and coordinating India's vast railway network changed the everyday environment in colonial India. Not many could remain insensible to such changes: even if one never boarded a train, one was faced with vastly altered landscapes, new forms of measuring, organizing, and scheduling time, and swiftly changing channels through which contagion now spread. Those whose property had been commandeered for railway construction—from surveys to preparing the permanent way, as well as allied activities like brick making or housing workmen—were affected before railway travel actually materialized. As more and more of the permanent way was laid, people across the country found their physical surroundings altered by thousands of miles of track, interspersed with signals, crossings, gates, bridges, and embankments. Neither were these changes only visual. Instead, as Chapter 3 argues, structures like railway embankments had a material impact on people's lives and livelihoods. Similar to other parts of the world, railway companies in India utilized embankments as a cost-effective mechanism for dealing with substantial changes in gradient as well as for laying tracks across low-lying, deltaic areas with uneven terrain. However, problems arose when railway companies built high embankments without providing adequate drainage outlets for the rain and floodwater that these structures trapped. The height of the embankment blocked old drainage patterns without providing new ones and converted seasonable flooding that used to be beneficial for cultivation into calamitous events that destroyed lives, crops, and property. Facing repeated losses, many sought redress; more often than not, however, they found themselves marginalized by the needs of railway construction, with arguments about 'public improvement' effacing the human cost of such undertakings.

Other everyday negotiations elicited by railways were no less substantive even if some were less explicitly adversarial. Chapter 4 traces how in the half-century between 1854 and 1905 the time of a single meridian was standardized as supra-local railway time, synchronized with the time of the Greenwich meridian in England, and then deemed civil time (continuing as India's national time). Standardized railway time was spawned by the needs of coordinating safe interchange between multiple, intersecting, railway networks spread across India's longitudinal breadth. However, the fact that railway time was gradually mandated as civil (and national) time meant that it permeated the daily lives and routines of more than just railway passengers. Thus, train schedules, railway timetables, and station clocks were not merely the technical instruments that railway passengers needed on an everyday basis. Instead, they became artefacts that influenced and changed everyday understandings of time, speed, and mobility among the colonized population at large, whether these were expressed in wide-ranging demands for train schedules to better reflect people's daily routines or in nostalgic laments that the speed of railways had erased the sensory excitement of journeying on foot. Significantly, while reified ideas of colonial (and metropolitan) time-sense informed the discussions and decisions of the colonial state, the ways in which people in colonial India actually apprehended temporal standardization remained analogous to similar processes in different parts of the world.

While the speed of railway travel compressed distance, it simultaneously expanded the purview of other influences, not least that of disease. Chapter 5 examines how a widening network of trains and tracks began to be linked with the spread of contagious diseases and with facilitating the epidemic spread of cholera and plague. Epidemic outbreaks during fairs, festivals, and pilgrimages were said to be aggravated by the frequently unhygienic conditions of railway travel as well as the fact that railways substantially increased the number of people who could congregate at each event. Even those who did not travel could not ignore what trains brought—disembarking passengers were associated with the entry of contagious diseases into areas far from centres of contagion. At the same time, some among India's medical and sanitary establishment repudiated the suggestion that diseases like cholera travelled through channels of communication; significantly, however, they argued their case by correlating the timing, spread, and intensity of epidemics with the presence or absence of railway links in various areas. Meanwhile, railway infrastructure itself began to be used to contain the spread of other diseases like plague, saving the state from the commercial and financial consequences of invoking general quarantine. Instead, thousands of railway passengers faced a web of preventive surveillance, being medically examined and possibly detained, as well as having their belongings inspected, cleaned, or destroyed. Some tried to evade this intrusion, which remained severest towards third-class passengers, the poor, and the itinerant. However, the perceived success of such surveillance encouraged colonial India's medical and sanitary establishment to suggest it as a routine mechanism of control, not only over health and disease but also over popular mobility.

After examining how few could ignore the palpable changes wrought by railways in their immediate environment—physical, temporal, and epidemiological—Chapters 6 and 7 together examine how railways and railway spaces lay at the heart of military control, political action, and dissent in colonial India. Chapter 6 explores how railways were viewed as being qualitatively different from other, previous forms of military links, their potential for swift transport seen to overcome challenges not only of distance but also of disease and seasonality. The state's ensuing anxiety about protecting railway links was reflected in the increasingly severe penalties prescribed for any interference with railways; this same anxiety, however, generated space for railway sabotage as a form of both public protest and political action. In the mid- to late nineteenth century, interfering with or sabotaging railway property became a way for people not only to draw administrative attention to their immediate needs and complaints or to settle local jealousies and conflicts but also part of more organized forms of anti-colonial radicalism. However, even as railway sabotage became a mechanism to challenge imperial control, train journeys themselves became a staple part of planning and executing it, its organizers relying—much like the state itself did—on the regular, uninterrupted, and timely functioning of railways.

Moving from sabotage to mass politics, Chapter 7 explores how colonial India's trains, platforms, and stations became everyday spaces central to popular action. Nationalist elites used railways to engender mass support, physically transporting themselves and their ideas of *satygraha* across India; at the same time, railway spaces were also where popular radicalism challenged elite dictates about the content and limits of political action. Thus, while crowded train doorways, politically tense railway platforms, and burnt signal rooms certainly marked the nation reclaiming railways from imperial control, yet railway spaces were notoriously contingent, being as amenable to nationalist rituals and collections as to the making of 'rogues,' as some less than obedient *satyagrahi*s were described in an elite lexicon. To maintain control over mass action, nationalist elites sought to exclude such dissident acts from the purview of nationalism, ousting those who sabotaged railway infrastructure from the bounds of *swaraj* itself. Thus, how one deployed railways became central to distinguishing citizen from denizen, a process acutely visible in 1947–48, when railway trains became the vehicle in which millions experienced their past and future being sundered from each other.

Everyday life and the state

In exploring how people encountered, navigated, and refashioned railways, I use 'everyday' in its most colloquial sense—as a space of continuous, daily, negotiation between people and the technology that permeates their lives.[15] At the same time, the book relies upon critical insights addressing two specific concerns. The first stresses how everyday life is indispensable to retrieving as historical and political subjects those who have been deemed anonymous, silent, and subordinate. The second pertains to understanding use or 'consumption' as simultaneously productive and transgressive, encompassing a range of tactics through which people actively inhabit (or consume) the abstractions that they are confronted with, whether technology or infrastructure. Most immediately, these concerns inform much of the work done by scholars of the Subaltern School as well as those invested in the study of *Alltag* or everyday life.[16] Neither need introduction but their methodological influence is succinctly captured in Dorothee Wierling's description of *Alltag* as the domain in which people 'exercise a direct influence—via their behaviour—and on their immediate circumstances.'[17] Equally relevant is the assertion that *Alltag* 'is not limited to the so-called basic facts of human existence; it is more than the routine of daily labor; it is not just private or shaped by "small" events.'[18] On the one hand, this allows for the purview of *Alltag* to extend beyond the domain

---

[15] In his *Everyday Technology: Machines and the Making of India's Modernity* (Chicago: University of Chicago Press, 2013), David Arnold explores the 'small' everyday machines that people negotiate with on a daily basis—from bicycles to typewriters—and their importance to how Indians both understood and constituted 'modernity' in the colonial context. David Arnold and Erich deWald also stress how 'everyday technology' illuminates inner histories and local narratives. See their 'Everyday Technology in South and Southeast Asia: An Introduction,' in *Modern Asian Studies* 46, 1 (January 2012): 1–17.

In contrast, Gyan Prakash and Kevin Kruse use 'everyday' to depict 'a distinct space of routines produced and governed by modernity.' *The Spaces of the Modern City: Imaginary Politics and Everyday Life* (Princeton: Princeton University Press, 2008), 12.

[16] A significant part of the seminal work of Subaltern Studies' scholars resides in the multi-volume *Writings on South Asian History & Society* published by Oxford University Press from 1982 onwards. The emphasis on studying the everyday is discussed in Alf Ludtke, ed., *The History of Everyday Life: Reconstructing Historical Experiences and Ways of Life* (translated by William Templer, Princeton: Princeton University Press, 1995); Ben Highmore, *Everyday Life and Cultural Theory* (London: Routledge, 2002); and Michael Sheringham, *Everyday Life: Theories and Practices from Surrealism to the Present* (Oxford: Oxford University Press, 2006).

[17] Dorothee Wierling, 'The History of Everyday Life and Gender Relations: On Historical and Historiographical Relationships,' in Ludtke, *History of Everyday Life*, 150–51.

[18] Wierling, 'The History of Everyday Life,' 150.

of the individual, private, and domestic with which the category is often associated. On the other hand, it permits a conceptually broad use of the idea of transgression, including within it those acts through which people actively inhabit the large-scale technological abstractions that they routinely face and, in so doing, demonstrate 'the everyday's capacity to disrupt the systems that seek to encapsulate it.'[19]

The emphasis on transgression also underscores the extent to which people's attempts to navigate the new and alien technology of railways involved negotiating with the state. In colonial India the state not only had substantial financial investment in railway profits but also a good degree of control over mandating the nature of railway facilities. Thus, it both informed and regulated how people experienced railway travel and railway infrastructure: What kind of accommodation would be provided to which groups of passengers? To what standards of passenger comfort would railway companies be held accountable? Which of the many popular suggestions for changes and improvements would merit attention and redress? When and where would railway time become civil time? How much state protection would be afforded to railway property? Would those who interfered with it be criminalized through the legalities of malicious damage or of treason? These are just some of the questions that suggest how vital aspects of popular experience with railways technology were mediated

---

[19] Michel de Certeau, *The Practice of Everyday Life* (Berkeley: University of California Press, 1988 [1984]), 165–76. Specifically, he discusses the relationship (and conflict) between strategic use and tactical use, with the former defined (or authorized) by the producer and latter representing the manipulations of the consumer. What is of import here is how, in the act of consumption, the consumer 'invents' in texts something different from what they 'intended,' thus detaching them from their origins. De Certeau discusses such creative consumption in relation to the ascendancy of the written word in Western culture, yet his concern with 'society as text' (166–67) makes his insights relevant to broader discussions of technological change. Also, Sheringham, *Everyday Life*, 48.

De Certeau's ideas of consumption *as* production can be used to engage with Pierre Bourdieu's argument that transgressive practices ultimately, even if indirectly, bolster established structures as well as with Roy and McLeod's arguments about people and societies accepting or rejecting technology en masse. Pierre Bourdieu, *Outline of a Theory of Practice* (1977); Roy McLeod and Deepak Kumar, eds., *Technology and the Raj: Western Technology and Technical Transfer to India 1700–1947* (New Delhi: Sage, 1995), 19. They can also be correlated with Georg Simmel's explication of how people (and societies) simultaneously internalize and counter structural impositions, especially 'The Metropolis and Mental Life' (1903).

by a diverse range of state actors—at multiple levels, in various departmental bodies and organizations, embodying varied and contradictory concerns.[20]

People's everyday relationship to railway technology was not only structured through their relationship with the state but also recorded through it. Methodologically, historians of South Asia have long been concerned with how many of the historical sources that speak to the trials and tribulations of ordinary people are recorded in state-generated official documents, frequently under conditions of conflict and duress—in Shahid Amin's evocative words 'Peasants do not write, they are written about.'[21] As Ranajit Guha emphasized in his canonical study of peasant insurgency, such 'elitist' evidence—which stamps 'the interests and outlook of the rebel's enemies on every account of our peasant rebellions'— is a 'staple' of most historical writing on the colonial period.[22] Thus, speaking of courtroom records, Amin points out how historians (among others) have learned 'to comb' such state-generated documents for the voices of subaltern populations, describing these records as texts in which 'peasants cry out, dissimulate or indeed narrate.'[23] Consequently, even as they

---

[20] Without suggesting that the British-Indian colonial state and its postcolonial successor are identical, it is useful to think in terms of C.J. Fuller and John Harriss' discussion of exactly how important a role the Indian state plays in the daily lives of Indians and the range of relationships that it mediates, especially in relation to infrastructure. C.J. Fuller and John Harriss, 'For an Anthropology of the Modern Indian State,' in C.J. Fuller and Véronique Bénéï, eds., *The Everyday State and Society in Modern India* (New Delhi: Social Science Press, 2000), 1–30.

[21] Shahid Amin, *Event, Metaphor, Memory: Chauri Chaura 1922-1992* (Delhi: Oxford University Press, 1995), 1.

[22] Ranajit Guha, *Elementary Aspects of Peasant Insurgency in Colonial India* with a foreword by James Scott (Durham: Duke University Press, 1999, first published in 1983), 14. Significantly, Guha stresses that while 'folklore' can be seen as a way of combating such bias, yet this remains limited—not only in quantity but also because 'it can be elitist too.' Of course, Guha is speaking specifically in the case of peasant militancy but his point emphasizes how sources conventionally seen as more 'authentic' accounts of popular experience require the same interpretive analysis that state-generated records do (14-15).

[23] Amin, *Event, Metaphor, Memory*, 1. There are a host of studies of popular culture and of subaltern populations in western Europe that rely heavily on state-generated documents, from courtroom records to church records. Some of the well-known ones include Carlo Ginzburg's *The Cheese and the Worms: The Cosmos of a Sixteenth Century Miller* (1980); Natalie Zemon Davis' *The Return of Martin Guerre* (1983); and David Sabean's *Power in the Blood: Popular Culture and Village Discourse in Early Modern Germany* (1984). While

raise a host of interpretive concerns, state-generated records remain invaluable to studying the everyday. Further, Guha highlights the historical *relationships* that such documents allow one to recover, stating that:

> It is of course true that the reports, minutes, despatches, etc. in which policemen, soldiers, bureaucrats, landlords, usurers, and others hostile to insurgency register their sentiments amount to a representation of their will. But these documents do not get their content from that will alone, for the latter is predicated on another will—that of the insurgent.[24]

Thus, while it is indisputable that the colonial state in India collected information for its own purposes of control and classification, it is equally true that in the process it generated an overwhelming corpus of historical sources about people's everyday concerns, complaints, problems, and distress. To take an example, the literal, physical, experience of travel for many of the poorest among India's travelling public—relegated to goods vehicles during times of heavy traffic like fairs, *melas*, and pilgrimages—is found in complaints documented in official pilgrim committee reports generated by local governments under orders from the sanitary and medical establishment. Even when such complaints elicited no action, with many being written off by officials who blamed passengers for the discomforts they were forced to endure, they *do* detail the conditions of travel: long bogies, ventilated only through small *jhilmil*-patterned openings, the floors dirty and the interiors coated with the residue of sharp and flinty *kankar*, sticky jaggery, or the dust of powdered chillies.

Equally importantly, a large proportion of such state-generated records (stretching across railway, public works, home, medical, sanitary, police, judicial, and legislative proceedings) provide detailed analyses from multiple railway companies working across various regions, and dealing with questions specific to their areas. Such records are important in comparing experiential similarities and differences across regions and railway lines: for instance, how the more general problem of overcrowding in the third class became fatal in those specific areas where the summer months brought dramatically high temperatures. Equally important in plumbing the local depths of people's

---

Ginzburg and Davis' texts remain contained within the sixteenth century, Sabean's text stretches through to the beginning of the nineteenth century.

[24] Guha, *Elementary Aspects of Peasant Insurgency*, 15.

experiences are the native newspaper reports series that, while collated by the
state for its own purposes, engage extensively with local issues and concerns.
It is the local specificity available in this series that allows one, for instance,
to explore how people in different areas sought to reorganize train schedules
so that these better met their needs: from demands to change the time of the
interchange between the Delhi–Ghaziabad and Ghaziabad–Meerut trains to
that of a halt at Manakpur, or another for rescheduling the night Olavakode
train to meet the special train connecting Tirur to Calicut. Thus, while far from
an unmediated link to the everyday life of ordinary people, official documents
remain important to recovering many of their experiences.

Many such sources register another interpretive layer, for recognizing that
which Niraja Jayal has termed the 'representational mode' of colonial politics,
means recognizing how several of the concerns and demands of subaltern
populations were communicated to the state through elite mediation.[25]
Thus, while *Alltag* remains substantively concerned with the concerns of
ordinary people, especially the subaltern and marginalized, this book also
includes a discussion of how the more privileged in colonial society negotiated
with railways. Three historical considerations inform this decision. First,
subalternity was the dominant Indian experience of railway travel. While
some Indians could and did travel in the first or second classes, yet almost
90 per cent of all railway passengers in colonial India—and, consequently,
an even higher percentage of Indian passengers—travelled in the third class.
This means that many who could be included conventionally among elites
travelled in the third class. Second, the presence of railways was both broad
and deep enough to affect the entire colonized population. Thus, while elite
and privileged groups in colonial society negotiated railways with resources
different from those available to subaltern populations, yet many of the changes
that both faced remain comparable—from standardized time to the spread of
epidemic contagion, from changing landscapes to the politicization of railway
spaces. Third, in its role as one of the largest public spaces in colonial India, the
railway was, in fact, where the content of the categories of elite and subaltern

---

[25] In her discussion of the colonial 'Subject-Citizen,' she points out how imperial
perceptions of India as a society composed of disparate communities engendered a
modernist representational mode of rule in which individuals could represent these
diverse communities. Niraja Gopal Jayal, *Citizenship and Its Discontents: An Indian
History* (Boston: Harvard University Press, 2013), 39.

was negotiated. In which group should we locate those financially elite Indians who could afford to travel first class but remained excluded from first-class retiring rooms that were, in practice, reserved for European and Anglo-Indian passengers? Or, how should we understand the case of those high-caste Hindus who could only afford third-class travel but who continued to insist that they were, ritually speaking, social elites who should have segregated carriage space? That high-caste Hindus harassed 'untouchable' passengers in third-class carriages certainly highlights the discriminatory politics of elite and subaltern in railway spaces, but it also points to the fact that these self-proclaimed elites were travelling in the same space as those whom they chose to harass.

Habitation, local and global

In asking how people *inhabit* large-scale technological change, the book stresses habitation or consumption as historical production. It thus complements scholarship that assesses the impact of railway technology in colonial India through questions about capital, labour, management, and bureaucracy. Daniel Thorner's detailed explication of the process through which British investment in Indian railways was secured forms the earliest critical scholarship on the subject.[26] Subsequently, Dipesh Chakrabarty's essay on 'railway-thinking' among Bengal's commercial elites contextualized their support for railways within the range of choices presented by the colonial economy, while Ian Derbyshire's and Mukul Mukherjee's analyses of the United Provinces and Bengal respectively, focused on how railways transformed inter-market commodity flows, agricultural prices, and wages in each area.[27] The economic impact of railways continues to inform more recent debates. Tahir Andrabi and Michael Kuehlwein argue that railways played a 'surprisingly modest role'

---

[26] Daniel Thorner, *Investment in Empire: British Railway and Steam Shipping Enterprise in India 1825–1849* (Philadelphia: University of Pennsylvania Press, 1950); and *idem*, 'Capital Movement and Transportation: Great Britain and the Development of India's Railways,' *Journal of Economic History* 11, 4 (Autumn 1951): 389–402.

[27] Dipesh, Chakrabarty, 'The Colonial Context of the Bengal Renaissance: Early Railway Thinking in Bengal,' *Indian Economic Social History Review* 11 (January 1974): 192–206; Mukul Mukherjee, 'Railways and their Impact on Bengal's Economy, 1870–1920,' *Indian Economic and Social History Review* 17, 2 (1980): 191–209; Ian D. Derbyshire, 'Economic Change and the Railways in North India,' *Modern Asian Studies* 21, 3 (1987): 521–45.

in grain price convergence in British India. In contrast, analyzing the period between 1874 and 1912 through the lens of total factor productivity, Dan Bogart and Latika Chaudhary see railways as 'an important engine of growth for the Indian economy.'[28]

Questions about labour and management are equally central to railway history. The most substantive treatment remains Ian J. Kerr's discussion of the processes involved in building India's railways, especially the management and control of the vast labour force that was involved.[29] More recently, Manu Goswami and Ravi Ahuja have explicated railways within a larger colonial ideology of infrastructure and public works, while Laura Bear has penned a rich ethnographic history of India's 'railway caste,' the term designating the large numbers of Anglo-Indians for whom railway service became the single largest source of employment.[30] While Bear correlates the economic and the 'intimate' historical selves of these workers when exploring their marginalization in the narration of race and nation, Nitin Sinha examines labour politics through analyzing strikes by railway workers, especially at the large locomotive workshop at Jamalpur.[31] This complements Ian Kerr's early analysis of how, during the nineteenth century, the railway workforce used collective action to protest arrears and reductions in wages, demand higher wages, dispute supervisory practices, and complain about working

---

[28] Tahir Andrabi and Michael Kuehlwein, 'Railways and Price Convergence in British India,' *Journal of Economic History* 70, 2 (June 2010): 351–77, quote on 352; Dan Bogart and Latika Chaudhary, 'Engines of Growth: The Productivity Advance of Indian Railways, 1874–1912,' *Journal of Economic History* 73, 2 (June 2013): 339–70, quotes on 341, 358.

[29] Ian J. Kerr, *Building the Railways of the Raj* (Delhi: Oxford University Press, 1995). An overview of the subject can be found in John Hurd and Ian J. Kerr, *India's Railway History: A Research Handbook* (Leiden: Brill, 2012).

[30] For Manu Goswami, see Chapter 3 of her *Producing India: From Colonial Economy to National Space* (Chicago: University of Chicago Press, 2004), 103–31; Ahuja, *Pathways of Empire*; Laura Bear, *Lines of the Nation: Indian Railway Workers, Bureaucracy, and the Intimate Historical Self* (New York: Columbia University Press, 2007). She argues that when estimated in 1923, 'nearly half of the Anglo-Indian community was employed or associated with the railways as dependents of employees' (8–9).

[31] Nitin Sinha, 'Entering the Black Hole: Between "Mini-England" and "Smell-like Rotten Potato", the Railway-Workshop Town of Jamalpur, 1860s–1940s,' *South Asian History and Culture* 3, 3 (2012): 317–47.

conditions.[32] Smritikumar Sarkar's recent discussion of how the colonial state acquired land for the initial burst of railway construction has not only foregrounded a little explored subject but also linked it with contemporary concerns about land acquisition for public works.[33]

Lisa Mitchell's essay on the practice of pulling alarm chains to stop trains also elides the temporal divide of colonial and postcolonial, tracing the colonial genealogy of a form of political action that remains common in contemporary India.[34] Her piece also signals a way to understand the impact of railways distinct from questions of political economy, market integration, monetization, commercialization, labour, management, and bureaucracy. Mitchell is not alone. Ian Kerr's more recent work focuses on two such questions: how railways changed the nature of pilgrimage traditions in colonial India and how railways have been represented in cultural mediums.[35] Both issues have been further explored, the former in Ravi Ahuja's work on changing circulatory regimes and the latter in Marian Aguiar's literary analysis of the motile representation and signification of railway spaces.[36] In its textual focus, Aguiar's text can be paired both with Prabhjot Kumar's analysis of how railway space is configured in fictional and cinematic representations of Partition and Harriet Bury's

---

[32] Ian J. Kerr, 'Working Class Protest in 19th Century India: Example of Railway Workers,' *Economic and Political Weekly* 20, 4 (26 January 1985): PE34–PE40.

[33] Smritikumar Sarkar, 'Land Acquisition for the Railways in Bengal, 1850–62: Probing a Contemporary Problem,' *Studies in History* 26, 2 (August 2010): 103–42. Dennis Weitering's 'Sharing the Burden: Licensed Porters of Dadar Railway Station, Mumbai, and Their Search for Work, Income and Social Security,' in Ian J. Kerr, ed., *27 Down: New Departures in Indian Railway Studies* (with CD) (Delhi: Orient Longman, 2007) shifts the discussion of railway labour into a more contemporary context.

[34] Lisa Mitchell, '"To Stop Train Pull Chain": Writing Histories of Contemporary Political Practice,' *Indian Economic Social History Review* 48, 4 (2011), 469–95.

[35] Ian J. Kerr, 'Reworking a Popular Religious Practice: The Effects of Railways on Pilgrimage in 19th and 20th Century South Asia,' in *idem*, ed., *Railways in Modern India* (Delhi: Oxford University Press, 2005 [2001]), 304–27; and Ian J. Kerr 'Representation and Representations of the Railways of Colonial and Post-Colonial South Asia,' *Modern Asian Studies* 37, 2 (2003): 287–326.

[36] Ravi Ahuja, '"The Bridge-Builders": Some Notes on Railways, Pilgrimage and the British "Civilising Mission" in Colonial India,' in Harald Fischer-Tiné and Michael Mann, eds., *Colonialism as Civilizing Mission: The Case of British India* (London: Anthem Press, 2003), 195–216; Ahuja, *Pathways of Empire*; Marian Aguiar, *Tracking Modernity: India, Trains, and the Culture of Mobility* (Minneapolis: University of Minnesota Press, 2011).

suggestion that late-nineteenth century descriptions of railway journeys were vital to articulating the spatial relationship between definitions of regional and national in colonial India.[37]

Many of these works represent not only an increasing interest in understanding how railways affected social relations, political action, and cultural production, but also suggest a different historiographical impetus, moving away from questions about the theoretical potential of railways to galvanize capitalist processes and their historical failure to practically do so in colonial India.[38] From Thorner's explication of how colonialism retarded the capitalist possibilities generated by railways to Sumit Sarkar's explanation of why the 'normal multiplier effect' of railway investment was lacking in India, the 'transition narrative' (or rather its failure) has informed much of the vital scholarship on the subject.[39] Even those who disagree with such conclusions of failure do not necessarily repudiate the transition narrative itself: Derbyshire emphasized how railways opened up numerous marketing possibilities in the traditionally 'constrained' economy of the United Provinces and ensured that there were no significant regional food shortages after 1900, while Mukherjee explained how railways began to dominate as bulk-carriers in Bengal.[40]

Critiquing developmental narratives of modernization as well as the binary opposition with 'tradition' that these frequently employ, scholars like Bear, Goswami, and Aguiar have instead foregrounded interstitial groups and spaces and highlighted the extent to which the modernizing railway project was executed through processes that traditionalized Indian society and culture. Thus, Bear discusses how the Anglo-Indian railway family fused *jati* with

---

[37] Harriet Bury, 'Novel Spaces, Transitional Moments: Negotiating Text and Territory in Nineteenth-Century Hindi Travel Accounts' and Prabhjot Parmar, 'Trains of Death: Representation of Railways in Films on the Partition of India,' both in Kerr, *27 Down*. In this context, see also Sinha's discussion of the fluidity of the category of 'interior' in his *Communication and Colonialism*.

[38] Cf. Dipesh Chakrabarty's critique of developmental teleology as 'the central problematic of the study of colonial India.' *Provincializing Europe: Postcolonial Thought and Historical Difference* (Princeton: Princeton University Press, 2000).

[39] Thorner, *Investment in Empire*; Sumit Sarkar, *Modern India, 1885–1947* (Delhi: Macmillan, 1983), 37–38, 129.

[40] Mukherjee, 'Railways and their Impact' and Derbyshire, 'Economic Change and the Railways,' 525, 540–43. Similarly, in his general assessment of the colonial economy, Tirthankar Roy stressed how the inter-regional crop movements made possible by railways decreased the incidence of famine. Tirthankar Roy, *The Economic History of India: 1857–1947* (Delhi: Oxford University Press, 2000), 263–65.

'political sentiments and class sensibilities,' Goswami comments on how the liberating and levelling railway project actually ensconced prescriptive hierarchies, while Aguiar uses literary analysis to highlight the presence of counter-narratives to modernity 'within the Indian context.'[41] Cumulatively, their work critiques a developmental teleology that intertwines spatial and historical movement and it instead turns the spotlight on 'miscegenations' through which processes of modernization are articulated in colonial contexts.[42] The intervention is especially important because, to quote Alan Trachtenberg: 'Nothing else in the nineteenth century seemed as vivid and dramatic a sign of modernity as the railroad.'[43] However, even as it acutely sensitive to how modernity's abstractions are shaped under colonial compulsions, the analytic of 'colonial-modernity' continues to examine railways through somewhat normative distinctions between tradition and modernity, albeit now in relation to social forms and cultural practices rather than economic processes.[44] Further, in theory, frameworks of vernacular or hybrid recognize that everywhere a normative modernity is articulated through local specificities; in practice,

---

[41] Cf. Bernard Cohn's work on traditions of modernity. Aguiar, *Tracking Modernity*, xiii–xviii; Bear, *Lines of the Nation*, 9. Cf. Laura Bear, 'Miscegenations of Modernity: Constructing European Respectability andRace in the Indian Railway Colony, 1857–1931,' *Women's History Review* 3, 4 (1994): 531–48; Goswami, *Producing India*, 112–31.

[42] Bear, 'Miscegenations of Modernity.'

[43] Alan Trachtenberg in Wolfgang Schivelbusch's, *The Railway Journey: The Industrialization of Time and Space in the 19th Century* (Berkeley: University of California Press, 1987), xiii. A glance at the scholarship on railways confirms the preoccupation with modernity: Ian Carter, *Railways and Culture in Britain: The Epitome of Modernity*. (Manchester: Manchester University Press, 2001); Todd S. Presner, *Mobile Modernity: Germans, Jews, Trains* (New York: Columbia University Press, 2007); and Michael Beaumont and Michael Freeman, eds., *The Railway and Modernity: Time, Space and the Machine Ensemble* (Oxford: Peter Lang, 2007).

[44] Partha Chatterjee, *Our Modernity* (author's translation of Srinjan Halder Memorial Lecture, 1994) (Rotterdam/Dakar: SEPHIS and CODESRIA, 1997), 3; Gyan Prakash, *Another Reason: Science and the Imagination of Modern India* (Princeton: Princeton University Press, 1999), 201–2; Dipesh Chakrabarty, 'Witness to Suffering: Domestic Cruelty and the Birth of the Modern Subject in Bengal,' in Timothy Mitchell, ed., *Questions of Modernity*, Vol. 11 of Contradictions of Modernity (Minneapolis: University of Minnesota Press, 2000), xviii, 49–86; and David Arnold, *Science, Technology, and Medicine in Colonial India*, The New Cambridge History of India, Vol. III–5 (Cambridge: Cambridge University Press, 2000) 17.

however, the hyphenated modern frequently remains the marker of colonial contexts, distinguishing these structurally from other non-colonial (and hence non-hyphenated) ones.

While sharing many of these critical concerns, this book simultaneously frames processes of negotiating technology as a global one. Suggesting this is not to minimize historical specificity but instead to formulate it in dialogue with shared and related experiences in other parts of the world. The Indian experience with railways was indisputably specific: it would not be an exaggeration to argue that when they rode a train or encountered the railway, many Indians learned as much about the colonial-capitalist structure of the British-Indian state as they did about railway technology. Early railway construction was financed within a specific colonial guarantee of metropolitan venture capital, railway policy was buffeted between imperial commitments to profit versus 'improvement,' and conditions of travel were premised on imperial perceptions of a colonized population. Railway passengers faced discomforts endemic to systemic subordination even as their demographic strength made them a constituency increasingly important to a colonial state seeking legitimacy in the face of an emerging nationalist agenda. At the same time, several kinds of negotiations had global analogies, whether it involved the spread of suburban living spurred by railways, the introduction of supra-local standardized time, the spread of epidemic contagion, or the extensive degradation of natural habitats exploited for railway construction. What remained historically specific were not necessarily the changes and challenges themselves but instead the combination of resources and constraints through which people could navigate them.[45]

In facilitating this dialogue between local and global effects of railway technology, the lens of the everyday replaces the apocryphal colonial imagined by imperial minds with a material and historical one. It does this by demonstrating that despite technological change in the colony being premised on constructed

---

[45] To understand India's transition to a capitalist mode of production, Kerr's 1995 study on colonial labour processes not only traced how historical practices specific to railway construction in India showed real and formal dimensions of the labour process at the same work site but also stressed how this duality was 'generally present in the advance of capitalism everywhere.' Kerr, *Building the Railways*, xii–xiii, 9, 13–14, 54, 86, 126, 191–93. Chakrabarty's *Provincializing Europe* and Neil Harvey's *Uneven Development: Nature, Capital and the Production of Space* (1984) offer possible ways to engage with similar ideas.

and reified ideas of colonial 'tradition,' such imaginings could not be—and were not—always executed in practice. The case of female railway passengers is an instructive example here. Scholars have highlighted the colonial paradox that Indian women became modern railway passengers while travelling in special *zenana* carriages that were intended to replicate colonial traditions of extreme female seclusion.[46] Officials and elites at the apex of Indian society certainly insisted that respectable Indian women would use railways only if assured of heavily secluded *zenana* accommodation. Such suggestions also led some railway companies to experiment with building heavily secluded carriages. However, in most cases, constraints of cost and rolling stock dictated otherwise and *zenana* carriages never became commonplace. Thus, most Indian women continued to travel in the usual females'-only carriage, no different from those provided for women passengers in other parts of the world.[47] Eventually, some railway companies painted the word *zenana* on regular females'-only carriages (having failed to import plates of female figures that were to have designated these carriages). However, when travelling in a carriage that was specifically marked as *zenana*—and thus invoked an idea of ineluctable colonial difference—Indian women were actually travelling in a railway space that was rather global.

Similar dialogues between local and global are suggested in different parts of the book. The continuing discomfort of third-class passengers in India cannot be explained without understanding the extent to which they were seen to be 'peculiar' in comparison with passengers in England (which was the model for railway planning in India). Similarly, the discussion about standardized railroad time here cannot be understood outside of official discussions about the temporal 'irrationality' of Indians. At the same time, popular reactions to temporal standardization in India remain analogous to those in other places where local time was replaced with supra-local time and civil time synchronized with railroad time. It was not simply in India that railway embankments provided a cost-effective engineering strategy for building railways across uneven terrain; however, when poorly built embankments wreaked havoc, a colonial bureaucracy privileged the interests of railway companies over those of cultivators. India's medical and sanitary establishment could hardly analyze the relationship between spreading railways and increasing epidemics outside

---

[46] Bear, *Lines of the Nation*, 12, 36–62; Goswami, *Producing India*, 104, 117.

[47] Ritika Prasad, 'Smoke and Mirrors: Women and Railway Travel in Colonial South Asia,' *South Asian History and Culture* 3, 1 (January 2012): 26–46.

of the international discussions on the subject. However, hesitant to disrupt trade, a colonial state officially supported non-contagionism in relation to diseases like cholera well after contagionist views had prevailed globally. Neither can one ignore the fact that while railways were seen everywhere as invaluable for the speed with which they could concentrate armies, in India their value was seen as exponentially greater for reasons specific to terrain, climate, and epidemic history. Thus, even as it remains definitively bound up with the material history of colonial India, the book relates local specificities to global similarities; simultaneously, it argues that understanding how railways transformed people's lives in colonial India offers important cues for understanding how this technology transformed everyday life everywhere. It is both a local story of global negotiations and a global story of local negotiations.

The Nature of the Beast?
An Elementary Logic for Third-Class Travel

The people of India were unlikely to be railway passengers. So concluded the East India Company's Court of Directors in 1845, when faced with the first commercial proposal for building railways in colonial India.[1] Arguing that India's population had been rendered immobile by poverty, a landscape of isolated habitations, and religious restrictions, the Court suggested that railway companies seek most of their profit here by transporting merchandise and livestock rather than people. Pointing to existing circuits of circulation and mobility, some interlocutors disagreed, arguing that railways would, in fact, attract passengers.[2] However, for purposes of early railway planning, it was the Court's view that prevailed.

The Court's expectations notwithstanding, railway travel became rather popular. Though the increase in passengers was quite startling from the 1870s onwards, railways attracted people right from the start. Half a million

---

[1] Horace Bell, *Railway Policy in India* (London: Rivington Percival, 1894), 4.

[2] See W.P. Andrews, *Indian Railways and Their Probably Results* (London: T.C. Newby, 1848 [1846]), 34–38. For discussions of patterns of mobility in India, both precolonial and pre-railways, see Chatterjee 'Discovering India,' and Sinha, *Communication and Colonialism* (he also shows how the colonial state resorted to the same metaphor of native immobility when discussing roads, 32); Ahuja, *Pathways of Empire*; and Markovitz, Pouchepadass, and Subrahmanyam, *Society and Circulation*.

travelled in the opening year—1853–54—even though only 35 miles of track was open at the time.[3] Despite the disruption in railway construction during 1857–59, the number of passengers continued to grow. The 3.89 million who travelled in 1860 represented a 680 per cent increase over 1854.[4] In 1870, by which time the colonial state had begun to involve itself directly in railway construction—while continuing to support and subsidize companies like the East Indian Railway (EIR) and the Great Indian Peninsular Railway (GIPR)—18.22 million passengers travelled across more than 4,500 miles of track.[5] Over the next three decades, passenger figures catapulted, aided by the substantial expansion in the size of the railway network. In 1900, more than 175 million passengers traversed the roughly 25,000 miles of track open by then.[6] By 1911, annual passenger traffic was over 389 million; statistically speaking, this meant that each person comprising India's population of 315 million was a railway passenger at least once that year (Figures 1.1 and 1.2).[7]

The growth indicated in these figures is significant. Even more important is that almost 90 per cent of these passengers travelled in the third class, generally the lowest class of railway travel available across the country. Further, third-class traffic was comprised overwhelmingly of Indians—'native passengers' to use the historical nomenclature. The limited exception would be small groups of 'poor whites,' the label being used to designate pauperized elements among domiciled Europeans and Eurasians.[8] Conditions in the third class thus defined everyday railway travel for the overwhelming bulk of the colonial population.

---

[3] *Statistical Abstract Relating to British India from 1840 to 1865*, 58.

[4] Ibid., 58–59.

[5] *Statistical Abstract Relating to British India from 1867/8 to 1876/7*, 89–90. This fixes mean mileage in 1870 at 4,586, while Morris D. Morris and Clyde B. Dudley list it as 4,771 route miles and 5,367 total running miles in 'Selected Railway Statistics for the Indian Subcontinent, 1853–1946–47,' in *Artha Vijana* XVIII, 3 (September 1975): 1-150, figures on 13.

[6] *Statistical Abstract Relating to British India from 1894–95 to 1903–04*, 138.

[7] *Statistical Abstract Relating to British India from 1903–04 to 1912–13* (London: HMSO, 1915), 136; E.A. Gait, *Census of India, 1911*, volume I: India, part I: Report (Calcutta: Superintendent of Government Printing, 1913), 85.

[8] Satoshi Mituzani estimates that one in six was destitute. *The Meaning of White: Race, Class, and the 'Domiciled Community' in British India, 1858–1930* (New York: Oxford University Press, 2011), 10–11, 86. This was despite the fact that railway companies consistently hired domiciled Europeans and Eurasians to upper-level subordinate positions. In 1923 'nearly half of the Anglo-Indian community' was employed or associated with railways as dependents of employees. Bear, *Lines of the Nation*, 9.

Figure 1.1. Growth in Passenger Traffic (in millions).

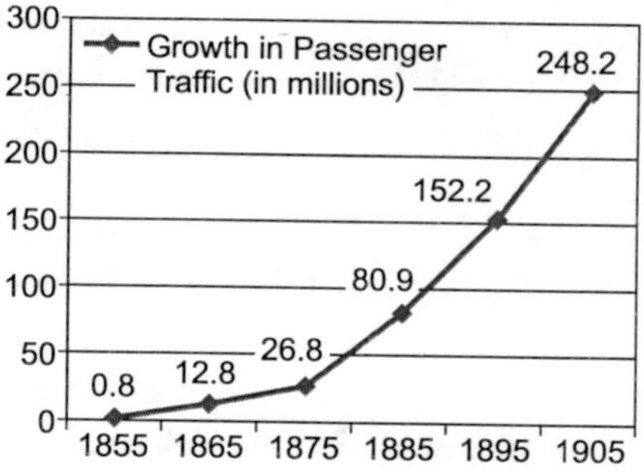

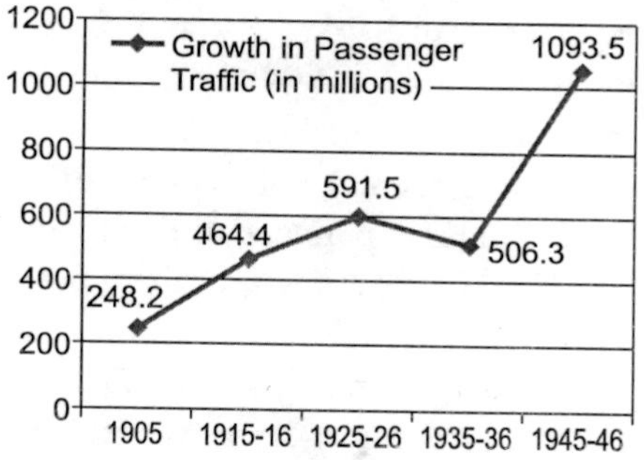

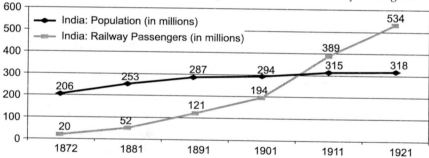

Source: Tabulated from data in *Statistical Abstract Relating to British India: from 1840 to 1865* (London: HMSO, 1867), 58–59; *from 1867/8 to 1876/7* (London: HMSO, 1878), 90; *from 1876/7 to 1885/6* (London: HMSO, 1887), 178; *from 1885–86 to 1894–95* (London: HMSO, 1896), 161; *from 1903–04 to 1912–13* (London: HMSO, 1915), 136; *from 1910–11 to 1919–20* (London: HMSO, 1922), 138; and Morris D. Morris and Clyde B. Dudley, 'Selected Railway Statistics for the Indian Subcontinent, 1853–1946–47,' in *Artha Vijana* XVIII, 3 (September 1975): 1–150, figures on 33–37 (double counted series).

Figure 1.2. Growth in Population Compared to Growth of Railway Passengers.

Sources: Tabulated from data in *Statistical Abstract Relating to British India: from 1867/8 to 1876/7* (London: HMSO, 1878), 90; *from 1876/7 to 1885/6* (London: HMSO, 1887), 6, 178; *from 1885–86 to 1894–95* (London: HMSO, 1896), 161; *from 1894–95 to 1903–04* (London: HMSO, 1905), 138; *from 1903–04 to 1912–13* (London: HMSO, 1915), 136; and Morris D. Morris and Clyde B. Dudley, 'Selected Railway Statistics for the Indian Subcontinent,' 1853–1946–47,' in *Artha Vijana* XVIII, 3 (September 1975): 1–150, figures on 35; *East Indies Census: General Report on the Census of India, 1891* (London: HMSO, 1893), 22; H.H. Risley and E.A. Gait, *Census of India, 1901*, volume IA: India, part II: Tables (Calcutta: Superintendent of Government Printing, 1903), 3; E.A. Gait, *Census of India, 1911*, volume I: India, part II: Tables (Calcutta: Superintendent of Government Printing, 1913), 3; J.T. Martin, *Census of India, 1921*, volume I: India, part II: Tables (Calcutta: Superintendent of Government Printing, 1923), 3; http://censusindia.gov.in/Census_And_You/old_report/census_1921.html.

Its spaces brought them together, publicly, in unprecedented numbers and its structural discomforts and routine indignities created a shared body of knowledge, not only about the details of railway travel but also of the extent to which their practical experience of technological change was mediated through an ideology of colonial difference.[9]

Passenger experience was not identical across the country. While railway companies varied in size, capital outlay, the combination of private and state ownership through which each was controlled, and the local conditions under which each operated, yet railway policy and law were centrally constituted. Equally importantly, aspects of third-class travel remained comparable across region and railway line. Most prominent was the limited space provided to third-class passengers and the rampant overcrowding that defined their railway experience. Equally important was the fact that, until the early 1900s, hardly any third-class carriages had lavatories. This was particularly difficult given the inability of third-class passengers to leave their carriages at intervening stops, whether to use the facilities or to procure food and water. Equally significant was the use of insanitary goods wagons to transport people who had paid for third-class tickets. Many of these conditions stemmed from the structure of early railway planning, especially a colonial belief that Indians would not take up railway travel. However, a host of railway functionaries and state officials continued to insist that such discomfort was caused by physiological and psychological 'peculiarities' attributable to 'native' passengers: their purportedly inexplicable instinct and preferences, supposed incapacity for rational thought, and lack of formal education.

Did conditions in the third class remain unchanged, unmitigated, and uncontested across almost a century? The number of third-class passengers certainly continued to grow. However, early commentators were adamant that this was *despite* the discomfort experienced. Thus, a bitterly critical piece in Allahabad's *Nur-ul-Absar* insisted that 'excepting the speed of a railway journey, the Natives of India are never heard to speak in favour of this.'[10] Discursively, the practice of attributing passenger discomfort to native 'peculiarity' continued through the colonial period. However, it could not stem the increasing tempo of demands to improve conditions in the third-class. Local newspapers played a

---

[9] Cf. Partha Chatterjee's discussion of the 'rule of colonial difference' in his *Nation and Its Fragments: Colonial and Postcolonial Histories* (Princeton: Princeton University Press, 1993), 16–18.

[10] *Nur-ul-Absar* (Allahabad), 15 August 1872, in Native Newspaper Reports (henceforth NNR): Punjab, Northwest Provinces (NWP), Oudh, and Central Provinces (CP).

key role in publicizing many of these demands, their rather public descriptions gaining the attention of a colonial state increasing its surveillance of public opinion.[11] On occasion, third-class passengers wrote in to railway companies as well as to state functionaries, from district collectors to the viceroy. Frequently, they spoke not only for themselves but also on behalf of a wider constituency of passengers, urging officials to remember their *duty* to them. Other critiques were penned by emerging nationalist elites, both provincial and national. Seeking the right to represent the national body, they stressed how conditions in the third class demonstrated the colonial state's inability to protect the welfare of Indians.

This stream of newspaper articles, letters, and petitions undoubtedly represents a systematic attempt across the decades to alleviate the conditions in which third-class passengers travelled. However, it also raises the question of whether the average third-class passenger was able to negotiate better conditions of travel. In a conventional sense, individual negotiations remained somewhat limited; however, the collective strength of third-class passengers gave them a substantial negotiating capacity. Thus, improving conditions in the third class became an important claim to representational power for both the colonial state and those challenging its legitimacy—this was not altogether surprising given that the vast body of third-class passengers was becoming increasingly isomorphic with an emerging body of potential citizens. The use of the term citizen here is not intended to elide the obvious contradictions of citizenship in a colony or the fact that only limited groups could inhabit even the limited and anomalous category of subject-citizen.[12] The recurrence of the language of duty signals this fact amply. Instead, the term suggests ways in which ordinary third-class passengers could and did *collectively* exercise influence: by travelling in large numbers, by making up the backbone of passenger traffic and receipts, and by becoming a group that political elites— whether colonial or national—could no longer ignore.

Did the critiques and suggestions bear fruit? Unevenly, it would seem. State officials and private railway companies had never been completely in agreement over the amenities (or lack of) for third-class passengers. The colonial state was obviously committed to profit, especially owing to the early terms of guarantee.

---

[11] C.A. Bayly discusses post-Rebellion surveillance of print in the epilogue to *Empire and Information: Intelligence Gathering and Social Communication in India, 1780–1870* (Cambridge: Cambridge University Press, 1996).

[12] Cf. Jayal, 'The Subject-Citizen: A Colonial Anomaly,' in her *Citizenship and its Discontents*, especially 39–48.

However, some of its functionaries also deployed the language of duty to suggest at least some modicum of comfort for the expanding numbers who comprised third-class passengers. This was intended to deflect critiques as well as to show that a colonial state could, in fact, alleviate the distress of its subjects. However, even when it wished to intervene, the state could not always enforce its statutory, administrative, or legal authority. Specific railway companies challenged some orders as financially unviable and others as impractical, while simply ignoring others. Further, the state itself did not speak in one voice. On several occasions, officials remained disinclined to intervene in what was described as the detailed operations of railways; equally, even when penalties were prescribed for railways that flouted orders, these were not necessarily enforced. As a result, conditions in third-class travel were addressed unevenly: lavatories were eventually provided but overcrowding persisted; railways were discouraged from using goods wagons for passengers but the practice began to be regulated rather than penalized or abolished.

Experiencing the Third Class

In India, railway travel was formally organized around three classes of accommodation, based on fare per mile. All railway lines offered first, second, and third classes, while some had a fourth or 'coolie' class, intended to attract people seen 'walking between towns and villages on the public roads and railway tracks parallel with a railway.'[13] Many of these were 'itinerant livestock traders' unable to provide water or feed for their livestock while on a railway.[14] Some railways, such as the GIPR, EIR, and Eastern Bengal Railway (EBR), did experiment with a seat-less fourth class that conveyed passengers in wagons meant for livestock or merchandise. In the late nineteenth century, some also experimented with an intermediate class, between the second and third classes, though it was not until World War I that these became more common. While not identical with it, this structure approximated the British model (though by 1865, British trains had as many as seven classes of travel).[15]

---

[13] Prog. of Railway Conference on Rolling Stock and Method of Working Traffic, 1871, in PWD: Railway, May 1871, nos. n/a, Oudh Prog., IOR.P/42, BL.

[14] Varady, Rail and Road Transport in Nineteenth Century Awadh, 129.

[15] After that, the 'history of classes on British railways now became one of reduction.' Jack Simmons, 'Class Distinctions,' in Jack Simmons and Gordon Biddle, eds., *The Oxford Companion to British Railway History: From the 1660s to the 1990s* (Oxford: Oxford University Press, 1997), 85. The first British passenger service in 1830 had only first

Given the gloomy prognosis for passenger traffic built into early railway planning, third-class fares in India were designed to attract large numbers. While third-class passengers often comprised the bulk of the traffic in other contexts, their proportion in India was distinct. In 1854, barely a year after railways began running, third-class passengers comprised 73.0 per cent of all passenger traffic in Bengal Presidency. This was more than double the 30.7 per cent for England that year.[16] The percentage increased and, between 1854 and 1859, the third class comprised as much as 95 per cent of passenger traffic on the three railway lines running in India.[17] Writing of England, Charles Lee took pains to stress how slowly third-class traffic grew there, pointing both to the impetus generated by the Great Exhibition—two decades after passenger trains began running there—and the role of the penny-a-mile 'Parliamentary trains' sanctioned in 1844.[18] In India, the proportion of third-class traffic was established right from the start of railway travel and stayed relatively stable through the colonial period, hovering around 90 per cent of total passenger traffic (see Table 1.1 and Figure 1.3). The demographics of the third class also remained remarkably stable. While not all natives travelled in the third class, yet almost everyone who travelled in the third class was native. 'Poor whites'

---

and second classes but a few years later a third class comprising of little more than open wagons was introduced. However, the third class was promoted with the introduction of 'Parliamentary trains' in 1844—requiring that all railways provide at least one service daily, with fares no more than a penny a mile, and affording basic standards of safety: C.E. Lee, *Passenger Class Distinctions* (London: Railway Gazette, 1946). The model of three classes, however, was not unique to Europe. James Zheng Gao describes the same in China, though here the railways' 'principal business' stemmed from second-class passengers. See his *Meeting Technology's Advance: Social Change in China and Zimbabwe in the Railway Age* (Westport: Greenwood, 1997), 158–59.

The British model was distinct from the early north American context, defined by 'the absence of the definite division of the service into three or four classes, as is the practice in Europe.' Emory R. Johnson, 'Characteristics of American Railway Traffic: A Study in Transportation Geography,' *Bulletin of the American Geographical Society* 41, 10 (1909): 610–21, quote on 620. However, the author suggested that 'the demand for cheap transportation in America will cause our railroads to break up the present "first" class into two grades, and thus virtually introduce the European third-class service' (617).

[16] Govt. of India (PWD) to Court of Directors, no. 30, 31 July 1856, Railway General Letters, 1852–61, National Archives of India, Delhi (henceforth, NAI).

[17] Julian Danvers (Secretary, Railway Dept., India Office), *Report to the Secretary of State for India on Railways to the End of the Year 1859* (London: HMSO, 1860).

[18] Lee, *Passenger Class Distinctions*, 6, 13, 17.

certainly travelled in the third class but their numbers were rather limited.[19] Europeans and Anglo-Indians remained scarce in the third class even after 1868, when many railways began reserving a special compartment for the two groups (Chapter 2).[20] Wealthy Indians could certainly afford first- and second-class fares but these classes of travel, even taken together, usually comprised less than 10 per cent of passenger traffic. Invariably, the third-class passenger was Indian; overwhelmingly, Indians—almost 90 per cent of them—experienced railway travel as a third-class passenger.

Table 1.1. Percentage of Third-Class Passengers on Different Railways, 1854–59

	1854	1855	1856	1857	1858	1859
Great Indian Peninsular	86.17	91.59	92.63	93.79	94.46	89.95
East Indian		85.80	92.50	93.50	93.90	94.80
Madras				94.98	96.93	95.68

Source: Tabulated from data in Julian Danvers (Secretary, Railway Department, India Office), Report to the Secretary of State for India on Railways to the End of the Year 1859 (London: HMSO, 1860).

Railways being a commercial venture, fares were intended to determine and distinguish the amenities available to different classes of passengers. However, the practical difference in comfort rather exceeded the gap merited by differences in fare. This was despite the fact that third-class passengers provided the dominant share of railway revenue. In his 1894 assessment, the consulting engineer for railways, Horace Bell, quoted a railway manager who believed 'it would pay him to give every first-class passenger twenty rupees to stay away;' Bell insisted that receipts from classes other than the third had 'no practical effect on the revenues of Indian railways.'[21] A decade later, special commissioner Thomas Robertson who was sent to India to assess the working of railways here, emphasized how unappreciative railway administrations were of their third-class traffic, which he described as 'the backbone of the passenger

---

[19] Mitzuni estimates that, in 1911, there would have been roughly 47,000 domiciled Europeans and 160,000 Eurasians, the two groups included in the category of 'poor whites.' Their total population would thus be about 200,000 in a year when third-class passenger traffic was 389,863,000. Mitzuni, Meaning of White, 72; Statistical Abstract from 1903–04 to 1912–13, 136.

[20] Before 1911, Anglo-Indians were known as Eurasians.

[21] Bell, Railway Policy in India, 190–91.

Figure 1.3. Third-Class Passengers as a Proportion of Passenger Traffic.

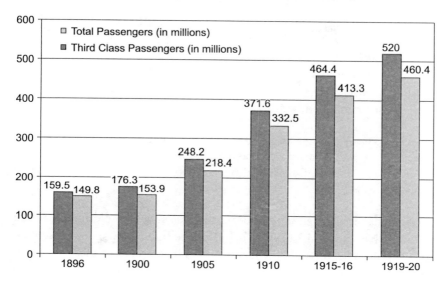

Source: Tabulated from data in *Statistical Abstract Relating to British India: from 1894–95 to 1903–04* (London: HMSO, 1905), 138; *from 1903–04 to 1912–13* (London: HMSO, 1915), 136; *from 1910–11 to 1919–20* (London: HMSO, 1922), 138.

business of every railway in India.'[22] His conclusion was endorsed by the *Indian Railway Gazette*.[23] In 1915, the President of the Railway Board—which had in 1904 replaced the railway branch of the Public Works Department (PWD)—remarked on the 'ample margin' available to improve conditions for third-class passengers.[24] However, even in 1947, a railway employee was categorical that any person who wished to be 'fit to carry out their business and duties' at the end of a train journey must eschew the third class.[25]

[22] Thomas Robertson (Special Commissioner for Indian Railways), *Report on the Administration and Working of Indian Railways, 1903* (Calcutta: Superintendent of Government Printing, 1903), 60–61.

[23] 'Some Passenger Statistics,' *Indian Railway Gazette: A Monthly Journal Devoted to Railways, Engineering and Matters of General Interest* 2, 6 (1 June 1908): 120–21 (BL).

[24] R.W. Gillian, President, Railway Board to R.S. Highet, Agent, EIR, 18 October 1915, Railway Traffic (henceforth, RT): A, January 1917, no. 760-T.-16/3-6, NAI; R.W. Gillian, President, Railway Board, Office Notes, 2 October 1917, RT: A, March 1918, no. 552-T.-17/1-24, NAI.

[25] V.V. Modak, *Railway Travel in India* (Bombay: V.V. Modak, 1947), 8–23.

A 'herd' of humans: the question of space

Overcrowded carriages dominated the experience of third-class travel. Whether it was the *Jabbulpore Samachar* writing of 'passengers huddled together' or the *Rohilkhand Akhbar* complaining that there was 'no limit to the number of persons thrust into a carriage so that sometimes they hardly find room to stand and breathe freely,' the problem was widespread.[26] An official from the North-West Provinces described:

> natives... penned up in carriages, 10 or 12 in a compartment, with seats 14 inches wide and 15 inches between them, with their legs dangling down in a way the most uncomfortable to them, and with no space to lie down to get any real rest.[27]

An imbalance between the number of third-class tickets sold and the rolling stock available was significantly to blame. Since Indians were not expected to embrace railway travel with any fervour, the Government of India suggested that third-class fares must be pitched low rather than high so as to 'induce the Natives to try the Railway.'[28] Having pledged to make up shortfalls in the 5 per cent dividend that railway companies had promised their—mostly British—investors, the government was wary of fares being 'pitched so high that the millions may not be induced to travel.'[29] However, being protected by this government guarantee, railway companies preferred to start with higher fares.[30] Occasionally, the government acquiesced to this, such as when the

---

[26] *Jabbulpore Samachar* (Hoshangabad), 1 July 1873 and *Rohilkhand Akhbar* (Moradabad), 14 June 1876, both in NNR: Punjab, NWP, Oudh, and CP. Also *Koh-i-Nur* (Lahore), 13 January 1872; and *Dabdaba-i-Sikandari* (Rampur), 10 August 1874.

[27] Note by Colonel A. Fraser, 29 July 1873, Papers Received from the North-West Provinces, appendix to PWD: Railway Prog., in PWD: Railway, October 1875, nos. 71–85, NAI

[28] Despatch no. 6, 18 May 1855 from the Home Govt. to the Governor-General, Railway Letters from Court of Directors, 1852–61, NAI.

[29] Govt. of India to Govt. of Madras (1869), quoted in Bell, *Railway Policy in India*, 189, 194–95.

[30] James C. Melville (East India House) to J.T. Walker, Chairman, Madras Railway Company, 21 May 1856, Enclosure 3, Despatch no. 14 of 21 May 1856 from Home Govt. to the Governor-General of India, Railway Letters from Court of Directors, 1852–61, NAI. Focusing on goods traffic, Daniel Thorner argued that government never fully persuaded railways of the logic of rock-bottom rates; however, he also stressed the

Madras Railway pointed out that wages, conveyance, and fuel cost much more there than in Bengal Presidency.[31] Generally, however, its inclination was to suggest low third-class fares, capping the per mile rate that passengers could be charged. Thus, the starting third-class fare on the EIR was capped at ¼ *anna* per mile (with a second-class fare being ¾ *anna* per mile and the first-class fare 2 *anna*s per mile).[32] Except for 'a bundle or a small carpet bag' that was carried free, passengers were to be charged for their luggage 'at a moderate rate.'[33]

When escalating figures for third-class traffic indicated the increasing popularity of railway travel, companies became reluctant to tamper with this success by raising fares.[34] Instead, they sought profit by ensuring 'the greatest economy of space and load' in third-class carriages, a yardstick tailor-made for overcrowded conditions.[35] The practice of overcrowding, however, was neither understood nor explained through the dictates of economy or the increasing disjunction between the space available in third-class carriages and the number of third-class tickets sold. Instead, railway functionaries argued that it was the specific attributes and inclinations of Indian passengers that engendered the overcrowded conditions of which they complained. More than one attributed

---

comparative element in fares. Thus, he quotes the Acworth Committee's assertion that 'Indian railway rates and fares have always been among the lowest, if not actually the lowest in the world,' but suggests the importance of distinguishing 'the absolute level of Indian railway rates as compared with other countries and the level at which Indian rates might have been pitched had the companies pursued a different kind of rate policy, say a policy designed to attract and develop a maximum volume of traffic.' He quotes Thomas Robertson saying that fares and rates in India, 'judged from the stand-point of the actual money payment made, are considerably lower than those charged in England; but for a comparison to be of any value, consideration must be paid to the circumstances of the two countries.' In 'Capital Movement and Transportation,' especially 396–97. Varady describes how suggestions by some O&RR shareholders that rates 'remain minimal' was disregarded. The government held up approval of the requested increase for more than two years, eventually authorizing a compromise: Varady, Rail and Road Transport in Nineteenth Century Awadh, 76–77.

[31] Bell, *Railway Policy in India*, 188–89, 194–95, 247.

[32] Despatch no. 6, 18 May 1855 from the Home Govt. to the Governor-General, Railway Letters from Court of Directors, 1852–61, NAI.

[33] Ibid.

[34] Govt. of India (PWD) to Court of Directors, no. 42, 25 November 1856, Railway General Letters, 1852–61, NAI.

[35] Imbrie Miller, Superintending Engineer, State Railways, Conference on Rolling Stock, 1871.

overcrowded conditions to a native preference for carriages without seats, combined with the overwhelming inclination to 'save a pie'.[36]

At a conference on railway stock convened in 1871, F. Firebrace of the Calcutta and South-Eastern Railway insisted that if given a choice—and at similar fares—Indian passengers preferred carriages without seats to those with them.[37] He was impervious to contrary evidence. When the government made fares for regular third-class carriages with seats equal to that of fourth-class carriages without seats, Firebrace himself observed a 'great rush' towards carriages with seats.[38] This fact, however, did not change his conclusion about the innate preferences of Indians. Instead, he attributed the rush to the fact that local Calcutta trains usually carried either *baboos* or field workers.[39] He explained that being clerical staff and administrators, *baboos* needed carriages with seats to keep their clothes clean. For field labourers, Firebrace explained the preference using arguments of social capital: since carriages with seats were 'considered by English people to be of a higher class than those without seats.' At the same time, he insisted that Indian passengers would 'put up with every inconvenience in order to save themselves the extra pie per mile.' He was convinced that at the right fare he could induce the majority of third-class passengers to ride in a ballast truck attached to a passenger train. Given these conclusions, he advocated 'great economy' as *the* yardstick to determine what facilities should be provided in 'low-priced Native transportation.'[40] Imbrie Miller, superintending engineer of state railways, concluded that the third-class passenger could hardly expect more than that railways increase the size of third-class compartments to 4 feet 4 inches and make sure they were separated by bulk-heads to limit overcrowding.[41]

---

[36] Note by F. Firebrace, Manager, Calcutta and South-Eastern Railway, 4 January 1871, Appendix C, Conference on Rolling Stock, 1871. One pie = 1/3 paisa, 1/12 anna, or 1/192 rupee.

[37] Ibid.

[38] Ibid.

[39] Ibid.

[40] Imbrie Miller, Conference on Rolling Stock, 1871.

[41] Ibid. In contrast, new stock for the 'Upper Class' was to be long carriages on bogie trucks that travelled quietly and with 'less jolting than the short Indian stock.' It was to have sky-lights and double roofs 'to exclude the smoke and dust,' easily accessible bathrooms and water closets, and wide longitudinal sleeping berths capable of being converted into lateral seats, so passengers could use side windows conveniently for 'the journey is made more tedious by confining the prospect to the inside of the carriage.'

Right from the start of railway travel in India, railway companies had been cautioned against forcing excessive numbers into carriages. An 1854 order permitted them to sell tickets only if there was room in the train.[42] However, since rolling stock varied by company, the government could not fix an absolute number of passengers permissible per carriage. Practically, this gave railway administrations latitude in inflating the number of passengers they considered permissible in a third-class carriage. Thus, in 1859, the governor-general pointed out that the EIR's policy of allotting 56 passengers in each third-class carriage meant that each person had less than 17 inches of sitting space.[43] Though he thought 20 inches should be the minimum allotted to every passenger, he insisted on at least 17.[44] Railways were also ordered to paint outside of each third- or fourth-class carriage the number of passengers permitted in it and were prohibited from carrying passengers in excess of this number.[45]

The government's displeasure about the 'very objectionable' fact of overcrowding did not necessarily translate into remedial action.[46] Partly, this was because its contractual and administrative control over railway companies was combined with its disinclination to interfere in their 'detailed management.'[47] In theory, railways remained under the purview of the PWD, the state possessing the right to issue executive orders as well as appoint consulting engineers and railway inspectors to regulate and assess their working.

---

[42] Draft for Regulating Railways in British India, enclosure in PWD: Railway, 13 April to 16 November 1854, Bengal Prog., IOR.P/163/20, BL (included with IOR.P/163/22).

[43] A. Fraser, Under-Secretary to Govt. of India (PWD) to Junior Secretary, Govt. of Bengal, 7 September 1859, PWD: Railway, 15 September 1859, no. 90, Bengal Prog., IOR.P/16/36, BL. Note by C.J. Hodgson, Consulting Engineer, Bengal, EIR, 13 August 1859, PWD: Railway, 18 August 1859, nos. 107–08, Bengal Prog., IOR.P/16/36, BL.

[44] A. Fraser, to Junior Secretary, Govt. of Bengal, 7 September 1859; Note by C.J. Hodgson, 13 August 1859.

[45] Colonel R. Stratchey, Secretary to Govt. of India (PWD), to Local Governments and Administrations, 27 August 1864, in PWD: Railway, September 1864, NAI.

[46] Secretary, Govt. of India to Under-Secretary, NWP (PWD), 27 August 1864, PWD: Railway, 30 September 1864, nos. 23–26, United Provinces (UP) and North-West Provinces (NWP) Prog., IOR.P/217/37, BL. Also, 'Railway Administration for Convenience of Passengers,' 27 August 1864, PWD: Railway, September 1864, no. 7, NAI.

[47] Railway Circular 13R, 27 August 1874, in PWD: Railway, 30 September 1864, nos. 23–26, UP and NWP Prog., IOR.P/217/37, BL.

In practice, this control was offset by the view that government should not assume regulatory positions for this would 'weaken the entire responsibility of the Railway Companies.'[48] Consequently, overcrowding continued to dog the railway journeys of third-class passengers, while railway companies continued to deny that they issued more tickets than there was space available on trains.[49] If faced with proof of overcrowding, they attributed it to a peculiar habit that they argued was endemic to native passengers: of 'following one another like sheep into a crowded carriage.'[50] Some suggested that every railway employee was 'patently aware that native passengers abhorred empty carriages.'[51] The local press not only noted the suggestion made by railway officials that native passengers possessed a sheep-like herd mentality but also inverted it. Whether it was the *Gramvarta Prakashika* from Comercolly or Bangalore's *Vrittanta Patrika*, they emphasized, instead, how third-class passengers were being 'driven and huddled like sheep into the railway carriages' or else, to quote the *Bengalee*, being treated as 'dumb, driven cattle.'[52]

Overcrowding was particularly dangerous in hot areas. Railway officials accepted that there was a higher frequency of passenger deaths on lines that traversed areas subject to hot and dry winds, like those in the EIR's northwest division.[53] However, they refused to correlate it with overcrowding or to heed suggestions that fewer passengers be allowed to travel in each carriage during summer months.[54] Instead, railway companies preferred to attribute such deaths

---

[48] Ibid.

[49] For a sample of the complaints: *Urdu Muir Gazette* (Meerut), 16 June 1871; *Shola-i-Tur* (Kanpur), 10 September 1872 and 22 March 1873; *Akhbar-i-Anjuman-i-Hind* (Lucknow), 25 September 1874; *Koh-i-Nur* (Lahore), 15 August 1874; *Mufid-i-Am* (Agra), 15 April 1875, *Mutla-i-Nur*, 7 November 1876, all in NNR: Punjab, NWP, Oudh, and CP.

[50] Deputy Agent, EIR, to Consulting Engineer, Govt. of India, Allahabad, 1 October 1859, PWD: Railway, October 1859, nos. 49–52, NWP Prog., IOR.P/237/26, BL.

[51] Deputy Agent, EIR, to Consulting Engineer to Govt. of NWP (PWD), 1 December 1863, in PWD: Railway, 30 November 1863, nos. 33–34, 55–59A, UP and NWP Prog. IOR.P/217/34, BL.

[52] *Gramvarta Prakashika* (Comercolly), 23 November 1878, and *Bengalee* (22 March 1901), in NNR: Bengal, *Vrittanta Patrika* (Bangalore), 31 May 1888, in NNR: Madras.

[53] Deputy Agent, EIR, to Consulting Engineer to Govt., NWP, 18 July 1865, in PWD: Railway, 31 October 1865, nos. 1–3, UP and NWP Prog., IOR.P/217/38, BL; Prog. of Railway Conference, September 1882.

[54] Deputy Agent, EIR, to Consulting Engineer to Govt., NWP, 18 July 1865.

to passengers being old, ill, or unfit to travel.[55] While they could not enforce reductions in passenger load, local officials in hot areas remained anxious about the link between overcrowding and the passenger deaths reported to them by railway administrations, as was required by law.[56] Thus, when EIR officials informed the government of the North-West Provinces of a woman travelling from Allahabad who was taken ill and died at Mohwar station, the railway's officials were instructed to ascertain not only cause of death but also the numbers of third-class carriages that were attached to the train in which she was travelling *and* the number of tickets issued for these.[57] The traffic manager explained to the railway's agent that it was 'very desirable' that her death 'may be proved not to be due in the remotest way to an over-crowded carriage.'[58]

Since they did not accept that there was systemic overcrowding, railway officials refused suggestions about decreasing the number of passengers permitted in third-class carriages, even for long-distance trains. Few acquiesced to the suggestion made at the 1882 railway conference in Simla that 'we should hear of fewer deaths in trains if this number was [kept] limit[ed] in hot weather.'[59] The Oudh and Rohilkund Railway (O&RR) and GIPR considered the suggestion, though eventually disagreeing with the proposition that long-distance trains should have only six passengers in each lateral compartment.[60] Overcrowding continued, including during the hot months, with some cases being rather extreme: in May 1890, a Madras newspaper complained that on the South Indian Railway 'at times, 64 passengers are huddled into a carriage which is provided with seats for 32 only.'[61]

---

[55] Traffic Manager (Upper Division) to Deputy Agent, EIR, Allahabad, 11 July 1865, in PWD: Railway, 31 October 1865, nos. 1–3, UP and NWP Prog., IOR.P/217/38, BL.

[56] J.J. Grey, Magistrate of Howrah to Commissioner, Burdwan Division, 5 February 1859, in PWD: Railway, 20 January 1859, no. 67; and 24 February 1858, nos. 106–09, Bengal Prog., IOR.P/16/33, BL.

[57] Traffic Manager to Deputy Agent, EIR, 17 February 1864, PWD: Railway, 30 September 1864, nos. 23–26, UP and NWP Prog., IOR.P/217/37, BL.

[58] Traffic Manager (Upper Division) to Deputy Agent, EIR, Allahabad, 11 July 1865.

[59] Prog. of Railway Conference (Simla), September 1882, Home: Public B, October 1882, nos. 143–44, NAI.

[60] David Ross, Manager, Sindh, Punjab, and Delhi; Delegate for the Eastern Bengal; H.F. Payne, Oudh and Rohilkund; Mr. Conder, Great Indian Peninsular; Urban Broughton, Eastern Indian; Traffic Manager's memorandum, Bombay, Baroda, and Central Indian, in Prog. of Railway Conference (Simla), September 1882.

[61] *Vettikkodiyon* (Madras), 24 May 1890, in NNR: Madras.

In and out of their pen: the question of lavatories

Until the early twentieth century, food, water, and lavatory facilities for third-class passengers were provided at railway stations, making it necessary for them to disembark at stations at which trains halted. However, many railway employees remained 'unwilling' to let third-class passengers out of carriages as needed and required, as well as being very slow to open carriage doors, arguing that they found the process excessively tedious.[62] Consequently, in many instances when trains halted at stations, third-class passengers were either left locked inside their carriages or else had to wait for a substantial period before being allowed to disembark.[63] A local official recorded that:

> when I arrive at a station, I am at once let out on the platform, while the Natives are detained, penned up in a crowded state till the ticket-collector has taken their tickets—a very slow process when there are many passengers.[64]

The *Jubbalpore Samachar* similarly concluded that '3rd and 4th class passengers once shut up in their pens must not expect to get out of them, except at the different stations to which they are bound.'[65]

In a particularly severe incident that occurred in June 1872, third-class passengers travelling on the Sindh, Punjab, and Delhi Railway were left locked up in their carriages for 13 hours 'without even getting water.'[66] The engine and five carriages of the down train from Lahore went off the line near Akarah station; finding it difficult at the time to replace the engine, railway officials had to leave the train overnight in that state. The traffic manager denied the incident, but it generated substantial press, especially when it was pointed out that the subsequent enquiry had been conducted by the very officers charged with the lapse and that it had been restricted to first- and second-class passengers. The *Koh-i-Nur*'s editor was emphatic that if district officers made alternative enquiries from third-class passengers 'the statement

---

[62] Arrangements for Comfort and Convenience of Passengers, 23 September 1875, in PWD: Railway, October 1875, nos. 71–85, NAI.

[63] *Hindu Prakash* (Amritsar), 21 August 1874; *Jabbulpore Samachar* (Hoshangabad), 1 July 1873; and *Benares Akhbar* (Benaras), 21 October 1875, all in NNR: Punjab, NWP, Oudh, and CP.

[64] Note by Colonel A. Fraser, 29 July 1873, Papers received from the NWP.

[65] *Jabbulpore Samachar*, 1 July 1873.

[66] *Meerut Gazette* (Meerut), 22 June 1872 and *Koh-i-Nur* (Lahore), 3 August 1872, both in NNR: Punjab, NWP, Oudh, and CP.

will appear to be too well founded,' while the *Nur-ul-Absar* chastised the Punjab government for relying on the statement of the railway company.[67] The government continued to insist that the problem could be alleviated if railway companies ensured that only one of the two carriage doors remain locked at stations, while also employing adequate numbers of ticket examiners to swiftly unlock doors at halts.[68] It emphasized that while safety regulations required that carriages be locked when the train pulled out of a station, they also required railway employees to 'pay immediate attention to any indication shown by the passengers of their desire to alight.'[69] Even as reports of third-class passengers remaining locked up in carriages trickled in, railway companies argued that they were complying with all requirements.[70]

When combined with the fact that halts remained inadequate in number and too short in duration, the practice of leaving third-class passengers locked in carriages heightened the demand that lavatory facilities be provided for them. Initially, railway administrations had been instructed to provide conservancy arrangements at stations. Privies and urinals were to be provided for European passengers and *tatti*s, or enclosures made of bamboo, grasses, or reeds, for natives.[71] When lavatory facilities for first- and second-class passengers began to be provided in trains, railway administrations repeatedly rejected the suggestion that these be provided in the third class. The issue was prominent in the railway conference in 1882, especially since the military department had demanded lavatories in third-class carriages for troop trains.[72] While willing to increase halts in number and length, railway officials argued that the 'habits' of third-class passengers were amply provided for by the facilities at stations.[73]

---

[67] *Koh-i-Nur*, 3 August 1872; *Nur-ul-Absar* (Allahabad), 15 August 1872, in NNR: Punjab, NWP, Oudh, and CP.

[68] Arrangements for Comfort and Convenience of Passengers, 23 September 1875; Prog. of Railway Conference, September 1882.

[69] General Rules and Regulations for Railways in India in conformity with Section 8 of Indian Railways Act, 1879, in PWD: RT, March 1880, no. 329, NAI.

[70] Prog. of Railway Conference, September 1882; see the *Amrita Bhodini* (Tirupatur), 5 April 1888, in NNR: Madras.

[71] Secretary, Govt. of India to Under Secretary, Govt. of NWP, PWD (Railway), Railway Circular 13R, 27 August 1874, in PWD: Railway, 30 September 1864, nos. 23–26, UP and NWP Prog., IOR.P/217/37, BL; Report on Sanitary Condition of Railway Stations by Committee appointed by the Lieutenant-Governor, NWP, PWD: Railway, 15 July 1865, nos. 11–13, in UP and NWP Prog., IOR.P/217/38, BL.

[72] Prog. of Railway Conference, September 1882.

[73] Remarks by delegates for Eastern Bengal and Madras railways, Prog. of Railway Conference, September 1882.

Some like the GIPR cited failed experiments with water closets, describing them as 'a complete nuisance, besides being a source of danger to health.'[74] Others argued that providing lavatory facilities would create 'considerable expenditure' and lessen the carrying capacity of third-class carriages by as much as 'six or seven per cent,' while still others pointed out that the resulting effluvium would harm the permanent way, creating a vast demand for labour to keep it clean.[75] Eventually, the very extent of third-class traffic was cited as a reason to withhold lavatory facilities. Bombay's consulting engineer argued that seeing that it was 'difficult to keep a closet in a 1st class compartment occupied by two or three European travellers sweet and clean during a long journey,' he could hardly imagine 'one used by 30 or 40 native passengers.'[76]

Early experiments were abandoned but complaints continue to come in.[77] An *inamdar* and conciliator from Poona addressed a detailed one to the viceroy in 1901.[78] Ramachandra Gungadhar Karwe first explained that he had travelled extensively by rail: from Poona to Calcutta, *via* Nagpur; from Poona to Lucknow, Allahabad, Banaras, and Gaya, returning *via* Agra, Jaipur, Ajmer, Ahmedabad, and Bombay; and also from Poona to Madras, and as far down as Londha junction. In his travels, he had been constantly conscious of how railway companies restricted lavatory facilities to the first and second classes, while drawing their income from third-class passengers. Similar to the Calcutta *Sanjivani*'s argument that railways would not 'of their own motion,' introduce lavatory facilities in the third class, Karwe's petition invoked the government's duties in this context, beseeching Lord Curzon, to heed the strictures of equity, justice, and 'mercy toward the poor' in alleviating the suffering of 'his poor ra[i]yats.'[79]

---

[74] In some of its two-compartment carriages in the third class, the railway had provided two closed closets in the centre of the carriage, each 4'2" × 1' 9" and fitted one with a commode and one with a cast-iron plate flooring with a hole in it, while in some others it had tried two closed closets, each 2'3" × 2' 6, both fitted with a cast-iron flooring with a hole in it. Note Reviewing Reports regarding Provision of Latrines in Lower Class Carriages on Indian Railways. *Railway Circulars of 1883* (Calcutta: PWD Press, 1884), NAI.

[75] Note Reviewing Provision of Latrines; Prog. of Railway Conference, September 1882.

[76] Bombay Govt., quoting Consulting Engineer for Railways, Bombay, in letter of 18 June 1884, in Note Reviewing Provision of Latrines.

[77] Prog. of Railway Conference, September 1882; Note Reviewing Provision of Latrines.

[78] Babu Ramachandra Gungadhar Karwe, to Secretary, Govt. of India (PWD), 3 December 1901, PWD: RT: A, April 1902, nos. 1–7, India Prog, IOR.P/6379, BL.

[79] *Sanjivani* (Calcutta), 16 February 1895, in NNR: Bengal.

Though it is unclear whether Curzon ever read this specific memorial, he severely chastised railway companies for their reluctance to provide lavatories in third-class carriages, describing their decision as 'old-fashioned, prejudiced and mistaken.' He was equally dismissive of the argument that excreta would be 'perpetually falling from the closets in such volume as to befoul the line and frighten off the gang men,' as of the suggestion that water closets would be used 'for immoral purpose' when trains stopped at stations.[80] Neither did he endorse the idea that passengers who wanted lavatory facilities should pay to travel first or second class. To keep the line in front of the platform clean, he suggested a mechanical arrangement 'by which the bottom of every pan was closed as soon as a train entered a station, and released as soon as it leaves.'

While expressed more vehemently, Curzon's views corresponded with the government's stated desire to meet 'the not unreasonable' demand for lavatories in third-class carriages.[81] The Railways Act of 1890 had instructed railways 'to provide latrine accommodation to one compartment reserved for females when the train of which it is a part runs for a distance exceeding 50 miles.'[82] In July 1895 and again in October 1896, the PWD had issued circulars to railway companies, suggesting they provide lavatory facilities in the third class.[83] These went un-heeded but complaints increased as faster trains with fewer halts became more common.[84] In 1902, local governments were ordered to ensure that railways began providing lavatories 'as early as possible,' first in all intermediate- and third-class carriages on mail and fast passenger trains that did not stop at every station, and then 'as opportunity arises' in all third-class carriages (except for on suburban trains running for

---

[80] Karwe to Secretary to the Governor-General of India, 3 December 1901; Lord Curzon, 1902a (8 February), in Curzon, Viceroy of India 1898–1905: Official Printed Material on India: Copies of Official Papers 1899–1906, BL.

[81] Govt. of India (PWD: RT), Circular 2, 31 January 1885, in Govt. of India, *Railway Circulars of 1883*.

[82] N.C. Kelkar, Secretary, Poona Sarvajanik Sabha to President, Railway Board, 24 June 1907, in RT: A, August 1907, nos. 92–104, India Prog., IOR.P/7634, BL; T.R. Wynne, Reply to Mr. Dadabhoy, Imperial Legislative Council, 25 February 1910, in RT: A, April 1910, nos. 71–72, India Prog., IOR.P/8472, BL.

[83] Govt. of India (PWD: RT) to Secretaries to Govts of Madras, Bombay, and Burma (PWD, Railway); Chief Commissioner of Assam; Agent to the Governor General of Rajputana; and Consulting Engineers at Calcutta, Lucknow and Assam, 26 February 1902, in PWD: RT: A, April 1902, nos. 1–7, India Prog., IOR.P/6379, BL.

[84] Ibid.

less than 50 miles).[85] New carriage stock built for these classes was required to have lavatory accommodation. The 1902 order seemed to have had some teeth and by 1908, an estimated 5,364 third-class carriages had been fitted with lavatories.[86]

Turn-of-the-Century Stocktaking

The organization of railway administration changed significantly at the turn of the century. The railway branch of the PWD, which had been the main administrative body for managing railways, was abolished on the recommendation of the 1903 Robertson report. In 1905, government control over railways was transferred to a new Railway Board. This was to comprise of 'specially qualified railway men' from Britain, their home-training being intended to inoculate them against 'local traditions and prejudices.'[87] The Board was subject to the control of the governor-general, its president being a member of the viceroy's council. This administrative shake-up was seen as a harbinger of substantial improvement, especially since it came in the wake of Robertson's sharp indictment of railway administrations for mistreating their revenue-generating third-class passengers. The state's increasingly direct relationship with railways also increased the hope that passenger grievances would get more attention. From a meagre 63 miles in 1870, state-owned lines had grown to about 20,000 miles in 1904, even though the state did not directly administer all the lines it owned, leasing the working of some to railway companies (Table 1.2).[88]

These institutional changes had little immediate impact. Railway administrations continued to decline responsibility and its officers continued to attribute problems to 'sheep-like' tendencies of third-class passengers who were, they insisted, afraid to enter empty carriages and instead followed each other into crowded ones. The Robertson report had challenged this claim, arguing that passengers, especially if they were going on a long journey, 'would not wilfully overcrowd themselves, if sufficient accommodation was

---

[85] PWD: RT: A, April 1902, nos. 1–7, India Prog., IOR.P/6379, BL.

[86] T.R. Wynne, Reply to Mr. Dadabhoy, Imperial Legislative Council, 25 February 1910.

[87] Some railway questions, especially those related to commercial aspects of railway administration, were transferred to the Dept. of Commerce and Industry, newly formed in 1905. See Robertson, *Report*, 16–19.

[88] *Statistical Abstract from 1867/8 to 1876/7*, 88; *Statistical Abstract from 1894–95 to 1903–04*, 139–40. For combinations of financial and administrative control, Robertson, *Report*, 3–5.

provided.'[89] The contention did little to alter the position adopted by railway administrations, which insisted that they adhered to existing legislation, as prescribed in the Railway Acts of 1879 and 1890.[90]

Table 1.2. Railway Ownership, 1904 (in miles)

All-India	**27,565**
Total State	20,943
Some Larger State-Owned Lines Worked by the State	
• Eastern Bengal Railway	971
• North-Western Railway	3,186
• Oudh and Rohilkund Railway	1,158
Some Larger State-Owned Lines Worked by a Company	
• Bengal and North Western Railway*	871
• Bengal–Nagpur Railway	1,696
• Burma Railway	1,340
• East Indian Railway	1,933
• Indian Midland Railway	805
• Madras (North-East) Railway	497
• Rajputana-Malwa Railway	1,682
• South Indian Railway	1,123
• Southern Mahratta Railway	1,042
• Tirhoot Railway	535
Guaranteed Companies	1,408
• Bombay, Baroda, and Central India Railway	504
• Madras Railway	904
Assisted Companies	1,713
Unassisted Companies	42
Native States	3,385
Foreign Lines**	74

* Property of Bengal and North-Western Railway Company 'but classed for convenience among State Lines.'

** Karaikkal-Peralam; Pondicherry; West of India Portuguese.

Source: Tabulated from data in *Statistical Abstract Relating to British India from 1894–95 to 1903–04* (London: HMSO, 1905), 136–38.

---

[89] Robertson, *Report*, 61.
[90] Abstract of Act IV of 1879, Enclosure to PWD (Railway) Circular no. 18, 24 August 1883, in Govt. of India (PWD), *Railway Circulars of 1883*. Louis P. Russell and Vernon B.F. Bayley, eds., *The Indian Railways Act IX of 1890* (second edition, Bombay and London: Thacker and Co., 1903), 160.

Subject to the approval of the governor-general, section 63 of the 1890 Act required railways administrations to fix the maximum number of passengers they could carry in each compartment and/or carriage.[91] They had to conspicuously exhibit this number inside or on carriages, both in English and in a relevant local language. Since such legislation remained toothless, so section 63 began to be described ironically as the 'Sardines section.'[92] Railways also remained averse to the suggestion that issuing fewer tickets would decrease overcrowding. Some like the manager of the EIR explained his refusal by citing his solicitude for passengers who wished to travel, while the agent of the Bombay, Baroda, and Central Indian Railway (BBCI) argued that such limits would engender 'much unpleasantness and accusations against staff.'[93] Meanwhile, there is no available evidence that section 93 of the Railways Act—which provided for a penalty of 20 rupees for each day that a railway contravened section 63—was invoked in practice.[94]

In some less public pronouncements, a few railways did admit that overcrowding stemmed from the gap between available passenger accommodation and the number of tickets issued. Responding to an enquiry instituted by the Railway Board immediately after it had been established, the South Indian Railway (SIR) agreed that its rolling stock was insufficient to accommodate its third-class passengers.[95] Others explained how they were trying to match third-class rolling stock to number of passengers, or else why finances militated against this solution.[96] The extent of shortages became apparent in 1910, when the Board admitted that only 210—or 38 per cent—of the 546 coaching vehicles added to rolling stock that year were meant for

---

[91] Section 8 (b) in Act IV of 1879 described in H.E. Trevor, *The Law Relating to Railways in British India* (London: Reeves and Taylor, 1891), 256.

[92] *Indian Engineering* of January 1908/9? quoted in question posed by Mr. Dadabhoy, Legislative Council meeting, 12 March 1909, RT: A, April 1909, no. 147, India Prog., IOR.P/8193, BL.

[93] G. Huddlestone, Traffic Manager, EIR to Agent, EIR, 24 June 1907, RT, January 1908, nos. 103–15, NAI; Agent, BBCI to Consulting Engineer (Railways), 18 June 1907, RT: A, August 1907, nos. 92–104, India Prog., IOR.P/7634, BL.

[94] Russell and Bayley, *Indian Railways Act IX of 1890*, 222.

[95] Agent, SIR to Consulting Engineer (Railways), Madras, 23 July 1907, RT, January 1908, nos. 103–15, NAI.

[96] Report by Railways on the Measures Adopted for the Comfort and Convenience of 3rd Class Passengers Travelling by Rail, RT, January 1908, nos. 103–15, NAI.

the third class.[97] Thus, in a year that 332.5 million third-class passengers comprised roughly 90 per cent of passenger traffic, only 622 (or 44 per cent) of 1,427 coaching vehicles under supply were third-class bogie carriages.[98] Officially, however, the Board refused to acknowledge that these numbers showed an inadequate increase in third-class stock, simply stating that they 'do not admit that the steady increase in up-do-date 3rd class carriages which is being made yearly is inadequate.'[99]

The situation changed somewhat during World War I when deployment of third-class carriages for troops meant even more overcrowding in ones still earmarked for passengers. Consequently, the Board was more willing to recognize 'the genuineness of the complaints as to overcrowding,' especially given the figures elicited by passenger censuses undertaken on large railways.[100] However, precisely because railways were heavily involved in transporting war material and troops, so nothing but rebuilt obsolete stock was available to alleviate the problem.[101] In the face of increasing public criticism, the Railway Board stressed improvements introduced since 1905, especially the 'substitution of new and improved carriages generally of the bogie type and of the same dimensions as those for passengers of the higher classes.'[102] However, overcrowding could only be alleviated, pointed out a member of

---

[97] R.T. Wynne, Reply to Sachidananda Sinha, Imperial Legislative Council meeting, 18 September 1911, in RT: A, October 1911, no. 104, NAI; R.T. Wynne, Reply to Mir Asad Ali, Imperial Legislative Council, 9 September 1913, in RT: A, October 1913, India Prog., IOR.P/9246, BL.

[98] R.T. Wynne, Reply to Sachidananda Sinha, 18 September 1911 and Reply to Mir Asad Ali, 9 September 1913; *Statistical Abstract from 1903–04 to 1912–13*, 136.

[99] R.T. Wynne, Reply to Sachidananda Sinha, 18 September 1911 and Reply to Mir Asad Ali, 9 September 1913.

[100] Assistant Secretary, Railway Board, to railways, 23 June 1916, RT: A, June 1917, no. 172-T.-16/1-23, India Prog., IOR.P/10198, BL; R.W. Gillian, Reply to M.B. Dadabhoy, 27 September 1916, RT, October 1916, no. 900T./1, India Prog., IOR.P/9979, BL. R.W. Gillian, Reply to Khan Bahadur Mir Asad Khan, Imperial Legislative Council, 15 March 1916, RT, June 1916, no. 547-T/1-2, NAI. Appendix to Notes in the Railway Board, RT: A, March 1918, no. 552-T.-17/1-24, NAI. (In this summary, the file quoted was RT: A, June 1917, no. 172–T.16/1-23)

[101] Appendix to Notes in the Railway Board (quoting RT: A, May 1916, no. 553-T.-16/1).

[102] These 'modern carriages' were to be fitted with lavatories, upper berths, racks, and roofs of improved design with greater heat resisting properties. Memorandum of Measures since 1905, reply by R.W. Gillian to S.N. Banerjee, Imperial Legislative Council, 9 March 1916, in RT: A, March 1918, no. 552-T.-17/1-24, NAI.

the Railway Board, if there were fewer third-class passengers: the Board thus asked Indian members of the Legislative Council to urge their constituents to avoid 'unnecessary travel.'[103]

The intermediate class as safety valve

During these war years, the Railway Board suggested that railways companies offer an intermediate class—between second and third—as a slightly more expensive alternative to those truly distressed by conditions in the third class. Towards the end of the nineteenth century, some railways had experimented with intermediate carriages on specific trains and routes. Thus, by the time the Board began stressing the idea in 1917, intermediate accommodation was selectively available on the GIPR as well as on the Madras and Southern Mahratta Railway.[104] However, others opposed the idea, the BBCI stressing that intermediate carriages would engender 'dead weight' and increase working costs without increasing profits.[105] The Board recognized that railway companies profited most from third-class carriages but pointed out that if increasing numbers of third-class passengers began paying the higher intermediate-class fare, profits would accrue eventually.[106] Meanwhile, even if they were restricted to long-distance trains, intermediate-class carriages would 'meet a public demand,' permitting railway authorities and the Board to counter critiques about how poorly third-class passengers were treated. As the Board's president pointed out in a private communication: if railways 'can get 50 per cent more for the comforts of an Intermediate class, they cannot be expected to provide the same conveniences for a 3rd class fare.'[107]

While the intermediate class certainly drew passengers, its statistical significance remained limited when compared to third-class traffic (Figure 1.4). Even on the GIPR, which was quite amenable to the idea, intermediate-

---

[103] R.W. Gillian, Reply to B.D. Shukl, Legislative Council, 27 February 1918, RT: A, March 1918, no. 552-T-17/1-4, NAI.

[104] Assistant Secretary, Railway Board to Agent, BBCI, 4 October 1916, RT: A, October 1916, no. 760-T/1-2, NAI.

[105] Quoting the agent of the BBCI, R.J. Kent, Joint Secretary to Govt. of Bombay (PWD) to Secretary, Railway Board, 20 July 1916, in RT: A, October 1916, no. 760-T./1-2, NAI.

[106] Officiating Assistant Secretary, Railway Board to Agent, BBCI Railway, 4 October 1916.

[107] R.W. Gillian, President, Railway Board, Office Notes, 2 October 1917.

class traffic hovered around 1 per cent of third-class traffic during the period between 1912/13 and 1915.[108] In the quarter century between 1896 and 1920, annual figures for intermediate-class traffic hovered between 6 and 10 million (with some spikes and dips between 1914 and 1918), making it between 2 and 3 per cent of total traffic. In the same period, third-class traffic increased from 150 to 460 million, ranging between 87 and 94 per cent of total passenger traffic.

Figure 1.4. Intermediate-Class Traffic *versus* Third-Class Traffic.

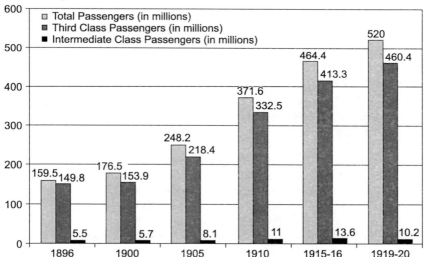

Source: Tabulated from data in *Statistical Abstract Relating to British India: from 1894–95 to 1903–04* (London: HMSO, 1905), 138; *from 1903–04 to 1912–13* (London: HMSO, 1915), 136; *from 1910–11 to 1919–20* (London: HMSO, 1922), 138.

In the wagon: the passenger as merchandise

While it encouraged an intermediate class as a possible alternative, the Railway Board was also confronted by the fact that railway companies transported passengers holding third-class tickets in goods wagons meant for livestock and merchandise. Though not identical, some of these wagons were similar to the 'open carriages' used for cheap railway transport in England. English 'open carriages' were formally abolished in 1844 with the introduction of Parliamentary trains subject to minimum standards of safety and security, which

---

[108] RT: A, October 1916, no. 760-T./1-2, NAI.

included ensuring that vehicles were enclosed and provided with seats.[109] In India, however, wagons continued to be used throughout the colonial period. Railway administrations usually blamed their use on the excessive rush of passengers around large festivals like the *maha* Kumbh. While the *maha* Kumbhs were renowned for the numbers of people who congregated on auspicious days, there were numerous pilgrimage sites that attracted people on a fairly regular basis.[110] However, passengers were transported in 'specials' and 'mela rakes' even during annual festivals 'varying very little in number of visitors from year to year,' or when they were visiting 'holy places to which people go all the year round.'[111] Neither did this practice cease over time.[112] Railway companies also ignored the extent to which passengers documented under the rubric of 'pilgrim traffic' included those travelling for a combination of reasons: commerce and exchange was, in fact, a central facet of many *mela*s.[113] Ironically, even as they blamed the use of goods wagons on the rush of passengers, especially that part of it designated as 'pilgrim traffic,' railway companies continued to advertise the facilities available to passengers travelling 'to religious festivals.'[114]

---

[109] Jack Simmons, 'Parliamentary Trains,' in Simmons and Biddle, *British Railways History*, 369. Susan Major argues that 'open carriages and goods wagons' were used as 'excursion carriages' during the excursion boom in Britain (1840–60), continuing as late as 1872 (293). Given the extent to which excursions were dominated by the poor and working classes of England, the descriptions point to possible analogies that one can see in the treatment of subaltern masses across national contexts. Susan Major, 'The Millions Go Forth': Early Railway Excursion Crowds, 1840–1860, unpublished D. Phil dissertation, Railway Studies, University of York, August 2012.

[110] Kerr, 'Reworking a Popular Religious Practice,' 308–9; Kama Maclean, *Pilgrimage and Power: The Kumbh Mela in Allahabad, 1765–1954* (Oxford and New York: Oxford University Press, 2008).

[111] 12-yearly *mela*s: Kumbh at Hardwar, Kumbh Magh at Allahabad, twelfth year fair at Puri, Pushkaram of the Godavari and the Krishna, Mahamakam at Kumbakonam, and Sinhast at Nasik. W.W. Clemesha, Sanitary Commissioner to Govt. of India to Secretary, Dept. of Education, 27 September 1916, RT: A, 655-T-16/6-34, November 1917, NAI. For how railways increased pilgrimage traffic, Kerr, 'Reworking a Popular Religious Practice'; and Ahuja, 'The Bridge Builders.'

[112] Memorial by Secretary, Indian Association, to Secretary, Govt. of India (PWD), 4 October 1901, in PWD: RT: A, May 1902, nos. 60–64, India Prog., IOR.P/6378, BL.

[113] Varady, Rail and Road Transport in Nineteenth Century Awadh, 140–41; Anand Yang, *Bazaar India: Markets, Society, and the Colonial State in Bihar* (Berkeley: University of California Press, 1999), Chapter 3.

[114] See for instance, 'Publicity and Third Class Traffic,' *Indian State Railways Magazine*,' April–September 1932, 475–76, Rail Museum Archive, Delhi.

The use of goods wagons for passengers was criticized right from the start, being denounced in the press, through petitions, in committees, at railway conferences, and in political forums.[115] However, the most comprehensive criticism came from the provincial pilgrim committees of 1913–14 (even though these were less concerned with the discomfort of passengers relegated to wagon stock and more with the question of how wagons that lacked partitions, seats, and lavatories exacerbated the potential for infectious contact).[116] In the wake of cholera and plague epidemics, the argument began carrying increasing weight—by the early twentieth century, India's sanitary establishment abandoned its support for a non-contagionist theory of cholera transmission (see Chapter 5). The pilgrim reports did not ask railway companies to stop using all wagon stock but only those that were constructed entirely of steel and completely unventilated.[117] It did, however, suggest how goods wagons could be made more sanitary when used for passengers. Railway administrations remained unwilling, many returning to earlier arguments about wagons without seats being particularly suited to native passengers. Ironically, even as some railways described 'ruses' used by pilgrims to secure seats in coaches rather than wagons, others remained adamant that passengers preferred wagons because these offered room to sleep and to stow belongings. The London Board of the Barsi Light Railway serving the pilgrimage town of Pandharpur averred that Indians were *fortunate* to have 'a supplementary means of travel which is denied passengers in the West.'[118] Others argued that

---

[115] *Urdu Dehli Gazette* (Agra), 24 April 1875 and *Rohilkhand Akhbar,* 15 July 1874, in NNR: Punjab, NWP, Oudh, and CP; W.H.L. Impey, Secretary to Govt. of NWP and Oudh (PWD: Railway), to Secretary, Govt. of India (Home), 8 May 1894, in Home: Public B, December 1894, nos. 137–38, NAI; Babu Brijnandan Pershad, in Prog. of Railway Conference, O&RR, December 1903; Memorial by Secretary, Indian Association, to Secretary, Govt. of India (PWD), 4 October 1901, PWD: RT: A, May 1902, nos. 60–64, India Prog., IOR.P/6378, BL; Question by Sachidananda Sinha, Imperial Legislative Council, 18 September 1911, in RT: A, October 1911, no. 104, NAI.

[116] *Report of the Pilgrim Committee, Bihar and Orissa, 1913* (Simla: Government Central Branch Press, 1915), 31, 34, appended to RT: B, July 1916, no. 655-T/1-5, NAI; *Report of the Pilgrim Committee: Bombay* (Simla: Government Monotype Press, 1916), in Railway Board: Traffic A, October 1916, no. 895-T.-16/1, NAI. Also, W.W. Clemesha, Sanitary Commissioner to Govt. of India, Office Note, 7 March 1916, in RT: A, November 1917, no. 655-T-16/6-34, NAI.

[117] *Report of Pilgrim Committee, Bihar and Orissa*, 39; *Report of Pilgrim Committee, Bombay.*

[118] Agent O&RR's weekly confidential report to President, Railway Board, 27 April 1916, RT: A, March 1916, no. 393-T-16/1-13, NAI; Note by Board of Barsi Light Railway,

eliminating wagons would prevent passengers—as many as three-fourths—
from going on pilgrimage.[119]

Future assessments revealed that with the exception of the SIR, goods
wagons continued to be used to convey passengers.[120] The prohibition of
goods wagons for transporting humans was broached again after World War
I, in particular through a Council of State resolution suggested by Lalubhai
Samaldas. Though eventually adopted in 1922, the resolution was amended to
the more toothless recommendation that steps be taken 'as far as practicable'
to stop the practice.[121] Subsequently, railway administrations agreed to
inform the Railway Board of instances in which they used goods wagons for
passengers, as well as the number of wagons used.[122] That railways still used
goods wagons was attested to by the paraphernalia of reports and figures sent
in by railway administrations documenting such instances.[123] As with goods
wagons, passenger censuses became the official means to address and defuse
criticism about overcrowding, without having to increase third-class passenger
stock or the amenities available for third-class passengers.[124] The Board had
initially suggested that censuses be done at varying times during the year, each
railway company choosing when and on which route. By 1931, it decided that
one annual census in June would suffice, this month having been identified
as having maximum passenger traffic.[125]

Enclosure to letter from Board to Agent, 30 January 1919, RT: A, 655-T-16/54, June
1919, NAI.

[119] Agent O&RR to Secretary, Railway Board, 27 July 1917, in RT: A, November 1917,
no. 393-T-16/23-26, India Prog., IOR.P/10198, BL.

[120] Agent, O&RR to Secretary, Railway Board, 30 September 1916; Agent, NWR to
Secretary, Railway Board, 25 October 1916; Agent, MSMR to Secretary, Railway
Board, all in RT: A, 655-T-16/6-34, November 1917, NAI; W.W. Clemesha, Sanitary
Commissioner, to Secretary, Dept. of Education, 27 September 1916, in RT: A, 655-
T-16/6-34, November 1917, NAI.

[121] Resolution in Council of State, in RT: A, March 1922, no. 780-T.-21/1-24, NAI.

[122] RT: B, August 1929, no. 490-T/32-71, NAI.

[123] RT: B, August 1929, no. 490-T./32-71, NAI; Meeting of the Committee of Passenger
and Traffic Relief Association, held on 25 July 1935 with Chief Commissioner and
Financial Commissioner of Railways, in RT: B, July 1936, no. 490-T/323-347, NAI;
RT: B, January 1940, no. 490-T./384-409, NAI.

[124] RT: B, May 1931, no. 2942 T/C/1-43, NAI.

[125] C.P. Colvin, Railway Board, to Ernest Jackson, Agent, BBCI, 29 May 1930, in RT: B,
May 1931, no. 2942 T/C/1-43, NAI; Railway Board to agents and managers, 6 May
1930, in RT: B, May 1931, no. 2942 T/C/1-43, NAI.

The Curious Power of the 'Irrational' Native

Arguments about how it was the instincts and peculiarities of native railway passengers that doomed them to the discomforts associated with third-class travel gradually became part of a more public narrative about the nature of colonial society. A telling example is a 1929 piece in the *Indian State Railways Magazine* by H. Sutherland Stark, a journalist who believed that while laymen should generally avoid making suggestions to experts, yet he had been able to 'study and observe facts' about third-class passengers that had escaped 'ordinary attention.'[126] Part of a range of magazines and supplements published by railways from the mid-1910s onwards, the *Indian State Railways Magazine* was considered part education and part publicity: a mélange of railway news from India and abroad, technical material and related advertisements, serialized stories, and observations about India and Indians.

From disorder to discomfort

Stark elaborated on the 'psychology of the Indian third-class passenger,' which he described as being 'full of peculiarities.' He explained that the 'vision of a train' created a 'brain storm' in their minds, one that symbolized a clash between 'the progressiveness of the West'—represented by railway travel—and the 'somnolence of the East'—embodied in the passengers themselves. Despite his opinion of Indians as a 'staid and even lethargic' people, whose actions 'in field or in factory' moved to 'the slowest beats of the metronometer,' he had found a self-possessed third-class passenger to be a commodity 'comparatively unknown in Hindustan.' Reconstituting metaphors of inertia and somnolence that had been belied by the extent of third-class traffic, Stark insisted that third-class passengers travelled as if in 'a dream,' one in which they *created* the debilitating conditions of which they complained.

While he described himself as being 'unversed in the secrets of railway administration and traffic control,' Stark's conclusions virtually mirrored the arguments continuously espoused by railway companies. From when they entered the railway's premises to when they exited at their destination, he found

---

[126] H. Sutherland Stark, 'Educating the Third Class Passenger,' *Indian State Railways Magazine*, April 1929–September 1929, 924–26. Rail Museum Archives, Delhi. Possibly, he was a sports correspondent—discussing hockey legend Dhyan Chand, M.L. Kapur mentions a certain H. Sutherland Stark as 'London representative of 'Sports,' a magazine of Lahore' writing at the same time. *The Romance of Hockey* (Indian Hockey Federation: Ambala Cantt., 1968?), 38.

native passengers to be people beset with panic. Their 'mental unpreparedness' for railway travel, combined with their lack of both 'self-possession' and 'method,' led to the crowded conditions of booking offices and station platforms. In Stark's words, farmers who would usually be too lazy or inert to pursue a wandering ox would, 'in a frenzy, hurl themselves at a half-open doorway in a suicidal effort to board a moving train.' Everyone would surge around a booking window 'in a disorderly rabble,' without anyone having the correct fare: instead, there was 'much untying of clothes and bundles' at the counter. Unlike people 'anywhere else,' no native passenger seemed to have heard of a queue or to possess any idea of method. Duplicating the arguments of railway companies, he argued that unlike in 'a Western land' where travellers awaiting a train would 'spread themselves out evenly over the platform,' Indian village folk would cluster immediately in front of the station building, thus overcrowding the third-class carriages at the centre of the train. He was perplexed as to why large parties from villages 'which ordinarily harbour three or four distinct and even hostile groups' would 'force their way into an already full carriage.' Further, that 'neither threats not cajolery will induce them to stir, on the plea that they must not be separated.'

Stark concluded that it was because they were 'insufficiently taught how to travel like sane human beings' that these passengers inflicted upon themselves 'needless' anxieties and discomfort. He believed that railway companies had done all that they could, especially since the end of World War I. Thus, the solution lay in educating passengers, both to 'cure' them of incorrect habits and to 'prepare th[e] minds' of growing generations. He suggested that local staff at wayside and village stations be given training courses and manuals that prepared them to help passengers behave in 'a calm and self-restrained manner.' Railways should also undertake a larger project of 'broadening the outlook and rationalizing the behaviour' of the masses: introducing railway literature as part of the curriculum of village schools, developing stories that would tell the masses how journeys could be made comfortable, publishing books designed to instruct people on how to utilize 'in a rational manner the amenities offered by the railways,' and offering lectures at small stations. Railways were to be more than a technology of transport; they were to become a *preceptor* that would inculcate in the masses 'self-composure and mass orderliness.'

Unenfranchised but impossible to ignore

While third-class passengers may have been designated as disorderly and irrational, neither the colonial state nor an aspiring nationalist one could ignore the fact that—numerically at least—they represented the bulk of the colonial public. Structurally conflating third-class passengers with Indian passengers allowed railway and state officials to use a narrative that explained away the discomforts faced by the former through the 'peculiarities' of the latter. However, this same conflation converted third-class passengers into a politically invaluable constituency. While lacking any formal rights of franchise, they had become nevertheless a demographically overwhelming body of potential citizens. Their negotiating power stemmed not necessarily from direct interventions but from their demographic strength, the latter giving them political voice, albeit one frequently mediated through elite (and often self-ascribed) representatives. Subjects they certainly were—perhaps, twice over—but in an expanding area of representational politics, their needs, concerns, and demands became increasingly impossible to ignore.

This is proved by the extent to which third-class passengers occupied the time of the Imperial Legislative Council, especially after 1909. Even before 1909, representational associations—whether the British Indian Association, the Indian Association, or the Poona Sarvajanik Sabha—had petitioned for the improvement of conditions under which third-class passengers travelled.[127] After 1909, the engagement increased, involving a host of council members from different parts of the country: whether Sachidananda Sinha or Mir Asad Ali, M.B. Dadabhoy or S.N. Banerjee, K.V. Rangaswamy Ayyangar or B.D. Shukl.[128] A telling example of how the troubles of colonial India's

---

[127] Petition by the British Indian Association (NWP) to Viceroy and Governor-General of India, Aligarh, 16 October 1866, in Home: Public B, December 1866, nos. 50–51, NAI; Surendranath Banerjea, Honorary Secretary, Indian Association, to Secretary, Govt. of India (PWD), 4 October 1901, PWD: Railway A, May 1902, India Prog., IOR.P/6378, BL; N.C. Kelkar, Secretary, Poona Sarvajanik Sabha to President, Railway Board, 24 June 1907.

[128] Question by Mr. Dadabhoy, Legislative Council meeting, 12 March 1909; T.R. Wynne, Reply to Mr. Dadabhoy, Imperial Legislative Council, 25 February 1910; R.T. Wynne, Reply to Sachidananda Sinha, Imperial Legislative Council, 18 September 1911; R.T. Wynne, Reply to Mir Asad Ali, Imperial Legislative Council, 9 September 1913; R.W. Gillian, Reply to Khan Bahadur Mir Asad Khan, Imperial Legislative Council, 15 March 1916; R.W. Gillian, Reply to M.B. Dadabhoy, 27 September 1916; Memorandum of Measures taken by the Railway Board since 1905, laid during reply by R.W. Gillian to S.N. Banerjee, Imperial Legislative Council, 9 March 1916; R.W. Gillian, Reply to K.V.R. Ayyangar, Imperial Legislative Council, October 1917, no. 555-T.-17/1, India Prog., IOR.P/10198, BL; R.W. Gillian, Reply to B.D. Shukl, Legislative Council, 27 February 1918.

massive body of third-class passengers became more visible as popular politics became increasingly integral to formal mass nationalism lies in the politically charged discussion that ensued in the wake of a long journey from Bombay to Madras undertaken in 1917 by the rising nationalist leader M.K. Gandhi. Decrying conditions to which third-class passengers were subject, Gandhi invited the press and the public to join him in a *crusade* against a grievance that had 'too long remained unaddressed.'[129] The crusade was launched in a scathing letter to the press published in *The Statesman* (29 September 1917) and *The Leader* (4 October 1917). A copy was sent to the Department of Commerce and Industry, which dealt (in addition to the Railway Board) with the subject of railways. Reminding his audience of the extent to which he had travelled across India between 1915 and 1917—'up north as far as Lahore, down south to Tranquebar, and from Karachi to Calcutta' enabling him to have covered 'the majority of railway systems'—Gandhi expounded on the extent of overcrowding and the egregiously insanitary facilities. Insisting that conditions in the third class vitiated even 'simple justice,' he argued that the real issue was not one of resources or of war economies but instead one of sympathy with third-class passengers and a due recognition of their rights.

While Gandhi suggested various measures through which railway companies could improve the comforts of third-class travel, he also held that the abysmal conditions in the third class had blunted people's sense of cleanliness and decency.[130] In a speech later that year, Gandhi stated that the indignities of third-class travel were 'visibly deteriorating the Nation' and creating degraded human beings who scrambled 'like mad animals' for seats in compartments, were content to 'wallow in dirt' during the actual journey, swore and cursed just to get standing room, were 'served their food like dogs and eat it like them,' and 'bend before those who are physically stronger than they were.'[131] Thus, like Stark would do later, he argued that third-class passengers themselves needed to be educated—or re-educated—and that railway travel offered a chance to

---

[129] RT: A, March 1918, no. 552-T.-17/1-24, NAI. The letter to the Secretary, Govt. of India (Commerce and Industry) was sent on 31 October 1917. The entire text was later published in a publication titled M.K. Gandhi, *Third Class on Indian Railways* (Lahore: Gandhi Publications League, 1917?).

[130] Gandhi, *Third Class on Indian Railways.*

[131] M.K. Gandhi, Address at All-India Social Service Conference, Calcutta, 31 December 1917, *Amrita Bazar Patrika*, 2 January 1918, *Collected Works of Mahatma Gandhi* (henceforth *CWMG*), Vol. xiv (Ahmedabad: Publications Division, Ministry of Information and Broadcasting, 1965), 121–28.

create a civic body of citizens. By neglecting the third-class passenger, both the state and the civil society had lost the opportunity of giving 'a splendid education to millions in orderliness, sanitation, decent composite life, and cultivation of simple and clean tastes.' He suggested that political volunteers travel on trains not only to see that passengers left and boarded trains without a scramble and that guards and railway officials curbed overcrowding but also to educate passengers and inculcate in them a sense of their civic duties.[132]

Gandhi's challenge galvanized the Railway Board, whose officials feared an impending agitation on the issue. They sought to respond swiftly, 'without bringing against ourselves a general accusation against the Indian people.'[133] Though he believed that Gandhi was 'honest' and 'reasonable,' the Board's chairman R.W. Gillian was concerned about the political potential of what he described as Gandhi's natural sympathy for third-class passengers and of the hardship encountered by 'his people.' Gillian's diagnosis was astute. At a conference in Godhra soon after his letter was published in newspapers, Gandhi diagnosed the condition of third-class passengers as symptomatic of India's colonial condition. He also argued that its persistence across the decades pointed to a subject people who were unable or unwilling to challenge such subordination. Arguing that suffering in third-class travel was borne because of an attitude of submission, he stated categorically that the fact that 'we tamely put up with the hardships of railway travelling is a sign of our unmanliness.'[134] Rallying the forces, Gandhi advised volunteers that nothing else provided as much facility to nationalist workers for effective service 'as the relief of agony through which the 3rd class railway passengers are passing.'[135]

It is possible to read some of the actions that both Gandhi and Stark deemed 'symptoms' of mental chaos differently, seeing them instead as popular negotiations with authorized formats of railway travel. The cluster around the ticket office instead of a queue, the many small bags and bundles carried in lieu of the expected luggage, and perhaps even the refusal to break up groups travelling together could be those daily resistances through which ordinary people inhabit structures, localize abstractions, and individualize large-scale processes

---

[132] Ibid.

[133] R.W. Gillian, President, Railway Board, Office Notes, 2 October 1917 and 3 December 1917.

[134] M.K. Gandhi, Speech at Gujarati Political Conference, Godhra, 3 November 1917, *CWMG*, Vol. xiv, 44–66.

[135] Gandhi, Address at All-India Social Service Conference, Calcutta, 31 December 1917.

of historical change.[136] Recently, Lisa Mitchell has also pointed out that before it became a political tactic in the 1930s, the practice of alarm-chain pulling to stop trains was 'widely popularised as an effort to get authorities to address the problem of overcrowding,' especially in the late nineteen tens and twenties.[137]

None of this erases the fact that defining aspects of third-class travel continued to involve both indignities and discomforts that were not of people's choosing and that stemmed both from the inadequate investment in third-class rolling stock and—at best—an equivocal commitment to providing amenities for this class of passenger. At the same time, however, structural determinants did not mean that third-class passengers were unable to negotiate. The sheer collective strength of third-class passengers meant that improving conditions of travel for them became an important claim to representational power—both for the colonial state and for nationalist elites challenging its legitimacy. As shown above, public appeals, both in the press and from those passengers who wrote and petitioned, reminded the colonial state of its duty; simultaneously, nationalist challengers spoke of how conditions in the third class vitiated the rights that Indians had. Thus, the demographic congruence between the categories of third-class passenger and Indian passenger made them an emerging body of citizens, in that they could compel political elites to recognize and address—or at least be seen to address—them as a constituency that possessed rights.[138]

Further, if shared rituals are a vital aspect of citizenship, then third-class travel provided a critical platform for its emergence in colonial India.

---

[136] James Scott offers a critical understanding of the centrality and limitations of practical and material—Brechtian—practices of resistance. While railway passengers were not poaching or deserting, to take two of the practices important to the peasants that Scott writes about, his insistence on such practices being 'ordinary' tactics of 'first resort' used by 'relatively powerless groups' is important here, as is his suggestion that they 'typically avoid any direct, symbolic confrontation with authority.' See his introduction to James C. Scott and Benedict J. Kerkvliet, eds., *Everyday Forms of Peasant Resistance in South-East Asia* (London and New York: Frank Cass and Co., 1986).

[137] Mitchell, 'To Stop Train, Pull Chain,' 478.

[138] Though he focuses on relatively recent forms of entanglement between elite and subaltern society, Partha Chatterjee's discussion of 'the moral assertion of popular demands' is quite evocative here; equally important is his discussion of how the Indian state *cannot* ignore groups and associations whose daily struggles often involve violation of law and whose modes of seeking redress often lie outside formal definition of civic engagement. *The Politics of the Governed: Reflections on Popular Politics in Most of the World* (New York: Columbia University Press, 2004) 30–41.

The routine discomforts and indignities that held together the third-class experience exposed millions of Indians—collectively and simultaneously—to the intertwined structures of capitalist profit, colonial control, and state paternalism that determined the practical details of their travel experiences. The fact that many of the structural discomforts in third-class travel continued across decades meant that such experiences were shared across time as well as space. Thus, even as India's third-class passengers joined millions across the globe in negotiating a new, popular, technology of travel, they were also differentiated from millions by the fact that their encounter with technological change was intertwined with their practical experience of colonialism. The everyday details of third-class travel meant that for large numbers of Indians, these two histories—of negotiating technological change and of negotiating colonialism—often resided in the same experience.

Demand and Supply?
Railway Space and Social Taxonomy

In 1873, the editor of the *Ahmedabad Samachar* filed a complaint against the Bombay, Baroda, and Central Indian Railway (BBCI) for making him share a third-class railway carriage with a sweeper. Branding the complaint as one based upon 'a vain superstition of the Hindoo religion,' Ahmedabad's small cause court referred the case to the Bombay High Court, which dismissed it.[1] About 35 years later, in 1911, Mathradas Ramchand, a pleader travelling from Karachi to Hyderabad on the North-Western Railway (NWR) also lost a legal battle. This time, it was Mathradas who challenged the railway's right to segregate paying passengers by delimiting certain second-class carriages as 'Europeans only.' The judicial commissioner of Sind disagreed with his claim and instead upheld the railway's right to exclude Indians from any carriage marked 'Europeans only.'[2] A decade later, in 1921, Venkataramana Ayyangar faced an even more perplexing situation. He described to members of the Madras Legislative Council how his motor-driver Jnanamuttu had failed to procure him a retiring room at Erode station—until he decided

---

[1] *Dabdaba-i-Sikandari* (Rampore), 20 October 1873, in NNR: Punjab, NWP, Oudh, and CP.

[2] Mathradas Ramchand *versus* Secretary of State for India, Judgment in Court of the Judicial Commissioner of Sind, High Court of Appeal, 1st Appeal no. 53 of 1911, in RT: B, July 1913, nos. 14–15, NAI.

to don a hat and give his name as John Matthew. Then, the station-master acquiesced.[3]

As these incidents suggest, railway space spurred public conversations about contact and access, rights and privileges, and inclusion and exclusion. On the one hand, the everyday routines of railway travel engendered a series of shared experiences among colonial India's vast body of passengers (Chapter 1). On the other hand, train compartments and carriages, waiting and retiring rooms at stations, refreshment rooms, and dining cars were everyday spaces in which strangers found themselves in unprecedented situations of proximity. The ensuing conversations about distinction, difference, and distance—invoking (and combining) arguments of class, rank, race, or gender—resulted in negotiations that ranged from public protestations to litigious conflict. Caste status, socio-religious taboos on contact, and arguments of respectability and hygiene were amalgamated to counter the possibilities of physical proximity, especially in overcrowded spaces. Demands for exclusive reserved space invoked distinctions of gender as well as hierarchies of race and rank, while prescriptions of ritual purity and pollution dominated conversations about food, water, and commensality.

Colonial authorities routinely described such discussions as demonstrating the peculiarities of Indian society, specifically an excessive commitment to social and religious distinctions. Of course, both ascriptions of difference and the way in which these were negotiated in railway spaces here were contextually specific, being tied to norms prevalent in colonial society as well as to attempts to circumvent and reinvent these. However, what was not specific was the fact that the public nature of railway spaces allowed people to simultaneously pursue ideals of a horizontal society *and* reinstate hierarchies of difference. Protracted conversations about the public, legal, and statutory mechanisms through which difference could be both erased and enforced in railway space was a global phenomenon for, even where the state did not control railways as directly as it did in colonial India, these were usually subject to laws for common carriers.[4]

---

[3] Venkataramana Ayyangar addressing the Madras Legislative Council 'Resolution re: Racial Distinctions among Railway Passengers,' 5 March 1921, RT, October 1921?, no. 47-T.-21/6-21, NAI.

[4] Amy Richter, *Home on the Rails: Women, the Railroad, and the Rise of Public Domesticity* (Chapel Hill: University of North Carolina Press, 2005), 23; Isaac F. Redfield, *The Law of Railways: Embracing Corporations, Eminent Domain, Contracts, Common Carriers of Goods and Passengers, Constitutional Law, &c. &.c.* (Boston: Little Brown, 1867), 9–10; Simmons and Biddle, *British Railway History*, 255–57.

Thus, both Amy Richter and Kenneth Mack demonstrate how railroads were critical to working out gender, class, and racial hierarchies in the north American South, both before and after de jure segregation was instituted.[5] In fact, 'railroad stories' offer 'some of the earliest and starkest examples of a much larger effort to create, impose, and resist new racial identities' in north America.[6] The 'black lady' as railway passenger was a particularly complicated case since she claimed privileges accorded to women passengers by claiming access to ladies' cars 'rather than riding in the mixed race, predominantly male smoking car that rail companies identified as suitable for all black passengers.'[7] Barbara Welke has documented how black women brought a majority of the legal challenges to racial segregation on common carriers.[8] A different politics of difference manifested itself in attempts by American railroad companies to segregate immigrants from other passengers: Jeffrey Richards and John MacKenzie describe the 'separate waiting rooms' provided for immigrants and labourers at various larger stations.'[9]

Despite such distinctions, the open-style American coach car 'sustained many Americans' sense of themselves as members of a classless society.'[10] The correlation between a socially level passenger body and a democratic polity was so strong that 'many passengers clung to it even in the era of speciality cars and racial segregation.'[11] Some commentators in fact distinguished north America from the 'Old World' by comparing themselves favourably with European arrangements of passenger stratification, 'frequently said to be the result of social stratification and the existence of class feeling.'[12] Ironically, British commentators simultaneously applauded how 'the universal and levelling

---

[5] Richter, *Home on the Rails*, 5; Kenneth W. Mack, 'Law, Society, Identity, and the Making of the Jim Crow South: Travel and Segregation on Tennessee Railroads, 1875–1905,' *Law & Social Inquiry* 24, 2 (Spring 1999): 377–409, quotes on 378, 382.

[6] Richter, *Home on the Rails*, 5.

[7] Ibid., 99–103.

[8] Barbara Welke, *Recasting American Liberty: Gender, Race, Law, and the Railroad Revolution, 1865–1920* (Cambridge and New York: Cambridge University Press, 2001), 297–99.

[9] Jeffrey Richards and John MacKenzie, *The Railway Station: A Social History* (Oxford and New York: Oxford University Press, 1986), 147.

[10] Richter, *Home on the Rails*, 17.

[11] Ibid., 17. Specialty services included Pullman cars, 'parlor' coaches and extra-fare trains.

[12] Some, however, explained it as being caused by the low average income of the industrial classes in Europe. Quoted in Johnson, 'Characteristics of American Railway Traffic,' 617.

tendency of the railway system' had changed British society, citing examples of English lords travelling with strangers who were their social inferiors.[13]

While British railroads did not formally struggle with statutory racial segregation—like in north America—or with accommodating religious and racial privilege—like in colonial India—they were hardly immune to discussions of hierarchy and stratification. Suggesting intricate calibration, albeit one underpinned explicitly by economic and financial distinctions, John Simmons writes of how, by 1865, there were seven classes of travel on British railways.[14] Even without formal distinctions in travel space, social hierarchies were expressed materially, whether in stories of railway officials behaving differently to different classes of passengers, or of the bishop and the blacksmith who could travel together but 'will not be permitted to take luncheon side by side in the first-class refreshment room, if the blacksmith, like the bishop, wears the apron of his calling.'[15] Neither can one underestimate the extent to which economic distinctions translated into social ones. Writing of China, James Zheng Gao describes how, though railways were accessible to all, 'travellers were separated by social class.' Consequently, first-class cars were only occasionally occupied, usually by foreigners and some government officials; second-class cars, which dominated business on lines like the Shanghai–Nanjing and Shanghai–Hangzhou–Ningbo, were occupied by the 'middle class;' while third-class cars remained the preserve of 'migrant laborers and peasants.'[16] Thus, while social taxonomy was materialized in historically specific ways, the new public space of railways was rarely free of differentiation and contestation, for space and amenities as much as for recognition of race, rank, and privilege.

In colonial India, there is evidence both of a history of complaints, demands, and litigation premised on arguments of difference, and of complex struggles through which passengers, railway companies, and the state narrated, negotiated, normalized, contested, and resolved such questions. Within colonial society, articulations of difference centred on demands for privileged access and differential space; such demands were most frequently made by colonial elites who, while hardly a cohesive demographic, remained dogged in their claims for

---

[13] Samuel Sidney, *Rides on Railways Leading to the Lake & Mountain Districts of Cumberland &.c &.c.* (London: William S. Orr, 1851), 12.

[14] Jack Simmons, 'Class Distinctions,' in Simmons and Biddle, *British Railway History*, 85.

[15] Ibid., 86; Richards and MacKenzie, *The Railway Station*, 138.

[16] Gao, *Meeting Technology's Advance*, 158–59.

preferential treatment. Claims combining arguments of social rank, religious taboos, and hygiene were exacerbated in the context of female passengers, a group seen to need special protection in a place as public as a railway. All demands were not equal, however. Thus, railway and state administrators usually rejected demands for a restructuring of travelling space even as they paid minute attention to prescriptive hierarchies and taboos when organizing food and water for native passengers. However, even as administrators labelled demands that railway carriages be stratified along differentials of rank and religion as being logistically and financial unviable, these very demands were used to explain de facto racial segregation in railway space, specifically the reserved compartments, carriages, and retiring rooms provided for Europeans and Anglo-Indians. Officially, such reservation was explained as a way to protect native passengers from offensive contact; in a colonial context, however, it was obviously critiqued and legally challenged as an explicit form of racial privilege. In practice, normative definitions of race were complicated by the fact that native passengers—*if* they had adopted (that which was described as) European forms of dress and style of living—were occasionally allowed into some reserved spaces.[17] However, even as it undercut strictly physiological definition of race, this 'concession' made dress and lifestyle not only visible markers of affiliation but also of an assumed hierarchy of civilizations.

Irrespective of whether exclusionary demands were aimed at maintaining privilege or securing creature comforts, the fractious public conversations and legal confrontations that they generated compelled millions of railway passengers—and hence colonial society at large—to grapple with fundamental questions about inclusion and exclusion on an everyday basis. Further, even as arguments for affinities based on wealth, rank, and 'breeding' coalesced entitlement with cultural syntax rather than the somatic of race, there was a concerted drive to eliminate any form of racial privilege during railway travel.[18]

---

[17] Emma Tarlo's *Clothing Matters: Dress and Identity in India* (Chicago: University of Chicago Press, 1996) offers a valuable discussion of 'the building up and casting aside of different identities by means of clothes' as well as of '"re-dress:" the choosing of alternative images with the rediscovery of the self that this sometimes implies' (1).

[18] Cf. Ann Stoler and Frederick Cooper's discussion of how racism 'has long depended on hierarchies of civility, on cultural distinctions of breeding, character and psychological disposition, on the relationship between the hidden essence of race and what were claimed to be its visual markers.' 'Between Metropole and Colony: Rethinking a Research Agenda,' in Frederick Cooper and Ann Laura Stoler, eds., *Tensions of Empire: Colonial Cultures in a Bourgeois World* (Berkeley: University of California Press, 1997), 34.

However, such challenges to racial hubris did not necessarily prevent more local forms of exclusion. Particularly harsh was the treatment meted out to 'untouchable' passengers by some high-caste Hindus. Such behaviour generated tremendous anxiety among Indian nationalists who had begun to see railway travel as a microcosm of the social democratization necessary to a horizontal national community. Thus, regardless of whether they were instituted or not, demands for such segregation attracted substantial critique from within colonial society, more so as nationalist fervour increased in the early decades of the twentieth century.

Narrating Difference in Colonial Society

Reserved carriages: distinctions in space

In 1844, Mr. Ghose of the Calcutta-based mercantile firm Kelsall and Ghose had explained to railway promoters that for railway travel to be 'generally and eagerly availed of' railway spaces must be organized to separately accommodate 'Mahomedans, the high- and low-caste Hindoos.'[19] Intermittently through the late nineteenth century, religious and caste differences were amalgamated into more public demands that railway companies distinguish between 'respectable' and 'common' and that they stop treating all third-class passengers as one (*sab ko ek lakri se hakna*).[20] That a third-class fare allowed 'a sweeper or a *chamár*' access to the same carriage as a high-caste Hindu was seen by some to demonstrate a shocking 'want of respect and regard' to 'caste, rank, and position' as well as to social and religious taboos on proximity.[21] A few argued that it also demonstrated complete unconcern for hygiene.[22] Complaints urged that by not insisting on separation between respectable and common and between high and low caste, the state had abdicated its commitment to justice as well as its post-1857 commitment to maintaining colonial traditions.[23] A correspondent

---

[19] Messrs Kelsall and Ghose to R.M. Stephenson, 12 August 1844, in Railways: Home Correspondence, 1845–48, IOR.31478 L/PWD/2/43, BL.

[20] *Urdu Akhbar* (Delhi), 16 November 1871; *Hindu Prakash* (Amritsar), 17 July 1874; *Mufid-i-Am* (Agra), 15 April 1875; *Aligrah Institute Gazette* (Aligarh), 23 July 1875; *Mutla-i-Nur*, 7 November 1876, all in NNR: Punjab, NWP, Oudh, and CP.

[21] *Dabdaba-i-Sikandari* (Rampore), 20 October 1873; *Hindu Prakash* (Amritsar), 17 July 1874; *Vidya Vilas* (Jammu), 2 November 1874, *Aligarh Institute Gazette* (Aligarh), 23 July 1875; *Urdu Akhbar* (Delhi), 16 November 1871, in NNR: Punjab, NWP, Oudh, and CP.

[22] Ibid.

[23] Ibid.

for the *Lawrence Gazette* did not know whether he was more shocked by the fact that a brahman was 'pushed' into a compartment with a sweeper or the fact that such desecration occurred on a state-owned railway.[24]

Caste hierarchy remained the chief organizing principle for demands focused on maintaining spatial distance but religious distinctions were not absent. Though suggested less frequently, there were demands that Hindu and Muslim passengers be accommodated in separate railway carriages, especially in the confines of the frequently overcrowded third class where physical contact was most likely.[25] On occasion, arguments deploying caste and religious difference coincided, as happened during a large conference organized by the Oudh and Rohilkund Railway (O&RR) at Lucknow in 1903. The 200-odd delegates who attended this conference comprised a motley group, ranging from members of district and municipal boards, to *vakil*s and pleaders, bank managers, doctors, newspaper editors, and managers of commercial and mercantile firms.[26] Fifty-seven had been nominated by local officials of areas where the railway had a substantial presence, and the others invited by the railway administration. The frequent use of the appellation of *ra'is*, combined with the fact that each was allowed to being with him 'two servants' who would be accommodated in the third-class, suggests that many of them were familiar with the upper classes of travel or else would have preferred that, finances permitting.

Some delegates reiterated that 'sweepers, *chamar*s and other low-castes' must be separated from high-caste Hindus, while others demanded separate carriages for '*dvija*' brahmans.[27] Pandit Sri Panchana Tripathi Jyotishi of Bhagalpur, however, argued that separate carriages were required for 'Hindus, Mohammedans and low-caste people,' while D.C. Sinha from Barrackpur insisted that separate accommodation in all classes should be provided for Hindus, Muslims, and Christians.[28] In a demographic calculus based on religious identity, Khunni Lal Shastri from Bareilly argued that since Hindus outnumbered Muslims in the wider population, so: '2/3rd of carriages on trains

---

[24] *Lawrence Gazette* (Meerut) 1 June 1875, in NNR: Punjab, NWP, Oudh, and CP.

[25] *Khair Khwah-i-Alam*, 15 August 1874, in NNR: Punjab, NWP, Oudh, and CP.

[26] Prog. of Oudh and Rohilkund Railway (O&RR) Conference, December 1903, Lucknow, 1–3 December 1903, in PWD: RT: A: June 1904, nos. 74–75, NAI.

[27] Suggestions from residents of Saharanpur; Manant Kanh Das for rai's of Hardwar; Babu Brijnandan Pershad (rai's, Moradabad); Babu Moksha Das Mitter, (rai's, Benaras); and Ganesh Shastri (Secretary, Jatri Kalesh Nibarini Sabha, Benaras), all in Prog. of O&RR Conference, December 1903.

[28] Prog. of O&RR Conference, December 1903.

should be set apart for Hindus and the rest for Mahomedans.'[29] Carriages for different communities were to be located at different ends of each train.

Such demands were not unequivocal. In fact, suggestions to separate railway passengers based on caste or religion failed to be included in lists of formal resolutions carried out at the 1903 conference. When voiced, such suggestions also generated public outrage. The editor of Etawah's *Al Bashir* not only demanded to know how such ideas of segregation could be broached by 'educated patriotic Hindus who aspire to create nationality in India,' but also warned of the political consequences of such exclusionary beliefs. He argued that if some Hindus were averse to being seated in the same railway carriage as Muslims 'even for a few hours,' then Muslims would be compelled to 'promote loyalty to Government...and depend upon their own efforts and resources for advancement and progress.'[30] Significantly enough, he believed that demands for separate carriages *contravened* tradition rather than enforced it. Such demands indicated to him that—unlike 'forty years ago'—now Muslims had become just another demographic minority in India, akin to Anglo-Indians and native Christians. (Though the editor himself did not speak of it, both Anglo-Indians and native Christians were also groups whose practical choices during railway travel, especially if these gained them access to space reserved for Europeans, were seen to bespeak choices about identity and belonging.[31])

Railway administrations rejected most of the early demands that railway compartments or carriages reflect caste or religious distinctions. Often they did this by pointing out how financially and logistically unfeasible such accommodation would be—officials envisioned trains with carriages meant for high-caste Hindus running empty, even as other passengers were left clamouring at stations.[32] The occasional experiments that did get sanctioned

---

[29] Khunni Lal Shastri (Bareilly), Prog. of O&RR Conference, December 1903.

[30] *Al Bashir* (Etawah), 1 December 1903, in NNR: United Provinces.

[31] In *Lines of the Nation*, Laura Bear discusses how arguments of 'blood, loyalty, and habits of life' marked Anglo-Indians as being 'outside the project of a nationalism that demanded a peculiar kind of genealogical "Indianness" on the part of its members' (9–10).

[32] Mr. Burt, O&RR, Prog. of Railway Conference, O&RR, December 1903. Two railways in Kathiawar seem to be an exception. In 1916, the Jamnagar Railway stated that one compartment in third-class carriages was being set aside on all of its trains 'for the exclusive use of low caste passengers' and the Bhavnagar State Railway that 'a separate 3rd-class compartment is as a rule, but not invariably [?] provided...for the exclusive use of passengers of low caste.' Manager, Jamnagar Railway to the Secretary, Railway

failed in practice. In the context of nineteenth-century Awadh, Robert Varady shows how Oudh and Rohilkund officials made gestures towards providing stratified accommodation by sanctioning an experiment in which 'natives of higher ranks' could travel in a first-class carriage by paying a higher fare; another carriage was set aside for 'natives of a respectable position' who were willing to pay 50 per cent more than the third-class fare. However, finances militated against such 'concessions,' which were 'neither widespread [or] efficient, nor long-lasting.'[33]

Cognizant of official reactions, later petitions widened the range of arguments presented. The petitions sent to the viceroy in 1914 from the Tirtha Yatra Klesha Nivarini Sabhas at Kumbakonam, Vedagriham, Bangalore, and Arsikere (in present-day Tamil Nadu and Karnataka) certainly replicated earlier complaints in that they described the 'promiscuous huddling together' entailed in railway journeys and pointed out that such proximity violated rules of commensality, leaving Hindu pilgrims 'unable to eat or even drink water because people of other castes were present in the same compartment.'[34] They also reiterated earlier arguments of profitability, claiming that if railway companies accommodated demands such as theirs, they would see 'a large increase' in the number of pilgrims travelling by train. At the same time, the petitions added two hitherto unused arguments. Combining earlier narratives of cleanliness and hygiene with India's recent epidemic history, they stressed the dangers of infectious contact in overcrowded third-class carriages. They insisted that in 'the present times of plague and other epidemics' separate carriages were necessary to forestall contact of sanitary bodies with people they deemed as 'not clean enough.' Having experienced—or at least witnessed—the mammoth system of detention and surveillance of railway passengers at the height of the plague epidemic in the late 1890s and early 1900s (Chapter 5), the petitioners could hardly have been ignorant of the potency of this argument. Should railways and government still demur, they pointed out that there was

---

Board, 2 November 1916; Manager, Bhavnagar State Railway to Secretary, Railway Board, 2 December 1916, both in RT, December 1916, India Prog., no. 893-T/1-6, IOR.P/9979, BL.

[33] Varady, Rail and Road Transport in Nineteenth Century Awadh, 155–56.

[34] Letters to the Viceroy from the Tirtha Yatra Klesha Nivarini Sabhas at Kumbakonam (3 August 1914), Vedagriham (27 August 1914), Bangalore (17 October 1914), Arsikere (17 October 1914); and from the Advaita Sabha (Kumbakonam), 30 September 1914, all in RT, April 1916, no. 165 T.- 16/1-14A, NAI. Each of the five petitions was dated differently but contained identical text.

a clear precedent for their demand since railways *already* reserved carriages for Europeans and Anglo-Indians.

Perhaps it was the strain of war economy on passenger travel, possibly combined with the fact of an impending Kumbh in 1918, which prompted the *sabha*s to make the demand at this specific juncture. However, these same war economies meant the petition had scant chance of success. State officials and railway companies dealt with the 1914 demands much like they had dealt with the 1903 ones: the *sabha*s were informed of the impracticability and wastefulness of separate railway accommodation for different castes or creeds. In January 1916, the Railway Board officially declined the petition, stating that since accommodation set aside for different castes 'would be more or less empty,' it would serve no purpose but to accentuate the very 'crowding and congestion' that was frequently complained of.[35]

A question of honour: women, respectability, and seclusion

Questions of proximity, distance, and contact were most acute in relation to the question of female passengers. Initially, officials had been preoccupied with secluding 'ladies of rank,' this concern both informed and endorsed by specific groups of colonial elites. The landed and aristocratic members of the British Indian Association—describing themselves as 'Native gentlemen of the highest rank'—were outraged that 'Native ladies of respectable birth and breeding' were expected to use the females'-only carriages provided for native women.[36] Many railways had begun to reserve these early on, the provision itself resembling 'ladies' compartments' provided in Britain and in north America.[37] Colonial elites, however, rejected females'-only carriages, insisting that these were unacceptable to any but 'lower-class' women who, railway administrators

[35] A.G. Stowell, Railway Board to President, Tirtha Yatra Klesha Nivarini Sabha (Kumbakonam, Vedagriham, Arsikere, Bangalore) and Secretary Advaita Sabha (Kumbakonam), 24 January 1916, in RT, April 1916, no. 165 T.- 16/1-14A, NAI.

[36] Govt. of India, PWD: Railway, Circular no. 22, 29 October 1866, Home: Public B, December 1866, nos. 50–51, NAI; Petition by the British Indian Association (NWP) to Viceroy and Governor-General, Aligarh, 16 October 1866, in Home: Public B, December 1866, nos. 50–51, NAI.

[37] Carter, *Railways and Culture in Britain*, 172; D. Lardner, *Railway Economy: A Treatise on the New Art of Transport* (London: Taylor, Walton, and Mayberly, 1850), 401. In 1836, the Cumberland Valley Railroad Company provided a 'ladies compartment,' as did the Philadelphia, Wilmington & Baltimore Railroad two years later. Richter, *Home on the Rails*, 93–95.

insisted, were 'always visible to every one.'[38] Thus, several railways abolished females'-only carriages, citing male concern with seclusion and arguing that respectable Indian women were reluctant to travel separate from male 'relatives' and 'protectors.'[39]

While this was stressed as a specifically Indian norm, female respectability in railway spaces was a more general preoccupation, as was the correlation between privacy and respectability. An inverse correlation between female visibility and societal respectability was critical to the process through which middle-class women in Victorian England were pushed 'into the seclusion of the private sphere as a mark of class status or superiority.'[40] Barbara Welke has described how the norms of public conduct 'binding middle-class white women' when travelling or in a public space amounted to a 'socialized helplessness,' while Amy Richter explains how, in north America, there was increasing emphasis on how a female passenger could maintain privacy—'the basis of her respectability'—in the midst of strangers encountered during a railway journey.[41] Neither was the disinclination of Indian women to travel alone exceptional: it was because many women refused to travel separate from their male escorts that some railway companies in north America allowed male escorts to accompany their female charges in ladies' cars; female travellers in Britain—'certainly of the upper and middle classes'—also accepted the need for a male escort when travelling.[42] Similarly, it was not only in India that females'-only carriages were seen as problematic: a late-nineteenth century review conducted by the Board of Trade found 'Ladies' only' compartments

---

[38] For historical assessments of seclusion see Antoinette Burton, *Dwelling in the Archive: Women Writing House, Home, and History in Late Colonial India* (Oxford and New York: Oxford University Press, 2003), 66 and Janaki Nair, 'Uncovering the Zenana: Visions of Indian Womanhood in Englishwomen's Writings, 1813–1940,' *Journal of Women's History* 2, 1 (Spring 1990): 8–34.

[39] J.M.H. Shaw-Stewart, Consulting Engineer, Railways (Madras), to Secretary, Govt. of India (PWD: Railway), 26 June 1869; C.A. Orr, Secretary, Govt. of Madras (PWD: Railway) to Secretary, Govt. of India (PWD), 16 July 1869, both appended to Minute by William Muir, 17 July 1869, United Provinces Prog. (PWD: Railway), July–November 1869, IOR.P/442/61, BL.

[40] Kumkum Sangari and Suresh Vaid, eds., *Recasting Women: Essays in Indian Colonial History* (New Brunswick: Rutgers University Press, 1999 [1989]), 11.

[41] Welke, *Recasting American Liberty*, 57; Richter, *Home on the Rails*, 5–6.

[42] Richter, *Home on the Rails*, 93–95; John Simmons, 'Women's Emancipation,' in Simmons and Biddle, *British Railway History*, 566.

in British trains to be 'noticeably under-used,' a conclusion that the British press endorsed.[43]

Such analogies found little purchase, however, among colonial authorities. Instead, they broadened the purview of female seclusion in India, diagnosing it—contrary to historical evidence—as a colonial rather than elite norm.[44] This was in stark contrast with the representation of Indian elites, who stressed seclusion as a norm that distinguished rank. Thus, the petition from the British Indian Association stated explicitly that special provisions were *not* required for 'the lower classes.'[45] However, this specificity was lost in the official discussions that ensued around the time of a 'gross outrage' in 1867, when Samuel Horn, a European travelling in a third-class carriage on the East Indian Railway (EIR) violated an Indian woman travelling in the same carriage (despite her being accompanied by a male relative).[46] The woman died when trying to escape by jumping out of the moving train. The incident coincided with increasing official emphasis on the question of female passengers and, in the late 1860s, local administrations in Madras, Bombay, Bengal, Punjab, NWP, Awadh, and the Central Provinces were charged by the governor-general to consult railway officials and 'chief Native gentlemen' in their jurisdictions on the needs of Indian women travelling by rail.[47] In the deliberations that ensued, the governor-general emphasized the need for railway accommodation to address 'habits of seclusion common in the East,' citing the extent to which railway functionaries and local and provincial administrators had concluded—to quote William Muir, Lieutenant-Governor of the NWP—that 'respectable men, however poor' would not allow 'their women to be herded together away from themselves.'[48]

---

[43] Simmons, 'Women's Emancipation,' 566; 'Assault on Women in Railway Carriages,' *The Times* (London), 5 August 1896.

[44] As both Nair and Burton note, whether Hindu or Muslim, secluded women in India were 'high-caste or upper class;' further, seclusion remained 'confined to certain classes and regions, there being large areas of India, and of course, other classes where women were far more "visible".' Burton, *Dwelling in the Archive*, 66; Nair, 'Uncovering the Zenana,' 11.

[45] Petition by the British Indian Association, 16 October 1866.

[46] Govt. of India, PWD (Railway) Prog., July 1868, no. 71, NAI.

[47] They were to focus on women in 'the upper grades of society,' but not limit their enquiries to them. Note by Major Hovenden, Consulting Engineer (Bengal), 31 August 1869, United Provinces Prog. (PWD: Railway), July–November 1869, IOR.P/442/61, BL.

[48] Minute by William Muir, 17 July 1869; Observations of Governor-General, 10 November 1869, United Provinces Prog. (PWD: Railway), July–November 1869, IOR.P/442/61, BL.

Muir was not alone in making such generalizations. Thus, speaking of how best to facilitate 'private ingress and egress' to and from trains, a government circular on passenger conveniences suggested that Indian women adopt 'the costume commonly worn in Turkey and Egypt where seclusion of their sex is *as general* as it is in India' (emphasis added).[49] When combined with official assumptions that females'-only carriages were unviable because in India it was difficult 'getting family parties of the lower classes to divide,' such conclusions widened the purview of female seclusion beyond what actually existed in practice.[50] Further, the discursive correlation of female seclusion with respectability made seclusion during railway travel a mechanism for social mobility; failure to subscribe to this correlation excluded one from the purview of respectability.[51] This concatenation of arguments meant that female seclusion—described by Muir, among others, as one of the 'great retarding elements to social improvement and elevation'—was actually generalized as an arbiter of respectability in colonial India.[52]

Discursive correlations notwithstanding, in practice strictly secluded accommodation was rarely accessible. First-class carriages were the most amenable to secluded travel, especially if these had all required conveniences, negating the need to leave it 'for any purpose.'[53] However, first-class carriages were only accessible to a miniscule portion of the population. Few could afford to reserve even an entire second- or third-class carriage, especially since a lot of rolling stock remained unsuited to being portioned off into smaller (hence cheaper) compartments. Even when fares were scaled, the proposition remained expensive. On the Madras Railway, reserving a second- or third-class carriage

---

[49] Arrangements for Comfort and Convenience of Passengers, 23 September 1875, Govt. of India (PWD: Railway) Circular no. 17, PWD: Railway, nos. 71–85, October 1875, NAI.

[50] Govt. of India circular (May 1868) to local administrations: PWD: Railway, no. 71, July 1868, NAI.

[51] Drawing from M.N. Srinivas' ideas of 'Sanskritization' in *Religion and Society Amongst the Coorgs of South India* (Oxford: Clarendon Press, 1952).

[52] Quoted in a review of Muir's *Annals of the Early Caliphate* in *The British Quarterly Review*, Vol. LXXVII, January and April 1883 (London: Hodder and Stoughton), 446–47.

[53] Some railways tried to adopt suggestions that palanquins be brought to the train's door, to prevent 'respectable' women from having to walk from their conveyances to the railway carriage. Commissioner of Dacca, quoted in note by Major Hovenden, 31 August 1869; Minute by William Muir, 17 July 1869; *Urdu Akhbar* (Delhi), 24 September 1870, in NNR: Punjab, NWP, Oudh, and CP.

could cost up to the equivalent of 50 tickets. In Punjab, one had to pay five-eights the charge of the whole to reserve a first- or second-class compartment, while reserved accommodation in a second- or third-class carriage on the Eastern Bengal Railway (EBR) required the payment of five and eight fares respectively.[54]

As a result, there were increasing suggestions for moderately priced 'family compartments' in the third and intermediate classes: designed like coupes, they were to be 'entirely shut off' from the rest of the carriage, protected by venetian blinds and provided with conveniences 'separate from the seat.'[55] In practice, however, such family accommodation was provided sparingly, even after 1869. The EIR did introduce a resolution through which third-class carriages were to be fitted for the convenience of *purdah* ladies, with one end of the compartment separated from the rest, next to which would be another compartment, separated from the rest.[56] However, this was the exception rather than the rule since most officials and railway functionaries envisaged such accommodation as being extended, at best, to the second class, which represented only between 0.75 and 2.25 per cent of passenger traffic.[57] Almost 15 years later, the Government of India still found itself coaxing state-run railways—over which it had maximum control—to adapt carriages in the intermediate class (below second class but above third class) to the needs of female seclusion, venturing to suggest that other privately-owned railway lines might consider such accommodation.[58] Again, while some like the Punjab Northern did try to provide intermediate-class carriages in which canvas

---

[54] L. Conway-Gordon, for Joint Secretary and Consulting Engineer, Govt. of Punjab (PWD: Railway) to Secretary, Govt. of India (PWD), 2 July 1869; Note by Captain F.S. Stanton, Consulting Engineer, Govt. of Oudh (Railway), 17 June 1869, enclosures to United Provinces Prog. (PWD: Railway), July–November 1869, IOR.P/442/61, BL.

[55] Minute by William Muir, 17 July 1869; Commissioner of Dacca, quoted in Note by Major Hovenden, 31 August 1869. Also, C. Stephenson, Board of Agency, EIR to Consulting Engineer to Govt. of Bengal (PWD), 27 August 1869; Memorandum by J.S. Trevor, Consulting Engineer for Railways, Bombay, 20 August 1869; Resolutions by the Govt. of Bombay (PWD: Railway), 3 September 1869, all enclosures to United Provinces Prog. (PWD: Railway), July–November 1869, IOR.P/442/61, BL.

[56] 149 of 1867. This was available for the hire of five seats 'by any native travelling with females.' C. Stephenson, to Consulting Engineer, Govt. of Bengal, 27 August 1869. Bear, *Lines of the Nation*, 50.

[57] *Statistical Abstract from 1894–95 to 1903–04*, 138; *Statistical Abstract from 1903–04 to 1912–13*, 136; *Statistical Abstract from 1910–11 to 1919–20*, 138.

[58] Railway Circular III, 1 March 1883, in *Railway Circulars of 1883*.

screens were provided to allow 'upper-class natives' to travel secluded with
their families, yet intermediate-class travel, if and when available, hovered
between 2.5 and 3.5 per cent of total passenger traffic.[59]

The extent to which 'respectable' women were using females'-only carriages
even after 1869 is attested to by the anxiety about enforcing respectability
in these. In 1874, the Bengal government was insisting that females'-only
compartments be made more private to better serve *paradanishin* or veiled
women, while the *Jaridah-i-Rozgar* was complaining about Christian
missionary women who tried to convert *gosha* or secluded native women
travelling in females'-only compartments.[60] The press stressed the 'serious
inconvenience' that 'respectable Hindu ladies' faced in travelling 'in the same
carriage with women of the lower classes, such as sweepers, *chamar*s, and the
like,' arguing that the aggravation was enhanced because the latter carried 'flesh
and other nasty things with them.'[61] Female privacy was negated, declaimed
the *Nur-ul-Absar*, if 'respectable Hindoostanee ladies are made to sit in the
same carriages with *ayas* and women of other low castes.'[62] There were also
complaints that respectable women encountered prostitutes when travelling
in such carriages: the *Allyghur Institute Gazette* decried as 'aggravating' the
fact that 'some prostitutes' seated themselves in a compartment 'occupied by
Hindoostanee ladies.'[63]

While some officials like the Commissioner of Dacca argued that it would
be 'unwise in these days of social improvement' to introduce any system
that perpetuated caste prejudice, most others focused on the logistical and
financial unviability of such measures.[64] Bombay Presidency's consulting
engineer for railways believed that 'Borah and other Mahomedan ladies' would

---

[59] *Statistical Abstract from 1894–95 to 1903–04*, 138; *Statistical Abstract from 1903–04 to 1912–13*, 136; *Statistical Abstract from 1910–11 to 1919–20*, 138. Though it had been introduced by some railways in the late nineteenth century, it remained limited to specific trains and routes even as late as 1917, when the Railway Board was still urging railways to consider providing an intermediate class on long-distance trains.

[60] L.C. Abbott, Under Secretary, Govt. of Bengal to Secretary, Govt. of India (PWD), 24 July 1874, PWD: Railway, October 1875, nos. 71–85, NAI. *Jaridah-i-Rozgar* (Royapetta, Madras), 28 May 1892, quoting the *Najmul Akbar*, in NNR: Madras.

[61] *Oudh Akhbar* (Lucknow), 6 June 1875, in NNR: Punjab, NWP, Oudh, and CP.

[62] *Nur-ul-Absar* (Allahabad), 15 May 1872, in NNR: Punjab, NWP, Oudh, and CP.

[63] *Allyghur Institute Gazette* (Aligarh), 15 September 1873, in NNR: Punjab, NWP, Oudh, and CP.

[64] Commissioner of Dacca, quoted in Note by Major Hovenden, 31 August 1869.

welcome segregation since they were 'more particular' than 'Parsi and Hindu ladies,' but insisted that paucity of numbers made the demand impossible to accommodate.[65] Some officials, particularly in Oudh and the North-West Provinces tried to devise ways in which 'higher castes of Hindoo ladies' could be separated from both those of a different caste or from 'Mahomedan ladies.'[66] However, for many railway administrations, such accommodation would only increase the 'useless dead load hauled about by trains.'[67] That this was true across areas and irrespective of whether they were state-controlled or private was proved by a governmental enquiry in the early 1880s, which included lines ranging from the Sind, Punjab, and Delhi Railway, Oudh and Rohilkund Railway, East Indian Railway, and Eastern Bengal Railway, to the Great Indian Peninsular Railway, Bombay, Baroda and Central Indian Railway, Madras Railway, and South Indian Railway.[68] In 1890, section 64(1) of the revised Railways Act finally mandated females'-only compartments in the lowest class on every passenger train as legally required of all railways in British India. If the train was to run for a distance exceeding 50 miles, then one such reserved compartment was to be provided with a water closet.[69] The continued use of such females'-only compartments is apparent both in demands to discontinue its use—such as the *Hitavadi*'s challenge of 1905—as well as in complaints bemoaning its absence—such as Narayan Rao Paranjpay's in 1906 about how the Calcutta and Bombay mails were not fulfilling this legal requirement.[70]

After the turn of the century, however, the discussion about protecting female honour during railway travel became less embroiled in discussions of

---

[65] Memorandum by J.S. Trevor, Consulting Engineer for Railways, Bombay, 20 August 1869.

[66] Meerut's Commissioner speculated about some '2nd and 3rd class carriages [being] divided into three compartments, one end for Hindoo ladies, the other end for Mahomedan ladies; and the centre for male members.' Quoted in United Provinces Prog. (PWD: Railway), July–November 1869, IOR.P/442/61, BL.

[67] Memorandum by J.S. Trevor, Consulting Engineer for Railways, Bombay, 20 August 1869.

[68] Statement Showing Measures Adopted on Principal Railways in India towards Providing Reserved Accommodation for Native Females, Railway Circular III, 1 March 1883, in Govt. of India, Public Works Dept., *Railway Circulars of 1883*. The MSMR stated that this was available to all female passengers, even though 'practically they are used only by natives.'

[69] Russell and Bayley, *Indian Railways Act IX of 1890*, 161.

[70] *Hitavadi* (Calcutta), 25 July 1905, in NNR: Bengal; Narayan Rao Paranjpay to Manager, EIR, 17 July 1906, RT, January 1908, nos. 103–15, NAI

religious and social hierarchies. Instead, threats to respectability were causally linked with the leniency of punishment allegedly meted out to European and Eurasian railway employees who dishonoured Indian women.[71] The focus on railway employees was not new. Public complaints had for long highlighted how ticket examiners and collectors harassed Indian women: 'purposely' inconveniencing *paradanishin* women on the pretext of examining or collecting their tickets, 'carrying on jokes' with them, or detaining them at stations under some pretence, 'generally giving as the reason that the girls or boys with them are older than they have been represented.'[72] Around the turn of the century, however, the press not only began to emphasize the increasing seriousness and frequency of offences against female passengers, ranging from theft and unwanted attention to sexual assault, but also to link this with the 'partiality' shown 'by our judges and magistrates owing to racial predilections.'[73]

In this narrative, European and Eurasian offenders were clubbed together, the deliberate focus on them emphasized by the numerical preponderance of native railway employees—in 1900, an overwhelming 337,383 natives, were employed by railways as compared to 5,229 Europeans and 7,364 Eurasians.[74] Such reports did not argue that Indian employees did not commit such crimes. Instead, they stressed the rising frequency with which European and Eurasian railway employees abducted and molested Indian women. It explained their boldness through the lenient punishment meted out to them, this itself stemming from the racial structure of judicial prejudice. This shift corresponded with a larger one: Elizabeth Kolsky describes how in the late nineteenth century, newspapers across India were reporting daily on the menace of 'white violence' and the 'scandalous acquittals of Britons accused of brutalizing natives.'[75] Consequently, some commentators urged Indian

---

[71] For a lengthier discussion of this, see Prasad, 'Smoke and Mirrors,' especially 33–46.

[72] *Koh i-Nur* (Lahore), 12 March 1870; *Aina-i-Aib-Numa-i-Hind* (Lahore), 17 February 1872 and 23 March 1872; *Rajputana Social Science Congress Gazette* (Jaipur), 7 July 1876, in NNR: Punjab, NWP, Oudh, and CP. *Urdu Akhbar*, 1 May 1873, in Précis of Complaints in the Native Press, appended to PWD: Railway, no. 71–85, October 1875, NAI; Response to Govt. of India Enquiry about the Comfort and Convenience of Native Passengers, PWD: Railway, no. 71–85, October 1875, NAI.

[73] *Rahbar* (Moradabad), 28 August 1906, in NNR: Agra and Oudh.

[74] *Statistical Abstract from 1894–95 to 1903–04*, 138.

[75] Elizabeth Kolsky, *Colonial Justice in British India: White Violence and the Rule of Law* (New York: Cambridge University Press, 2010), 185–86. She contends that this perception is supported by the historical record (190).

women to defend themselves against the depredations of 'white-skinned railway employees,' the Calcutta *Sanjivani* even urging them to carry scimitars concealed on their person when travelling by train.[76]

Catering to Difference?

Unlike in the case of railway compartments and carriages, food and water supplied on Indian railways began to be calibrated according to differences in diet, socio-religious taboos on touching and handling, and other rules of commensality. Some of the demands received by railway administrations spoke more generally about the needs of native or third-class passengers.[77] On occasion, railway administrations also used (fairly broad) ascriptions of class to designate what kinds of refreshments passengers could afford. Thus, the agent of the EIR argued against refreshment rooms that would be patronized only by 'upper-class' natives, while the Madras and Southern Mahratta Railways (MSMR) described how refreshment rooms 'resorted to by the middle and upper classes' offered items cooked in *ghee* or clarified butter, while 'the poorer classes of Indians' usually bought inexpensive fare cooked in oil from platform stalls.[78] However, the general discussion about refreshments and eating spaces remained saturated with questions of religion and caste.

Rules of commensality: supplying food and water

Such demands came from a variety of sources. An early one was made in 1866 by the elite and propertied members of the British Indian Association of the North-West Provinces. They asked that railways provide separate refreshment rooms for Hindus and Muslims, similar to those already provided for European passengers.[79] The popular press intermittently reprinted similar demands,

---

[76] *Sanjivani* (Calcutta), 27 July 1905, in NNR: Bengal; *Anand* (Lucknow), 9 October 1906 and *Hindustani* (Lucknow), 10 October 1906, in NNR: Agra and Oudh; and *Howrah Hitashi*, 12 December 1903, in NNR: Bengal.

[77] *Benaras Akhbar* (Benaras), 21 October 1875, in NNR: Punjab, NWP, Oudh, and CP; Extract from Resolution at Fourth Session of Central Provinces and Berar Provincial Conference, Nagpur, 16–18 November 1915, in RT: A, January 1917, 69-T.-16/1-6, NAI.

[78] Agent, EIR to Consulting Engineer to Govt. of India (Railways), Calcutta, 15 February 1902, in PWD: RT: A, May 1902, nos. 60–64, India Prog., IOR.P/6378, BL; R. Todd, Agent, MSMR to Secretary, Railway Board, 27/28 September 1918, Railway Board: Traffic A, November 1918, no. 328-T.-18/1-7, NAI.

[79] Petition by British Indian Association, NWP, to Viceroy, Aligarh, 16 October 1866.

which were presented in concerted form at a railway conference in Lucknow in 1903 that had been organized by the O&RR. While speaking to general rules of commensality, the demands made by the Tirtha Yatra Klesha Nivarini Sabhas in 1914 stressed the restrictions and taboos that caste Hindus and Hindu pilgrims were subject to during travel.[80] In contrast, a demand made in 1914–15 by a passenger-protection society criticized the fact that food supplied at many stations catered solely to the culinary inclinations of a numerically preponderant Hindu community.[81] The petition contended that 'Hindu and Muhammadan food' varied a great deal, and since Hindu vendors were unable to supply meat, so Muhammadan passengers either had to be content 'with the Hindu food—*puri* and sweets—or carry food with them.' While accepting that the food required for Muslim passengers would vary by region, it suggested a 'Muhammadan menu' to be supplied by Muslim vendors, in refreshment rooms at large stations and on refreshment cars in trains.

Unlike with separate carriages, both colonial and railway officials were sympathetic to demands that facilities for food and water be organized around socio-religious taboos on commensality; the only exception was where such segregated facilities would limit the carrying capacity of third-class rolling stock. In general, however, state officials tabulated available facilities under the rubric of 'Hindu' and 'Muslim' refreshments, often clarifying that brahmins were employed to ensure the purity of food and water made available to high-caste Hindus. Railway administrations also appointed separate Hindu and Muslim food inspectors to regulate cleanliness and quality of wares. Thus, the person catering on the EIR had four food inspectors, described as: 'Senior Hindu,' 'Junior Mahomedan,' 'Senior Mahomedan,' and 'Junior Hindu.'[82]

Initial directives had recommended that refreshment rooms for European passengers be complemented with 'suitable arrangements for the supply of food for Natives.'[83] Subsequently, the distinction was attributed to the eating

---

[80] Prog. of O&RR Conference, December 1903; Letters to the Viceroy from the Tirtha Yatra Klesha Nivarini Sabhas, August–October 1914.

[81] Extract from a letter from the General Secretary, Passenger Protecting Society of India, July 1914; General Secretary, Passenger Protecting Society of India to Railway Board, 20 January 1915 and 7 July 1915, all in RT: A, December 1915, nos. 343–68, India Prog., IOR.P/9574, BL.

[82] R. Cowley, acting Traffic Manager, Calcutta, to Agent, EIR, RT: A, January 1917, no. 69-T.-16/1-6, NAI.

[83] Railway Circular 13, PWD: Railway, 27 August 1864, PWD (Railway), 30 September 1864, nos. 23–26, NWP Prog, IOR.P/217/37, BL; Railway Circular 22, 29 October 1866.

habits of the two: it was suggested that since native passengers 'do not as a rule take their meals at regular hours,' so they were best served by platform vendors and stalls, while refreshment rooms were necessary for European passengers who ate 'at particular times' and could not obtain their preferred diet locally.[84] The system of vendors supplying 'native refreshments' continued throughout the colonial period. Contracted vendors paid a tax or a license fee to the railway administration, undertook to sell 'good and fresh' products, to be clean, dress in uniform, and sport badges if these were provided.[85] They priced their offerings in consultation with civil officers but station-masters retained the right to authorize prices and to dismiss vendors.[86] At smaller stations, eatables arranged on trays or barrows were vended alongside stationary railway carriages. At junctions or changing stations with longer halts, vendors sold their wares in stalls either on or outside the station platform. Stalls were awarded by auction and maintained by paying rent to railway administrations.[87] Passengers usually disembarked to purchase refreshments, though at selected stations stall-vendors sent their employees around the train with wares arranged on *thalīs* or trays.[88]

Fruit, parched grains, nuts, 'country sweetmeats,' breads, biscuits, tea, coffee, tobacco, cigarettes, and *paan* (betel) were commonly sold at stations by those designated as general vendors.[89] At least in later decades, some

---

[84] Consulting Engineer, Govt. of India (Railways), Calcutta to Secretary, Govt. of Bengal (Railways), 21 February 1902.

[85] Arrangements for Improving Supply of Refreshments to Native Passengers, RT: A, May 1908, nos. 227–51, India Prog., IOR.P/7918, BL. Also, Rules Relating to Licenses at Stations on O&RR; and Arrangements for Supply of Food for Indian Passengers on the NWR, both in RT: A, March 1917, no. 69-T.-16/7-8, NAI.

[86] Arrangements for Improving Supply of Refreshments to Native Passengers; Consulting Engineer (Railways), Calcutta, to the Secretary to Govt. of Bengal (Railway), 21 February 1902, PWD: RT: A, May 1902, nos. 60–64, India Prog., IOR.P/6378, BL; Vendor's agreement on the EIR, included as appendix to Agent, EIR to Consulting Engineer to Consulting Engineer to the Govt. of India for Railways, Calcutta, 15 February 1902, in PWD: RT: A, May 1902, nos. 60–64, India Prog., IOR.P/6378, BL.

[87] Memorandum on Refreshment Arrangements on the EIR, included as appendix to Agent, EIR to Consulting Engineer to the Govt. of India for Railways, Calcutta, 15 February 1902.

[88] Rules Relating to Licenses at O&RR Stations.

[89] Arrangements for Improving Supply of Refreshments to Native Passengers; Rules Relating to Licenses at O&RR Stations; Arrangements for Food for Indian Passengers, NWR.

stations had separately designated Hindu and Muslim vendors, who supplied refreshments specifically graded as 'Brahmin's food, sweetmeat, tea and coffee,' 'Non-Brahmin's food, sweetmeat, tea and coffee,' 'Mahomedan food, tea and coffee,' and 'Hindu tea and coffee.'[90] Some vendors and stalls provided food tailored to the needs of Hindu passengers travelling on a fast-day, who would eschew food with gram, wheat, or other flour in favour of sweets made with milk.[91] Refreshment lists differentiated *kacha* items—prepared with water and not eaten outside the *chowka* or kitchen—from *pukka* ones cooked in milk or in *ghee*.[92]

Assessments made at the turn of the century showed Indian passengers being served dominantly by platform vendors and stalls, while European passengers continued to be served in the refreshment rooms set aside for them. However, over the decades, demands had increased that native passengers also be provided with refreshment rooms.[93] Such demands were often conjoined with complaints about the inadequate number of platform vendors, or the fact that high license fees made their wares unnecessarily expensive.[94] To make the point, some compared the nominal rates paid by those running European refreshment rooms with the extortionate ones allegedly charged for stalls selling native refreshments. On the Great Indian Peninsular Railway (GIPR), for instance, the annual fee for a European refreshment room was fixed at Rs. 360, while those for native stalls went as high Rs. 3,500 per annum.[95] Similarly, the firm of Messrs. G.F. Kellner & Co. contracted by the EIR since 1892 was heavily subsidized by it, including paying only a nominal rent for the refreshment room that they ran.[96]

---

[90] RT: A, December 1915, nos. 343–68, India Prog., IOR.P/9574, BL; RT: A, January 1917, no. 69-T-16/1-6, NAI; RT: A, October 1920, no. 552-T.-17/86-88, NAI.

[91] GIPR Supplement to Traffic Instruction Book; Appendices to Rules regarding Sale of Refreshments at O&RR Stations; Arrangements for Supply of Food and Other Refreshments for Indian Passengers on NWR.

[92] Ibid.

[93] Secretary, Indian Association, to Secretary, Govt. of India (PWD), 4 October 1901.

[94] *Akhbar-i-Anjuman-i-Panjab* (Lahore), 8 August 1873; *Benaras Akhbar* (Benaras), 21 October 1875; and *Lauh-i-Mahfuz* (Moradabad), in NNR: Punjab, NWP, Oudh, and CP.

[95] RT: A, August 1907, nos. 92–104, India Prog., IOR.P/7634, BL.

[96] Secretary, Indian Association, to Secretary, Govt. of India (PWD), 4 October 1901; PWD: RT: A, May 1902, nos. 60–64, India Prog., IOR.P/6378, BL; RT: A, August 1907, nos. 92–104, India Prog., IOR.P/7634, BL.

1907 and after: dining cars and refreshment rooms

Around 1907, not long after being instituted, the Railway Board recommended that refreshment rooms for Indians be opened at stations where long-distance trains halted for a half-hour or more.[97] Also, that refreshment or dining cars be provided on mail and passengers trains. Not only had popular demands for these increased over the decades but also the Madras and Southern Mahratta Railway (MSMR) had recently undertaken a successful experiment with refreshment cars on selected trains.[98] Several railway administrations disagreed, stating that it was impossible to provide enough refreshment cars to accommodate colonial norms of commensality, particularly those caste and religious prejudices that they described as being endemic to north India. They also argued that such dining accommodation would reduce the third-class accommodation available in trains, without increasing passenger traffic or receipts.[99]

Some were eventually persuaded to try running refreshment cars but the experiments remained short-lived. The EIR withdrew these a few months after introducing them on its short-distance trains between Calcutta and Mokameh and on a long-distance express between Howrah and Mughal Serai.[100] Its officials recognized that refreshment cars were unsuited to short-distance trains but attributed the failure on the long-distance express to the prejudices of high-caste Hindus averse to eating 'in the same compartment as a Mohamedan or a low-caste Hindu.'[101] Even the fact that the food was supplied by a 'reliable firm of Hindoos' had been inadequate. However, the experiment also failed on the BBCI, which had provided separate eating compartments for Hindus

---

[97] PWD: RT: A, May 1902, nos. 60–64, India Prog., IOR.P/6378, BL; Secretary, Railway Board to President, IRCA, 14 August 1907, in RT: A, August 1907, nos. 92–104, India Prog., IOR.P/7634, BL.

[98] General Traffic Manager's Office, MSMR, Madras, 4 March 1911, and W.H. Wood to W.B. Wright, MSMR, 13 March 1911, both in RT: A, April 1911, nos. 15–16, Part I, NAI.

[99] Agent, BNR to Junior Consulting Engineer, Govt. of India (Railways), 17 July 1907, in RT: A, August 1907, nos. 92–104, IOR.P/7634, BL; C.H. Cowie, Manager, O&RR to Secretary, Railway Board, 20 October 1911; H.T. Taylor, Offg. Manager, EBSR to Secretary, Railway Board, 10 June 1911; and G.C. Godfrey, Acting Agent BNR to Secretary, Railway Board, 8 September 1911, all in RT: A, May 1914, nos. 10–25, NAI.

[100] R.S. Highet, Acting Agent, EIR, to Secretary, Railway Board 16 September 1912 and 17 May 1913, both in RT: A, May 1914, nos. 10–25, NAI.

[101] Ibid.

and Muslims on its Ahmedabad–Delhi express, as well as on Bengal–Nagpur Railway (BNR).[102] The BBCI attributed the failure to competition posed by platform vendors, combined with the disinclination—or inability—of third-class passengers to leave their carriages.[103]

Despite the doubts voiced by its administration, refreshment cars were fairly successful on the North-Western Railway (NWR).[104] Initially, the railway assigned one refreshment car on its Lahore–Delhi train to serve separate Hindu and Muslim meals. Promising results encouraged it to assign a second car on this route as well as to declare its intention to introduce these on other passenger trains.[105] Instead, a war-time reduction in passenger train services meant that all refreshment cars on the line were withdrawn in 1916.[106] In private, members of the Railway Board expressed surprise that refreshment cars had succeeded on railways 'as far apart' and serving such disparate areas as was traversed by the NWR and MSMR.[107] In a more public response in 1916, however, the Board's president stated that except in the Punjab, refreshment cars had failed owing to 'to the caste prejudice of passengers.'[108] Alternative explanations focusing on the inability of passengers to access these cars found no space in his 1916 response; they did, perhaps, inform the more circumspect response of 1919, which stated that refreshment cars had been withdrawn because they were not adequately utilized.[109]

---

[102] Home Board (London) to Agent, BBCI, 29 September 1911; Agent, BBCI to Secretary, Railway Board, 23 October 1911; General Traffic Manager to Agent, BBCI, 13 July 1911; and Agent, BNR, to Secretary, Railway Board, 2 April 1914, all in RT: A, May 1914, nos. 10–25, NAI.

[103] Home Board (London) to Agent, BBCI, 29 September 1911; Agent, BBCI to Secretary, Railway Board, 23 October 1911.

[104] H.A. Cameron, Traffic Superintendent, to Manager, NWR, 3–4 May 1911, RT: A, May 1914, nos 10-25, NAI.

[105] C.H. Cowie, Agent, NWR to Secretary, Railway Board, 23 October 1913, in RT: A, May 1914, nos. 10–25, NAI; C.H. Cowie, Agent, NWR, to the Secretary, Railway Board, 23 September 1915, in RT: A, December 1915, nos. 343–68, India Prog., IOR.P/9574, BL.

[106] Question and Answer, Imperial Legislative Council, 6 February 1919, RT: A, March 1919, no. 105/T.-19/1-3, India Prog., IOR.P/10624, BL.

[107] R.W. Gillian, Office Note (Railway Board), 13 May 1916, in RT: A, January 1917, 69-T.-16/1-6, NAI. Note was also signed by A.R. Anderson (18 May 1916) and F.D. Couchman (19 May 1916).

[108] Memorandum of Measures taken by Railway Board since 1905, tabled in Imperial Legislative Council Meeting, 9 March 1916, RT: A, May 1916, no. 553-T./1, NAI.

[109] Reply to K.K. Chanda, Imperial Legislative Council, 6 February 1919, RT: A, March 1919, no. 105/T.-19/1-3, India Prog., IOR.P/10624, BL.

Unlike with refreshment cars, the experiment with refreshment rooms for native passengers was wider and more sustained, at least from the nineteen teens onwards. 'Hindu' refreshment rooms were more common, many splitting their offerings into vegetarian and non-vegetarian meals.[110] However, some railways provided separate refreshment rooms for both Hindus and Muslims, each run by 'caterers of proper caste.'[111] Some stations also had a separate lessee for selling food to Muslim passengers, who could ask railway staff to wire ahead and ask for as many '1st or 2nd class' meals as had been requested.[112] At larger stations, specific 'Mahomedan' meals were offered, the menu including *chapatti*s, *paratha*s, rice and *pulao, korma, tarkari gosht*, and *kabab*, rounded off with *kheer or halwa*, and tea, coffee, and milk.[113] Sometimes, *shirmall, salan, kallia*, and *kofta* were also included.[114] One of the more elaborate in organization, many stations on the MSMR had provided not only a 'a general stall for the sale of sweets for all castes' and 'a kitchen with a Brahmin cook who cooks for all castes' but also a separate dining room each for brahmins and non-brahmins, as well as a 'Muhammadan cook' and separate dining rooms for Muslim passengers.[115]

Similar practices of calibration governed the supply of water to railway passengers. From early on, most third-class passengers had been unable to get off at stations to procure water from hydrants and *surahi*s provided on station platforms.[116] Consequently, they relied on watermen appointed by railway companies, who carried buckets from which they doled out cups of water to

[110] GIPR Supplement to Traffic Instruction Book; Appendices to Rules regarding Sale of Refreshments at O&RR Stations; Arrangements for Supply of Food and Other Refreshments for Indian Passengers on NWR.

[111] A.T. Stowell, Asst. Secretary, Railway Board to M.K. Gandhi, 22 January 1918, RT: A, March 1918, no. 552-T.-17/1-24, NAI.

[112] GIPR Supplement to Traffic Instruction Book; Appendices to Rules regarding Sale of Refreshments at O&RR Stations; Arrangements for Supply of Food and Other Refreshments for Indian Passengers on NWR.

[113] Ibid.

[114] Ibid.

[115] E.S. Christie's report on the MSMR in C. Dove Wilson, Senior Govt. Inspector, Railways, Circle no. 7, Madras, to Secretary, Railway Board, 12 November 1918, RT: A, January 1919, no. 69-T.-16/13–17, India Prog., IOR.P/10624, BL; R. Todd, Agent, MSMR to Secretary, Railway Board, 27/28 September 1918, RT: A, November 1918, no. 328-T.-18/1-7, NAI.

[116] *Hindu Prakash*, cited in *Karnamah* (Lucknow), 2 August 1874.

passengers, or filled up the small *surahi*s that many carried with them. However, their numbers were inadequate, especially during the summer months, as a slew of public complaints showed.[117] Officials were not only sympathetic to the need for increasing the supply of water at stations but also rather particular about conforming to dictates of purity and pollution. Thus, many were particularly concerned that high-caste Hindus be served by 'Brahmin watermen.'[118] Most officials agreed that more watermen were needed, with many specifying the need for separate Hindu and Muslim watermen, or else for brahmin watermen and *bhistee*s, the latter to supply everyone except high-caste Hindus.[119] Railways were urged to employ adequate numbers of water-carriers and to ensure that there were enough of 'both Hindu and Mussulman' ones.[120] Some like the Sindh, Punjab, and Delhi Railway (SPDR) described how they ensured that passengers were served by 'Hindu watermen and Mahomedan bhisties,' while others like the GIPR arranged watermen 'of different castes' for 'various classes of passengers.'[121]

On occasion, such extensive calibration was critiqued rather than endorsed, as well as replaced with suggestions that 'perhaps the division lies between

---

[117] *Koh–i–Nur* (Agra), 18 May 1872; *Kavi Vachan Sudha* (Benaras), 20 July 1872; *Meerut Gazette* (Meerut), 22 June 1872; *Mufid-i-Am* (Agra), 15 January 1873; *Karnamah* (Lucknow); 2 August 1874, *Urdu Dehli Gazette* (Agra), 17 April 1875, in NNR: Punjab, NWP, Oudh, and CP. Also, later, General Secretary, Passenger Protecting Society of India, Lucknow to Secretary, Railway Board, 17 May 1917, RT: A, June 1918, no. 552-T.-17/25-67, India Prog., IOR.P/10396, BL.

[118] Chief Commissioner (Central Provinces), summing up investigations of Commissioners of Nagpur, Narbuda, and Jabalpur. T.W. Armstrong, Secretary to Chief Commissioner of Central Provinces (PWD) to Secretary, Govt. of India (PWD), 19 March 1874. In one instance, it was stated that 'certain Mohamedans do not use water or green and fresh things touched by Hindus.' M. Agha Hassan Khan in Prog. of O&R Railway Conference, Lucknow, December 1903.

[119] Commissioner, Allahabad (20 August 1869); Magistrate, Allyghur (21 August 1869); Magistrate, Boolundshuhur (3 September 1869); Magistrate, Meerut (21 August 1869); Magistrate, Moozuffernuggur (13 August 1869); Magistrate, Saharunpoor (26 August 1869); Magistrate, Agra (7 September 1869); Magistrate, Mynpoory (31 August 1869); Commissioner, Agra (16 September 1869); and memorandum by E. Palmer, Chairman, of Agency, EIR, 29 January 1870, all in Papers received Unofficially from NWP, PWD: Railway, October 1875, nos. 71–85, NAI.

[120] Prog. of Railway Conference, September 1882, Home: Public B, October 1882, 143–44, NAI.

[121] Ibid.

vegetarians and non-vegetarians.'[122] K.S. Venkataram Ayyar who reached this conclusion in 1918 did not suggest that this had always been the case; instead he argued that education, combined with 'more social intercourse, advance of social reform and [a] broad view of things' had changed public perceptions and that 'people have not the same caste scruples as they used to have.' However, even as he described how rules of commensality among Hindus were becoming more relaxed, he insisted that there was 'no use of mingling all classes of Indians.' He believed that there were enough Muslim passengers that separate refreshment rooms could be provided for them, at least at large stations; in these, he recommended that 'peculiar food such as *pulavu* or *biriyani* with curry may be sold' and tables and benches provided since 'Mahomedans are accustomed to take food in plates unlike Hindus.'

Practising Colonial Difference

Even as spaces of commensality continued to be structured around arguments of difference, questions about physical separation remained contentious. Railway companies had rejected demands that carriages accommodate distinctions of caste or religion; however, they continued to reserve space for Europeans and Anglo-Indians. The problem was exacerbated by the fact that many such reserved compartments ran either empty or half-empty. This not only offered a stark contrast with overcrowded third-class carriages but also undermined official arguments about financial and logistical compulsions. While such spaces were often designated as 'European only,' it was understood that they were open to Anglo-Indians (earlier known as Eurasians), the latter either assumed in or subsumed under the prior category. While race was—and was seen as—the primary axis for such differentiation, the issue was complicated by the fact that 'native' passengers in 'European costume' were sometimes allowed into reserved carriages. During railway travel, attire not only allowed some passengers to reconfigure boundaries of racial affiliation but also offered choices seen to bespeak a cultural homogeneity that could temporarily efface distinctions between 'native' and 'Englishman.'

---

[122] Notes made by Rao Bahadur K.S. Venkataram Ayyar (Negapatam), Appendix C in C. Dove Wilson, Senior Govt. Inspector, Railways, Circle no. 7, Madras, to Secretary, Railway Board, 12 November 1918.

Reserved carriages: learning one's place

Even as they publicly embodied racial distance, compartments reserved for European passengers were officially attributed to Indian demands for segregated space—which railway companies had already rejected. In the late 1860s, official intervention was spurred by the death of an Indian woman who had been sexually violated by a European co-passenger.[123] This led the governor-general not only to insist on ensuring that railway companies continued to provide separate carriages for women, but also that they separate Indian and European passengers, particularly in the third class. Local governments were to encourage a 'complete separation of Europeans from Natives in the 3rd-class,' as well as to examine what arrangements for such separation existed in other classes of travel.[124] This incident became central to official explanations that described how accommodation reserved for Europeans and Anglo-Indians was intended to protect native passengers.

While demands to separate 'natives' and 'Europeans' certainly existed, they usually came from Indians travelling in the first or second classes. Many had found that their ability to afford a first- or second-class fare did not protect them from the disdain of Europeans and Anglo-Indians, who often thought it 'derogatory to their position to have Hindustanees seated in the same carriage as them.'[125] Newspapers reported that Indians could not, 'generally speaking,' travel in the first and second classes 'without fear of being ill-treated' by their co-passengers; further, that even the intermediate class was 'rarely accessible to Natives, on account of [it] being occupied chiefly by Europeans and Eurasians.'[126] Public accounts provided evidence of such incidents. Thus, the *Mayo Gazette* described how a high-court pleader with a first-class ticket from Benaras to Allahabad was turned out of his carriage at Mughal Serai because a European entered it; the *Shola i-Tur* recounted how a *sudder suddoor* travelling second-class was, 'without provocation,' abused by an European 'intent on using force'; and the *Hindu Prakash* narrated how a European passenger tried to turn out a 'native Christian' head-master travelling intermediate class from Multan to Amritsar.[127]

---

[123] Railway Circular 11R, 2 July 1868, PWD: Railway, July 1868, no. 71, NAI.
[124] Ibid.
[125] *Shola i- Tur* (Kanpur), 22 March 1873, in NNR: Punjab, NWP, Oudh, and CP.
[126] Ibid.
[127] *Mayo Gazette*, 10 July 1872, quoted in PWD: Railway, October 1875, nos. 71–85, NAI; *Shola i-Tur* (Kanpur), 22 March 1873; *Hindu Prakash* (Amritsar), 3 July 1874, in NNR: Punjab, NWP, Oudh, and CP.

Though such incidents occurred in all classes of travel, the second class seems to have been particularly fractious. Especially if travelling with their families, many Indians travelling first-class chose to reserve the entire carriage, thus minimizing contact with strangers. The second-class had a more textured demographic, including Europeans who could not afford the first-class, and Indians unwilling to travel third-class.[128] Further, many Indians in the second-class saw themselves as higher in social rank than many of their European co-passengers, complaining bitterly about being compelled to travel with a 'low class' of Europeans, often 'on the tramp.'[129] They were referring to 'poor whites,' the appellation used for the less well-off among domiciled Europeans and Eurasians/Anglo-Indians. While not a vast presence in absolute terms, 'poor whites' complicated racial claims to privileged access, not least because many of them were seen as being 'hopelessly degraded'—'low and licentious' as it were.[130]

Such claims of respectability, when combined with ill-treatment stemming from racial hubris, resulted in popular demands that Indian passengers in upper railway classes be provided with separate travelling accommodation.[131] The fact that such demands continued intermittently through the decades led railway and government officials to explain reserved accommodation as an Indian demand. Thus, in 1916 when K.K. Chanda challenged railway administrations for reserving 'compartments and carriages for Europeans, or Europeans and Eurasians only,' the Railway Board attributed such reservation to demands for segregation made by Indians themselves.[132] It returned to the oft-quoted 1903 conference in Lucknow organized by the O&RR in which four of the 19 proposals discussed were listed under the rubric of 'Separate Accommodation for Europeans and Natives.'

The conference, however, lacked the explanatory weight attached to it. While some like Mahant Kahn Das from Hardwar and M. Agha Hussain

---

[128] PWD: Railway, May 1871, nos. 5–12, Oudh Prog., IOR.P/42, BL.

[129] Petition by the British Indian Association, NWP, Aligarh, 16 October 1866.

[130] Mitzuni, *Meaning of White*, 53–57. He estimates that in 1911, their population would be 200,000 (72). Harald Fischer-Tine, *Low and Licentious Europeans: Race, Class and 'White Subalternity' in Colonial India* (New Delhi: Orient BlackSwan, 2009).

[131] *Shola i- Tur* (Kanpur), 22 March 1873.

[132] K.K. Chanda, Question in Imperial Legislative Council, 27 September 1916, in RT: A, October 1916, no. 899-T./1, NAI. *Sindh Law Report* (5), 140, clause 10; Robert Gillian (President, Railway Board), Reply to K.K. Chanda, Imperial Legislative Council, 27 September 1916, in RT: A, October 1916, no. 899-T./1, NAI.

Khan from Fyzabad had endorsed separate first- and second-class carriages 'for Natives and Europeans,' others had challenged both the principle and the practice.[133] Some like Moksha Das Mitter from Benaras considered separate accommodation 'undesirable' but suggested that *if* it was formally instituted, then Europeans should be excluded from compartments not reserved for them.[134] Sunder Lal Misser of Calcutta was equally concerned with symmetry, insisting that if separate carriages were provided, then 'there should be no distinction' in those provided for Indians.[135] Their concerns highlighted the fact that carriages reserved for Europeans and Anglo-Indians did not formally preclude such passengers from using unreserved carriages. While no formal resolution (or legislation) resulted from this conference, its proceedings became important to the official arsenal: even in 1921, the Manager of the Bengal-Dooars Railway was quoting 'a Hindu society in Lucknow' that asked that Europeans and Anglo-Indians 'not be brought in touch with Hindus.'[136]

Demands for reservation existed in concert with public critiques of the practice. A 1910 piece in the *Amrita* that actually recommended separate carriages as a way to protect 'respectable 2nd class travellers in India' had to point out that 'of course many an Indian gentlemen would object to this arrangement.'[137] Many already had. A 1908 order to provide separate first- and second-class carriages for 'European & Indian gentlemen on main routes' was verbally contravened because of strong public objection, while in 1911 the Railway Board explained that some railways did not provide separate accommodation in the second-class owing to the 'strong objection' raised 'by Indians themselves.'[138] Notwithstanding the occasionally rescinded order, railways continued to reserve some accommodation for Europeans and Anglo-Indians, though different lines chose in which classes they would do so.

---

[133] Summary of Proposals, Prog. of O&RR Conference, 1903.

[134] 'Separate Accommodation for Europeans and Natives,' Prog. of O&R Conference, 1903.

[135] Ibid.

[136] Manager, Bengal Dooars Railway to Secretary, Railway Board, 16/17 September 1921, in RT, 1922, no. 229-T.-21/ 15-38, India Prog., IOR.P/11225, BL. The manager's letter referenced the Railway Board's file on the 1903 conference. The file noted in the margins in the 1921 file is the same as that for proceedings of the O&R conference: RT: A, June 1904, nos. 74–75.

[137] *Amrita*, 19 January 1910, in RT: B, March 1911, nos. 33–34, NAI.

[138] For the 1908 order, RT: B, April 1921, nos. 1–6, NAI. Railway Board to Secretary to Govt. of Eastern Bengal & Assam (PWD), 7 March 1911, RT: B, March 1911, nos. 33–34, NAI.

In point of law: challenging reserved accommodation

As part of maintaining reserved accommodation, railway administrations evicted Indian passengers from designated carriages, even if these were running empty. Some of those thus evicted turned to litigation, challenging both the legality of such reservation and the act of eviction. Though the legal battle failed to overturn the practice, it engendered a sustained debate on three related issues: whether such reservation was legally permissible under the Indian Railways Act of 1890; why Indian passengers were not allowed to travel in reserved space when these remained unoccupied by Europeans and Anglo-Indians; and whether Indians entering such reserved carriages became trespassers who could be forcibly removed by the railway, even if they had paid the fare for that class of travel.

These challenges were substantively explicated in a 1908 case in which the litigant, Mathradas Ramchand, challenged the right of the state-owned North-Western Railway to remove him from a second-class carriage. Mathradas argued that his second-class fare entitled him to *any* second-class accommodation that was unoccupied; further, that reserving space for Europeans violated section 42 of the Railways Act, which prohibited railway administrations from showing 'undue or unreasonable preference' to any particular person or description of traffic, as well as from subjecting any to 'undue or unreasonable prejudice or disadvantage.'[139] The additional judicial commissioner of Sind declined to assess the charge of illegality posed under section 42, arguing that the provisions of section 41 precluded railway administrations from being sued for omissions or violations of the Act.[140] He dismissed Mathradas' suit.

Mathradas appealed, but unsuccessfully. Sind's judicial commissioner not only endorsed the restrictions of section 41 but also—by equating such reservation with the division of railway accommodation into first, second, and third *classes* based on fare (sections 66 and 113) and the separate accommodation reserved for females (sections 64 and 119)—argued that railways had a right to reserve carriages for the European and Anglo-Indian community.[141] In his

---

[139] Indian Railways Act, 1890, reproduced in Bell, *Railway Policy in India*.

[140] Russell and Bayley, *Indian Railways Act*, 72, 52. Section 41 permitted Mathradas to complain to the Governor-General, who could refer the case to Railway Commissioners (section 28) or a special tribunal of a High Court judge and two lay commissioners, one experienced in 'railway business.'

[141] Several of these sections were identical to earlier regulations, like those introduced in 1853 and 1854. See 'Regulations for EIR,' 13 April 1854, no. 2, Bengal Prog., IOR.P/163/20-22, BL.

opinion, the boards marked 'Indians' and 'Europeans' were 'definite intimation' of the fact that Mathradas' ticket only entitled him to a seat in *a*—and not *any*—second-class carriage. Thus, he became a trespasser when he did not enter the carriage earmarked for Indians. Bypassing the fines prescribed in sections 109(1), 112, and 113 for passengers who entered a reserved or full carriage or else travelled without a sufficient ticket, the commissioner deployed section 122, which allowed railway employees to remove anyone 'unlawfully' on railway premises.[142]

The logic that if railways could separate by sex, then they could segregate by race was not specific to India; it was similar to legal arguments deployed in the Jim Crow American South, and described—again, similarly—as a mechanism to 'prevent personal collisions and preserve peace and order.'[143] However, in India, the issue of separation and segregation continued to be intertwined with problems of overcrowding, at least in relation to third-class travel. Thus, the question of reserved compartments—especially of those only partially occupied—was complicated by a 1911 order in which the Railway Board authorized railway administrations to prosecute passengers who prevented others from entering into compartments that were not fully occupied. By raising the penalty from a mere fine, as defined under section 109(2), the Board hoped to communicate its strong objection to the practice of passengers refusing to let others into compartments that they deemed were legally full.[144] Instead, it found itself blindsided by questions about reservation: Indians wanted to know how this order affected those of them who chose to travel in reserved compartments when these were either partially or fully unoccupied. In private, the Board noted that this was not permissible but declined any official pronouncement; some of its members declared that such questions were ruses intended to obtain 'an opinion or pronouncement' that could be subsequently

---

[142] Russell and Bayley, *Indian Railways Act*, 228, 230–32, 240. Sections 117–20 allowed passengers to be removed only if they were smoking without permission, drunk, suffering from infectious diseases, interfering with the comfort of fellow passengers; riding on the footboard or roof; or entering a carriage or place set apart for women. Russell and Bayley, *Indian Railways Act*, 237–39.

[143] Adelbert Hamilton, 'Discrimination in Railway Facilities,' *The American Law Register* 32, 7, new series, volume 23 (July 1884): 417–34; Richter, *Home on the Rails*, 99–103.

[144] RT, May 1911, nos. 102–5, NAI. 109 (2) made it punishable to resist 'lawful entry of another passenger into a compartment…not already containing the maximum number of passengers exhibited therein or thereon under section 63.'

quoted as an official ruling.[145] Thus, Mr. Anrudh Singh from Calcutta who had sent one such letter was referred to the concerned railway for answers.[146] However, excepting the South Indian Railway, which explicitly ordered guards and station-masters to ensure that Indians were not allowed to occupy reserved compartments, railway manuals generally remained silent on the subject.[147]

However important they were to challenging the formal contradictions in railway policy, litigation and public complaints generally failed to prevent railway companies from reserving carriages or from evicting Indian 'trespassers' from these, irrespective of whether they ran empty or not. The grievance only increased in the early twentieth century, when it merged with broader nationalist opposition to multiple forms of racial segregation. Governor-General Reading could hardly have been surprised to receive a biting letter in 1921 asking him to either abolish such reservation, or face a *satyagraha* in which Indian passengers would occupy reserved compartments, refusing to vacate them regardless of any action undertaken by railway administrations. The author, V.V. Kelkar, President of the Railway Grievances Committee of Bhusawal first criticized reservation in principle, asking why compartments were reserved for 'these Anglo-Indians and Europeans' when in various parts of the world 'other races, nationalities and castes, differing in manners, customs, dress, civilization and so forth travel amicably together in the ordinary third-class compartments'?[148] He was equally infuriated by the fact that Indians were not allowed to use reserved carriages even when these ran empty. His letter described them as being 'mercilessly dragged out' while trains ran on 'defiantly with such emptied compartments.' His complaint drew sustenance from statistics that showed that on the GIPR only 25 of the 250 seats reserved for Europeans and Anglo-Indians were usually occupied on trains passing through Bhusawal daily.[149] Asking if reserved compartments expressed a sense of 'race superiority' or a fear that Europeans and Anglo-Indians were incapable of travelling without molesting others, Kelkar's committee denounced the

---

[145] Office Notes, RT, January 1917, no. 3-T/17/1-2, NAI.

[146] Ibid.; Asst. Secretary, Railway Board to Anrudh Singh, Calcutta, 15 January 1917, in RT, January 1917, no. 3-T/17/1-2, NAI. A.N. Mitra forwarded his complaint to the EIR (Calcutta, 22 March 1917) to the Railway Board. RT: B, July 1917, no. 169-T./16/22-24, NAI.

[147] Office Notes, RT, no. 3-T/17/1-2, January 1917, NAI.

[148] V.V. Kelkar, President of the Railway Grievances Committee (Bhusawal) to Lord Reading, Viceroy and Governor-General, 20 August 1921, in RT, September 1921, no. 229-T.-21/1-14, NAI.

[149] Ibid.

'ignominious peace' involved in giving up 10 seats for every single European and Anglo-Indian.[150]

While accepting that unoccupied reserved accommodation infuriated Indian passengers who were squashed in overcrowded compartments, the Railway Board continued to deny that the practice was racially motivated.[151] Instead, it reiterated that reservation stemmed from the 'prejudices and dislikes' expressed by Indians, and was necessary to avoid the 'unpleasantness and ill-feeling' that could be sparked by any 'trifling incident.' The issue remained unresolved, leading to further litigation. Thus, in his suit against the BBCI, Partab Daji tried to limit the rights of railway companies to define trespass. Like Mathradas, he failed: Justices Piggott and Walsh of the Allahabad High Court ruled that any prohibition against undue preference in section 42 had 'no application to reservation of a particular passenger carriage for any *class* of the travelling public' (emphasis added).[152] This interpretation was challenged by Narayan Krishna Gogate who refused to leave a reserved third-class compartment. The presiding magistrate M.C. Kelkar not only agreed with Gogate's argument that railway companies had not provided specifically for racially-based reservation under section 47 (as they had for women passengers) but also argued that any attempt to legalize such reservation was *ultra vires*, given the mandatory provisions of section 42 against undue preference.[153] However, in the absence of 'any clear ruling' from the Bombay High Court, he was legally bound to the prior Allahabad ruling despite disagreeing with it.[154]

Sartorial politics: the life of Macaulayan hierarchies

As the question of reservation smouldered, it intersected a related debate: who could—or could not—claim to be a European or Anglo-Indian passenger. In

---

[150] Ibid.

[151] W.D. Waghorn, President, Railway Board to C.L. Corfield, Assistant Private Secretary to Viceroy, 31 August 1921, in RT: A, September 1921, no. 229-T.-21/1-14, NAI.

[152] See RT: A, September 1921, no. 229-T.-21/1-14, NAI.

[153] The defence argued *vide* Justice Saha's decision in Javedkar *versus* GIPR (Bom. L.R, Vol. XXIII, 309). In this case, the complainant cited was not the railway on which the accused had been travelling by down passenger from Bhusawal to Pachorak on 17 February 1922 but instead Mahadu Vithu, Railway Police Constable, Jalgaon, who had instructed the accused to leave the carriage.

[154] Judgment no. 8 of 1922 in the Court of 1st Class Magistrate, Jalgaon, East Khandesh, Enclosure to Memorandum by V.V. Kelkar, in RT, (?)1922, no. 229-T.-21/15-38, India Prog., IOR.P/ 11255, BL. The prosecution stood on a ruling on section 109 by the Allahabad High Court (ILR, Vol. XLII, 327).

the world of railway travel at least, the categories were far from self-explanatory. Some months before V.V. Kelkar described how anyone wearing 'a European hat and even a tattered European coat and pantaloon' was allowed into compartments reserved for Europeans and Anglo-Indians, Venkataramana Ayyangar had encountered something similar. As he told his colleagues in the Madras Legislative Council, his motor-driver Jnanamuttu had been unable to secure him a retiring room at the Erode station. However, when Jnanamuttu returned some minutes later, now wearing a hat and calling himself John Matthew, the station-master said: 'Here is a room.' Attire certainly did not provide unfettered access since Indians 'in European costume' could and were evicted by railway guards, either 'according to his sweet will or when a so-called European objects.'[155] However, during railway travel, a hat, coat, and pantaloon did, on occasion, allow some to reconfigure boundaries of racial affiliation.

The practice was certainly not new to 1921, when both Kelkar and Ayyangar emphasized it. Even in 1873, a railway official had articulated his concern that separate retiring accommodation at stations for Indian passengers travelling in the first and second classes would offend many 'native gentlemen' who, he believed, preferred consorting with European gentry to being 'intermixed with castes and classes of his countrymen with whom he is not accustomed to associate.'[156] Half a century later, the Railway Board's president was told that it was 'well understood' that compartments that were reserved for Europeans and Anglo-Indians were generally available to those Indians 'who have adopted European dress & customs.'[157] In this sartorial politics of inclusion and exclusion, attire signalled a cultural homogeneity that minimized differences between 'native' and 'Englishman.' As the EIR's agent explained, the 'usual' first- or second-class passenger, 'whether Indian or non-Indian,' was seen as 'more cultured, tolerant and self-controlled.'[158] The feeling was certainly not restricted to railway officials or the colonial state. Lachmi Prasad Sinha was not alone in insisting that what made the practice of reserving compartments more

---

[155] Starred Question, Legislative Assembly by Rai Bahadur Lachmi Prasad Sinha (Admitted in List 87-A, Serial 29), for 15 January 1923, in RT: A, April 1923, 47-T-21/60-86, NAI.

[156] Note by W.W. Greathead, 1 August 1873, in Appendix, PWD: Railway, October 1875, nos. 71–85, NAI.

[157] Office Note (A.G. Stowell, Assistant Secretary Railway Board), Railway Board, 21 June 1917, in RT: B, July 1917, no. 169-T.-16/22-24, NAI.

[158] EIR Agent to Secretary, Railway Board, 25 October 1921, in RT: A, 1922, no. 229-T.-21/15-38, India Prog., IOR.P/11225/BL.

offensive was that even 'literate and high-class Indians' dressed in European attire were evicted from them.[159]

Retiring rooms provided at stations further exacerbated discussion on the relationship between attire and 'manners.' In theory, railways offered retiring rooms at stations for first- and second-class passengers. In practice, Indians with first- or second-class tickets were often excluded, these rooms having been marked as 'European-only' by railway administrations. Like with reserved compartments, passengers designated as Anglo-Indian were allowed into these waiting rooms. On occasion—as in the case of Jnanumuttu or 'John Matthew'— Indians in European attire were allowed into retiring rooms marked 'European only.' Official responses attributed this to the fact that unlike Europeans and Indians 'who have adopted the European style of living,' those Indians living 'in the Indian style' would naturally prefer *serai* accommodation available in the town to retiring rooms at stations.[160] The Railway Board suggested that such segregation was restricted to 'certain railway lines in South India.'[161] However, while the Madras and Southern Mahratta Railway (MSMR) and the South Indian Railway (SIR) were most *explicit* about excluding Indians from retiring rooms— this restriction being inscribed in railway guides for certain stations like Guntakal, Arkoram, Renigunta, and Bellary—the practice itself seemed to be more general.[162] In 1874, the *Dabdaba-i-Sikandari* was writing of Allahabad railway station when describing how 'a native gentleman' was turned out of a retiring room, whilst in 1914, Munshi Mahadeo Rao was informed that retiring rooms at Kathgodam station had been reserved for Europeans since it had first opened about 30 years ago.[163] Similarly, K.K. Chanda's critique of

---

[159] Starred Question, Legislative Assembly by Lachmi Prasad Sinha, for 15 January 1923.

[160] Secretary, Railway Board to T. Balaji Rao Nayadu Garu, Nellore, Mr. Konda Venkatappayya Paniulu, Guntur, and P.S.T. Saye, Barrister, Guntur, 24 June 1920, in RT: A, April 1921, no. 304-T-.20/2-15, India Prog., IOR.P/11065, BL. Secretary, Railway Board to P. Siva Rao, quoted by L. Davidson, in Prog. of the Madras Legislative Council, 15 July 1920, and P. Siva Rao, Prog. of the Madras Legislative Council, 15 July 1920, both in RT: A, April 1921, no. 304-T-.20/2-15, India Prog., IOR.P/11065, BL.

[161] Extract from Prog. of the Indian Legislative Council (Simla), 2 September 1920, in RT: A, April 1921, no. 304-T-.20/2-15, India Prog., IOR.P/11065, BL.

[162] Office Notes, RT, January 1917, no. 3-T/17/1-2, NAI. P. Siva Rao, Prog. of the Madras Legislative Council, 15 July 1920, in RT: A, April 1921, no. 304-T-.20/2-15, India Prog., IOR.P/11065, BL.

[163] *Dabdaba-i-Sikandari* (Rampore), 10 August 1874, in NNR: Punjab, NWP, Oudh, and CP; Q & A in the United Provinces' Legislative Council (Nainital), 14 September 1914, in RT, October 1914, no. 71, India Prog., IOR.P/9497, BL.

the practice in 1916 was not restricted to Madras, while a sharply critical 1920 editorial titled 'Racial Bar' was published in the *Searchlight* out of Patna.[164]

Perhaps because railway guides in Madras were most explicit about excluding Indians, some of the most engaged discussions occurred in the Madras Legislative Assembly. Members not only objected to the fact that Indian passengers were excluded from first- and second-class retiring rooms, but also criticized the occasional concession of providing them with separate retiring rooms. They were equally hostile to the suggestion that Indians would be admitted into first- and second-class retiring rooms *only* if they dressed in European attire.[165] T. Arumainatha Pillai could not comprehend the fundamental difference between Indian passengers 'in their own dress' and those who 'put on a hat.' P. Siva Rao found it grossly unsatisfactory that Indians, 'whatever their position in life may be and whatever their habits,' should be shut out from first- and second-class retiring rooms, while C.V.S. Narasimha Raju pointed out that Indians and Europeans often shared rest-houses maintained by local boards and the PWD.[166]

Faced with these demands, railway administrations threatened to shut down retiring rooms altogether. Consequently, a significantly toned down resolution emanated from the Madras assembly, suggesting that retiring rooms be provided for Indians on stations in Madras Presidency where there were 'similar' provisions 'for other communities.' Despite the less demanding language, the resolution was defeated by the decisive vote of the vice-president.[167] While he formally challenged it on a technicality—arguing that it had been moved without the prior consideration of the railway department—the vice-president chastised the resolution as an attempt to abolish 'those concessions which our European fellow subjects are at present enjoying.' An enraged *Searchlight*

---

[164] K.K. Chanda, Question in the Imperial Legislative Council, 27 September 1916, in RT: A, October 1916, no. 899-T./1, NAI; *Searchlight* (Patna), 1 August 1920.

[165] Prog. of the Madras Legislative Council, 15 July 1920.

[166] Ibid.

[167] *For*: Arumainatha Pillai; K. Venkatapayya Pantulu; P. Siva Rao; Rai Bahadur T. Namberumal Chetti Garu; B. Venkatapathi Raju; Raja of Ramnad; Rai Bahadur T. Balaji Rao Nayudu Garu; C.V.S. Narasimha Raju; B.V. Narasimha Aiyar; Rai Bahadur N. Subba Rao; Rai Bahadur T.N. Sivagnanam Pillai Avargal; Khan Bahadur A.T.G.M. Ahmad Tambi Marakkayar. *Against*: L. Davidson, CSI; C.G. Todhunter, CSI; R.A. Graham, Surgeon-General; R. Littlehailes; Diwan Bahadur L.D. Swamikannu Pillai Avargal; M.D. Devadoss; T. Richmond; J.H. Thonger; E.S. Lloyd; W.J.J. Howley, CSI, Advocate-General.

attributed his negative vote to his Anglo-Indian 'spirit,' alleging that he would prefer that retiring rooms be abolished altogether rather than that they be thrown open to Indians.[168] Such a charge re-emphasized the contested identity of certain groups of railway passengers, just as V.V. Kelkar had earlier inquired why it was that 'native Christians, Goanese and Parsis' could usually use reserved compartments.[169]

A losing battle, or keeping reservation alive?

In April 1921, the Madras assembly resolved that retiring rooms for Indian passengers should be provided at every station that offered one for European passengers.[170] The larger issue, however, remained unresolved. Even as the SIR explained that it was allowing Indians who conformed to 'European habits' unrestricted use of first- and second-class retiring rooms, as well as providing separate retiring rooms for those with 'Indian habits,' demands were renewed that railways open retiring rooms to all 'irrespective of race, colour or caste.'[171] Public ire increased as railways continued to reserve compartments for Europeans and Anglo-Indians. Four large lines—the MSMR, SIR, Bengal-Nagpur, and North-Western, together covering approximately 9,500 miles in 1920—agreed to limit reserved space to a single compartment of 10 seats, the facility restricted to intermediate and third classes in mail and fast passenger trains.[172] However, four other large lines—which together controlled another 9,000 miles—refused the Board's suggestion to so restrict

---

[168] *Searchlight* (Patna), 1 August 1920.

[169] Kelkar to Reading, 20 August 1921.

[170] Assistant Secretary, Railway Board to Secretary, Govt. of Madras, PWD (Railway), 2 April 1921, in RT: A, April 1921, no. 304-T-.20/2-15, India Prog., IOR.P/11065, BL.

[171] Agent, SIR, to Secretary, Railway Board, 16 April 1921, in RT: A, April 1921, no. 304-T-.20/2-15, India Prog., IOR.P/11065, BL. Serial no. 1 of List no. 18-A of Admitted Questions and Resolutions of the Legislative Assembly; Memorandum from Assistant Secretary, Railway Board, no. 304-T.-20, 10 February 1921, both in RT: A, April 1921, no. 304-T-.20/2-15, India Prog., IOR.P/11065, BL. Also, RT: B, October 1921, no. 47-T.-21/6-21, NAI.

[172] Assistant Secretary, Railway Board to Agents, 8 September 1921, RT: A, September 1921, no. 229-T.-21/ 1-14, NAI; Assistant Secretary, Railway Board to various railway, 21 April 1922, in RT: A, (?)1922, no. 229-T.-21/ 15-38, India Prog., IOR.P/11225, BL.

reserved compartments.[173] Only three lines specified that they reserved no accommodation, but at a total of 2,565 miles, they comprised only 6 per cent of railway mileage in 1920.[174] In October 1922, the Indian Railway Conference *endorsed* the practice of reserving carriages, although it suggested that Indians in European dress be allowed into these.[175]

It was as this time that the Anglo-Indian and European Domiciled Association reiterated that differences in 'modes of living' necessitated reserved accommodation for Anglo-Indians and Europeans, especially given that many of them were in 'straitened circumstances, moving about the country seeking employment.'[176] In the immediate post-war boom of 1919, many domiciled Europeans and Anglo-Indians had resigned from their jobs, whether in railways or elsewhere, to take advantage of new employment opportunities; however, this 'booming economy' collapsed in 1923, leaving many unemployed.[177] In private, members of the Railway Board accepted that this group 'naturally wished to retain a privilege they have so long enjoyed.'[178] However, since they could not completely ignore 'Indian vocal opinion' they hoped that time would resolve the issue.[179] In the ensuing battle of attrition, reservation lost some ground: by 1924, company lines abolished reservation in the intermediate class, with state-managed railway being instructed to do the same.[180] Most railways settled for reserving one small third-class compartment (see Table 2.1).

---

[173] EIR, BBCI, EBR, and GIPR, in RT: A (?) 1922, no. 229-T.-21/15-38, India Prog., IOR.P/11225, BL.

[174] *Statistical Abstract from 1910–11 to 1919–20*, 140–44.

[175] Memorandum from Legislative Assembly, 18 January 1923, in RT: A, April 1923, no. 47-T-21/60-86, NAI. C.M. Hindley, Response to Lachmi Prasad Sinha, 8 February 1923, Legislative Assembly Debates, Vol. II, no. 33, in RT: A, April 1923, no. 47-T-21/60-86, NAI.

[176] Secretary, Anglo-Indian and European Domiciled Association to C.D.M. Hindley, 29 January 1923, RT: A, April 1923, no. 47-T-21/60-86, NAI.

[177] Mitzuni, *Problem of White*, 93.

[178] S.D. Manson, Office Note (Railway Board), 7 March 1923, RT: A, April 1923, no. 47-T-21/60-86, NAI.

[179] Ibid.; Extracts from Discussions in the Legislative Assembly about Mr. Hussanally's Resolution for Abolition, 10 March 1923, in RT: A, April 1923, no. 47-T-21/60-86, NAI.

[180] It would apply to the EIR when it shifted from Company to State management at the end of 1924. Mr. C.D.M. Hindley (Chief Commissioner, Railways), Reply to Question no. 84, (Admitted in List no. 175-A), in RT: C, April? 1924, no. 834-T/ 1-6, NAI.

Table 2.1. Reservation for Europeans and Anglo-Indians, *ca.* 1924

Railway	*Facility*
North-Western	• One third-class compartment on fast and passenger trains
Oudh & Rohilkund	• One third-class compartment on the Punjab & Dehra Dun mail
East Indian	• One third-class compartment on mail and passenger trains
Great Indian Peninsular	• Third-class accommodation on mail and express trains
Bombay, Baroda & Central Indian	• One third-class compartment on mail and fast passenger trains (*Abolished completely that year)
Bengal Nagpur	• One third-class compartment on mail and fast passenger trains
South Indian	• One third-class compartment on the Mettupalayam, Manglaore, and Ceylon Boat mails, and Trivandrum Express
Burma	• One third-class compartment on four mails and two fast trains
Madras & Southern Mahratta	• *On Broad Gauge*: Two third-class compartments on the Calcutta mails, and one third-class compartment on the Bombay and Bangalore mails, and four other trains. In addition one third-class compartment on 12 local trains • *On Metre Gauge*: One third-class compartment on the Poona–Bangalore mail and passenger trains

Source: Tabulated from RT: C, April(?) 1924, no. 834-T/1-6, NAI.

Denouements

Even as reserved compartments for Europeans and Anglo-Indians were castigated as discriminatory, 'untouchable' Antyaja passengers found themselves harassed by high-caste Hindus, especially in Kathiawar. The latter hoped that being subjected to such ill-treatment would compel untouchables to keep their distance from them during the course of railway travel. In nationalist circles, however, acute anxiety was generated by the fact that such incidents occurred '*even* in railways,' as emphasized by M.K. Gandhi.[181]

The issue was obviously not new to the 1920s and 1930s; however, during these decades it became a visible symptom of inclusion and exclusion in the national society being constructed. The racial politics of railway space had been apparent to Gandhi ever since he had been thrown out of a first-class

---

[181] M.K. Gandhi, Presidential Address, Kathiawar Political Conference, Bhavanagar, 8 January 1925, *in Young India*, 8 January 1925, *CWMG*, Vol. xxv (Ahmedabad: Publications Division, Ministry of Information and Broadcasting, 1967), 550–64.

railway carriage in South Africa in 1893.[182] It was also paramount, however, in the mind of one of Gandhi's primary interlocutors B.R. Ambedkar, who had ceased to take discrimination 'as a matter of course' after a bitter experience at Masur railway station.[183] The sheer joy of his first railway journey had been thwarted when Ambedkar witnessed the revulsion of a station-master who had just been told by the child that he was a *Mahar*, a group classified as untouchable in Bombay Presidency. Ambedkar continued to reflect on the inherent contradictions in high-caste Hindus ostracizing untouchables during railway travel in an attempt to maintain caste purity. In the heated politics of the mid-1930s, he wrote:

> It must be a source of silent amusement to many a Non-Hindu to find hundreds and thousands of Hindus breaking Caste on certain occasions, such as railway journey and foreign travel and yet endeavouring to maintain Caste for the rest of their lives![184]

Even as it generated demands for separation and incidents of discrimination, the railway carriage was *expected* to flatten the social space of colonial India. Soon after returning to India, Gandhi had emphasized that railway passengers must desist from any form of differentiation during travel, whether based on caste, class, region, or religion; instead, he insisted that railway passengers should realize themselves 'all as children of India who have for the once assembled under one roof.'[185] Laudatory surprise is thus writ large in Gandhi's

---

[182] M.K. Gandhi, *The Story of My Experiments with Truth* (1927), English translation by Mahadev Desai (Navjivan Publishing House: Ahmedabad, 1940), 92–93.

[183] Born in 1891, Ambedkar dates the incident to when he was about nine. Ambedkar, 'Waiting for a Visa.' The text (estimated to have been written around 1935 or 1936), can be found in *Dr. Babasaheb Ambedkar: Writings and Speeches*, Vol. 12, edited by Vasant Moon (Bombay: Education Department, Government of Maharashtra, 1993), part I, 661–91.

[184] The 1935 speech, planned for the Jat-Pat-Todak Mandal of Lahore, was actually not given. It was, however, printed in Ambedkar's *Annihilation of Caste, with a Reply to Mahatma Gandhi* (various editions, this one: Jullundar: Bheem Patrika Publications, 1968).

[185] M.K. Gandhi, 'Railway Passengers,' before 26 July 1916, *CWMG*, Vol. xiii (Ahmedabad: Publications Division, Ministry of Information and Broadcasting, 1964), 284–87. The extract was in a pamphlet distributed in Gujarat in 1916–17 (*Mahatma Gandhini Vicharsrishti* [from Gujarati]). A summary appeared in the *Kathiawar Times*, 26 July 1916.

description of 'the exceptional assortment of passengers' he encountered in
a third-class journey from Madras to Bombay in 1917.[186] Or in Mulk Raj
Anand's *Coolie*, when the protagonist Munoo emerged from hiding in a third-
class carriage to be greeted by veritable cross-section of Indian society: Seth
Prabha Dyal from Kangra, 'a Mohammedan peasant,' 'a Sikh peasant,' and 'a
young Hindu student.'[187] In a later moment in the same story, however, Munoo
awoke at Ambala junction to the voices of hawkers shouting, 'Hindu sweets,'
'Muhammadan Bread,' 'Hot Tea,' 'Cold Water.'[188] This was the same cry that
had dismayed Maulana Abul Kalam Azad, who imagined its divisive effects
on the millions of railway passengers who heard it every day.[189]

---

[186] *Statesman*, 29 September 1917.

[187] Mulk Raj Anand, *Coolie*, 1936, in the *Mulk Raj Omnibus*, edited and with an
introduction by Saros Cowasjee (Delhi: Penguin/Viking, 2004), 187–92.

[188] Mulk Raj Anand, *Coolie* (1936), 272.

[189] Quoted in M.K. Gandhi's 'Curse of Untouchability,' *Harijan*, 1 June 1940, *CWMG*, Vol.
lxxii (Ahmedabad: Publications Division, Ministry of Information and Broadcasting,
1978), 108–9.

Three

Crime and Punishment
In the Shadow of Railway Embankments

On 8 September 1919, three villages in Monghyr district lay submerged.[1] They were within a half-mile of the railway embankment that supported a branch line of the Bengal and North-Western Railway (BNWR) running from Sahebpur Kamal to Monghyr Ghat (Figure 3.1).[2] That night, two separate groups of villagers—25 from Durakpur and Samastipur and seven from Kurha—cut the railway embankment along mile 1, hoping to drain the high floodwater being held up by it. They were discovered by a railway patrol but all except one person from Kurha escaped. He was arrested and charged under section 126 of the Railways Act. Intended to punish malicious interference with railway property, this allowed for imprisonment up to 10 years, or else transportation for life. On the same night, seeing Ganges waters rising, a police watch was

---

[1] Note on Embankment Cutting on Bengal and North-Western Railway, file IM-3 of 1920, nos. 1–5, PWD: Railway: A, Bihar and Orissa Prog., IOR.P/10744, 1920, BL. Monghyr, the most westerly district of the Bhagalpur division, was subdivided into Monghyr, Jamui, and Beguserai, the headquarters being at Monghyr on the southern bank of the Ganges, which flowed through the district from west to east. L.S.S. O'Malley, *The Gazetteer of Monghyr District* (revised edition, Patna: Superintendent of Government Printing, Bihar and Orissa, 1926), 1–2. List of railway stations from Appendix I (271).

[2] O'Malley, *Monghyr District* (1926), 1–2.

ordered on culvert 18 at mile 101-5 of the main BNWR embankment.[3] The previous night, someone had been caught trying to open the culvert, while a few nights earlier people from nearby villages had removed the sleepers that formed the culvert's sluice.[4] In the former instance, the person was charged under section 126 of the Railways Act; in the latter instance, a case of theft was registered under section 379 of the Indian Penal Code.[5]

Figure 3.1. Sahebpur Kamal to Monghyr Ghat (Monghyr district)
= four miles on BNWR branch line

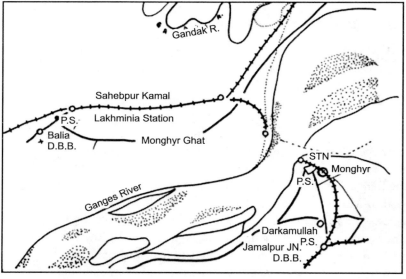

Illustration based on map section from O'Malley, *Monghyr District* (1926).

1919 was not the first or last year that railway embankments would be cut by people who believed that these blocked natural drainage and aggravated seasonable inundation and flooding, thus endangering lives and damaging property and livelihoods. Neither was deltaic north Bihar the only area where railway embankments were held responsible for severely exacerbating popular distress during times of heavy rainfall and flood. A correlation between the

---

[3] 1st Special Report, file IM-3 of 1920, nos. 1–5.

[4] 1st Special Report; Obstruction Report, 10 September 1919, file. IM-3 of 1920, nos. 1–5.

[5] Under-Secretary, Govt. of Bengal (PWD) to Secretary, Govt. of Bengal and Orissa (PWD), Calcutta, 14 October 1919, file IM-3 of 1920, nos. 1–5.

building or extension of railway embankments and increasing episodes of unseasonable, prolonged, or excessively damaging flooding was recorded in different parts of the country. Though the precise way in which a railway embankment affected the nature, course, and duration of flooding in an area varied, the affected public remained adamant that railway embankments were central to their distress. When faced with rising floodwater—repeated appeals for relief notwithstanding—some took matters into their own hands. They either cut embankments that were holding up floodwater or forcibly opened culverts that railway administrations had either blocked off or refused to open. Railway administrations described such attempts as sabotage and demanded that the perpetrators be charged with criminal action, both because they interfered with railway property and because damaged or collapsed railway embankments could result in accidents.[6] They also asked that such railway embankments be placed under armed patrol so as to prevent any stoppage in traffic, the costs to be borne *collectively* by the populace of surrounding areas. What they were usually unwilling to do, however, was increase waterways.

The disruption caused by railway embankments was part of the profound and long-lasting impact that a range of colonial projects of 'improvement' had on India's natural environment. Colonial India was not alone: the environment and ecology of British colonies—and colonized spaces more generally—were transformed both by the empire's 'ferocious agendas of extraction' and its 'fastidiously pursued interventions for improvement.'[7] At the same time, some of the ways in which railway construction affected the natural environment were also shared more globally, from the visible transformation of the landscape, to the growth of (what came to be defined as) smoke and noise 'pollution.'[8] The frequently debilitating consumption of wood by railways—for fuel, carriages, sleepers, cross-ties, posts, and fittings—was also a global concern, depleting forests as well as drastically affecting people whose lives were integrated with these.[9] Given the powers of extraction appropriated by imperial states, colonized

---

[6] Trevor, *Law Relating to Railways*, 300-1, Section 126.

[7] Deepak Kumar, Vinita Damodaran, and Rohan D'Souza, eds., *Environmental Encounters in South Asia* (Delhi: Oxford University Press, 2011), 4.

[8] Gordon Biddle, 'Railways, Their Builders, and the Environment,' in A.K.B. Evans and John Gough, eds., *Impact of Railways on Society in Britain: Essays in Honour of Jack Simmons* (Burlington: Ashgate, 2003); Jack Simmons, *The Railway in Town and Country, 1830–1914* (North Pomfret, Vt.: David & Charles, 1986); Peter Thorsheim, *Inventing Pollution: Coal, Smoke, and Culture in Britain Since 1800* (Athens: Ohio University Press, 2009).

[9] D.G. Donovon, 'Forests at the Edge of Empire: The Case of Nepal,' *Environmental Encounters in South Asia*, 248, table 10.3; Hurd and Kerr, *India's Railway History*, 200.

spaces were particularly vulnerable.[10] However, if the railway's hunger for timber engendered extensive commercial intrusion into Zambezi's teak forests, they also elicited the prognosis of a 'timber famine' by an American president.[11]

In colonial India, railways required large quantities of timber for fuel and sleepers.[12] Contemporary estimates indicated that in the 1870s over a million wooden sleepers were required for railway construction.[13] Further, while the use of coal fuel increased in the late nineteenth century, wood fuel continued to be consumed, with over 300,000 tons being used each year even in the last decade of the century.[14] The Himalayan forests were affected, as were Burma's teak (*Tectona grandis*) forests; the prohibitive cost of transporting Burmese teak down to northern India led to an increased focus on *sal* forests (*Shorea robusta*), stretching from the western *terai*, down to Bengal—and on the *deodar* forests (*Cedrus deodara*) of the upper Ganges and Indus basins.[15] Thus, discussing environmental change in north India, Robert Varady pegs railways unequivocally as 'agents of deforestation,' linking them with allied problems like soil erosion.[16]

---

[10] For colonial control over India's forests (and how railway needs spurred state appropriation), see Madhav Gadgil and Ramachandra Guha, *This Fissured Land: An Ecological History of India* (Berkeley: University of California Press, 1993), Chapter 4.

[11] Vimbai C. Kwashira, *Green Colonialism in Zimbabwe, 1890–1980* (Amherst: Cambria Press, 2009), 135–81; Arnulf Grübler, *Technology and Global Change* (Cambridge and New York: Cambridge University Press, 1998), 28.

[12] Less so initially for carriages since locomotives and rolling stock were imported from England.

[13] Each mile of railway construction was estimated as requiring more than 860 sleepers, with each lasting between 12 and 14 years. D. Brandis in *Indian Forester*, V (1879), quoted in Guha, *Fissured Land*, 122, n. 4.

[14] 'Fuel on Indian Railways,' *The Railway News*, London, 27 October 1900, reprinted in *The London News: Finance and Joint-Stock Companies Journal*, LXXIV, July–December 1900 (London: Railway News' Offices, 1900), 615.

[15] Amiya Kumar Bagchi, *Private Investment in India, 1900–1939* (London and New York: Routledge and Kegan Paul, 2000 [1972]), 332–33; Richard P. Tucker, 'Forests of the Western Himalaya and the British Colonial System (1815–1914),' in Ajay Singh Rawat, ed., *Indian Forestry, a Perspective* (New Delhi: Indus Publishing, 1993) 179–83; Elizabeth Whitcombe, *Agrarian Conditions in Northern India: The United Provinces under British Rule, 1860–1900* (Berkeley: University of California Press, 1972), 94–95. In *Himalayan Forests and Forestry* (New Delhi: Indus Publishing, 2000), S.S. Negi lists 26 Himalayan species marked out for railway sleepers (157).

[16] Robert Varady, 'Land Use and Environmental Change in the Gangetic Plain,' in Sandra B. Frietag, ed., *Culture and Power in Banaras: Community, Performance, and*

No less critical to people's everyday lives was the railways' hunger for land. Leveraging the 'risks' involved, private English companies who initially built railways in India secured a promise of free land from the Government of India.[17] This meant that in the early decades—especially in the 1850s and 1860s—the state acquired the land for private railway companies and then ceded it to them free of charge (Figure 3.2).[18] State facilitation of railway construction, especially for purposes of land appropriation, was globally familiar in the period. In countries like France, the state was directly involved, while in areas like north America, private railway companies received state aid in the form of land grants.[19] Even where railway companies directly purchased land and where landed interests were especially protected through competitive compensation—like in Britain—the state facilitated the process through Acts of Incorporation.[20] However, the guaranteed system in India was distinguished by the fact that the state ceded all land for the permanent way free to private companies, a concession further augmented by a state-guaranteed return on private investment drawn from public revenues: 'private enterprise at public risk' as Daniel Thorner termed it.[21]

The state acquired the required land by designating railways as public works. In Bengal and Bombay, Act XLII of 1850 extended the state's power to acquire land and immovable property to include that required for railway construction.[22] Similar powers were authorized in Madras through Act XX of

---

Environment, 1800–1980 (Berkeley: University of California Press, 1989), 243; Varady, Rail and Road Transport in Nineteenth Century Awadh, 190–91.

[17] For a detailed discussion of the process, see Thorner, *Investment in Empire*.

[18] In 1870 itself, private, guaranteed, railways accounted for 4,711 of the 4,775 miles of track that existed. *Statistical Abstract from 1867/8 to 1876/7*, 88. Class A land for the permanent way was ceded permanently, while class B and C land for executing construction and providing and preparing materials was to be returned by railway companies to government.

[19] L.C.A. Knowles, *Economic Development in the Nineteenth Century: France, Germany, Russia and the United States* (London: Routledge, 2006 [1932]), 209–36; David Salomons, *Railways in England and in France: Being Reflections Suggested by Mr. Morrison's Pamphlet and by the Report drawn up by Him for the Railways Acts Committee* (London: Pelham Richardson, 1847), 56–57.

[20] Ibid. R.W. Kostal, *Law and English Railway Capitalism, 1825–75* (Oxford: Oxford University Press, 1994), 145–80.

[21] Thorner, *Investment in Empire*, Chapter 7.

[22] Provided for in Bengal Regulation I of 1824 and Bombay Act XXVIII of 1839, respectively.

Figure 3.2. Length of Track, 1854–70 (in miles)

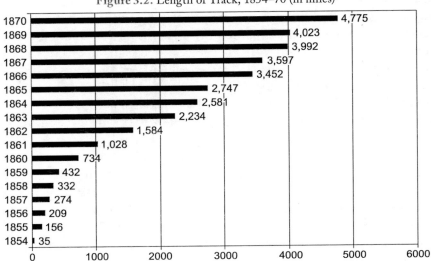

Source: Tabulated from data in *Statistical Abstract Relating to British India: from 1860 to 1869* (London: HMSO, 1870), 30–31; *from 1840 to 1865* (London: HMSO, 1867), 58–59; *from 1867/8 to 1876/7* (London: HMSO, 1878), 88.

1852 but procedures for land acquisition for public purposes were made uniform under Act VI of 1857.[23] The principle of arbitration held till 1870; then the Land Acquisition Act X (1870) referred disputed cases to civil courts that would determine the amount of compensation when the local collector could not settle it by agreement.[24] The degree of disruption was heightened by the quantities of land required: land was needed not only for the permanent way and stations but temporarily for conducting surveys, extracting and preparing material to build the permanent way, and building temporary accommodation for those employed on the works. Thus, distinguishing railways from other public works, Smritikumar Sarkar argues that: 'Never before had land been acquired for public works on such a massive scale.'[25]

From the start, reports came in describing how such land acquisition affected property: whether it was the 'excitement among the Natives of Patna' or the

[23] Passed on 1 May 1857. Charles Dickenson Field, *Chronological Table of, and Index to, the Indian Statute-Book from the Year 1834* (London: Butterworths, 1870), 112.

[24] Book Circular no. 15 of 1870, 28 August 1870, in *Punjab Record or Reference Book for Civil Officers*, Vol. 5 (W.E. Ball, Manager, 1870), 27.

[25] Sarkar, 'Land Acquisition for the Railways in Bengal, 1850–62,' 105.

consternation among Delhi's residents at the 'knocking down and blowing up [of] houses,' the process engendered confusion and anxiety.[26] Government collectors and railway commissioners were accused of undervaluing land or compensating the wrong party, while there were frequent complaints against careless surveyors and railway officers empowered to enter people's property.[27] In early processes of arbitration, compensation was withheld until all claims were reconciled.[28] People described how railway construction caused damage, whether it was how processes like brick-making degraded their land, or how the proximity to new railway lines diminished the value of their property.[29] Despite the state's invocation of rights to appropriation, the process was not devoid of negotiation and contestation. As Sarkar has shown, land acquisition in Bengal between 1850 and 1862 involved 'numerous cases of protest, opposition and arbitration,' some of them resulting in route realignments, as well as a shifting away of lines from river towns to more marshy areas (subsequently linked up through feeder roads).[30]

For the public that was affected, the building of railway embankments shared many of the disruptions associated with land acquisition. Even before the embankment was actually built, the land and landscape was subject to myriad intrusions. Many railway embankments were built quite high, being

---

[26] PWD (Railway) to Court of Directors, letter no. 25 of 27 June 1856, Railway General Letters, NAI; *Delhi Gazette*, 18 August 1859.

[27] Bengal Public Works (Railway), 10 February 1859, nos. 152–53, IOR.P/16/33, BL; Bengal Public Works (Railway), 15 September 1859, nos. 78–81, July–October 1859, IOR.P/16/36, BL; Bengal Public Works (Railway), 20 October 1859, nos. 48–49, July–October 1859, IOR.P/16/36, BL; United Provinces Prog. (PWD: Railway), 30 September 1863, nos. 70–72, IOR.P/217/34, BL.

[28] Bengal Public Works (Railway), 21 April 1859, nos. 14–16, March–April 1859, IOR.P/16/34, BL; Bengal Public Works (Railway), 20 October 1859, nos. 1–4, July–October 1859, IOR.P/16/36, BL. Initially the railway company could not take possession of the land until all claims had been settled. However, the Bengal government suggested an amendment allowing the Railway Commissioner to take possession of the land immediately after the completion of the detailed measurements. Rivers Thompson, Junior Secretary to Govt. of Bengal, to Secretary, Govt. of India, PWD, 14 October 1859, Bengal Public Works (Railway), 20 October 1859, nos. 1–4, July–October 1859, IOR.P/16/36, BL.

[29] Bengal Public Works (Railway), May–June 1859, IOR.P/16/35, BL; Bengal Public Works (Railway) Prog., July–October 1859, nos. 152–54, IOR.P/16/36, BL.

[30] Sarkar, 'Land Acquisition for the Railways in Bengal, 1850–62,' 106, 139.

raised 12 to 16 feet above ordinary ground.[31] This not only made railway embankments higher than most embanked roads but also meant that they required larger quantities of earthwork.[32] To quote Ira Klein, railway builders 'moved hundreds of millions of feet of earth, and made thousands of miles of embankments.'[33] The disruption was heightened by the fact that embankments and cuttings were often constructed first during a two-fold working season.[34] Further, construction sites became temporary dwellings for migrant railroad workers, many of whom were drawn from outside of the surrounding areas, thus altering the social ecology in many places.[35]

In itself, laying railway lines on raised embankments was an accepted engineering strategy in areas with uneven terrain, being seen as less taxing and less expensive than many alternatives.[36] In colonial India, even some flat areas required embankments that raised the permanent way above flood-prone sections.[37] However, it was well recognized that such embankments altered drainage patterns; consequently, railway administrations were legally required to make and maintain works to mitigate the effects of such interference. In colonial India, railway administrations were to 'offset' any 'interruptions' to the use of land through which a railway line was constructed by building 'such and so many convenient crossings, bridges, arches, culverts, and passages.'[38]

---

[31] Ira Klein, 'Death in India,' *Journal of Asian Studies* 32, 4 (1973): 639–59, quotes on 645–46. Klein describes this to discuss how inadequate drainage in railway embankments was associated with malaria. This chapter does not address this link, which is addressed briefly in Chapter 5.

[32] J.A.S. Day, *A Practical Treatise on the Construction and Formation of Railways* (third edition, London: John Weale, 1848), 91; A.W. Skempton, 'Embankments and Cuttings on the Early Railways,' *Construction History* 11 (1996): 33–49, quote on 33.

[33] Klein, 'Death in India,' 645.

[34] Being followed by 'an earth consolidating rainy season,' after which came repairs and plate-laying. Kerr, *Building the Railways of the Raj*, 41; idem, *Engines of Change*, 39–40.

[35] For the demographics of construction workers, see Kerr, *Building the Railways of the Raj.*

[36] Day, *Practical Treatise on the Construction and Formation of Railways*, 90–103.

[37] Kerr, *Engines of Change*, 23.

[38] Article 11(1: a & b) of 1890 Act, Trevor, *Law Relating to Railways*, 186–87; clause 11(1) of 1890 Act, M. Teruvenkatachariar, *High Court Decisions of Indian Railway Cases with an Appendix Containing All the Indian Railway Acts, the Carriers' Act and Act XIII of 1855 Together with Index* (Trichinopoly: St. Joseph's College Press, 1901), 813–14. This was also true of embanked roads; however, railway embankments were usually higher and less liable to being 'topped.' For instances of threats posed by road embankments in colonial Orissa, see Ahuja, *Pathways of Empire*, 176, 184.

These arches, tunnels, culverts, drains, watercourses, and passages had to be planned so they would be '*sufficient at all times to convey water* as freely from or to the lands lying near or affected by the railway as before the making of the railway, or as nearly so as may be' (emphasis added).[39] These details having been determined in consultation with civil authorities, waterways were to be constructed 'during or immediately after' the railway line itself was laid out. Up to 10 years after the railway opened to public traffic, either those who owned or occupied affected land or local authorities could request further accommodation if they believed the waterways provided were insufficient. The additions were to be paid for by them or else by the railway, differences of opinion being referred to the governor-general.[40]

This legal mandate notwithstanding, railway embankments continued to be built with inadequate waterways; sometimes, railway administrations closed off or blocked waterways that had been sanctioned and built. During times of excess rainfall and flood, they either refused to open sluice gates or else blocked culverts with sleepers or rails. Consequently, the embankment held up accumulated rain or floodwater, preventing it from draining off. Explaining their decision, railway administrations argued that waterways—at least those that would allow high floodwater to drain unimpeded—weakened bridges and embanked structures, which were scoured by water rushing through them. Building stronger embankments and culverts or reinforcing existing ones entailed construction costs that they were reluctant to incur.

In theory, railway companies were liable 'for damages caused to lands in the neighbourhood of the lien by the Railway works, such, for instance, as damage to crops, by the stoppage of drainage by an embankment.'[41] District officers were required to help assess the damage and conciliate the parties involved but the government was not liable unless the railway could prove that its officers had refused to sanction the necessary works. In practice, however, railway administrations denied any correlation between inadequate or blocked waterways and impeded drainage, dismissing the suggestion that these trapped rain and floodwater or aggravated distress; instead, they relied on narratives stressing the unpredictability of India's climate. Where the correlation between

---

[39] Article 11 (1: a & b) of 1890 Act; clause 11 (1) of the 1890 Act. This was common with the construction of railway embankments, Gordon and Biddle, *British Railway History*, 135–36.

[40] Article 12 of 1890 Act, in Trevor, *Law Relating to Railways*, 186–87.

[41] Oudh: PWD and Railway: Prog. of Chief Commissioner of Oudh, June 1870, IOR.P/442/62, BL.

embankments and impeded drainage was more explicit, they argued that these same embankments protected land lying on their other side, drawing analogies with how *bandh*s had been used historically to prevent rivers from spilling and to exclude water from fields and habitations. This coincided with the specific interests of the colonial state since *bandh*s, as Dinesh Kumar Mishra points out, were not only important to how the state controlled the 'agro-ecological setting' but also to securing permanence 'in both its administrative and revenue policies.'[42]

The situation was complicated by the range of local interests involved.[43] In specific cases, local administrators endorsed the popular opinion that inadequate waterways in railway embankments severely exacerbated damage to life, crops, cattle, and property. They were spurred by the distress of those affected, the fact that severe and unseasonable flooding added substantially to their administrative burden, and their reluctance to provide the large punitive patrols that railway companies began demanding. The fact that the destroyed crops affected revenue created further dissonance between railways and civil authorities. However, other officers chose to support the demands of railway companies. By the early to mid-twentieth century, many civil engineers had grown wary of the effects of embankments but despite this the liability entertained by railways remained difficult to prove conclusively. The colonial state did— gradually, and in theory— ascribe to itself some degree of responsibility. However, it usually failed to recognize specific cases in which such liability would attach. Even where the link was more explicit, explanations of public improvement continued to obscure the human costs involved.

Railway Embankments and Flood Damage in North Bihar

Correlation *versus* causality

North Bihar was neither the first nor the only area where railway embankments were linked with severe and prolonged flooding. This was not because railway

---

[42] Dinesh Kumar Mishra, 'The Bihar Flood Story,' *Economic and Political Weekly* 32, 35 (1997): 2206–17, quote on 2206. Rohan D'Souza's discusses the relationship between agrarian capitalism and flood control in the Mahanadi delta in *Drowned and Damned: Colonial Capitalism and Flood Control in Eastern India* (Delhi: Oxford University Press, 2006).

[43] For the range of interests involved, see Praveen Singh, 'The Colonial State, Zamindars and the Politics of Flood Control in North Bihar (1850–1945),' *Indian Economic Social History Review* 45, 2 (2008): 239–59.

embankments here did not have this effect; describing its 'flood problem' in his 1948 report, P.C. Ghosh, previously an executive engineer in the Bihar PWD described north Bihar as 'a huge inland delta.'[44] Rather, it was because railways came to north Bihar comparatively late. While the section from Dalsingsarai to Darbhanga via Samastipur was opened in 1875, yet—with the exception of the Darbhanga State Railway—north Bihar's railway network developed in the mid- to late 1880s.[45] Thus, reports from many parts of the country describing the damage cause by railway embankments preceded accounts from north Bihar.

An early account came from Burdwan, where a railway embankment with 'insufficient waterway' was held responsible for 'thoroughly imped[ing] the drainage of the area after its completion in 1860.'[46] In 1877, villages south of Burdwan suffered 'great loss' from inundations of the river Damodar, the problem attributed to 'the construction by the East Indian Railway of an embankment to protect their property.'[47] Describing people's distress, the *Urdu Guide* wrote that: 'Thousands of dwellings have fallen, hundreds of lives been lost, countless number of cattle and a large quantity of grain been destroyed.'[48] The editor was emphatic that people living in these villages had 'never dreamt of such dangers and losses, before the construction of the railway.' That same year, after the monsoons, inhabitants of Dhubail village in Kushtea subdivision witnessed the damage caused by the construction of the Northern Bengal State Railway (NBSR). The line blocked the natural watercourses through which water drained into the Gorai river and the ensuing inundations destroyed crops on about 1,500 *beegahs* of land. People complained that the 'evil' could have been rectified by constructing culverts across the railway line, but this had not been done.[49]

Some such cases elicited compensation. The Oudh and Rohilkund Railway (O&RR) was held responsible for the damage caused by severe floods between 1870 and 1873 in the Ramganga Valley area of Bareilly, resulting from the fact

---

[44] P.C. Ghosh, *A Comprehensive Treatise on North Bihar Flood Problems: Being a Description of the River System and their Behaviours and Tendencies with Suggestions for Flood Mitigation* (Patna: Superintendent of Government Printing, 1948), iii.

[45] Mishra, 'The Bihar Flood Story,' 2208; Yang, *Bazaar India*, 49.

[46] Mishra, 'The Bihar Flood Story,' 2207.

[47] *Urdu Guide* (Calcutta), 22 September 1877, in NNR: Bengal.

[48] Ibid.

[49] *Grambarta Patrikasha* quoted in *Urdu Guide*, 22 September 1877. A *beegah* varies from a third of an acre to an acre.

that its embankment obstructed natural drainage.[50] The railway was asked
to pay a government-assessed compensation of Rs. 5,242 and to rectify the
situation. A similar link was proved in a case of disastrous flooding in 1892
in Dinajpur, a town usually 'free from natural visitations.'[51] The town lay on
the Behar section of the Eastern Bengal State Railway (EBSR); portions of
it had been completed gradually between 1887 and 1891, with the 'disastrous
flood' of 1892 following almost immediately after.[52] A subsequent enquiry
contended that the railway line, which bisected the district from east to
west, was in large measure 'responsible' for the damage. Lacking adequate
waterways, it had held up floodwater coming from the north.[53] Adding
waterways alleviated the problem and almost two decades later the *Eastern
Bengal Gazetteer* pointed out that since then 'no flood worthy of the name
had occurred' at Dinajpur.[54]

In several other cases, however, it was more difficult to prove a direct causal
link. When Jounpore and Azimgarh were inundated in 1871 following a steep
rise in the Gomati and Tonse rivers, railway engineers denied that the railway's
embankment had in any way affected the severity of the flood. They pointed
out that the floodwater had risen far above the embankment, running for days
at the same level on both sides of it. The commissioner of Allahabad division
agreed that the railway embankment was not holding up the floodwater;
however, he insisted that it did push floodwater to rise higher than it would
have risen ordinarily. In his view, the enormous structure 'raised to one level
height over a long range of country' had affected the topography and drainage
patterns in the area.[55] It stopped up natural drainage channels for rainwater,

---

[50] Whitcombe, *Agrarian Conditions in Northern India*, 93.

[51] F.W. Strong, *Eastern Bengal District Gazetteers: Dinajpur* (Allahabad: Pioneer
Press, 1912), 64. Also in Meghnad Saha, 'The Great Flood in Northern Bengal,' in
Ramachadra Chatterjee, ed., *The Modern Review: A Monthly Review and Miscellany*
Xxxii, 5 (November 1922): 605–11.

[52] The Eastern Bengal State Railway was originally known as the Northern Bengal State
Railway. The stations on the main line included Parbatipur, Bhawanipur, Phulwari and
Chorkai (identical with Berampur), while those on the Behar section from east to west
were Parbatipur, Chirirbandar, Kaugaon, Dinajpur, Birol, Radhikapur, Kaliyaganj,
Bangalbari, and Raiganj. Strong, *Dinajpur*, 92.

[53] Strong, *Dinajpur*, 64; Saha, 'Great Flood in Northern Bengal,' 605–11.

[54] Strong, *Dinajpur*, 64.

[55] F.O. Mayne, Commissioner, Allahabad Division to C.A. Elliot, Secretary, Govt. of
NWP, Allahabad, 7 October 1871, in 'Flooding of Towns of Jounpore and Azimgurh,'
Article VI, *Selections of the Records of the North-Western Provinces* (second series)

which had had to find other channels down into the valleys of the Gomati and Tonse. This increased the water accumulated in these valleys at the beginning of the flood, and hence increased the quantity of water collected in the rivers before the big flood came down.[56]

Thus, the growing belief in north Bihar that since railway embankments had been built in the area floods 'invariably' caused damage, no matter how seasonable they were, was not an isolated one.[57] Those affected by railway construction did not posit a naive relationship between railway embankments and flooding. As in many deltaic areas across the country, cultivators in north Bihar welcomed seasonable floods, relying on them for a rich deposit of silt, especially for a winter crop.[58] Consequently, they stressed how railway embankments that were built without adequate waterways generated a 'ponding effect,' either preventing floodwater from draining off as it had before these were built or else confining floodwater to a smaller area. By flooding the area to a greater depth than usual, this process transformed normal, seasonal flooding into calamitous events.[59]

As railway lines spread over north Bihar, the population became vigilant about inadequate waterways provided in embanked railway lines. The two large railway lines serving the area were the Tirhut (or Tirhoot) State Railway and the Bengal and North-Western Railway (BNWR), the first being constructed from the mid-1870s onwards and the later in the early 1880s.[60] Both remained the property of the state, though they were administered by the Bengal and North-Western Railway Company, which took over the running of the Tirhut State Railway in 1890.[61] The extent of the problem was visible in a petition

---

(Allahabad: Government Press, 1872), 183–84; Revenue Dept. Resolution 1517A, Nynee Tal, 25 September 1871, in 'Flooding of Towns of Jounpore and Azimgurh,' 23.

[56] F.O. Mayne to C.A. Elliot, 7 October 1871; Revenue Dept. Resolution 1517A (Nynee Tal), 25 September 1871.

[57] L.S.S. O'Malley, *Monghyr: Bengal District Gazetteers* (Calcutta: Secretariat Book Depot, 1909), 111.

[58] Describing northern Bengal—specifically the area around the Chaman *bil*—the *Rajashahi Gazetteer* explained how annual inundations fertilized soil and precipitated river-borne silt, making artificial irrigation unnecessary: quoted in Saha, 'Great Flood in Northern Bengal,' 605–11.

[59] O'Malley, *Monghyr* (1909), 111.

[60] The company was registered in England in 1882. Bell, *Railway Policy in India*, 42.

[61] Tirhut was the ancient name for 'a tract of country bounded on the north by the Himalayas, on the south by the Ganges, on the west by the river Gandak and on the east by the river Kosi.' In 1875, this was divided into two, 'the western portion being

sent by civil authorities and landowners of Bhagalpur district in May 1898, complaining that 30 miles of the Tirhut line (the Hajipur-Beghumserai-Kathiar extension) had been recently constructed without any drainage openings.[62] The Government of India, which had clearly received similar requests earlier, directed the consulting engineer at Lucknow to settle the issue of alignment and waterway as had been done in previous cases, by consulting with railway and local officials and affected landowners. More importantly, it insisted *suo moto* that the adequacy of waterways be assessed for the entire line starting from Garhara (mile 0, Figure 3.3), instead of just from miles 57 to 86, which had been the immediate cause for concern. Despite the area being replete with depressions and *nala*s that used to form natural drainage channels, the section showed no waterways planned for over 30 miles—only a single waterway was contemplated east of mile 0 until the Kosi river, at mile 31¼.[63]

Figure 3.3. Garhara (mile 0) on Tirhut Railway

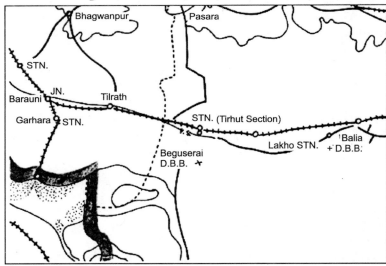

Illustration based on map section from O'Malley, *Monghyr District* (1926).

---

constituted into the district of Muzaffarpur, and the eastern and larger portion being formed into the district of Darbhanga. ' L.S.S. O'Malley, *The Gazetteer of Darbhanga District: Bengal District Gazetteers* (Calcutta: Bengal Secretariat Book Depot, 1907), 157–58.

[62] Secretary, Govt. of India (PWD) to Consulting Engineer (Railways), Lucknow, 31 May 1898, Bengal Public Works (Railway) Prog., no. 2, July 1898, IOR.P/5396, BL.

[63] Ibid.

The Monghyr floods of 1904–6

The effect of inadequate waterways was shown dramatically in the 1904 floods in Monghyr district, described as 'probably one of the severest floods ever experienced in the tracts affected.'[64] The northern portion of Monghyr was no stranger to floods. The principal effluents of the Ganges in the north—the Burh Gandak, the Baghmati, and the Tiljuga or Kamla (Figure 3.4)—were known to overflow their banks after heavy rainfall in the sub-Himalayan areas from where they began.[65] The floods were seasonable, with two exceptions. If water did not drain off quickly or subsided too slowly for cold-weather crops, it damaged the Gogri area, and if it occurred in August—before the crops had been harvested—rather than in September, then it damaged the southern strip.

Figure 3.4. Gandak, Baghmati, and Tiljüga/Kamla

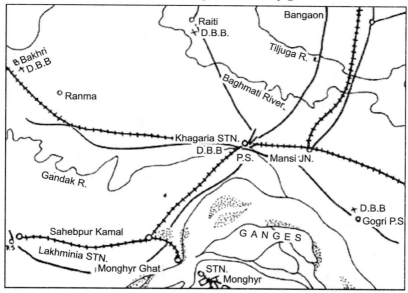

Illustration based on map section from O'Malley, *Monghyr District* (1926).

The problem was obvious in 1904, when the damage was greater than in the previous flood of 1901, even though the level of floodwater had been higher in 1901. The height of 25.75 feet reached by the floodwater in 1904 was two

---

[64] O'Malley, *Monghyr* (1909), 112.

[65] Ibid., 1–7, 111.

feet lower than the 27.75 feet it had reached on 8 September 1901.[66] However, in 1904, the water remained above 25 feet for 15 days unlike in 1901 when it was over 25 feet only for six days.[67] The damage caused in 1904 was attributed to the length of time that the floodwater had remained above 25 feet.[68] In the severely affected Beguserai subdivision, the part most affected was that which lay between the BNWR line and the Tirhut road.[69] Here,

> the water having topped and breached the road in its progress northwards, was stopped by the railway embankment, and then turned eastwards, a considerable current setting in between the road and the railway, which are not far apart.[70]

More than 1,125 *kutcha* houses were estimated to have collapsed, while the *bhadoi* crop, mostly maize, was severely damaged, with between 50 per cent and 75 per cent of it lost where it had not yet been harvested.

In an official enquiry, G.G. Maconchy, the superintending engineer in the PWD, emphasized the role of the railway embankment in the damage caused, specifically in Beguserai. While he accepted that tract had always been liable to floods, he argued that the floodwater topping the Ganges usually ran in a north-easterly direction towards the Burh Gandak, which traversed the country north of the railway. The discharge then fell either into the Gandak near its mouth or else rejoined the Ganges through the low lands in the area.[71] The Tirhut road and the railway, both of which crossed the flooded tract roughly from east to west, ran against the natural direction of the floodwater and blocked its discharge.

Like several other railway lines in northern Bihar, this one too was aligned with the Tirhut road, which itself had been built with bridges.[72] However, the bridges had been closed off in 1888 because of suggestions that the water rushing through the bridges led to excessive scouring, making them unsafe.

---

[66] This was the record for Monghyr since gauge was first taken. O'Malley, *Monghyr* (1909), 112–13.

[67] It reached 27.25 feet on 14 August 1904, but fell to 24.58 feet only on 29 August 1904. In 1901, it stayed above 25 feet only between 5–10 September, falling to under 18 feet by 11 September.

[68] O'Malley, *Monghyr* (1909), 112.

[69] Ibid., 113–14. Beguserai was the headquarter of Beguserai subdivision, lying about five miles north of the Ganges. The town was half a mile from the railway station, and the Tirhut Road ran east and west through it . O'Malley, *Monghyr District* (1926), 203.

[70] O'Malley, *Monghyr* (1909), 114.

[71] Quoted in O'Malley, *Monghyr* (1909), 119–20.

[72] Yang, *Bazaar India*, 49.

By the time the BNWR line was constructed, the Tirhut road had become 'an obstruction, lying right across the direction of the spill'; despite this, the railway line was aligned with it and built without any waterways except for three or four small sluices intended to let off residual drainage, after the main flood had subsided.[73] The railway, however, was significantly higher than the road and thus proved to be a more formidable obstacle to drainage than the road had ever been. Even with its waterways blocked off, the road could be breached by high floods. Since it was above high-flood level, the railway bank prevented floodwater from spreading northwards and eastwards gradually 'as it used to, without doing any particular harm.' Instead,

the spill was effectively stopped by the railway, which remained intact, and the flood was ponded up all along its south side, the depth above ground level being about 8 feet at Begusarai, while the ground on the north side was dry.[74]

This ponded-up floodwater drowned crops or else damaged them by flowing eastwards, rapidly breaching *bandhs*. To prevent future damage, it was suggested that the railway's structure be provided with sufficient waterways.[75] However, this solution was soon rejected, spurred by an enquiry into the subsequent floods of 1906. Focusing on areas in the Beguserai subdivision other than the ones examined in the 1904 report, Mr. B.K. Finnimore, another engineer in the PWD, stressed that the embankment had protected the land north of it during the Ganges flood and that those who owned land in this area opposed any more channels or openings.

In 1906 itself, flooding in the area around the newly constructed Mansi-Bhaptiahi extension was linked unequivocally with the construction of railway embankments in the area.[76] The 'unfortunate coincidence' of heavy local rainfall in 1905 had meant that the 'exceptional floods' that occurred soon after the railway was constructed were not attributed to it. But when the flooding was repeated 'in a more serious form' in 1906, attention turned to the railway's embankment, which ran across the natural drainage line of Gogri *thana* (figure 3.5).[77] Enquiries revealed the planned allowance of waterway as insufficient

---

[73] Quoted in O'Malley, *Monghyr* (1909), 119–20.

[74] Ibid.

[75] Ibid., 121.

[76] Mansi Junction to Bhaptiahi on BNWR = 61 miles. O'Malley, *Monghyr district* (1926), 271.

[77] O'Malley, *Monghyr* (1909), 116–17.

and increased waterways were again suggested since the issue was 'a matter of life and death' for cultivators in the area.

Figure 3.5. Mansi Junction, Gogri *thana*

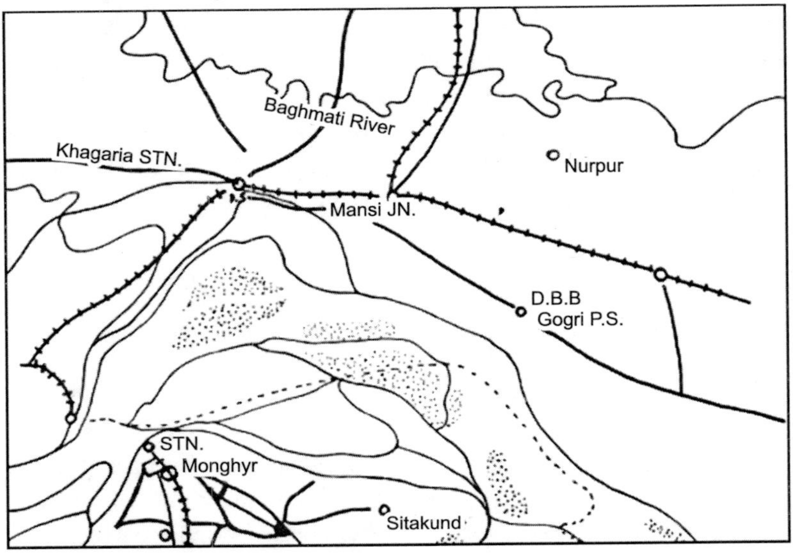

Illustration based on map section from O'Malley, *Monghyr District* (1926).

However, such diagnoses and suggestions only infrequently translated into effective interventions. In the occasional instance, railways were compelled to pay compensation, such as in 1886 when a BNWR embankment across the Banwari Chuck valley blocked drainage and destroyed standing crops; more generally, however, popular demands were 'stonewalled.'[78] The damage concerned local administrators and revenue officials but railways remained fairly intractable. It was in one such earlier moment—during the construction of a railway embankment connecting Baraunit to Katihar—that Bhagalpur's commissioner complained of how railway authorities 'keep us in dark and appear to avoid us and we suspect them of intentions that can only be called sinister.'[79]

Given that railways continued to refuse responsibility for damage, while continuing to plan lines and embankments with inadequate waterways, many

---

[78] Mishra, 'The Bihar Flood Story,' 2208; Singh, 'The Colonial State,' 254–55.

[79] Dated 11 April 1897, quoted in Mishra, 'The Bihar Flood Story,' 2208.

of those affected by railway embankments devised alternative means of redress. To drain off floodwater held up by railway embankments, they either cut the railway embankment, making a breach in it through which water could flow, or else opened and unblocked culverts by removing the sleepers and rails with which railway companies usually blocked them off. In both cases, their actions were deemed as sabotage against railway property which, in many cases, was simultaneously state property.

The Politics of Redress: Distress and 'Sabotage' in North Bihar

On the night of 6–7 August 1917, it was a desperate group of almost 500 people armed with *lathi*s and *kodali*s who came in boats from villages south of the BNWR line, determined to cut the railway embankment between Pasraha (in Monghyr district) and Narayananpur.[80] However, they were driven off by force—the inspector of railway police, Mr. Macdowell, fired a revolver, while another railway officer fired a 12-bore—and the breach blocked before the water forced its way through it. Another group was more successful, cutting a breach in the embankment about a mile further west, before being driven back.[81] Roughly an hour later, a patrolling trolley-man discovered another deep cut in the railway embankment, this time between Khagaria and Mili, while floodwater rushing through a 'natural' breach at Gochari overtopped the railway embankment between Pasraha and Mansi junctions (14 miles, Figure 3.6).[82]

The events of 6–7 August 1917 were hardly unanticipated. The armed patrols were there precisely *because* it was expected that people from surrounding areas would try to cut the railway embankment to release ponded-up floodwater. Such popular attempts at 'sabotage' thus represented the continued inadequacy of waterways, the continuing presence of flood damage, and the continuing failure of popular demands for redress, even when these were endorsed by official enquiries and local administrators.

---

[80] District Magistrate, Monghyr, to Commissioner, Bhagalpur Division, 11 August 1917; Investigation Report on Damage Done by Floods in August 1917 to the BNWR Embankments in the Monghyr and Bhagalpur Districts and the Measures Proposed for the Protection of the Embankments, both in Govt. of Bihar and Orissa Prog., PWD: Railway A, file no. 1V-F/1 of 1918, IOR.P/10296, 1918, BL.

[81] Investigation Report on Damage Done by Floods in August 1917.

[82] Ibid.; O'Malley, *Monghyr District* (1926), 271.

Figure 3.6. (Khagaria →) Mansi → Pasraha (→ Narayanpur)

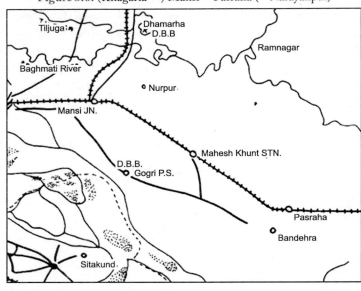

Illustration based on map section from O'Malley, *Monghyr District* (1926).
Pasraha to Mansi junction = 14 miles.

The story of embankment cutting

In the two years before 1917, the government had been repeatedly alerted to damage resulting from the construction of various sections of the BNWR. In 1915, before the flood season, Dwarkanath from Muzaffarpur had asked the local government to urge upon the BNWR the pressing need for more floodwater outlets.[83] In a meeting of the Bihar and Orissa council later that same year—this time after the floods—Lacchmi Prasad Sinha described how the construction of the embanked Khagaria–Rosera line of the BNWR without adequate waterways had obstructed the flow of water from the left bank of the Gandak river into the Baghmati, causing heavy flooding in the areas situated between the line and Khagaria and Beguserai (Figure 3.7).[84]

---

[83] F. Clayton to Dwarka Nath, 30 August 1915, file XIII C/7 of 1915, nos. 1–3, PWD: Railway: A, Govt. of Bihar and Orissa Prog., IOR.P/9802, 1915, BL.

[84] Council Question by Lacchmi Prasad Sinha Regarding Obstruction of Overflow of Water by Construction of the Khagaria–Rosera line, 26 November 1915, file XIII C/1 of 1915, nos. 1–4, 12 and file XIII C/8 of 1915: nos. 1–2, 6, PWD: Railway: A, Govt. of Bihar and Orissa Prog., IOR.P/10082, 1916, BL.

Houses had collapsed and there was 'serious damage to crops and the general property of the people.'[85]

Figure 3.7. Area between Beguserai and Khagaria

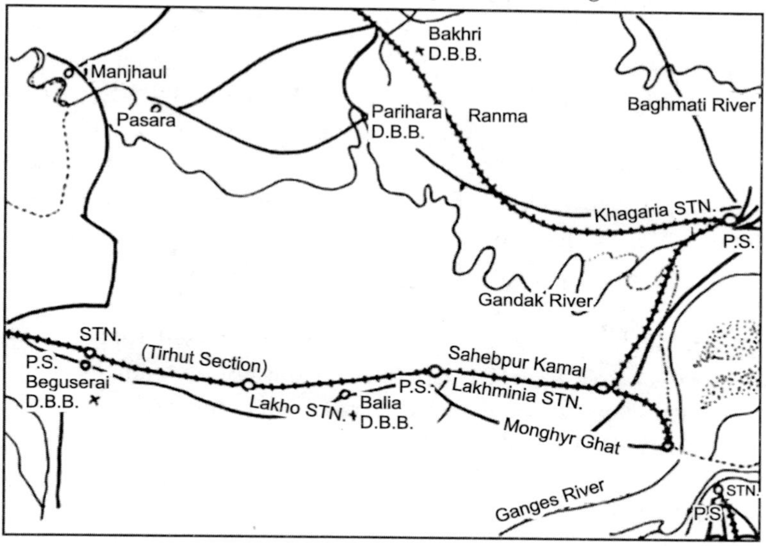

Illustration based on map section from O'Malley, *Monghyr District* (1926).

Both interventions had little effect. Dwarkanath was told that the revenue department would respond with a statement some time in the future.[86] To Lacchmi Prasad Sinha, the PWD's secretary simply reiterated the assertions of the railway's agent: there was no correlation between building of the railway embankment and the 'exceptionally' heavy floods that had occurred in the previous rainy season. He added that the drainage on this portion of the line had been evaluated and approved by the local government in 1913.[87] Repeating

---

[85] Council Question by Lacchmi Prasad Sinha, 26 November 1915.

[86] F. Clayton to Dwarka Nath, 30 August 1915.

[87] Reply by F. Clayton to Council Question of 26 November 1915 regarding the obstruction of the overflow of water by the construction of the Khagaria-Rosera line, file XIII C/1 of 1915, nos. 1–4, 12 and file XIII C/8 of 1915: nos. 1–2, 6, PWD: Railway, Bihar and Orissa Prog., IOR.P/10082, BL. The reply was forwarded to the Secretary of the Railway Board and the BNWR's J. Walker (agent, BNWR) to F. Clayton, Secretary PWD (Bihar and Orissa), 22 November 1915, file XIII C/1 of 1915, nos. 1–4 and 12 and File XIII C/8 of 1915: nos. 1–2, 6.

what had been argued earlier, the secretary insisted that the embankment protected those on the other side of it. Thus, even if it checked any part of the spill of the Burh Gandak towards the old Baghmati channel, it simultaneously protected the country round the Burh Gandak from spills from the Baghmati.[88]

In June 1916, people living in the villages of Babhangawan, Amarpur, and Gouripur told the district magistrate and collector of Bhagalpur how anxious they were about a recently constructed branch line of the BNWR, particularly the segment from Thana Bihpur to Mahadevpur Ghat. This had been built over a dead stream of the Ganges (Kalbalia, near Latipur station), without any waterways or culverts.[89] While the stream remained dry in the summer, it would swell up in the rainy season; in the absence of waterways, it would flood the villages on its bank. The villagers complained of the 'high floods' of 1914 and 1915 that had caused particular damage in Nartakia, Gouripur, Jamaldipur, Babhangawan, and Latipur.[90] They stressed that the Ganges had flooded the area between its bank and the railway embankment on 7 September 1915 because there were an insufficient number of culverts to drain off the floodwater.[91] Most of their cattle had been swept away and the villagers themselves had been saved only by the intervention of the district magistrate, Srish Chandra Ghosh, who arranged boats to convey people and cattle to the other side of the railway embankment.[92]

In this case, the district magistrate endorsed the urgent need to improve the drainage capacity of the railway embankment. However, no steps were taken: railway authorities insisted that additional culverts increased the risk

---

[88] Reply by F. Clayton to Council Question of 26 November 1915.

[89] Inspector-General of Police, to Chief Secretary, Govt. of Bihar and Orissa (Ranchi), 31 August 1917, PWD: Railway A, file 1V-F / 1 of 1918, Govt. of Bihar and Orissa Prog., IOR.P/10296, BL; Jogalkishor Ram Marwari, Gaya Prasad Chaudhuri and others of villages Babhangawan, Amarpur, Gouripur, etc., etc., petitioners, to District Magistrate and Collector, Bhagalpur, PWD: Railway A, file 1V-F/ 1 of 1918, Govt. of Bihar and Orissa Prog., IOR.P/10296, BL.

[90] Petition from villages of Babhangawan, Amarpur, Gouripur, etc., etc.; Inspector-General of Police, to Chief Secretary, Govt. of Bihar and Orissa (Bankipur), 19 August 1917, PWD: Railway A, file no. 1V-F/ 1 of 1918, Govt. of Bihar and Orissa Prog., IOR.P/10296, BL; Inspector-General of Police, to Chief Secretary, Govt. of Bihar and Orissa (Ranchi), 31 August 1917.

[91] S.C. Ghosh, Deputy Collector to Magistrate, 1 June 1916, quoted in Inspector-General of Police, to Chief Secretary Govt. of Bihar and Orissa (Ranchi), 31 August 1917.

[92] Petition from villages of Babhangawan, Amarpur, Gouripur, etc., etc.

of the entire embankment being washed away.[93] Consequently, the villagers apprehended that the 1916 monsoon would generate another 'disastrous flood.'[94] Thus, the inspector-general of police was not particularly surprised when, in September 1916, villagers cut the railway embankment to secure relief from the rising floodwater.[95] (September 1916 was the date to which Bihar and Orissa officials formally traced the practice of embankment cutting in this area. Floods were recorded in 1914 and in 1915 but no cases of embankment cutting officially recorded.[96])

The return of severe floods led to multiple cases of embankment cutting in 1917.[97] Like in 1916, members of the Bihar and Orissa council had pointed out the dangers of inadequate waterways in BNWR embankments months before the floods, citing these as the 'principal causes of the devastation' in the area.[98] They demanded government intervention to ensure that more waterways were provided, especially where lines had been breached in 1916, and asked for a comparative statement of the number of floods in the north Gangetic portions of the province before *and* after the construction of the BNWR lines in those areas.[99] Both requests were denied, the first being described as 'vague' and the second as being incommensurate with the labour and time that it would require.[100] Council members were told that railway authorities would be asked to rectify the problem if 'actual experience' showed waterways to be

---

[93] S.C. Ghosh, Deputy Collector to Magistrate, 1 June 1916.

[94] Petition from villages of Babhangawan, Amarpur, Gouripur, etc., etc.

[95] Inspector-General of Police to Chief Secretary, Govt. of Bihar and Orissa (Ranchi), 31 August 1917.

[96] The Bihar and Orissa department said it had not received records prior to 1911. Inspector-General of Police, to Chief Secretary, Govt. of Bihar and Orissa (Bankipur), 19 August 1917 and 31 August 1917.

[97] Inspector-General of Police, to Chief Secretary, Govt. of Bihar and Orissa (Bankipur), 19 August 1917.

[98] Question by Lachhmi Prasad Sinha, 22 November 1916, file no. XIII-C/5 of 1916, nos. 1–2; Question by Adit Prashad Singh, 22 November 1916, File no. XIII-C/4 of 1916, nos. 1–7, both in PWD Railway A, Govt. of Bihar and Orissa Prog., IOR.P/10101, 1917, BL. (The latter emphasized their effect in the entire Tirhut area, including the districts of Muzaffarpur and Darbhanga.)

[99] Question by Lachhmi Prasad Sinha and Adit Prashad Singh, 22 November 1916.

[100] Answers by Mr. Clayton to Lachhmi Prasad Sinha and Adit Prashad Singh, 22 November 1916, file XIII-C/4 of 1916, nos. 1–7, both in PWD: Railway A, Govt. of Bihar and Orissa Prog., IOR.P/10101, BL.

insufficient. Meanwhile, Tirhut's commissioner convened a special conference on flooding in north Bihar.[101]

The primary target in 1917 was the main line of the BNWR, which ran east to west parallel with the Ganges. Between eight and 10 feet above the level of the country and 'having no bridges or culverts,' it completely obstructed the flow of floodwater.[102] Running south to the Ganges, the railway had a branch line whose embankment also prevented the flow of water and raised the level of floodwater in the villages immediately west of it. The railway embankment protected the country to its north from the Ganges flood, unless the Kosi—the only outlet for floodwater from the north—was also in flood. In this case, the villagers living north of the railway embankment were completely 'at the mercy of the flood' and could only secure relief 'by cutting the railway embankment and letting the floodwater out into the Ganges over the country to the south of the Railway.'[103] Villagers who lived south of the railway embankment believed that cutting it would let the Ganges flood run north inland, while those living south of the main line and west of the branch lines 'undoubtedly' secured relief by cutting the railway embankment of this branch line.[104] In September 1916, the country on both sides of the embankment had been flooded but in 1917 the flood on the south side was higher than the flood on the north. Thus, on the night of 6–7 August 1917, villagers living in the south tried to cut the embankment between Pasraha and Narayananpur as well as Khagaria and Mili, even as floodwater rushing through a 'natural' breach at Gochari overtopped the railway embankment there.[105]

Though they were driven off by shots fired by a patrolling body of railway officers and policemen, a case of criminal damage was instituted under section 126 of the Railways Act, which penalized any attempt to interfere

---

[101] Answers by Mr. Clayton to Lachhmi Prasad Sinha and to Adit Prashad Singh, 22 November 1916 ('Information for the period before this Province was created is not available in this office.'). For reference to Dwarka Nath, file no. XIII C/7 of 1915, nos. 1–3, PWD: Railway A, Govt. of Bihar and Orissa Prog., IOR.P/9802, BL.

[102] Inspector-General of Police to Chief Secretary, Govt. of Bihar and Orissa (Bankipur), 19 August 1917.

[103] Ibid.

[104] Ibid.

[105] District Magistrate, Monghyr to Commissioner, Bhagalpur, 11 August 1917; Investigation Report on Damage Done by Floods in August 1917 to Bengal and North-Western Railway Embankments in Monghyr and Bhagalpur Districts and the Measures Proposed for the Protection of the Embankments, both PWD: Railway A, File no. 1V-F /1 of 1918, in Bihar and Orissa Prog., IOR.P/10296, BL.

with, sabotage, or wreck any railway property.[106] However, the enquiring officers had little success in identifying the alleged saboteurs: since the locality remained submerged, most people were simply struggling to save their lives and property.[107] Further, villagers on the western side of the line were 'heartily in sympathy' with the embankment-cutters, for they too were swamped by Ganges floodwater, the BNWR embankment preventing the water from flowing off.[108] Local officers also realized that the flood was severe enough that the line had been breached naturally in several places. Thus, on 7 August, when the deputy superintendent rushed to a spot between Pasraha and Narayanpur, he found that the 'thousands of men, women, cattle and children assembled on the line with much of their household goods' were innocent—the line had simply collapsed ('*Line ekdam baith gya*').[109]

Punishing the guilty?

In relation to the embankment cutting in August 1917, both the deputy superintendent and inspector-general of police were sympathetic to the plight of villagers. The latter went as far as to argue that: 'had any one in authority been present it is a question whether he would not have taken upon himself to cut the embankment to save lives and property.'[110] Even in the case of the cutting incident at Latipur station, which he believed was 'a little more wanton,' the deputy superintendent stressed how the embanked branch line had acted as a breakwater, holding up the Ganges flood.[111] He himself did not think that the police should press the cases that had been instituted since:

> The necessity for waterways or some system of relief has *constantly* been brought into evidence, and I would suggest the best way of preventing breaches in the future is for Government to insist on the railway doing whatever is necessary [emphasis added].[112]

---

[106] Trevor, *Law Relating to Railways*, 30–31.

[107] S.P., Bhagalpur to D.M., Bhagalpur, 13 August 1917, PWD: Railway A, file 1V-F/ 1 of 1918, Bihar and Orissa Prog., IOR.P/10296, BL.

[108] Ibid.

[109] Deputy Superintendent's report, quoted in Inspector-General of Police, to Chief Secretary, Govt. of Bihar and Orissa, Bankipur, 19 August 1917.

[110] Inspector-General of Police to Chief Secretary, Govt. of Bihar and Orissa (Bankipur), 19 August 1917.

[111] Deputy Superintendent's report, quoted in Inspector-General of Police to Chief Secretary, Govt. of Bihar and Orissa (Bankipur), 19 August 1917.

[112] Ibid.

Agreeing with this view, the inspector-general emphasized that the appropriate action would be to determine, first, the extent of the damage caused and, second, what relief could be provided if the railway constructed proper waterways.[113] He was disinclined to use—as had been suggested by the railway company—sections 107 and 144 of the Criminal Procedure Code, which allowed for executive measures either to keep the peace or pre-emptive measures to stall any 'nuisance or danger' that was apprehended. Believing it unlikely that villagers would try to cut the embankment if they were satisfied that their grievances were receiving due consideration, he preferred that some officers (armed with the means to communicate swiftly with the superintendent of police) watch over the relevant villages.

However, the commissioner of Bhagalpur division was less sanguine; he demanded both a protective and a punitive force beyond what district authorities were equipped to provide. He was adamant that while district authorities could prevent 'surreptitious cutting' of the line by small groups of people, they lacked the resources to prevent pre-arranged attacks by those 'determined to cut the line at all costs.'[114] Only a large police force could protect portions of the BNWR embankment during the remaining months of the rainy season, when floods were anticipated. In addition to prosecuting individuals involved in embankment cutting, he suggested that a punitive force be quartered on the villages 'to which responsibility can be brought home.'[115] The Railway Board also supported a 'more stringent' response and supported the BNWR's suggestion that collective responsibility be placed on those villages to which those suspected of cutting the embankment belonged.[116]

Such punitive action was taken in those parts of Monghyr and Bhagalpur that were designated as areas requiring 'special protection.'[117] In 1918 and

---

[113] Inspector-General of Police, to Chief Secretary, Govt. of Bihar and Orissa (Ranchi), 31 August 1917.

[114] Bhagalpur division included both Bhagalpur and Monghyr districts. Commissioner of Bhagalpur Division to Secretary, Govt. of Bihar and Orissa, 12 August 1917, PWD: Railway A, File no. 1V-F /1 of 1918, Govt. of Bihar and Orissa Prog., IOR.P/10296, BL.

[115] Ibid.

[116] Secretary, Railway Board, to Secretary, Govt. of Bihar and Orissa, PWD: Railway, 12 September 1917, PWD: Railway A, file no. 1V-F/1 of 1918, Bihar and Orissa Prog., IOR.P/10296, BL.

[117] Special Report, Case no. 23-3rd Report (W.H. Hodgson, Major, I.A., S.P. Monghyr), 10 October 1918, PWD: Railway A, file no. VIIE-1 of 1919, Bihar and Orissa Prog., IOR.P/10497, 1919, BL.

1919, an additional police force was stationed in some villages, their costs being borne by the local populace.[118] Villagers were compelled to supply *rasad* or provisions to this force of over 200 men and 'hundreds of rupees from every village was realised by force.'[119] Having failed to secure relief, despite appealing repeatedly to the authorities—including the lieutenant-governor of the province—and recounting their distress in the press, the tenants of Chai (Bhagalpur) and Fakria (Monghyr) held a combined conference on 18 June 1920 at Jhanjhara. Reports indicated that it was attended by nearly 8,000 tenants residing within the circumference of about 200 square miles from Mansi to Mahadeopur Ghat stations. Recounting how 'hundreds of lives' and 'cattle and properties' were lost when the Ganges flood breached the BNWR line at Mansi and Mahadeopur Ghat stations in 1917, submerging villages in six to nine feet of water, they demanded that four specific bridges and three places in the Babhara embankment be 'reopened forever.'[120] Copies of the resolution were to be sent not only to the press but also to the entire administrative hierarchy that would be involved in alleviating their distress: the viceroy, the lieutenant-governor of Bihar and Orissa, the commissioner of Bhagalpur, the collectors of Bhagalpur and Monghyr, and the agent of the BNWR at Gorakhpur. It was also sent to the nationalist hierarchy, including 'M. Gandhi and all the Congress spokesmen, secretaries of provincial and all-India Congress Committees.'[121]

It failed at each administrative level. Quoting an 1898 decision to construct the railway line without any flood openings, the BNWR argued that providing even a single waterway would endanger the line, generating 'great public inconvenience and loss.'[122] While unable to trace the 1898 decision quoted by the railway administration, the Railway Board endorsed the argument of the 1917 enquiry: that the waterways being petitioned for would afford 'little or no relief' to areas south of the line, but instead have 'a prejudicial effect' on the country lying to the north of it during a Ganges flood.[123] Officials in the Bihar

---

[118] Special Report, Case no. 23-3rd Report, 10 October 1918.

[119] Chai and Fakria Parganas Combined Tenants' Conference, 18 June 1920, file no. IP-3 of 1919, PWD: Railway A, Bihar and Orissa Prog., IOR.P/10744, BL.

[120] Ibid.

[121] Ibid.

[122] Agent BNWR to Secretary, Railway Board, 10 July 1920, file no. IP-3 of 1919, PWD: Railway A, Bihar and Orissa Prog., IOR.P/10744, BL.

[123] Ibid.; Secretary, Railway Board, to Secretary, Govt. of Bihar and Orissa, PWD: Railway, Simla, 22 September 1920, file no. IP-3 of 1919, PWD: Railway A, Bihar and Orissa Prog., IOR.P/10744, BL.

and Orissa PWD accepted the advice that the railway bank in itself had 'no appreciable effect' on the height of the flood but instead saved villages on the north side of it from damage.[124] While the lieutenant-governor sympathized with the distress caused by the previous floods, he accepted the arguments of BNWR officers and local officials; consequently, civil authorities were told to convince the petitioners that the openings they had requested were not only contrary to the interests of 'the Railway as well as the general public' but also militated against their *own* well-being.[125]

Blocking sluice culverts

Increased focus on embankment cutting drew attention to the fact that along with providing inadequate drainage outlets, railway administrations also blocked existing culverts, sanctioned in the original construction plans. This violated the terms on which official permission had been granted for laying the lines. Like inadequate waterways, it also contravened the legal requirement that drainage in railway embankments must be 'sufficient at all times to convey water as freely from or to the lands lying near or affected by the railway as before the making of the railway, or as nearly so as may be.'[126] The BNWR administration, however, insisted that blocking culverts—or refusing to open them as the case may be—was necessary to protect the structural integrity of railway embankments. In their view, preventing a discharge of water was the only way to ensure that the culvert, its masonry, and the line passing over it remained undamaged.[127] Consequently, the railway's engineers and management described as sabotage any attempts to let out floodwater by unblocking culverts, even though it was illegal for them to have closed off these in the first place.

Some local administrators highlighted the illegality of the railway's position in closing off culverts that had been sanctioned as part of approved construction plans. Consequently, they condemned attempts by railway administrations to

---

[124] C.B. Mellor, Secretary, Govt. of Bihar and Orissa, PWD, to Goswami Darbari Prasad, Secretary, Chai and Fakria Parganas Tenants' Conference, 17 October 1920, file no. IP-3 of 1919, PWD: Railway A, Bihar and Orissa Prog., IOR.P/10744, BL.

[125] Ibid.; Secretary, Railway Board, to Secretary, Govt. of Bihar and Orissa, PWD: Railway, Simla, 22 September 1920.

[126] Article 11 (1: a & b) of 1890 Act in Trevor, *Law Relating to Railways*, 186–87; clause 11 (1), of 1890 Act, Teruvenkatachariar, *High Court Decisions*, 813–14.

[127] Special Report, Case no. 23-3rd Report, 10 October 1918.

seek criminal penalty for those who tried to reopen these culverts. They were particularly irritated when they realized that many such incidents of sabotage had come after repeated complaints, which had been either ignored or rejected. Thus, when villagers from Rampur village cut the embankment between Salauna and Hassanpur Road at mile 94111,[128] Monghyr's superintendent of police was quite clear that at the 'root of the whole trouble' was the fact that railway authorities had blocked the culvert's two 4'-6" openings with sleepers.[129] As the water rose, they only gradually removed the sleepers. Consequently, the local populace saw:

> their crops and property being destroyed by the rising flood on the one hand, whilst on the other they find the only effectual means of letting out the water blocked up with sleepers.[130]

Not surprisingly, this culvert was close to where the embankment had been cut in 1915, and where police had been stationed in 1916 as a preventive measure. In fact, on the morning of 30 August when the embankment was cut, permanent-way men had been stationed at a culvert three quarters of a mile away, this being 'the practice during the rains' to prevent tampering.[131] The superintendent had little sympathy for railway authorities, suggesting that instead of blocking drainage openings with sleepers they should construct structurally sound culverts that would not be damaged by the very purpose that they were intended to serve.[132]

Railway authorities earned more flak when it was discovered that they had been alerted to the problem in earlier years. In 1915, E.S. Hoernle, then a subdivisional officer in Beguserai, had pointed out the lack of waterways in the line between Hassanpur Road and Salauna. While he had posted an armed

---

[128] Report from Resident Engineer BNWR (Mansi) to Chief Engineer BNWR (Gorakhpur), 31 August 1918, PWD: Railway A, file no. VIIE-1 of 1919, Bihar and Orissa Prog., IOR.P/10497, BL. The line that was cut was on the Tirhut State Railway between Salauna and Hassanpur Road on the Khagaria-Samastipur Chord Line on 30 August 1918 (Tirhut State Railway worked by BNWR). Salauna is on the Mansi-Samastipur branch of BNWR: List of railway stations in O'Malley, *Monghyr District* (1926), 271.

[129] Special Report, Case no. 23-3rd Report, 10 October 1918.

[130] Ibid.

[131] Report from Resident Engineer BNWR (Mansi) to Chief Engineer BNWR (Gorakhpur), 31 August 1918.

[132] Special Report, Case no. 23-3rd Report, 10 October 1918.

police guard to protect the line, he was acutely aware of the 'justice of the raiyats' complaints' and declared that had the danger from floodwater continued much longer he would have cut the line himself (after notifying railway authorities).[133] The next year, the railway administration had refused to open the culvert near Salauna Station, removing only three of the 16 sleepers in each span.[134] The water kept rising and the police were called in to guard the railway line. However, Beguserai's subdivisional officer, Mr. Meredith, was quite clear that the line itself was the 'chief obstacle' to the water dissipating.[135] He stressed the 'very large' damage caused to crops 'by its unbridged state,' explaining that even if the railway raised the flood level only to the lower estimate of three feet, this made 'all the difference between discomfort and actual danger.'[136] Meredith was incensed that this was the third year in a row in which such a situation had developed. Since railway authorities were 'too niggardly to provide proper waterway,' he insisted that they had no right to demand help from district authorities by arguing that any cutting of the bank would cause a stoppage of traffic or even a railway disaster.[137] He was especially critical of the BNWR, deeming its officers 'notorious' in this respect.[138] The current commissioner of Bhagalpur, who had served previously in the area affected, also emphasized the consistent disinclination of the railway administration to provide adequate waterways, sarcastically referring to their desire 'never to allow water to flow where it can be prevented.'[139]

Notwithstanding such critique, the revenue department endorsed the railway's claim that adequate waterways had been provided.[140] Thus, when the area flooded again, the railway blocked up a culvert as was 'their usual

---

[133] E.S. Hoernle's letter of 9 November 1915, quoted in J. Johnston, Commissioner, Bhagalpur, to Chief Secretary, Govt. of Bihar and Orissa, 20 November 1918, PWD: Railway A, file no. VIIE-1 of 1919, Bihar and Orissa Prog., IOR.P/10497, BL.

[134] Salauna station is on Mansi-Samastipur branch of the BNWR. Appendix I: List of railway stations in O'Malley, *Monghyr District* (926), 271.

[135] Quoted in J. Johnston, Commissioner, Bhagalpur, to Chief Secretary, Govt. of Bihar and Orissa, 20 November 1918.

[136] E.S. Hoernle's letter of 9 November 1915.

[137] Ibid.

[138] Ibid.

[139] J. Johnston, Commissioner, Bhagalpur, to Chief Secretary, Govt. of Bihar and Orissa, 20 November 1918.

[140] Ibid.

practice.'[141] The water remained hedged in, its level rising; villagers who were watching their crops and property being destroyed cut the line between Salauna and Hassanpur. Though insufficient evidence prevented any action from being taken, the villagers accused of cutting the embankment were charged under section 126 of the Railways Act.[142] The commissioner, however, chose to question how the railway administration had decided to accord itself the right to block culverts with sleepers and why no civil authorities had questioned its right (or lack of) to do so. He referred pointedly to section 11 (1) (b) of chapter III of the Railways Act which placed railways under a statutory obligation to provide adequate waterways. Thus, 'in blocking for its own convenience one of the sanctioned open waterways it acted in a *wholly illegal* manner' (emphasis added).[143] If the railway could not spare the expense to build its culverts strong enough to take any flow of water as was likely to be met with, then he believed that 'it has no right to save itself at the expense of the population of the surrounding country.'[144] He insisted that before it demanded punitive police or any other special measures of protection, the railway had to evaluate the legality and propriety of its own actions.[145] The critique built as the province's chief secretary pointed out to the railway company that they had not been given permission to reduce the discharging capacity of the culverts at any time; thus, the procedure had to be discontinued until it was sanctioned by the local government.[146]

'The Hand of Man'

Though their actions were challenged, railway administrators seemed to be able to skirt formal liability. This was despite increasing public agitation about the heightened frequency of floods in Bengal, Bihar and Orissa, Assam, and

---

[141] Ibid.

[142] Mr. Clayton, Secretary, Govt. of Bihar and Orissa, PWD, to Secretary, Railway Board, 25 March 1919, PWD: Railway A, file no. VIIE-1 of 1919, Govt. of Bihar and Orissa Prog., IOR.P/10497, BL.

[143] J. Johnston, Commissioner, Bhagalpur, to Chief Secretary, Govt. of Bihar and Orissa, 20 November 1918.

[144] Ibid.

[145] Ibid.

[146] Mr. Clayton, Secretary, Govt. of Bihar and Orissa (PWD), to Agent, BNWR, Ranchi, 16 February 1919, PWD: Railway A, file no. VIIE-1 of 1919, Govt. Bihar and Orissa Prog., IOR.P/10497, BL.

Burma, and rising complaints about the damage engendered by these. Between 1924 and 1929, the issue became prominent at a national level, sparked by demands that the worsening situation be addressed in a concerted manner, leading to the establishment of the all-India flood enquiry committee.[147]

Much of the ballast for arguments about worsening conditions itself came from a series of events in 1922 described as 'The Great Flood in Northern Bengal.' The official report attributed the floods that occurred in Rajashahi district to 'excessive rainfall' in northern Bengal, a statement that the astrophysicist Meghnad Saha (who was involved in the relief efforts) challenged as 'an ill-concealed attempt' to blame nature instead of railways.[148] Local accounts emphasized how the double railway line running from Sara to Santahar had held up the flood, causing 'devastating accumulation' of water for upwards of a fortnight; also that the flood stayed in Rajashahi, east and west of the line, even *after* the rains had practically ceased.[149] While the original metre-gauge line from Sara to Santahar had been constructed with flood openings, these were closed off or reduced when the new broad gauge line was constructed. Unable to drain off, the floodwater turned into a 'boiling sheet' whose height exceeded the average annual flood level by eight to nine feet.[150] The difference of level on the west and on the east side of the railway line amounted to between four and five feet: 'a clear indication that the railway line was blocking the free passage of water.' This assessment was corroborated by the fact that the elderly in the locality remembered such heavy rains but not such heavy floods.

The height and duration of the flood destroyed the winter paddy. Used to annual seasonal inundations, cultivators in the area grew a long-stemmed winter paddy that was sown before the rains and which—during the rainy season—grew apace, its stems growing 10 or 12 feet and upwards. Provided the water rose gradually, the crop was not affected by regular inundations. However, it could not tolerate a sudden rise in water, particularly if this did

---

[147] T. Ryan (Industries and Labour Secretary), extract from the official report of the Council of State debates, 19 September 1929, 144, in 'Resolution re: Prevention of Floods,' Economic and Overseas Dept., Govt. of India, file no. 5180 of 1924, IOR.L/E/7/1367, BL.

[148] Saha, 'Great Flood in Northern Bengal,' 609. Saha's teacher P.C. Ray was involved in the flood relief.

[149] Ibid., 606–8

[150] J.C. Roy of the Social Service League observes this in a letter to the *Amrita Bazar* published on 6 November, Saha, 'Great Flood in Northern Bengal.'

not subside immediately.[151] The flood in itself would not have been disastrous if the water had not been held up by the railway embankment, or if there had been numerous and sufficiently large bridges in it. However, after lying under water for over a fortnight, the crop was a total loss.

The embankment's role in the damage witnessed in 1922 was established by comparing it with the effects of the 1871 floods, believed to be one of the highest floods recorded in Rajashahi. In 1871, cattle had suffered from a loss of fodder, people had been driven to seek shelter in high places, and cholera had broken out in epidemic form after the water subsided. However, not being held up by railway embankments, the floodwater had risen slowly and subsided rapidly. Thus, in most places, the crop grew on 'uninjured, and managed to keep its head above waters.' This was not the case in 1922. Instead, many suggested that the 1922 rice crop of Rajashahi (and the *ganja* crop of Naogaon) could have been largely recovered if either the railway embankment had had enough waterways, or else had been cut open to let the water pass freely.

When combined with increasingly severe episodes of flood damage in other provinces, this led to a demand for a committee of experts to assess 'causes of the recurring floods all over India.'[152] However, the central government reiterated that given the diversity of local conditions, flood prevention was a provincial subject.[153] During the discussion in 1924 the central government recognized—in principle—that some responsibility could accrue to it under certain conditions.[154] However, in both 1926 and 1927, it denied knowledge of any specific cases in which it could be proved that floods had been caused or aggravated by high railway embankments.[155] Since it did not accept that the economic disasters facing agriculturalists and villagers had been 'greatly enhanced by the railway embankments,' so it could hardly accept that railway companies, the Government of India, or the Railway Board were 'primarily

---

[151] Quoted from *District Gazetteer of Rajshahi* (76), in Saha 'Great Flood in Northern Bengal,' 605–11.

[152] Extract from Official Report of Legislative Assembly debates, 24 September 1924 (4083, 4101) in 'Resolution re: Prevention of Floods,' Economic & Overseas Dept., Govt. of India, file no. 5180 of 1924, IOR.L/E/7/1367, BL.

[153] T. Ryan, extract from the official report of the Council of State debates, 19 September 1924.

[154] Ibid.

[155] Charles Innes replying to Majid Bakshi, Legislative Assembly debates, 28 January 1926, 339–40, Economic and Overseas Dept., Govt. of India, file no. 5180 of 1924, IOR.L/E/7/1367, BL.

responsible for the economic distress owing to floods enhanced by the railway embankments.'[156] Thus, liability remained theoretical.[157]

Instead, the central government emphasized that it had exerted itself 'to the utmost extent' in cases where there had been any 'reason to believe that excessive floods were due to central works such as Railways.'[158] It claimed it was unable to trace cases in which railway administrations had been compelled to enlarge waterways under pressure by provincial governments or the Railway Board; it did, however, know of 'several in which Local Governments and railway administrations have acted together ... to prevent a recurrence of flood damages.'[159] Further, 'in the case of certain railway works which were supposed to have contributed to floods,' the matter was deemed settled by local governments and railway authorities.[160] Even in 1929, despite the fact that the same resolution had been 'brought thrice in the Legislature,' the government insisted that there was no public demand for central intervention.[161]

Popular opinion was less forgiving. Writing about the 1922 floods in Rajashahi, Meghnad Saha emphasized the 'Hand of Man,' refusing to relegate people's distress to an 'Act of God' as railway authorities claimed.[162] Saha may not have been familiar with the specific distress of Monghyr's cultivators who had been living in the shadow of railway embankments; however, his analysis of the distress in Rajashahi in 1922 would have resonated with the former. Saha abstained from blaming railway engineers of 'purposely doing mischief,' preferring to emphasize instead their indifference to the people in areas through which the line was constructed. Simultaneously, however, he referred to a rumoured battle between the commissioner of Rajashahi and the chief railway engineer about the inadequacy of waterways in the Sara–Santhahar

---

[156] A.A.L. Parsons replying to K. Ahmed, Legislative Assembly debates, 30 August 1927, 3598, Economic and Overseas Dept., Govt. of India, no. 5180 of 1924, IOR.L/E/7/1367, BL.

[157] A.A.L. Parsons replying to B.R. Das, Legislative Assembly Debates, 30 August 1927.

[158] A.A.L. Parsons in Legislative Assembly debates, 30 August 1927, 3598.

[159] Ibid.

[160] T. Ryan (Industries and Labour Secretary), Council of State debates, 19 September, 1929, 144.

[161] Mr. Kumar Sankar Ray Chaudhury, quoted in Extract from the official report of the Council of State debates, 19 September 1929, 144, in 'Resolution re: Prevention of Floods,' Economic and Overseas Dept., Govt. of India, file no. 5180 of 1924, IOR.L/E/7/1367, BL.

[162] Saha, 'The Great Flood in Northern Bengal,' 611.

line: the commissioner had predicted that a reduction of waterways 'might lead to a disaster' but was unable to convince railway authorities to recognize the problem. Saha's conclusion was unequivocal: 'ultimately the peasant was sacrificed to railway interests.'[163]

---

[163] Ibid.; 15 years later, in his message to the 1937 Patna Flood Conference, the Bihar nationalist leader Rajendra Prasad was still urging that when embankments are held responsible for floods and a suggestion is made that they should be done away with, the embankment that ought to attract attention first of all were railway embankments (and district board roads), quoted in Mishra, 'The Bihar Flood Problem,' 2209.

Four

Railway Time

Speed, Synchronization, and 'Time-Sense'

In 1919, a shopkeeper from Gujranwala was charged with 'waging war against His Majesty.' Under section 121 of the Indian Penal Code, a martial law tribunal accused Jagannath of fomenting agitation in meetings held on 12 and 13 April and of taking 'a very active part' in having shops closed on 14 April.[1] The tribunal argued that these events were central in Gujranwala's decision to replicate the violence seen in Amritsar. Jagannath defended himself with an alibi, offering railway timetables as proof that he could not have committed the acts that he was being charged with. He explained that he had left Gujranwala for Kathiawar on 12 April by the 5.00 p.m. train. He also offered to produce witnesses to corroborate his presence in Dhoraji on 16 April—since it took 44 hours to reach Dhoraji from Delhi by the fastest train, so their testimony, combined with railway timetables, made it impossible for him to have been in Gujranwala after 6.00 p.m. on 13 April. The tribunal allowed him to summon witnesses who could prove this alibi but pronounced judgment without waiting for them.

---

* An earlier version of this chapter was published as '"Time-Sense": Railways and Temporality in Colonial India,' *Modern Asian Studies* 47, 4 (July 2013): 1252–82.

---

[1] Gandhi, 'Jagannath's Case,' 170–74.

'Jagannath's Case' became somewhat of an albatross around the imperial neck, with the legally trained nationalist leader M.K. Gandhi insisting that railway timetables 'completely established' his alibi.[2] Its explicit political valence aside, Jagannath's use of railway timetables as legal defence suggests the extent to which railway infrastructure had permeated everyday life in colonial India.[3] Important here is Jagannath's depiction as one among millions of ordinary Indians: 'a man of humble position and status,' a petty shopkeeper who was 'unknown to fame and unconnected with any public activity.'[4] Jagannath's alibi did not protect him legally since the tribunal did not wait for him to produce witnesses. However, his story shows how technical artefacts linked with railways—train schedules, railway timetables, and station clocks—had become integrated into people's lives. These both embodied and fostered a changing temporal order, one that someone like Jagannath had absorbed effectively enough to deploy creatively in his defence.[5] That Jagannath himself was 'ignorant of Urdu as well as English' suggests that he likely read a timetable in Gurmukhi, which itself suggests that popular demands for railway timetables in local scripts had been successful. Given that the annual number of railway passengers in 1918–19 was nearly 460 million, Jagannath was one of a remarkable number of people who regularly encountered and negotiated train schedules and timetables; the eventual institution of railway time as civil and national time in colonial India further broadened the purview of such temporal reorganization.[6]

The centrepiece of this reorganization was the standardization of railway time across India, a process prompted by increasing railway mileage and the ensuing need to coordinate interchange across multiple lines. This concern was exacerbated by the longitudinal distance separating Bengal and Bombay presidencies, where the earliest railway lines had been built. The process itself took about half a century. Discussions began in 1854 and it was in 1870 that the time of a meridian passing through Madras ($80^0 27'$E)—'Madras time'— was agreed upon as an all-India railway time. Another 35 years later, in 1905, all-India railway time was shifted to another meridian, at $82^0 5'$E. Unlike

---

[2] Ibid.

[3] Ibid. For a brief discussion of the origin and expanded use of the term 'infrastructure,' see Ahuja, *Pathways of Empire*, 79.

[4] Gandhi, 'Jagannath's Case,' 170–74.

[5] Cf. Michel de Certeau's discussion of creative tactics in *Practice of Everyday Life*, esp. 165–76.

[6] *Statistical Abstract from 1910–11 to 1919–20*, 138.

Madras time, the latter was exactly 5 hours and 30 minutes ahead of the time of the Greenwich meridian, chosen as the international prime after the 1884 International Meridian Conference in Washington DC.[7]

Neither the fact of temporal standardization nor the fact that railway time was—gradually—established as civil time was specific to colonial India. However, it is equally true that in colonial India (as well as in colonial contexts more broadly), the process was perceived to be much more than a technical mechanism for coordinating the safe movement of railways. Just as railways themselves were deemed a speedy mechanism that would literally transport colonized societies into a normative historical modern, so a uniform railway time, synchronized with Greenwich time, was intended to make colonized populations temporally modern and 'rational.' Consequently, the process of standardizing railway time was saturated with presumptions of colonial difference, articulated through binaries of colonial *versus* metropolitan time-sense. These reifications not only structured official discussions and policy decisions but also informed official expectations about how Indians would, or would not, navigate the ensuing changes.

While it certainly unfolded gradually, millions of Indians were affected by the process through which the time of a single meridian was selected as an all-India railway time (and, eventually, as civil time). People's 'time-sense' not only had to grapple with standardization but also with related questions of speed and mobility. Even before standard time became a material reality, people were confronted with the fact that railways simultaneously compressed and expanded both time and distance, speeding up certain journeys but making other, longer, ones possible. Popular reactions were varied and complex; equally important is that they were analogous to variations in how people across the globe responded to similar processes. Some grappled discursively with the speed of railway journeys, while others grappled materially with railway timetables. As train schedules oriented everyday life towards the changes being instituted, the punctuality of trains was as much under discussion as the punctuality of its passengers. People negotiated with the mathematical abstraction of timetables, asking railway companies to print them in local scripts. They also asked that train timings be changed to better accommodate their everyday needs, whether in getting them to work on time or being better adapted to the new urban–suburban structure of their week. The heterogeneous ways in which

---

[7] Derek Howse, *Greenwich Time and the Discovery of Longitude* (Oxford: Oxford University Press, 1980), especially 'Greenwich Time for the World, 1884–1939.'

Indians accepted, contested, and appropriated railway time is to be expected, given the increasing size of the colonial travelling public and the growing relationship between railway and civil time. However, recovering the details of this heterogeneity remains vital to re-establishing the historical modern as a time shared by colonizer and colonized.

1854–1905: Standardizing Time in Colonial India

In the nineteenth century, the question of establishing railroad time generated extensive discussion across the globe. Clock-time was already in use, spurred by two separate imperatives: the horological precision required by ships crossing oceans and the demands of industrial work-discipline.[8] However, it was the demands of coordinating railway transport that effectively spurred the spread of supra-local standardized time.[9] In Britain, the rise of the mail-coach service in the late eighteenth century had nudged some towards thinking about standardization but it was the need to coordinate a widespread railway network that galvanized the introduction of a supra-local standard.[10] Several English railway companies began to standardize time on individual lines in the 1840s but there was little coordination until the Railway Clearing House was established as a forum for more general decisions. It was not till 1847

---

[8] Sumit Sarkar discusses how, from the sixteenth century onwards, 'one basic European quest in horological technique was for an effective combination of precision and portability in calculating time on ships crossing oceans.' In contrast, he sees such precise calculation of time as 'a less pressing requirement for the Indian Ocean-centred South Asian overseas trade, which could follow coasts or cross the Arabian Sea using regular monsoon winds.' 'Colonial Times: Clocks and Kali-Yuga,' in his *Beyond Nationalist Frames: Postmodernism, Hindu Fundamentalism, History* (Bloomington: Indiana University Press, 2000), 18–19. For capitalist work-discipline, see E.P. Thompson, 'Time, Work-Discipline, and Industrial Capitalism,' *Past and Present* 38 (December 1967): 59–97. Jacques Le Goff, *Time, Work, and Culture in the Middle Ages* (Chicago: University of Chicago Press, 1980) discusses work and time discipline in the middle ages, especially in relation to merchant's time, church time, and labour time.

[9] David S. Landes, *Revolution in Time: Clocks and the Making of the Modern World* (Cambridge: Harvard University Press, 1983), 94; Wolfgang Schivelbusch, *The Railway Journey: The Industrialization of Time and Space in the 19th Century* (Berkeley: University of California Press, 1986 [1977]), 43–44; Todd S. Presner, *Mobile Modernity: Germans, Jews, Trains* (New York: Columbia University Press, 2007), 61–62.

[10] Eviatar Zerubavel, 'The Standardization of Time: A Socio-historical Perspective,' *American Journal of Sociology* 88, 1 (July 1982): 1–23, especially 6.

when it was suggested that Greenwich Mean Time (GMT) be introduced as the standard time on all lines.[11] Ian Bartky has pointed out that in north America, early discussions about standardization were generated by scientific pursuits that required 'simultaneous observations' from scattered points.[12] However, the public implementation of standardization remained linked with the demands of railroad superintendents and managers. An 1883 piece in the journal *Science* explained that while 'committees of various scientific bodies' had 'called attention to the urgent need of reform in the standards of time in use, and suggested plans for action,' it was railways 'which are naturally most interested in the movement [that] have recently taken hold of the matter in earnest.'[13] On 18 November 1883, five standards of time were adopted in north America, differing by consecutive hours.[14]

In colonial India, the half-century between 1854 and 1905 was rife with discussions about standardizing railway time here. The process involved three sequential steps. First, the local time of areas linked in a single railway was synchronized with the local time of the capital of the presidency or province that the line served. Second, this presidency or province time was replaced with an all-India railway time derived from a meridian passing through the centre of the country. Third, all-India time was mathematically synchronized with that of Greenwich, accepted as the world's prime meridian $(0^0 0' 0")$ after 1884.[15] The initial demands for standardization came from railway companies concerned with technical coordination and safety at junction points. However, administrators at local and national levels, most notably civil servants in the PWD, remained heavily involved in the discussions. Despite frequently conflicting positions among the people involved, the discussions reveal the remarkable extent to which technical policy decisions drew on reified and ahistorical assumptions about temporal sensibilities and practices in colonial India.

Time and distance

Practical discussions about standardizing railway time in colonial India were premised on the idea that colonized spaces and people were temporally distant

---

[11] Schivelbusch, *Railway Journey*, 43–44.

[12] Ian Bartky, 'The Adoption of Standard Time,' *Technology and Culture* 30, 1 (January 1989): 25–56, quote on 25.

[13] 'Standard Railway Time,' *Science* 2, 36 (12 October 1883): 494–96.

[14] Bartky, 'Adoption of Standard Time,' 25; 'Standard Railway Time,' 494–96.

[15] The difference calculable in complete hours. (For India, the half-hour was accepted).

from the historical present. One can recognize in this the process that Johannes Fabian has termed 'allochronism,' a 'conjuring trick' to separate in historical time those who actually exist in shared time.[16] For Fabian, allochronism is a 'systematic' tendency to place the referents of anthropology (or the colonized) in a time distinct from, and anterior to, those producing anthropological discourse (or the colonizer). In colonial India, such practices of allochronism dictated that discussions about standardization of railway time presumed a world of 'co-existent yet non-contemporary beings.'[17] In effect, the colonized were temporally distanced through imperial knowledge that defined a singular Indian sense of time, characterized it as pre-modern, and juxtaposed it against a normative idea of modern, both historically and temporally.

Characterizing time-sense in India as one that was cyclical and incapable of comprehending historical change was not a practice that was new to the mid-nineteenth century. Romila Thapar has traced much of this to eighteenth-century Indologists faced with the challenge of cross-referencing Biblical and Classical information with Indian texts.[18] Indological scholarship relied on temporal distancing devices (cyclical; repetitive) and adjectives (mythical) to distance in time societies and people who actually existed contemporaneously in the present.[19] These distancing devices persisted into mid- to late-nineteenth century discussions about standardizing railway time, as did the concomitant suggestion of a metropolitan time-sense that was linear and historical, and able to mark the uniqueness of particular events, while rendering them non-recurring. The ahistoricity of such reifications has been noted by a range of scholars who argue not only that Indians used both cyclic and linear time depending on function, but also that secularization of time in western Europe

---

[16] Johannes Fabian, *Time and the Other: How Anthropology Makes its Object* (New York: Columbia University Press, 2000 [1983]), quotes on x, 23, 31, 32.

[17] As described by Prathma Banerjee in her *Politics of Time: 'Primitives' and History-writing in a Colonial Society* (Delhi: Oxford University Press, 2006), 4. See also Fabian, *Time and the Other*, 31; the introduction to Akhil Gupta and James Ferguson, eds., *Culture, Power and Place: Explorations in Critical Anthropology* (London: Duke University Press, 1997); and Anthony Giddens, *The Consequences of Modernity* (Stanford: Stanford University Press, 1990), 174.

[18] Romila Thapar, *Time as a Metaphor of History: Early India* (Delhi: Oxford University Press, 1996), esp. 4–6. Also Ronald Inden, *Imagining India* (Bloomington: Indiana University Press, 1990); and the introduction to Peter Marshall, ed., *The British Discovery of Hinduism in the Eighteenth Century* (Cambridge: Cambridge University Press, 1970).

[19] Fabian, *Time and the Other*, 30.

was itself a nineteenth century phenomenon.[20] However, ahistoricity did not diminish the practical life of such reifications.

Synchronizing the colony

Almost as soon as passenger trains began running in India, the government's consulting engineer for railways began an official discussion about what time would be 'observed generally on Indian railways.' At the point that W.E. Baker initiated the conversation in 1854, railways were restricted to a discrete 35 miles in Bombay Presidency. The 121 miles added in 1855 were on the other side of the country, in Bengal Presidency. Baker argued that India's expanse meant that local mean time should be kept at each station on Indian railways.[21] Presidency officials in Madras and Bombay agreed with him. However, they did not argue their case by emphasizing how rail mileage was limited, as well as locked into two discrete pockets. Instead, they juxtaposed time-sense in India and England to make their case.[22] Without much elaboration, Colonel Pears who was the consulting engineer for railways at Fort St. George stated that in England the need for standardization derived weight from the number and influence of men of business for whom it was critical that 'there should be no mistake about time;' in India, he argued, the sun was 'the great natural time piece' and it would 'be very long before the mass of people could be made

---

[20] Thapar stresses how cyclic time co-existed with linear conceptions of time, especially in relation to genealogy. *Time as a Metaphor*, 4–6. Sumit Sarkar points out how classical Indology tended to ignore Indo-Islamic notions entirely as well as the presence of 'not one but several layers even in pre-Islamic Indian conceptions of time.' See his 'Colonial Times,' 15. For Europe, see also Stephen Kern, *The Culture of Time and Space, 1880–1918* (Cambridge: Harvard University Press, 1983), especially 10–35 and Henri Lefebvre, *The Production of Space*, translated by Donald Nicholson-Smith (Oxford: Blackwell, 1991), 22–23. Relevant here is the argument made by Ashis Nandy about imperialism involving 'internal' colonization (of difference) in metropolitan contexts before it expanded outwards: see his *The Intimate Enemy: Loss and Recovery of Self under Colonialism* (Delhi: Oxford University Press, 1983).

[21] Home: Railway A, 4 August 1854, no. 57, NAI; Home: Railway, 4 August 1854, no. 58, NAI; *Statistical Abstract from 1840 to 1865*, 58.

[22] J.J. Pears, Consulting Engineer for Railways (Fort St. George) to Chief Secretary, Fort St George, 12 September 1854, in Home: Railway A, 15 September 1854, nos. 89–91, NAI; Captain Crawford, Superintending Engineer for Railways (Bombay) to H.E. Goldsmith, Chief Secretary, Govt. of Bombay, 21 August 1854, in Home: Railway A, 15 September 1854, nos. 60–61, NAI.

to understand a railway time.'[23] He added that railway travelling was common in England but presumed that in India there would be too many people who 'live at a distance from the Railway and feel its influence but little, travelling by it rarely.'

The East Indian Railway (EIR), however, remained dissatisfied with local mean time being the standard. To make their case, its officials invoked, like Baker had, India's vastness; however, the EIR's traffic manager turned the argument on its head. J.C. Batchelor applauded England's decision to replace local time with Greenwich time, pointing out that the advantages of standardization 'on a large Railway system' like India's were too obvious to need reiteration.[24] He was aware of those who opposed standardized time in India on the grounds that, unlike India, England was a small country where the entire variation of time from one extreme to the other was limited. However, he argued that it was precisely India's size that necessitated standardization: As he explained, since the

> difference in time between here [Calcutta] and Delhi is 45 minutes, and between here [Calcutta] and Bombay [is] 63 minutes... the difficulty of constructing an intelligible Time Bill, without the establishment of some universal time will be great.

The EIR's agent E. Palmer emphasized the confusion that would result from such differences in time and suggested that a standard time be fixed 'for all India.'[25] Either Jabalpur time (79⁰93'E)—as suggested by Batchelor—or Kanpur time (80⁰21'E) was considered adequate to the task. To prepare timetables for the opening to Patna and Benaras, the EIR went as far as to seek permission to arrange for either Jabalpur or Kanpur time to be telegraphed throughout the line daily as the time 'by which all Railway Station clocks may be regulated from the 15th October next.'[26] A chagrined Government of India declined, insisting that stations on the EIR would follow presidency time—that of its capital, Calcutta—up to the 'extreme limit of local Bengal

---

[23] Pears to Chief Secretary, 12 September 1854.

[24] J.C. Batchelor, Traffic Manager, EIR to E. Palmer, Agent, EIR, 31 July 1862, in PWD: Railway, 15 August 1862, nos. 26–28, NAI.

[25] E. Palmer, Agent, EIR to Secretary (PWD), 4 August 1862, in PWD: Railway, 15 August 1862, nos. 26–28, NAI.

[26] Palmer to Secretary (PWD), 4 August 1862.

supervision,' continuing with Allahabad time from there to Delhi.[27] The more general question of time to be kept 'when the lines are opened through' would only be considered after the main lines were completed.[28]

In doing so, however, the government unwittingly sanctioned a move from local mean time to presidency time. The Secretary of State for India in London belatedly informed the Indian administration that their 1862 decision instituting Calcutta time as railway time on EIR stations in Bengal contravened their 1854 decision supporting local mean time.[29] While admitting this error, the Government of India decided to stay with the 1862 decision: by now, the EIR had worked for nearly a year up to Allahabad with Calcutta time, and from Allahabad to Delhi with Allahabad time.[30] The Secretary of State declared that he found the earlier plan of local mean time to be 'the more convenient' of the two options but did not press the point.[31]

Expressing its dissatisfaction with the government's orders, the EIR continued its demand for an all-India railway time. This time, its deputy agent Cecil Stephenson stressed how necessary this was for EIR guards and pointsmen to be able to ensure passenger safety.[32] At this point, the specific request focused on standardization on the EIR. However, the EIR was no longer the contained railway line it had been when such discussions had begun. Between 1855 and 1867, railway mileage in Bengal had burgeoned and the EIR had also spread westward out of the presidency: from 121

---

[27] PWD: Railway, 15 August 1862, nos. 26–28, NAI; and PWD: Railway, April 1864, nos. 78–81, NAI.

[28] R. Strachey, Secretary, Govt. of India (PWD), 11 August 1862 in PWD: Railway, 15 August 1862, nos. 26–28, NAI.

[29] Secretary of State for India to Govt. of India, 17 November 1864, in PWD: Railway, February 1865, nos. 14–15, NAI; also PWD: Railway, June 1864, no. 49, NAI.

[30] Govt. of India to Secretary of State for India, 17 November 1865, in PWD: Railway, February 1865, nos. 14–15, NAI. The Government of India informed the Secretary of State of their 1864 decision in a letter dated 13 June 1864; the latter expressed his objection in a letter dated 17 November 1864; and the Government of India responded in a letter dated 17 November 1865.

[31] PWD: Railway, July 1865, nos. 25–27, NAI; Secretary of State to Govt. of India, 17 November 1864.

[32] PWD Circular (no. 7): To Govts. of Madras, Bombay, NWP and Punjab; Chief Commissioners of Oudh and Central Provinces; Agent to Governor-General, Central India and Rajputana, 16 April 1864, in PWD: Railway, April 1864, nos. 78–81, NAI. Cecil Stephenson to Deputy Consulting Engineer, Govt. of Bengal (Railway), 19 May 1865, in PWD: Railway, July 1865, nos. 25–27, NAI.

miles in 1855, mileage had increased to 1,353 miles by 1868.[33] The Bengal government disagreed with Stephenson's conclusion, countering his concern for passenger safety with the argument that an all-India railway time would militate 'against the interests of the public of the large centres of business,' such as Calcutta and Bombay who were 'entitled to the greatest consideration.'[34] The EIR continued to stress that in resisting standardized railway time the government was disregarding passenger safety.[35] Bengal's deputy consulting engineer for railways chose to support the EIR's request and suggested that the local time of Madras (Madras time) be accepted as 'the Railway standard in India as London time is in England.'[36] However, Bengal's lieutenant-governor disagreed, stating that the institution of Madras time or that of 'any other foreign city' would be unacceptable to the public in Bengal, especially that of its important commercial centres.[37] The government had by this point instituted Madras time as an all-India telegraph time but rejected the idea of it being introduced as standardized railway time.[38]

Across the globe, spatially specific local time was considered to be the 'only valid standard' till about the mid-nineteenth century.[39] Any form of temporal standardization, whether the institution of railway time or national time, required that local time be substituted with supra-local time, capable of being divided into commensurable units. In contrast to local time, supra-local time broke the link between time and place, a process that Wolfgang Schivelbusch describes as a loss of temporal identity for regions whose local time was replaced.[40] Further, while supra-local time was theoretically inter-subjective, it actually privileged a specific location whose local time was selected as the

---

[33] *Statistical Abstract from 1840 to 1865*, 58; *Statistical Abstract from 1867/68 to 1876/77*, 88.

[34] J. Hovenden, Assistant Secretary, Govt. of Bengal (PWD: Railway), to Secretary, Govt. of India (PWD), 1 June 1865, in PWD: Railway, July 1865, nos. 25–27, NAI. C.H. Dickens, Secretary, Govt. of India (PWD), to Joint Secretary, Govt. of Bengal (PWD: Railway), 5 July 1865, in PWD: Railway, July 1865, nos. 25–27, NAI.

[35] PWD: Railway A, June 1867, nos. 128–31, NAI.

[36] Deputy Consulting Engineer, Govt. of Bengal (Railway), 22 April 1867, in PWD: Railway A, June 1867, nos. 128–31, NAI.

[37] Assistant Secretary, Govt. of Bengal (PWD: Railway) to Secretary, Govt. of India (PWD), 23 April 1867, in PWD: Railway A, June 1867, nos. 128–31, NAI.

[38] C.H. Dickens, Secretary, Govt. of India (PWD) to Joint Secretary, Govt. of Bengal (Railway), 21 June 1867, in PWD: Railway A, June 1867, nos. 128–31, NAI.

[39] Zerubavel, 'Standardization,' 5.

[40] Using Walter Benjamin's notion of aura in 'The Work of Art in the Age of Mechanical Reproduction' (1936): Schivelbusch, *Railway Journey*, 42.

standard. Thus, temporal standardization was challenged in various contexts across the globe, 'particularly by communities whose local times differed substantially from the standards they were to adopt.'[41] Despite Greenwich time being suggested as England's railway standard in 1847, railroad time was not accepted 'as anything but schedule time' until much later in the nineteenth century. Further, there was 'considerable psychological and social resistance' in Scotland, Ireland, and the west of England to standardization by those anxious to 'preserve the hour of their locality.'[42] Thus, even though GMT was known colloquially as 'Railway Time' in England, several small towns 'held out stubbornly'—Richard and MacKenzie note, in particular, 'Norwich, Ipswich, Yarmouth, and Cambridge in the east and Bristol, Bath, Exeter, and Portsmouth in the west.'[43]

Given India's breadth, challenges to temporal standardization by those whose local time varied substantially from the standard would have been not only expected but also congruent with reactions to similar changes in other parts of the world. However, possible equivocation about this new temporal ordering in the colony was read normatively, spurring the conclusion that a colonized population would be unequivocally hostile to temporal standardization as well as unable to comprehend it. One can see this in many an official conclusion. While Colonel Pears had argued in 1854 that the need for standardization in England derived weight from the number and influence of men of business, in India it was the public of the large centres of business such as Calcutta and Bombay who were deemed unwilling to accept any but local time.[44] The government's invocation in 1867 of native prejudice sounded fundamentally similar to Colonel Pears' 1854 suggestion that in India it would take very long for most to understand railway time. The fact that annual passenger traffic had increased almost 2,500 per cent—from 0.5 to 13.8 million—between 1854 and 1867 did not substantially affect the argument of the colony as a site of difference.[45]

---

[41] Zerubavel, 'Standardization,' 16–19.

[42] Schivelbusch, *Railway Journey*, 43–44.

[43] Richards and MacKenzie, *The Railway Station*, 95.

[44] Jim Masselos traces the complexity of reactions—especially to the question of civil time being synchronized with railway time—in Bombay in his 'Bombay Time,' in Meera Kosambi, ed., *Intersections: Socio-Cultural Trends in Maharashtra* (New Delhi: Orient Longman, 2000), 161–86.

[45] *Statistical Abstract from 1840 to 1865*, 58; *Statistical Abstract from 1860 to 1869*, 30–31. It would also explain why the same government that standardized time on the telegraph

In 1870, almost two decades after discussions had begun, Madras time—'now used by the telegraph and regulated from the only government observatory'—was suggested as a standard railway time, first to be adopted on the Great Indian Peninsular Railway (GIPR).[46] It was also advocated as civil time. However, caveats were put in place to allay official concerns: when the change was to be effected, Calcutta, Bombay, and Karachi, were to be allowed to continue with their local time for civil purposes.[47]

'Rationalizing' the colony

After the establishment of an all-India railway time, the next procedural step was to link this mathematically with a meridian accepted as an international base. This impetus became part of wider discussions about selecting a prime meridian and 'a single, universal time for the whole world.'[48] The India Office in London forwarded to the Government of India suggestions made by Sanford Fleming, a Canadian railway engineer who was advocating (as had the 1884 Washington Conference) a prime meridian corresponding with the time of the Greenwich meridian in England.[49] However, this choice of zero longitude was far from uncontested. France held out against Greenwich, and even the establishment in 1911 of Paris Mean Time—described by David Landes as 'nothing other than Greenwich Mean Time, without the word Greenwich'—was seen as instrumental to 'salving' national susceptibilities.[50] Similarly, the General Time Convention in north America hotly debated the choice of Greenwich. Many emphasized how they saw little reason to consider the time of 'an English observatory' in determining railway time in America. A particularly pithy riposte came from the scientist Simon Newcombe who

---

system was more hesitant to introduce it on railways: the former being dominantly an official instrument arguably posed less threat of affecting 'public' opinion. Mentioned in PWD: Railway, April 1870, nos. 136–37, NAI.

[46] Note from Colonel Kennedy (Bombay) to Major Williams (Madras), 28 March 1870, and Resolution by the Govt. of India (PWD), 28 March 1870, both in PWD: Railway, April 1870, nos. 136–37, NAI.

[47] Office Note, 1 November 1890, in PWD: RT, February 1891, nos. 39–43, NAI. Masselos' 'Bombay Time' depicts some of the effects of different railway and civil time in the city of Bombay. Burma kept Rangoon time.

[48] Sanford Fleming, Memorandum on Reckoning Time on a Scientific Basis, 20 November 1889 (Ottawa), in PWD: RT, February 1891, nos. 39–43, NAI.

[49] Fleming, Memorandum on Reckoning Time, 20 November 1889.

[50] Landes, *Revolution in Time*, 286; Kern, *Nature of Time and Space*.

stated: 'See no more reason for considering Europe in the matter than for considering the inhabitants of the planet Mars.'[51]

Figure 4.1. Meridians

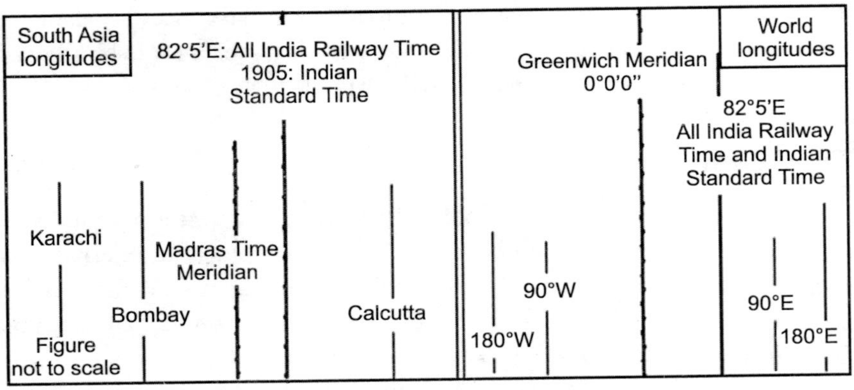

The Government of India did not fundamentally question the choice of Greenwich as base meridian. However, it was not immediately amenable to the idea of displacing Madras time—5 hours, 21 minutes and 10 seconds ahead of Greenwich—with another all-India time. Officials argued that there seemed 'no advantage' in exchanging the present standard of Madras time, especially if this would result in the establishment of time-zones regulated by meridians that passed 'through no important places.'[52] Instead, such changes should await a time 'when India's neighbours and the chief countries of Europe do so.' The Committee of the Royal Society disagreed with this assessment. To explain, it pointed to the doubt that 'attends all statements of time in the great majority of cases in India.' This Indian tendency, it argued, made it imperative to change railway time in India from Madras time to that of a longitude exactly 5 hours and 30 minutes east of Greenwich. The subtraction of 5 hours, 21 minutes, and 10 seconds required to translate events from Madras to Greenwich time was used to argue India's temporal irrationality, compared with countries where the calculation involved whole hours.[53] Even as the Royal Scottish Geographical

---

[51] In report by William F. Allen, Permanent Secretary of the Railroad's General Time Convention (1872–85). Bartky, 'Adoption of Standard Time,' 42–47, fn. 65.

[52] Office Note, 22 December 1890, in PWD: RT, February 1891, nos. 39–43, NAI.

[53] On a Proposal for an Indian Standard Time, enclosure to letter from J. Wilson, Secretary, Govt. of India (Revenue and Agriculture), Circular 7-48-2 (Meteorology), 13 July 1904, in PWD: RT: A, India Prog., IOR.P/6846, BL.

Society expressed the hope that 'all British stations' would adopt as their standard the nearest hour to Greenwich time, an official in the Government of India offered an argument of tutelage, concluding that when the time for such change arrived, then 'the experience of other countries will be available as a guide to the ultimate decision.'[54]

Early in the twentieth century, the imperial government circulated among railway companies just such a proposal, which it described as one that would allow colonial India to 'fall into line with the rest of the civilised world.'[55] Some like the GIPR objected, its agent in Bombay stressing the 'considerable inconvenience' that would result from upsetting 'the present standard adopted in India to which our business men of all nationalities are wedded by long usage.'[56] However, many other railway companies viewed this change as 'desirable,' resulting in what was described as a favourable 'consensus of opinion.'[57] The Government of India consequently replaced Madras time with a standard railway time 'exactly 5 ½ hours in advance of Greenwich' (and nine minutes in advance of Madras time).[58] The change was to be introduced at midnight between 30th June and 1st July 1905, though excluded from it were 'small local' railway lines where the change was seen to be 'inconvenient.' Railways in Burma followed a standard 6 ½ hours ahead of Greenwich (and 5 minutes and 23 seconds earlier than Rangoon time). Excluding such exceptions, the new all-India railway time was of a meridian roughly two degrees east of Madras, being 5 hours and 30 minutes ahead of Greenwich time.

---

[54] Royal Scottish Geographical Society, Note on Standard Time, 10 November 1898, in PWD: RT: A, India Prog., IOR.P/5682, BL; Govt. of India (Revenue and Agriculture) to George F. Hamilton, Secretary of State for India, 10 August 1899, in PWD: RT: A, India Prog., IOR. P/5682, BL.

[55] Quote in reply of Manager and Engineer, Bengal Provincial Railway, to Secretary to Govt. of Bengal, Railway Dept. 5 September 1904, in PWD: RT: A, January 1905, nos. 32–46, India Prog., IOR.P/7086, BL.

[56] Agent, GIPR to Consulting Engineer (Railways), 7 October 1904, in PWD: RT: A, January 1905, nos. 32–46, India Prog., IOR.P/7086, BL.

[57] Govt. of India Circular 7-71-22 from J. Wilson, Officiating Secretary to Govt. of India, 27 May 1905, in Home: Public A, July 1905, nos. 200–201, NAI; PWD: RT: A, January 1905, nos. 32–46, India Prog., IOR.P/7086, BL.

[58] Govt. of India Circular 7-71-22, 27 May 1905; *Statement Exhibiting Moral and Material Progress of India during 1904-05* (London: HMSO, 1906), 132. This was also to be telegraph time.

Negotiating with Time

Implementing the changes instituted between 1854 and 1905—from local mean time to presidency time, the institution of Madras time as railway time, and the 1905 establishment of a standard railway time linked with Greenwich time—was a gradual process. Further, the adoption of railway time as civil time was an even more vexed issue. Three decades after Madras time had been decreed as both railway and civil time in British India—with only Bombay, Calcutta, and Karachi being allowed to continue with their local time for civil purposes—the general manager of the Darjeeling Railway could be found describing the confusion caused by the simultaneity of railway time, telegraph time, office time, *cutchery* time, *bazaar* time, and church time, all in a small town like Darjeeling.[59] Neither was this specific to India. One can find descriptions of British visitors in Portugal in 1900 complaining of the difference between 'railway time' and 'town time' or how travellers in British Rhodesia found that while postal authorities worked on 'Cape time,' railway authorities worked on 'Beira time.'[60] However, given the continually increasing numbers of railways passengers, in India as elsewhere, millions had to regularly negotiate not only train schedules and railway timetables, but also the structure of temporal re-organization that underpinned railway time.

Time as narrative

The coming of the railway itself performed a temporal function, serving to demarcate historical time. There is brief yet explicit intimation of this in Bankimchandra's *Indira* (1873). The novel opens with the narrator-protagonist Indira lamenting that she could not take up her position as wife for her wealthy father believed that his son-in-law had not earned enough money to support his daughter. To rectify this, Indira's mortified husband resolved to travel to the west. 'There was then no railway,' states Indira, and 'the way to the west was very difficult.' Her husband travelled on foot and was long on the way till he 'finally reached the Punjab.' 'He who could do this,' she concludes emphatically, could also make enough money to support her.[61]

---

[59] General manager and chief engineer, Darjeeling-Himalayan Railway to Secretary, Govt. of Bengal (Railway), 24 August 1904, PWD: RT: A, January 1905, nos. 32–46, India Prog., IOR.P/7086, BL.

[60] Richards and MacKenzie, *The Railway Station*, 95.

[61] Bankimchandra Chattopadhyay, *Indira* (1873), translated by Marian Maddern, in *The Bankimchandra Omnibus*, Vol. 1 (New Delhi: Penguin, 2005), 253–338, quotation on 255.

This opening reference is startling in a novel in which railway travel does not really figure. A journey by boat when Indira is on her way to Calcutta is bracketed by two journeys on a palanquin: when Indira travels from her parental home to her in-law's house and when she returns with her husband to her in-law's house. Even Calcutta, linked in a functioning railway network, is approached by boat.[62] Bankim seems to deploy railways for temporal orientation: born in 1838, his adult life would have been co-terminus with the early spread of railways in Bengal, orienting his sense of historical time around railways. Neither was Bankim alone in organizing historical time through the presence and absence of railways. More than a decade after *Indira* was published, and in a rather different part of the country, M.K. Gandhi described planning his trip to Porbhandar with a strikingly similar sentiment, pointing out the limitations engendered by the fact that 'There was no railway in those days.'[63]

The slowness and arduousness that Bankim ascribed to the pre-railway journey confirms that this orientation is not merely descriptive. Indira contends that if her husband could travel on foot, he would not be daunted by the task of making money. Bankim seems to have both understood and endorsed the temporal acceleration generated by railways and the changes that this wrought in people's lives. In 'Bengal's Peasants', he wrote:

> Look at the railways, and the engines, which surpassing a hundred thousand of the horses of Indra in strength, make a month's journey in a day....Your father, who lives in Benaras, has this morning fallen fatally ill ...and by night you sit at his feet and care for him.[64]

Bankim's fascination with how the speed of railways allowed him to fulfil his filial obligations evokes the distinction that Ravi Ahuja suggests between absolute and relative distance, the first measurable in length, the second in transportation time and cost.[65] Bankim seems unequivocally enthusiastic about the possibilities engendered by temporal shrinkage, or the compression

---

[62] Ibid., 261–64, 265–69, 333.

[63] M.K. Gandhi, *Autobiography: The Story of My Experiments with Truth*, translated by Mahadev Desai and first published between 1927 and 1929 (Dover: New York, 1983), 33.

[64] Bankimchandra Chattopadhyay, 'Bengal's Peasants,' in *Sociological Essays: Utilitarianism and Positivism in Bengal*, English translation by S.N. Mukherjee and Marian Maddern (Calcutta: Rddhi, 1986), 116–17.

[65] Ahuja, *Pathways of Empire*, 49.

of travel time engendered by railways.[66] He exhibits no apprehension, such as is visible, for instance, in the German Romantic poet Heinrich Heine's characterization of railway travel from Paris to Germany as 'a terrible idea.'[67] Whereas the increased tempo of movement exhilarated Bankim, it suffocated Heine: imagining the impending completion of railway links, the latter felt 'the mountains and forests of all countries advancing on Paris.'[68]

Given Meenakshi Mukerjee's understanding of *Indira* as part of that strand of the nineteenth-century novel that sought to 'render contemporary Indian society realistically in fiction,' Bankim's enthusiasm records at least one sense of the response and possibility engendered by the speed of railways.[69] Crucial here is Partha Chatterjee's identification of Bankim as (anti-colonial) nationalist thought's moment of departure, embodying the assertion that for non-Europeans '[t]rue modernity' required combining 'the superior material qualities of Western cultures with the spiritual greatness of the East.'[70] When juxtaposed against Heine's anxieties, the reaction of this colonial elite—small but politically influential in the late nineteenth century—inverts the imperial structure of colonial time-lag, the 'first in Europe and then elsewhere' imperial rendering of temporality as has been explicated by Dipesh Chakrabarty.[71] Comparing Bankim's exhilaration with Heine's anxiety also emphasizes the global complexity and contradictions in responses to temporal standardization, showing how critiques of speed—or 'counternarratives' to quote Marian Aguiar's evocative phrase—are not, in fact, either particular or particularly salient to 'modernity outside of a Western context.'[72]

Multiple narratives were generated, however, when people faced the compression of time engendered by railways. In Intizar Husain's 'Kataa Huaa

---

[66] Schivelbusch, *Railway Journey*, 35.

[67] Presner, *Mobile Modernity*, 59–65, quotation on 61.

[68] Schivelbusch, *Railway Journey*, 37. This anxiety differs from the critique of railways (and industrialization) that was found in the writings of those like John Ruskin and William Morris.

[69] Meenakshi Mukherjee, *Realism and Reality: The Novel and Society in India* (Delhi: Oxford University Press, 1985), 16.

[70] Partha Chatterjee, *Nationalist Thought and the Colonial World: A Derivative Discourse?* (Minneapolis: University of Minnesota Press, 1998 [1996]), 50.

[71] Chakrabarty, *Provincializing Europe*, 8.

[72] Marian Aguiar, 'Making Modernity: Inside the Technological Space of the Railway,' *Cultural Critique* 68, 1 (2008): 66–85, quote on 67. Aguiar argues that 'Although these counternarratives exist along representations of technology across all cultural contexts, they highlight the particular expressions of modernity outside of a Western context.'

Dabba' (A Stranded Railroad Car, 1954), the elderly Mirza Sahib expresses his preference for travel before railways. For him, the speed of railways had robbed travel of enjoyment. On a train, he stated:

> You blink your eye and you've arrived at your destination. But there was a time when kingdoms fell and governments toppled by the time you reached where you were going; and the toddlers you'd left crawling on all fours—you returned to find them fathers worrying their heads over a suitable match for their marriageable daughters.[73]

Whereas Indira had invoked the rigours of pre-railway travel, Mirza Sahib invoked a romantic idea of it. For him, 'real' journeys were those before railways, when it took 'ages' to pass a single night of travel. One travelled 'hundreds and hundreds of miles, back and forth, with the end nowhere in sight and all traces of the starting point irretrievably obscured.' He thought back with excitement at the 'fear of tigers, of snake-bites, of highwaymen and yes, of ghosts too.' He remembered travelling 'by the dim star-lit sky overhead and the burning torches below.'[74] The speed of railways had destroyed this rich sensory tableau: now that the train was the fashion, concluded Mirza Sahib, 'I just don't feel like travelling anymore.'

Bankim had been exhilarated by the speed of railways and the possibilities created by compression of travel time; Mirza Sahib's melancholia is an eulogy for a past whose experiential depth was effaced by the speed of the new technology, a sentiment strikingly similar to the nineteenth-century English naturalist John Ruskin's lament about all travelling becoming dull 'in exact proportion to its rapidity.'[75] Schivelbusch's argument about the aesthetic freedom of the pre-industrial subject being 'discovered' precisely when pre-industrial

---

[73] Intizar Husain, 'Kataa Hua Dabba' (1954), translated by Muhammad Umar Menon as 'A Stranded Railroad Car,' in *idem*, ed., *The Colour of Nothingness: Modern Urdu Short Stories* (Delhi: Oxford University Press, 2006 [1998]), 25–36, quotes on 25–26.

[74] Husain, 'Kataa Hua Dabba,' 26.

[75] His tone remarkably similar to Mirza Sahib, John Ruskin wrote: 'The whole system of railway travel is addressed to people who, being in a hurry, are therefore, for the time being, miserable. No one would travel in that manner who could help it.' *The Seven Lamps of Architecture* (Mineola: Dover, 1989 [2nd ed., 1880), 121. For a detailed discussion on Ruskin on the disruptive presence of railways, see J. Mordaunt Crook's 'Ruskin and the Railway,' in A. K.B Evans and J.V. Gough, eds., *The Impact of the Railways on Society in Britain* (Farnham: Ashgate, 2003), 129-34.

methods of production and transportation were threatened by mechanization is certainly relevant.[76] However, irrespective of how romanticized it may be, Mirza Sahib's reaction demonstrates the heterogeneous responses to temporal shrinkage among the colonized.

While annihilating space by shrinking transport time, railways simultaneously expanded space by incorporating new—previously remote— areas into transport networks. Thus, railway travel both diminished and increased travelling time: railways allowed one to reach a destination faster, but as rail mileage expanded so did the time spent travelling. An example of the expansion of travel time, even as railways compressed distance, lies in the prodigious writings of the nationalist leader M. K. Gandhi during many hours of train travel. Gandhi's substantial collected works bear witness to the extent of writing (and dictating) that he did while travelling, hardly surprising when, to quote him, there were times when out of a month almost 15 nights were spent on trains.[77] In fact, stringing together the pieces written by Gandhi as he travelled on trains is akin to tracing a textual itinerary of how his message of *satyagraha* travelled through India.[78] Here, Gandhi's actual use of travel time, especially when juxtaposed against his unequivocal critique of railway technology in *Hind Swaraj* (1908/9), lends itself to the idea of consumption as a series of *explicitly* transgressive acts.[79] The politics of such transgression is heightened when juxtaposed against colonial arguments about native indifference to time: when the *Friend of India* concluded its discussion of passenger traffic by asserting that '[a] native...cares little for his time,' it echoed one of the many presumptions that had governed railway planning in India.[80]

---

[76] Schivelbusch, *Railway Journey*, 121.

[77] M. K. Gandhi, 'What to do When One Loses Temper,' *Navjivan*, 20 February 1921, *CWMG*, Vol. xix (Ahmedabad: Publications Division, Ministry of Information and Broadcasting, 1966), 373-75; quote on 373.

[78] The examples are strewn through *CWMG*. However, as an anecdote it is worth mentioning that when the Kohat disturbances threatened to become a conflagration, Gandhi suggested to Shaukat Ali that they travel together to Delhi since '[t]he train seems to be the best place for such a discussion.' Letter to Shaukat Ali, 23 February 1925, *CWMG*, Vol. xxvi (Ahmedabad: Publications Division, Ministry of Information and Broadcasting, 1967), 190–91.

[79] Cf. de Certeau, *Practice of Everyday Life*.

[80] 'The Traffic of the Bombay Railway,' *Friend of India*, 9 February 1854.

Being ahead of and behind time

The temporal re-structuring engendered by railways was most visibly manifested in timetables, which Jack Simmons argues was a word invented by railways.[81] It was train schedules that immediately and directly oriented everyday life towards the larger temporal changes being instituted. The early railway timetables were based on the 12-hour diurnal system, using ante-meridian (a.m.) and post-meridian (p.m.) notations: thus, a timetable published a fortnight after passenger trains had begun running in India showed trains leaving Bombay for Thana at 6.30 a.m. and 4.00 p.m., while those returning to Bombay left Thana at 8.45 a.m. and 6.50 p.m.[82] By the time the Canadian engineer Sanford Fleming penned his 1889 memorandum suggesting that the 24-hour notation be adopted on railway timetables globally, the format was being used on railways in India and Burma, as demonstrated by the rules recorded at the railway conference of 1882 (though both 24-hour and 12-hour timetables continued to be used, including by the same railway company).[83]

When Fleming highlighted the problems with the diurnal format—arguing that 'the misprint of a single letter, a.m. for p.m. or vice versa will easily arise to cause inconvenience, loss of time, probably loss of property, or loss of life'—the British railway establishment was among his intended audience.[84] The subject had been long under discussion: as early as March 1861, the periodical *Once a Week* had commented on the imprecision of Britain's Bradshaw timetables and guides, asking how many could immediately deduce whether 5 minutes past 12

---

[81] Derived from 'tide tables' used at ports from the sixteenth century onwards. He distinguishes timetables from the 'time-bills' of stagecoaches that, he argues, were not a schedule but a device used by the post-offices to check the punctuality of coaches. Jack Simmons, 'Timetables,' in Simmons and Biddle, *British Railway History*, 513.

[82] *The Bombay Times and Journal of Commerce*, 29 April 1853.

[83] Except for the Madras Railway, scheduled to change from 1 October 1890. Fleming, Memorandum on Reckoning Time, 20 November 1889. The system was used for telegraphs from the 1860s: see C. Douglas, Director General of Telegraphs in India, to E.C. Bayly, Secretary, Govt. of India, 3 September 1862, in PWD: Railway, 15 August 1862, nos. 26–28, NAI; Office Note, 4 December 1890, in PWD: RT, February 1891, nos. 39–43, NAI. Rule Ia, Prog. of Railway Conference, September 1882 in Home: Public B, October 1882, nos. 143–44, NAI. Notices for changes in the EIR timings within a week of each other show both formats in use in the same timetable. See notices in *Searchlight* (Patna), 23 September 1927 and 30 September 1927.

[84] Fleming, Memorandum on Reckoning Time, 20 November 1889.

at night was a.m. or p.m.[85] Its support for the 24-hour format was bolstered by
a belief that it was 'no great strain on the intellect,' for those who could read
and write would understand that 'a train arriving at 15.45 by the table, arrives
at 3.45 p.m. by the clock.'[86] More than three decades later, a report presented at
the International Railway Congress held in London in June-July 1895 pointed
out the 'great success' that the 24-hour system had had on 5,500 miles of
Canadian railway, on the more than 18,000 mile-long railway system in India,
and 'in all the doings of public life' in Italy.[87] A Mr. Robertson representing
the EIR highlighted how Britons in India quite easily adapted to 'the 24 hour
regime.'[88] To bolster his case, he added that 'the argument might be extended
to the natives, who daily use without difficulty the 24-hour dial.' Mr. Bell of
the Indian Government railways added that:

> I should say that it was not so much we who introduced this alteration into
> the public time-tables which are published, as that the public themselves by
> hearing the station masters and others began of their own accord to use this
> system of notation....The public began to use it, and *we followed rather than
> led the public* in our public tables [emphasis added].[89]

In his concluding remarks, the President suggested that if railways
everywhere 'followed the 24-hour system adopted in Indian time-tables, the
public would be the first to appreciate the reform.'[90] Public railway timetables
in Britain, however, adopted the 24-hour format only in 1964–65, more than
seven decades after railways in India had.

The question of railway time not only revealed how imperial discourse
remained insensitive to historical praxis but also demonstrated hierarchies
within Indian society. An 1866 petition to the viceroy by the British Indian
Association that requested shelter and accommodation at railway stations for
native third-class passengers premised its demand on the fact that most of

---

[85] *Once a Week*, March 1861, 273, Appendix C in PWD: Railway, 15 August 1862, nos.
26–28, NAI. Several of the early timetables using 12 noon have been reproduced in
Charles E. Lee, *The Centenary of Bradshaw* (London: Railway Gazette, 1940), 18–23.

[86] *Once a Week*, March 1861, 273.

[87] 'Question XV: The Twenty Four Hour Day,' Proceedings of the fifth session, London,
June–July 1895, in *Bulletin of the International Railway Congress Association*, Vol. xi
(1897) (Brussels: P. Weissenbruch and London: P.N. King and Son, 1897), 679.

[88] Ibid., 680–81.

[89] Ibid.

[90] Ibid., 686.

them could not be expected to arrive at the station at the 'proper' time.[91] Most of them, stated the petition, had an 'indefinite' idea of time, 'knowing little beyond pruhurs of three hours each.' Further that a large number came from surrounding villages and rural districts 'where no time is kept.' Obviously large segments of the Indian population were confronted by timetables that, at least till the late 1860s and early 1870s, used the Latin alphabet.[92] Considering the demographics and politics of the British Indian Association, its internalization of imperial views about temporal sense (or lack of) in the colony might not seem surprising. Yet, the petition also attacked the management of Indian railways: complaining of trains arriving 'so very irregularly and behind the time,' it faulted the imperial state on the very grounds on which it had sought dominance.[93]

This internalization of imperial critiques of the colony, as well as the fledgling paternalism towards a mass public that informs the 1866 petition, can be juxtaposed against a very different moment, embodied in a 1924 piece by M. K. Gandhi titled 'Time Sense.'[94] Excoriating the educated for being 'late for everything,' he argued that the masses waiting patiently for their leaders embodied forbearance. Whereas the British Indian Association had painted a picture of 'the poor, the ignorant and the helpless' masses, incapable of punctuality because they could not grasp the structure of temporality within which timetables existed, Gandhi—even as he stressed the need for time-discipline—dissociated punctuality from education. However, the question of punctuality was neither stable nor simple. Discussing the 'common charge' that Indians 'have no sense of time [and that] we are as a rule behind time'—an explicit reference to an allochronistic rendering of the colony—Gandhi instead argued:

> One who is too late is admittedly behind time. But it is equally true to say that one who is four hours before time is also behind time. He has neglected a hundred things....*He may succeed in catching his train, but he will be behind time for many other things probably more important* [emphasis added].[95]

[91] Petition by the British Indian Association, North-West Provinces, to Viceroy of India, Aligarh, 16 October 1866, in Home: Public B, December 1866, nos. 50–51, NAI.

[92] 'It is not every person who can say at once whether five minutes past twelve at night is A.M. or P.M.; and no wonder, for first of all these expressions are Latin abbreviations.' *Once a Week*, March 1861, 273.

[93] Petition by the British Indian Association, 16 October 1866.

[94] M.K. Gandhi, 'Time Sense,' *Young India*, 6 November 1924, *CWMG*, Vol. xxv (Ahmedabad: Publications Division, Ministry of Information and Broadcasting, 1967), 285–86.

[95] Gandhi, 'Time Sense.'

Re-inserting everyday life into 'empty' time

Even as time-sense functioned as a discursive battleground, railway passengers had to negotiate the everyday logistics of travel. Early demands made by the travelling public were for railway timetables to be translated into pertinent local language(s). Lahore's *Panjabi-i-Akhbar* had demanded in April 1871 that that the Sindh, Punjab, and Delhi Railway (SPDR) publish Urdu and Hindi translations of railway timetables for the 'benefit of the Native public.' Unlike many of the reforms demanded by the third-class travelling public, this was implemented quickly. In August 1871 the newspaper commended the fact that monthly tables were now being published in English, Urdu, and Hindi.[96] The demand gained momentum with the Railway Act of 1879 requiring that railways exhibit at each station a timetable in one or more local languages.[97] Delegates at the 1882 Railway Conference in Simla emphasized their compliance with this requirement.[98] Not all could match the zeal of the SPDR, which claimed to display timetables in English, Urdu, and Hindi, 'on the platforms, waiting sheds, outside verandahs, [and in] goods sheds,' in addition to supplying them to police *thana*s, court-houses, *daak* bungalows, hotels, and principal traders within a radius of 30 miles of each station.[99] However, others did provide them in waiting-sheds and at stations.[100] Public demands continued to stress the need for timetables in local scripts where this was not available.[101]

This preliminary demand was accompanied by the more vocal asking for train timings to be tailored to their convenience. As early as 1857, 'repeated applications' led the EIR's agent to authorize the 9.20 a.m. up and 10.12 a.m. down trains to stop at 'C[i]nnag[h?]ure' [Singhur?] and Bidabatty (near Serampore).[102] The demands only increased in the next few decades, across regions and railway lines. In August 1872, the *Koh-i-Nur* complained at length

---

[96] *Panjab-i-Akhbar* (Lahore), 5 August 1871, in NNR: Punjab, NWP, Oudh, and CP.

[97] Railway Conference, September 1882, Home: Public B, October 1882, nos. 143–44, NAI.

[98] In particular, representatives of the Sindh, Punjab, and Delhi, Eastern Bengal, Oudh and Rohilkund, Madras, South Indian, and Great Indian Peninsular railways.

[99] Note by Traffic Manager, SPDR, Railway Conference, Simla, September 1882.

[100] Delegate for Eastern Bengal Railway, Railway Conference, Simla, September 1882.

[101] *Andhrabhashasanjivani* (Masulipatna), no. 12 of December 1882, in Report on Telegu newspapers for December 1882, in NNR: Madras.

[102] Letters to Home Govt. no. 52, 30 October 1857, Railway General Letters, 1852–61, NAI.

about the trouble suffered by passengers owing to train timings between Delhi and Ghaziabad. Since the only up-train from Delhi started at 2.45 a.m. and left Ghaziabad for Meerut at 7. 35 a.m., passengers had to begin the journey from Delhi late at night and wait at Ghaziabad four or five hours for the Meerut train. They were similarly inconvenienced by the fact that the mail-train started from Lahore at 2.45 a.m., while the passenger train that started at 12 a.m. only reached the Phillour Pass at 8.00 p.m., leaving passengers to spend the night there before crossing the Pass.[103] Calcutta's *Sulabha Samachar* complained that trains on the Tirhut State Railway were not synchronized to connect with those on the EIR, the *Burdwan Sanjivani* suggested that the 7.20 up-chord could make time to halt at Mankpur if it omitted 'unimportant' stations, the *Kerala Patrika* asked for train timings in Malabar to be changed to afford 'greater convenience' to its public, and the *Swadeshamitran* demanded that the Madras Railway re-schedule the 9.00 p.m. Olavakode train to meet the special train connecting Tirur with Calicut.[104]

Train timings also became increasingly relevant to emerging time-structures of work and leisure. In certain urban areas, railways allowed specific groups to work on weekdays in the city and to return home on the weekends. Describing Britain, Dionysius Lardner has written of the 'epoch of suburbs' generated by the railroads, stating that: 'in all directions round the metropolis in which railways are extended, habitations are multiplied.'[105] In a letter to the Calcutta *Englishman* 'A Regular Passenger' complained that Monday morning trains between Pundooah and Howrah were inconvenient for those who worked in Howrah and visited their families on weekends.[106] He stated that since Monday morning passengers usually had to join their offices at nine—or at the very least before 10.00 a.m.—the Pundooah trains should start at 6.00 a.m. instead of 7.00 a.m. as present, thus allowing passengers to reach Howrah at half-past

---

[103] *Koh-i-Nur* (Lahore), 17 August 1872, in NNR: Punjab, NWP, Oudh, and CP.

[104] *Sulabha Samachar* (Calcutta), 15 January 1881, in NNR: Bengal; *Burdwan Sanjivani* (Burdwan), 9 April 1895, in NNR: Bengal; *Kerala Patrika* (Calicut), 18 February 1888, in NNR: Madras; *Swadeshamitran* (Madras), 21 May 1890, in NNR: Madras.

[105] Dionysius Lardner, *Railway Economy* (London: Taylor, Walton, and Mayberly, 1850), 36. See also Alan. A. Jackson, 'The London Railway Suburb,' in Evans and Gough, *Impact of the Railways*, 169–79.

[106] The improved communication with Calcutta made Howrah a suburb of Calcutta, 'enabling many of the people employed in the metropolis to reside on the right bank of the Hooghly.' *Imperial Gazetteer of India*, Vol. XIII (Oxford: Clarendon Press, 1908), 213–14.

eight.[107] The *Englishman* itself catered dominantly to the English community in Bengal as well as to a limited circle of bilingual Bengalis working in the context of a bureaucratic-capitalist time-discipline or *chakri*.[108] Nevertheless, among a limited set of people at least, the dual demands of work and family seem to have been split fairly discretely during the week, each circumscribed within its allotted days. Since the EIR link between Howrah and Pundooah was completed only in the second half of 1854, it is remarkable how quickly this urban–suburban organization of the week emerged, drawing on emerging bureaucratization, an urban-industrial order including clerical and mercantile firms, and the temporal shrinkage provided by the railways.[109] Neither was this necessarily restricted to more elite groups in colonial society. There is evidence of a pattern of daily and weekly commuters in disparate locations: whether employees at Jamalpur workshops who commuted to nearby villages using special workers' trains, or those who lived in the northern part of Bombay island and had to commute regularly to work owing to a housing shortage in the middle and lower part of Bombay island.[110]

Demands for convenient daily and weekly train timings continued to come in, whether from merchants and officials living at Saidapet and St. Thomas' Mount petitioning the South Indian Railway (SIR) to run trains starting at 8.00 p.m. from these stations, or employees at merchant offices in Calcutta complaining that there were only two trains after 6.00 p.m. to allow them to return to Hooghly, Bandel, or Chandrenagore.[111] Thus, station clocks and timetables became artefacts that marked the establishment of a new temporal order, albeit one that was realized gradually. In the demands of passengers for

---

[107] 'A Suggestion to the Traffic Manager of the Railway Company by A Regular Passenger,' *The Englishman and Military Chronicle*, 21 August 1857.

[108] Apropos Sumit Sarkar in *Writing Social History* (Delhi: Oxford University Press, 1997), especially 186–215, 282–357. He also discusses *chakri* in his 'Colonial Times.'

[109] G. Huddlestone, *History of the East Indian Railway* (Calcutta: Thacker, Spink and Co, 1906), 14.

[110] My thanks to Ian Kerr for this point. See L.S.S. O'Malley, *Bengal and Orissa District Gazetteers: Monghyr* (New Delhi: Logos: 2007 [1926]), 132 and S.M. Edwardes, *The Gazetteer of Bombay City and Island*, Vol. i (1909). The effect could even be in terms of carving up the year. Richard M. Haywood describes how because of 'the speed and ease of railway travel summer houses (dachi) began to be built' around Moscow, Klin, and Tiver, with some owners coming from as far away as St. Petersburg. *Russia Enters the Railway Age, 1842–55* (Boulder: East European Monographs, 1998), 524.

[111] *Bhaskara Gnanodayam* (Negapatam), 10 March 1893, in NNR: Madras; *Hitavadi* (Calcutta), 8 April 1904, in NNR: Bengal.

the alteration of train timings, one sees not only the spread of bureaucratic-capitalist structures, but equally a tempering of their theoretical abstractness with individual, local, and everyday concerns, effectively inserting the demands of daily life back into the empty homogeneity of standardized time.

The spread of railways also engendered a debate in which a disenchanted notion of leisure collided with sacred time (of a Judaeo-Christian God). In the 1850s, EIR officials in Calcutta found themselves isolated when attempting to generate profits through the running of excursion trains on Sundays. Both the Government of India and the company's directors in London insisted on limiting 'Sabbath trains' to the 'absolute necessities of the public.'[112] The government conceded that the EIR would eventually be able to run trains on Sunday but declined to encourage excursion trains on that day.[113] Thus, an EIR official in Calcutta petitioning for a passenger train from Howrah to Raneeganj on Sunday had to assure the company's Board that this would not be an excursion train. To enforce the important principle of limiting trains on the Sabbath, no reductions in fares could be made on Sundays; further arrivals and departures of even regular trains had to 'afford the Employees of the Company the opportunity of attending Divine Worship.'[114] The issue was aggravated when the Christian inhabitants of Calcutta insisted that government intervene to curtail 'this new practice' of Sabbath trains. The potency of the complaint was heightened because Sabbath-breaking was included among un-Christian acts supposed to have brought god's wrath upon the British state in the form of the 1857 Rebellion.[115] Thus, when the EIR's London Board discovered an announcement in the Calcutta papers advertising an excursion train 'on the occasion of a Hindu festival for a particular Sunday' the response was swift and stern. The railway's agent in Calcutta was admonished and excursion trains on Sunday were forbidden.[116]

This discussion mirrored an even more vocal debate taking place in Britain. Some in the church recognized that railways made many parishes more easily

---

[112] Letters from Home Govt., enclosure to despatch no. 19, 18 May 1858, Railway General Letters, 1852–61, NAI.

[113] Letters to Home Govt., 28 February 1856, Railway General Letters, 1852–61, NAI.

[114] Letters from Home Govt. enclosure to despatch no. 19, 18 May 1858.

[115] Don Randall, 'Autumn 1857: The Making of the Indian 'Mutiny,' *Victorian Literature and Culture* 31, 1 (2003): 3–17.

[116] Letters from Home Govt. enclosure to despatch no. 123, 8 December 1859, in Railway General Letters, 1852–61, NAI.

accessible but others saw facilities for Sabbath travel as 'Godless legislation.'[117] Groups like the Lord's Day Observance Society and the Anti-Sunday Travel Union were equally aggrieved by railway companies trying to fill their excess capacity on Sunday with excursion trains.[118] Local groups—from the Carlisle Lord's-Day Society to the Lord's-Day Society of Newcastle-upon-Tyne—strove to stop or at least limit Sunday travel, especially for pleasurable excursion trips, pointing out that it not only defiled the Lord's Day but also prevented many working on railways from attending divine worship.[119] The 'Sabbatarian extremists' in fact chose to view the Tay Bridge disaster of 28 December 1879 (when an iron railway bridge collapsed and there were no survivors) as 'a stern judgment' on Sunday train travel.[120] In India, however, the issue had a different valence, given the limited purview of Judaeo-Christian temporality in the colony. Forbidding Sabbath excursion trains can certainly be read as part of the homogenizing impulse of imperialism. At the same time, the very issue on which it was premised—Sabbath—also points to the multiple, contradictory, pulls through which the local sought to grapple with a flattened, homogenized, and 'empty' idea of inter-subjective temporality.[121]

A similar filling-in of empty time is visible in discussions about the public issue of timetables in 1912–13. In March 1912, the General Traffic Manager of the EIR had suggested that public timetables be issued on the first day of March, June, September, and December (instead of on the first of January, April, July, and October).[122] He explained his suggestions by invoking local seasonality. He concluded that March, April, and May were the hottest months over the larger portion of India; June, July, and August comprised 'most of the rainy season,' also being a time when timetables had to be altered on certain

---

[117] R.C. Richardson, 'The "Broad Gauge" and the "Narrow Gauge": Railways and Religion in Victorian England,' in Evans and Gough, *Impact of the Railways*, 101.

[118] Richardson, '"Broad Gauge" and the "Narrow Gauge,"' 103, fn. 10.

[119] 'Discussion on Sabbath Trains at the Annual General Meeting of the Newcastle and Carlisle Railway Company,' *Cowen Tracts* (1847) published by Newcastle University.

[120] Richardson, '"Broad Gauge" and the "Narrow Gauge"'; M. Robbins, *The Railway Age* (London: Routledge and Paul, 1962), 48; David Norman Smith, *The Railway and Its Passengers: A Social History* (Newton Abbot: David and Charles, 1988), 119–21. Susan Major offers a detailed analysis of Sabbatarianism in the context of railway excursions in Britain. See her The Crowds Go Forth, 139–88.

[121] Cf. Dipesh Chakrabarty's discussion in *Provincializing Europe* of a Universalizing History 1 intersected by local History 2.

[122] General Traffic Manager, EIR, to Agent, EIR, 15 March 1912, in Railway Board: Traffic A, January 1913, nos. 126–28, India Prog., IOR.P/9245, BL.

sections of the EIR line; August, September, October, and November covered 'the Autumn;' while December, January, and February 'comprise practically the cold weather of India.' However, his suggestion represented not simply the dictates of local seasonality but rather of seasonality as it affected the specific needs of Europeans in India. Thus, he explained that 1 March was when 'the exodus to Europe and Hills takes place;' the beginning of September marked 'the exodus from the Hills;' and timetables issued on 1 December could 'include all the Christmas concessions.' The new schedule was passed at a meeting of the Indian Railway Conference Association in 1912.[123] It exemplified two forms of local specificity, both cyclical and repetitive: the seasonality of colonial India and the migration patterns of an imperial population trying to renew their 'productive power' in the recreated England of India's hill stations.[124] Thus, even as railway timetables theoretically erased some natural rhythms, yet in practice they could not always remain insensible to other rhythms, in this case those that combined climate and season.[125]

The Hesitations of 'Now-Time'

How did the colonized, as passengers and population, negotiate the temporal re-structuring introduced through railways, both as speedy transport and as standardized time? How does the demand by a Lahore paper for railway timetables in Hindi and Urdu correspond with another for railway schedules to be altered to fit the urban–suburban week of passengers living in Pundooah and working in Howrah? Can one correlate Jagannath's deployment of railway timetables to defend himself against charges of treason with Gandhi's use

---

[123] Agenda for Indian Railway Conference Association (IRCA) meeting, Simla, 23 September 1912; letter from R.L. Bliss, Acting Secretary, IRCA to Secretary, Railway Board, 10–11 October 1912, in RT: A, January 1913, nos. 126–28, India Prog., IOR.P/9245, BL.

[124] Laura Bear discusses how the Committee on Colonisation believed that railways would provide Europeans with easy access to hill stations, allowing them to recuperate their 'productive powers.' *Lines of the Nation*, 32–33. Dane Kennedy has stressed the extent to which railways made hill-stations accessible in a way they were not before. *The Magic Mountains: Hill Stations and the British Raj* (Berkeley: University of California Press, 1996).

[125] Ravi Ahuja points out that 'while travel space on India's waterways or largely unsurfaced roads varied widely according to direction of river flows, weather, and season, the rhythm of railway transport could be regularised and codified in timetables.' *Pathways of Empire*, 62.

of railway time for scripting much of his oppositional politics, despite his trenchant critique of the technology? What results from juxtaposing Bankim's excitement about railway speed with Mirza Sahib's lament about how this very speed had destroyed 'real' journeys?

Most obviously, these responses delineate the complex ways in which people in colonial India negotiated an abstract administrative and technological change in their everyday life. They appear in fragments but it is precisely this structure that captures the polyvalence of historical responses.[126] Hence, one can read these negotiations as representing the complexity of everyday responses through a series of historical 'focal points.'[127] Some of these negotiations also represent, to borrow from Walter Benjamin, instances of 'now-time': moments in which the protagonists critically evaluate the present, even as they remain implicated in it.[128] The population of colonial India could hardly escape a world in which the speed of railways decreased and increased travel time, in which timetables and schedules marked the transition to standardized railway time, and in which many calendars were becoming alien, disenchanted, and homogenous. However, even as they navigated these changes, some of their responses, albeit tenuous, interrogate—even when they do not, or cannot, reject—that with which they were grappling with.[129]

Such moments that evaluate the relationship between time, speed, and railways have been captured in three works of fiction: Khushwant Singh's *Train to Pakistan* (1956), Saadat Hasan Manto's 'Kali Shalvar' (The Black Trousers, *ca.* 1940), and Intizar Husain's 'Kataa Hua Dabba' (A Stranded Railroad Car, 1954). All were written after the temporal restructuring that marked the period between 1854 and 1905, and by authors who were in fact born after 1905. However, the struggles of some of the characters with the changing temporality of speed and standardization offer instances that interrupt—to critique from within—that historical moment in which they are enmeshed.

---

[126] Cf. Gyandendra Pandey's argument that the minority or '"fragmentary" point of view' is one that 'resists the drive for a shallow homogenization and struggles for other, potentially richer definitions of the "nation" and the future political community.' 'In Defence of the Fragment: Writing about Hindu-Muslim Riots in India Today,' *Representations* 37 (Winter 1992): 27–55, especially 28–29.

[127] As described by Walter Benjamin in 'The Life of Students' (1915).

[128] See Michael Löwy, *Fire Alarm: Reading Walter Benjamin's On the Concept of History*, translated by Chris Turner (New York: Verso, 2005), 2.

[129] Löwy describes how Benjamin, inspired by both Marx and messianic influences, offered a 'modern critique of (capitalist/industrial) modernity,' using 'nostalgia for the past' as a revolutionary method of critique of the present. *Fire Alarm*, 2–3.

Mano Majra, the frontier village in *Train to Pakistan*, has become emblematic of competing narratives about South Asia's past, present, and future.[130] In her reading of the text, Marian Aguiar aptly highlights the extent to which the life of the village is emplotted through its relationship with railway trains passing through it.[131] The village is indeed 'very conscious of trains': it is introduced through its railway station; its denizens wake up and fall asleep to the sounds of passing trains; and shopkeepers and hawkers supplying these trains provide 'an appearance of constant activity.'[132] At first glance, having welded the natural circularity of everyday life with the linear impetus on which railways had been premised, Mano Majra seems to exist in a harmonious conjunction of time-scales, a 'natural/technological symbiosis' as Aguiar terms it.[133] However, Mano Majra's relationship with railways is perhaps more unstable than appears at first glance. Even though the presence of modernity through railways is indeed a 'fait accompli' as Aguiar suggests, yet Mano Majra also *distances* itself from this by reneging on its relationship with railways.[134] Just before he explains how railway timetables grid the life of the village, Singh states:

> Not many trains stop at Mano Majra. Express trains do not stop at all. Of the many slow passenger trains…only two are scheduled to stop for a few minutes. The others stop only when they are held up.[135]

Even while steeped in railway temporality, Mano Majra stands apart from it. Tellingly, the crowd at the railway station is not composed of bona fide passengers, oriented around railway timetables, but of hangers-on, *wasting time* in 'endless arguments about how late the train was on a given day and when it had last been on time.'[136]

Mano Majra's ambiguity becomes claustrophobia and fear in the relationship that Sultana—the protagonist of Manto's 'Kali Shalvar'—has with railway

---

[130] Cf. David Gilmartin's reading of it as 'an "authentic" world of community rooted in the reciprocities of local life.' 'Partition, Pakistan, and South Asian History: In Search of a Narrative,' *Journal of Asian Studies* 57, 4 (November 1998): 1069–95, see 1090, fn. 27.

[131] Khushwant Singh, *Train to Pakistan* (New York: Grove Press, 1956), 3–5. Marian Aguiar, 'Railway Space in Partition Literature,' in Kerr, *27 Down*, 39–67.

[132] Singh, *Train to Pakistan*, 3–5

[133] Aguiar, 'Railway Space in Partition Literature,' 48.

[134] Ibid.

[135] Singh, *Train to Pakistan*, 3–4.

[136] Ibid., 31.

trains. The night-train had delivered Sultana from the provincial cantonment town of Ambala to Delhi, a move analyzed by Aamir Mufti as 'a reorientation of life expectations along national lines.'[137] Delhi did not bring that which Sultana desired and consequently she begged her companion Khuda Baksh to return to Ambala with her. Return, however, was foreclosed. To Sultana's entreaty—'I'll pack and we can leave by the night train'—he responded: 'we can't go back now.' A despondent Sultana began spending her days watching the railway yard visible from her balcony: railway engines and carriages going by 'constantly, in one direction or the other.' The one that she empathized with, however, was 'that lone carriage [that] had been propelled on the tracks of life and then abandoned.' Though surrounded by movement—by 'other people...changing tracks'—Sultana feared she had no idea '[w]here she was headed for.' Fearfully, she thought:

> And then, one day, she would lose the impetus that had moved her and she would stop somewhere, at a place of which she knew nothing.[138]

In Intizar Husain's 'Kataa Hua Dabaa,' despair becomes temporal disorientation. When Shujaat Ali describes his father's first train journey to Delhi, the relationship between time, speed, and railways becomes phantasmagorical:

> As the train picked up speed, the same familiar feeling assaulted him: as if the car he was riding in had come unhitched and stood in the middle of nowhere while the rest of the train whistling and clattering, had steamed far away. Sometimes he felt that the train had started running backwards, pulling time along with it.[139]

---

[137] Aamir R. Mufti, 'Saadat Hasan Manto: A Greater Story-Writer than God,' *Enlightenment in the Colony: The Jewish Question and the Crisis of Postcolonial Culture* (Princeton: Princeton University. Press, 2007), 190. Saadat Hasan Manto, 'The Black Shalwar,' translated in Leslie A. Flemming and Tahira Naqvi, *Another Lonely Voice: The Life and Works of Saadat Hassan Manto* (Vanguard: Lahore, 1985), 206–19.

[138] Manto, 'The Black Shalwar.'

[139] Husain, 'Kataa Hua Dabba,' 29–30.

Contagion and Control
Managing Disease, Epidemics, and Mobility

In June 1916, an agent of the Bengal–Nagpur Railway (BNR) asked the Bengal government to clarify the link between railway travel and the spread of infectious diseases in India.[1] Recent official analyses of sanitary conditions along India's pilgrimage map not only implicated railways in disseminating infectious diseases but also suggested that the situation would deteriorate further: as railway communication became 'better and quicker,' infectious diseases would spread 'faster and further.' The Bengal government however, had a differing opinion, blaming the insanitary conditions of railway travel itself for outbreaks of epidemics, especially during periods of heavy traffic. Which was it to be, enquired the agent?

The decades in which India's railway network began carrying unprecedented numbers of people further, faster, and more frequently were the same ones in which cholera and plague effected substantial ravages among India's population.[2] While cholera epidemics preceded the advent of railways in

---

[1] Agent, Bengal–Nagpur Railway (Calcutta) to Secretary, Govt. of Bengal (Financial Dept., Medical Branch), 21 June 1916, in RT: A, November 1917, no. 655-T-16/6-34, serial no. 7/2, NAI.

[2] Between 1854 and 1900, the number of passengers travelling *annually* catapulted from 0.5 to 176 million. *Statistical Abstract from 1840 to 1865*, 58; *Statistical Abstract from 1894–95 to 1903–04*, 138.

colonial India, David Arnold estimates that at least 23 million people died
of the disease in British India between 1865 and 1947.[3] Similarly, Ira Klein
describes the savage impact of plague in the two decades after its outbreak
in Bombay in 1896, calling it 'India's most feared and one of its deadliest
maladies.'[4] He estimates a toll of at least 12 million, pointing out that 'India
was recorded as having suffered about 95 percent of the world's plague mortality
from the onset of the modern pandemic down to World War II.'[5] Both the
increasing speed and facility offered by railways were important in this context:
Arnold writes of how cholera's terror was exacerbated by 'the speed with
which the disease spread,' while Klein describes how 'plague rode the rails and
steamships' out of Bombay.[6] The colonial medical and sanitary establishment
further scrutinized the link between railways and epidemics because trains
facilitated mass travel to pilgrimage centres, places deemed as especially ripe
for the spread of contagion—the immersion of Hindu pilgrims in sacred tanks
or rivers was seen to provide 'almost ideal conditions for the rapid transmission
of the water-borne [cholera] vibrio.'[7] Even as contemporary accounts declared
it to be 'common knowledge' that pilgrims were 'responsible' for much of the
spread of infectious diseases in India, Ian Kerr, Ravi Ahuja, and Anand Yang
describe the correlation between spreading railway travel and an increase in
both the numbers of pilgrims and the frequency of pilgrimages undertaken.[8]

---

[3] When contextualized within 'the grim standards of India's other major diseases,' David
Arnold states that 'cholera was not an immoderate killer.' David Arnold, 'Cholera and
Colonialism in British India,' *Past & Present* 113, 1 (November 1986): 118–51, quotes
on 120, 123, 150. He also notes that 'the bulk of cholera victims came from the lower
classes' (118). Cholera declined in the 1920s, but returned during the Bengal famine
of 1943–44.

[4] Ira Klein, 'Plague, Policy and Popular Unrest in British India,' *Modern Asian Studies*
22, 4 (1988): 723–55, quotes on 724–25.

[5] Ibid., 724–25. Authorities suggested that plague deaths for Indonesia and China, the
'next worst afflicted,' were not even 2 per cent of India's totals. However, for both,
figures could be somewhat 'under-recorded for inland provinces, the less populous and
more lightly afflicted regions' (725).

[6] David Arnold, *Science, Technology and Medicine in Colonial India* (Cambridge: Cambridge
University Press, 2000), 81; Klein, 'Plague, Policy and Popular Unrest,' 737.

[7] Arnold, 'Cholera and Colonialism,' 138.

[8] *Report of Pilgrim Committee, Bihar and Orissa, 1913* (Simla: Government Central Branch
Press, 1915), 2, appended to RT: B, July 1916, no. 655-T/1-5, NAI; Kerr, 'Reworking
a Popular Religious Practice, 326; Ahuja, 'The Bridge-Builders,' especially 110–11.
Frequently, *mela*s were simultaneously commercial and religious. Anand Yang offers

Focusing on colonial Bihar, Yang writes of how railways 'widened the stream of pilgrims,' while Ahuja depicts not only 'considerable quantitative growth but also qualitative changes in the spatial, temporal, and social patterns of the Puri pilgrimage.'[9] Similarly, Kerr shows not only how railways increased the mass potential for participating in pilgrimage but also how pilgrimage 'began to overlap with tourism,' the act 'promoted and commercially wrapped' by railway companies.[10]

While the nexus between pilgrims, pilgrimage, and railway travel became central to official narratives about contagion and epidemic spread in India, railways affected its public health in other ways, too. In many accounts, it was railway construction and infrastructure (rather than travel) that was correlated with rising malaria, which Sheldon Watts describes as 'far and away India's most common killing disease,' at least in the 'eighty years before 1947.'[11] Watts recounts how, during the construction of the Great Indian Peninsular Railway in 1923–24, the correlation with malaria was reflected in the saying 'a death a [railway] sleeper.'[12] Borrow pits for embanking roads and railways became 'nurseries for mosquitoes,' while railway and road embankments, frequently 'heedless' of natural drainage patterns, generated waterlogging and flooding, thus creating breeding places for malarial mosquitoes.[13] Public accounts also

---

an excellent discussion of colonial Bihar in this context. See his *Bazaar India*, Chapter 3, esp. 117–20. Further, railways tabulated under 'pilgrims' passengers travelling to *mela*s that they had specified as commercial rather than religious: the O&RR's *mela* list included the 'Agricultural Exhibition and Mela' at Takia in December, while the BNWR tabulated 'important horse and cattle fairs' at Sonepore and Ballia in conjunction with *mela*s occurring at the time of eclipses. *Report of Pilgrim Committee, Bihar & Orissa*, Part I (1); Statement of Melas dealt with on O&RR, 1916, enclosure in Agent O&RR to Secretary, Railway Board, 27 July 1917, in RT: A, November 1917, no. 393-T-16/23-26, India Prog., IOR.P/10198, BL; Agent, BNWR to Secretary, Railway Board, 8/11 August 1916, RT: A, November 1917, no. 655-T-16/6-34, NAI.

[9] Yang, *Bazaar India*, 135–36; Ahuja, *Pathways of Empire*, 259–69.

[10] Kerr, Introduction, in *idem*, *Railways in Modern India*, 48, 313–14.

[11] Ira Klein, 'Death in India,' *Journal of Asian Studies* 32,4 (1973): 639–59, quotes on 645–46; Sheldon Watts, 'British Development Policies and Malaria in India 1897-c.1929,' *Past & Present* 165, 1 (1999): 141–81, quotes on 142–43. Nandini Bhattacharya argues that malaria was the principal cause of mortality in colonial India 'after cholera.' See her 'The Logic of Location: Malaria Research in Colonial India, Darjeeling and Duars, 1900–30,' *Medical History* 55 (2011): 183–202, quote on 186.

[12] Watts, 'British Development Policies,' 150, n. 23.

[13] Klein, 'Death in India;' Watts, 'British Development Policies,' 150, n. 23; Kerr, *Engines of Change*, 23.

recognized such links. Referencing an article in the *India Medical Record* that attributed malaria to the waterlogging of the country by railway embankments, an August 1901 piece in the *Amrita Bazar Patrika* urged popular agitation for redress.[14] Demonstrating another set of links, Nandini Bhattacharya has analyzed how malaria was linked to an influx of immigrant labour at a range of industrial sites, including those for railway construction.[15]

Thus, cholera and plague were certainly not the only ways in which railways affected public health in colonial India. Both were, however, central to a global debate on the relationship between railway travel and public health, part of a continuing discussion on how transport networks, including by river, sea, and road, affected the spread of infectious diseases. To bolster their argument, advocates of the contagion theory of cholera had frequently sought to demonstrate how it spread across vast ocean networks.[16] The mid-nineteenth century, however, was a particularly important moment in the debate. Between 1830 and 1870, ships' journey times were 'practically halved on many routes,' while steam power allowed for bigger vessels that could carry larger numbers and hence heighten the potential for infectious contact.[17] The speed of railways and the aggregation of people they afforded became similarly relevant. Outside India, specific railway links were being seen as crucial in the international spread of contagion, two important ones in this period being the Alexandria–Suez–Cairo and the Trans-Caucasian railways. Thus, in the mid-to late nineteenth century, many of the epidemiological questions about origin and transmission through transport technologies—and their public and policy implications—were scrutinized at a series of International Sanitary Conferences that addressed the issue transnationally. In many of these, pilgrims arriving from India as well as those returning from Mecca or Medina were frequently designated as central to the global dissemination of infection.[18]

Colonial India straddled a disjunctive space in discussions about cholera. In the late nineteenth century, its railway network became a veritable palimpsest for competing arguments about its cholera map. Data about the timing, spread,

---

[14] *Bengalee*, 5 April 1901, 14 August 1901; *Amrita Bazar Patrika*, 28 August 1901, in NNR: Bengal.
[15] Other sites included ports, jute mills, and tea gardens: Bhattacharya, 'The Logic of Location,' 190.
[16] Mark Harrison, *Contagion: How Commerce has Spread Disease* (New Haven: Yale University Press, 2012), 139–41.
[17] Ibid., 140–41.
[18] Ibid., 73, 144–46.

and intensity of cholera epidemics in various areas was correlated with the nature of railway links in those areas to repudiate miasmatic theories and instead support contagionist ones stressing transmission through infectious contact. Subsequently, however, the same burgeoning railway network was used to *repudiate* contagionism and deny infectious contact and mobility a causal role in cholera's epidemic spread. This not only made India different from the growing international medical consensus on contagionism but also directly affected public health—at least till the early 1890s, anti-contagionists endorsed 'cautious, piecemeal intervention' rather than an interventionist policy.[19] Scholars note how some of this contrary emphasis stemmed from the colonial state's anxiety about the financial and infrastructural costs of preventive intervention; it is equally plausible that the state was aware of how interventions like quarantine would hurt the commercial viability of railways, a technology that it was increasingly more directly invested in.

In the closing decade of the nineteenth century, contagionist views of cholera were re-instated in India, at least for preventive purposes. Soon after, however, railways became deeply involved in a different conversation, this time about the epidemic spread of plague. Despite the limited knowledge of plague etiology at this juncture, railways were deemed potent transmitters of infection in their capacity as carriers of both people and goods, especially infected grain. At the same time, they became instrumental in the state's attempt to contain plague without introducing general land quarantine, perceived as harmful to trade. Of the more than 150 million railway passengers who travelled each year between 1896 and 1898, a sizeable number came under scrutiny, given that some of the largest and most dense railway networks—the Bombay, Baroda, and Central Indian (BBCI), the Great Indian Peninsular (GIPR), the East Indian (EIR), and the North-Western (NWR)—served areas that were severely affected.[20] On sections of these lines, railway stations and trains became an intrusive disciplinary grid through which the state sought to contain the plague epidemic. The ensuing paraphernalia of medical surveillance and detention camps not only criminalized ill-health but also privation and unregulated mobility, wariness about the latter being a particular preoccupation of the colonial state.[21] Analyzing the measure, officials remained adamant that

---

[19] Arnold, 'Cholera and Colonialism,' 145.

[20] *Statistical Abstract from 1894–95 to 1903–04*, 139, 141.

[21] Whether because of the 'paranoid colonial mindset' as Nitin Sinha argues, or because of how peripatetic groups disrupted 'prevailing patterns of trade and transport, and the livelihoods supported by them.' He also argues that 'the British way of understanding

medical regulation of railway passengers was invaluable to retarding the spread of plague across India.[22]

Even as railway infrastructure became important to the state's ability to limit epidemic spread, railways themselves began to be deemed incubators of contagion. This was the conclusion reached by the provincial pilgrim committees that undertook a vast sanitary assessment after plague had ravaged the country for almost two decades. In this context, railways were not only blamed for generating dense gatherings of people; instead, their practice of transporting large numbers of pilgrims crowded into goods wagons intended for transporting merchandise and livestock was held responsible for both facilitating illness and increasing contagious contact. Reports emphasized the heightened risks of infectious transmission among people travelling in goods wagons, some even suggesting that railway passengers—rather than local medical or sanitary authorities—bear the costs of preventive sanitation, both at pilgrimage centres as well as for a more continuous and permanent system of medical surveillance along railway networks. Colonial knowledge about disease and medicine thus came to be actively structured by the antipodean possibilities created by technologies of rapid circulation. Railways became both vectors of epidemic contagion as well as networks through which disease could be disciplined; they could generate dense crowds and insanitary conditions, but could also, as some stressed, provide quick relief and avenues

---

criminality as entwined with mobility began much earlier [than 1857].' Sinha, *Communication and Colonialism*, 117, 190–91. Also earlier in his 'Mobility, Control and Criminality in Early Colonial India, 1760s–1850s,' *Indian Economic* and *Social History Review* 45, 1 (2008): 1–33. Anand Yang points out how David Jones—in *Crime, Protest, Community, and Police, in Nineteenth-Century Britain* (London, 1982)— shows that 'Victorian attitudes towards vagrants represented 'a continuing dialogue between the community and the outsider' and the 'convenient myth about the outsider as deviant and criminal.' David Jones, quoted in Anand Yang, ed., *Crime and Criminality in British India* (Tucson: University of Arizona Press, 1985), 11. See also Georg Simmel's, 'The Stranger' (1908).

Discussing leprosy, Biswamoy Pati and Chandi P. Nanda show how public health concerns were used to control the mobility of people and groups seen as 'undesirable;' equally, how the poor are 'more often than not' identified as the source of infection. 'The Leprosy Patient and Society: Colonial Orissa, 1870s–1940s,' in Biswamoy Pati and Mark Harrison, eds., *The Social History of Health and Medicine in Colonial India* (London and New York: Routledge, 2009).

[22] Plague Resolutions of the Govt. of Bombay, Home: Sanitary (Plague) B, September 1899, nos. 229–37, NAI.

of escape; they offered mobility even as they provided grids of surveillance and detention.

Cholera's Travels

The origin and transmission of cholera, described as one of the nineteenth century's 'most feared, but least explicable diseases,' was not resolved till its closing decades.[23] Colonial authorities initially adopted and then abandoned the contagionist view, which contended that the disease was transmitted through proximity and contact. However, in *both* instances, medical and sanitary officers deployed India's expanding railway network as a critical part of their argument. Thus, in the 1860s, India's expanding railway map was used as proof that cholera was indeed disseminated through contact; in the next two decades, the same railway map was used to support anti-contagionist views, putting India considerably at odds with international medical consensus.

From miasma to contagion: cholera takes the train

To determine preventive measures, the 1861 special commission on cholera in India replaced a miasmatic view of transmission—which held noxious or bad air to be the epidemic trigger—with a contagionist one.[24] This change corresponded with the opinion of the International Sanitary Congress held at Istanbul in 1866, which had concluded that cholera spread 'with a greater swiftness in proportion to the greater rapidity and activity' of human movement.[25] Being able 'in a short time' to carry contagion a great distance, railways were deemed the second most potent transmitter of cholera, after maritime communications.[26] Relying as it did on contact transmission rather than noxious air, the contagionist view drew further attention to the implications of railway transport, especially under crowded conditions.

Official analyses of the 1867 epidemic in north India emphasized how the spread of railways had increased the reach of cholera's contagious spread as

---

[23] Arnold, *Science, Technology and Medicine*, 81.

[24] Quoted in Henry Walter Bellew (Deputy Surgeon-General, Sanitary Commissioner, Punjab), *The History of Cholera in India from 1862 to 1881: A Descriptive and Statistical Account of the Disease as Derived from the Official Published Reports of Several Provincial Governments* (London: Trubner and Co., 1885), 6–7.

[25] Ibid., 7.

[26] Ibid.

well as the number of potential carriers. Referencing the over 3,500 miles of railway open in 1867, the officiating sanitary commissioner J.M. Cunningham argued that extension of railway communication had afforded facilities that were 'unprecedented' in any Kumbh, which was already one of the largest public gatherings in the country.[27] The government's sanitary commissioner G.B. Malleson found that pilgrims from Hardwar 'bore the disease with them to a distance varying from 50 to 300 miles in almost every point of the compass.'[28] Those seized weeks after they had left Hardwar were deemed to have been infected by pilgrims in whose company they had travelled.[29] For Malleson, this was more reasonable than arguing that the cholera germ had remained all that time undeveloped within their systems. The 1869 epidemic in Madras Presidency further deepened the perceived correlation between railways and cholera, especially around events that attracted large crowds, which then dispersed swiftly by train to distant places. Madras' sanitary commissioner found that:

> [the] extension of cholera by the Railway to Salem and Coimbatore, Bangalore and Conjeveram was *the most noticeable* feature of the Triputti [Tirupati?] festivals [emphasis added].[30]

He stressed that the disease subsequently assumed 'epic proportions' in Conjeveram, even if not in the other cities.[31]

Tangible anxiety about railways spreading contagion resulted in formal regulations governing the transport of ill and infectious passengers. In 1869

---

[27] 'Abstract of the Fourth Annual Report of the Sanitary Commissioner with the Govt. of India, 1867,' in *Report on Measures Adopted for Sanitary Improvements in India during the Year 1868 and up to the Month of June 1869 Together with Abstract of Sanitary Reports for 1867 Forwarded from Bengal, Madras, and Bombay* (London: Eyre and Spottiswoode, 1869), 11 (BL). For the figures, see *Statistical Abstract from 1860 to 1869,* 30. The *kumbh* is held every 12 years, the *ardh kumbh* every six years: Maclean, *Pilgrimage and Power.*

[28] G.B. Malleson (Sanitary Commissioner, Govt. of India) and J.M. Cunningham (Surgeon, Secretary), *Report on the Cholera Epidemic of 1867 in Northern India* (Calcutta: Superintendent of Government Printing, 1868), 131–32, 136.

[29] Ibid.

[30] W.R. Cornish (Sanitary Commissioner for Madras), *Report on Cholera in Southern India for the Year 1869* (Madras: Government Gazette Press, 1870), 12 (National Library of Medicine, Bethesda, MD).

[31] Ibid., 12.

itself, the Madras government suggested legislation to ensure that railways provided special carriages for people suffering 'from infectious or contagious diseases.'[32] The PWD— which had a railway branch instituted within it in 1864—was to ensure that this was adopted on all railway lines 'in the interests of public health.'[33] The ensuing rules of 1872 defined small-pox, cholera, measles, scarlet-fever, diphtheria, and whooping-cough as contagious diseases. A railway passenger suffering from any of these had to alert the station-master. If informed at least six hours before scheduled departure, he would provide the patient with a segregated carriage (or compartment) in the second or third class.[34] However, since the passenger would be charged for the entire space, such segregated travel remained prohibitively expensive. Any station-master who discovered a contagious passenger (or the corpse of one) had to empty and disinfect the affected space: the inside of the compartment or carriage was to be washed with boiling water, with one 'wine-glassful' of carbolic acid diluted in each gallon; further, sulphur was to be burnt in it, its fumes locked in for two hours by closing all doors and windows.[35]

Such procedures were fairly commensurate with precautions in other countries, which also prohibited persons suffering from infectious diseases from travelling on railways without identifying themselves, permitted railways to remove or exclude such passengers, and insisted on the disinfection of carriages in which they might have travelled.[36] In India, the 1872 order

---

[32] 'Death of Passengers on Indian Railways,' in *Medical Press and Circular*, 22 September 1869, digested in *Medical Press and Circular: A Weekly Journal of Medicine and Medical Affairs: From June to December 1869* (London: Medical Press and Circular Office, 1869), 251.

[33] Rules for the Conveyance by Rail of Persons Suffering from Contagious Diseases, Govt. of India (PWD: Railway), nos. 176–81 G.R., 2 February 1972, reproduced in *Abstract of Proceedings of the Sanitary Commissioner with the Government of India during the year 1872* (Calcutta: Office of the Superintendent of Government Printing, 1873), 22.

[34] Rules for the Conveyance by Rail of Persons Suffering from Contagious Diseases, 23.

[35] Ibid.

[36] George Findlay, *The Working and Management of an English Railway*, edited by S.M. Philip (London: Whittaker and Co., 1894), 336; 'The Law about Infectious Diseases,' *The Sanitary Record*, 13 February 1875, digested in *The Sanitary Record: A Journal of Public Health*, Vol. II, January–June 1875 (edited by Ernest Hart, London: Smith & Elder, 1875), 214; 'Railway Transport of Infectious Patients,' *The British Medical Journal* 2, 1607 (17 October 1891) describing resolutions at a meeting of the Hessian Medical Society at Darmstadt in Germany. Discussing north America, Thomas R. Crowder mentions legislation that made it illegal for those afflicted with communicable diseases

seems to be the first to formally regulate travel by passengers suffering from infectious illnesses. Previous railway legislation—1854 (no. XVIII), 1860 (no. LII), 1867 (no. XXXI), 1870 (no. XXX), and 1871 (no. XXV)— lacked concomitant provisions, as did the Contagious Diseases Act (1868).[37] The core of the 1872 order was duplicated in the Railways Act of 1890, which remained the substantive railway legislation throughout the colonial period. Sections 47(d) and 71 of the 1890 Act permitted railway companies to refuse to carry any passengers who were suffering from infectious or contagious disorders, except with special permission and under segregated conditions.[38] Though it was unclear how railway officials would identify those passengers who did not admit to being ill (or did not, in fact, know themselves to be infected), the law provided that anyone found contravening these regulations would be fined and forfeit his or her ticket. Employees who failed to properly segregate contagious or infected persons who had been permitted to travel were liable to a fine of one hundred rupees.

Reneging on contagionism: does cholera actually travel?

Around the time that the 1872 order was trying to regulate the carriage of contagious railway passengers, parts of the colonial establishment had begun to dispute that cholera was transmitted through such travel. This change was most forcefully expounded by J.M. Cunningham, who was sanitary commissioner of Bengal from 1869, becoming the Government of India's sanitary commissioner in 1875. This return to a non-contagionist view of cholera was instrumental in exonerating India's spreading railway network from playing a substantive role in generating or exacerbating cholera epidemics. Even more significantly, this renewed anti-contagionism relied on railways *themselves* to prove its case.

In his report on the 1872 epidemic in northern India, Cunningham argued that in the early part of the year, cholera was propagated along the eastern districts of the North-Western Provinces (NWP) and Oudh, 'where there are

---

'to ask for or to accept transportation from common carriers' like railroads, as well as the problems with enforcing such provisions. *The Sanitation of Railway Cars* (Washington: G.P.O., 1916), 5; also Richter, *Home and the Rails*, 23–24.

[37] Andrew Lyon, *The Law of India*, Vol. II: *The Miscellaneous Laws* (Calcutta: Thacker, Spink, & Co. and London: W. Thacker & Co., 1873), 501–13 and 194–200.

[38] Section 117 delineated such penalties. Russell and Bayley, *The Indian Railways Act IX of 1890*, 126, 174, 237.

no Railways and the means of communication are very slow.'[39] To emphasize that cholera was not disseminated through or along railway networks, he compared epidemics among European troops at Kanpur, Allahabad, Agra, Meerut, Ambala, Kasauli, and Mian Meer *before* and *after* these places were linked through railways. He concluded that cholera occurred no earlier in any of them in 1869 and 1872—after they were connected through railways— than it had in epidemics in 1845, 1856, and 1861.[40] Thus, Cunningham concluded that cholera did not travel more rapidly now than it used to do when there were no railways.[41]

When examining the spread of the 1875 epidemic, Cunningham sought to demonstrate that many areas with railway networks remained exempt from cholera; equally, that cholera remained prevalent in many areas lacking 'the great highways of traffic.'[42] He pointed out that a trunk line of railway 'on which there is much constant traffic' ran through that very part of the Central Provinces that escaped the epidemic, while in the Upper Provinces cholera spread over an area where transport networks were 'comparatively difficult and little used.'[43] Cunningham's conclusion was unequivocal: 'Over great part[s] of the country in which cholera was most severe,' he argued, 'there are no railways and the roads are often indifferent.'

As David Arnold points out, Cunningham's assertions made India 'distinct epidemiologically,' an argument that was analogous with the conclusion reached by the 1874 International Sanitary Conference that cholera 'developed spontaneously *only* in India' (emphasis added).[44] In 1877, Charles Gordon emphasized that except in India, railways had been pegged as 'the most active

---

[39] J.M. Cunningham (Sanitary Commissioner, Govt. of India), *Cholera Epidemic of 1872 in Northern India* (Calcutta: Superintendent of Government Printing, 1873), 15–16.

[40] The figures gave a monthly breakdown of the number admitted with cholera in these seven stations in the relevant years. Cunningham, *Cholera Epidemic of 1872*, 15–16.

[41] Ibid.

[42] Abstract of Report of Sanitary Commissioner with the Govt. of India for 1875, quoted in Abstract of Sanitary and Other Reports for 1875, reproduced in *Report on Sanitary Measures in India in 1875–76: with Miscellaneous Information up to June 1877*, Vol. ix (London: Eyre and Spottiswoode, 1877), 56.

[43] Ibid.

[44] Arnold, 'Cholera and Colonialism,' 145. A.B. Shepherd, 'Report on Practical Medicine,' in *A Biennial Retrospect of Medicine, Surgery and their Allied Sciences for 1873–74*, Vol. LXV edited by Mr. H. Power, Dr. Shepherd, Mr. Warren Tay, Mr. R.B. Carter, Mr. C.H. Carter, and Dr. T. Stevenson, (London: New Sydenham Society), 67 (Lane Medical Library, Stanford).

agents in the rapid extension of epidemics of cholera after sea transport.[45] The surgeon-general of British forces in Madras Presidency, who had served earlier in Bengal, was aware of a global series of examples of cholera being transmitted by rail: in 1865, out from Alexandria, and from Odessa to Alternberg; in 1869, from St. Petersberg, south-west to Moscow and 'similarly from Pesth to Trieste, Treviso and Genoa;' as well as in America, from 1832 onwards.[46] However, he argued that international commissions had contended that railways were 'less adapted to propagate an epidemic with such certainty as ordinary communication.'[47] He noted that this conclusion had not been substantiated as well as that it had been stated 'without probable cause.'[48] The only explanation he could offer was to cite (in the next sentence) Cunningham's 1872 report. In India, he concluded, the observation had been made that epidemics of the disease 'do not travel faster since the introduction of railways than they did before their introduction.'[49] Instead, Gordon pointed out how helpful railways had been in India in *preventing* intensification of cholera epidemics by permitting troops to be removed swiftly from infected stations, thus allowing them to escape any further attack.[50]

Soon after Robert Koch isolated the cholera bacillus, deputy surgeon-general Henry Walter Bellew further repudiated the contagionist emphasis on human intercourse and railway travel that had marked the earlier sanitary reports of 1861, 1867, and 1869.[51] Published at the close of Cunningham's tenure as sanitary commissioner, Bellew's *History of Cholera* insisted that facilities afforded by railways (and steam communication) had been 'attended to by

---

[45] Charles Alexander Gordon (Surgeon-General, Principal Medical Officer of the British Forces in the Madras Presidency, formerly of the Sanitary Commission of Bengal), *Notes on the Hygiene of Cholera* (London: Bailliere, Tindall and Cox and Madras: Gantz Brothers, 1877), 152.

[46] Ibid., 152–53.

[47] Ibid., 152.

[48] Ibid.

[49] Ibid., 152–53.

[50] Ibid., 154.

[51] Bellew, *The History of Cholera in India from 1862 to 1881*. As Sanitary Commissioner of the Punjab, Deputy Surgeon-General Henry Walter Bellew was secretary of a special committee to inquire into the question of cholera in the province. For a discussion of the immediate impact of Koch's discovery on Cunningham and the medical-sanitary establishment in colonial India, see Mark Harrison, *Public Health in British India: Anglo-Indian Preventive Medicine 1859–1914* (Cambridge: Cambridge University Press, 1994), 111–16.

no appreciable change in the prevalence or distribution of cholera' (emphasis added).[52] He stated that railways

> have not, by a single day hastened the appearance of the normal seasonal manifestations of cholera activity in localities habitually affected by the epidemic influence of the disease.

Nor had they 'operated to introduce cholera into tracts habitually exempt from its epidemic visitations.'

Like Cunningham had, Bellew also relied on examples of dense railway networks to support his anti-contagionism. Focusing on the Lahore and Multan line, he pointed out that daily railway communication between Bengal, the NWP, and the Punjab had not changed the seasonal cholera calendar in these areas.[53] He argued that Multan 'habitually escapes cholera' despite being 'in direct railway intercourse' with Lahore and Delhi; this was true even when the disease was 'raging at Lahore' and 'widely prevalent' in the northern districts of the Punjab, through which the Delhi line of railway ran.[54] Bellew instead attributed epidemics to weather, combined with the general state of public health, especially conditions of malnutrition and famine.

Scholars have noted both the financial and infrastructural obstacles to massive state intervention against cholera.[55] However, the extent to which political considerations played a role continues to be debated. Mark Harrison disagrees with Sheldon Watts that Cunningham was 'pressurized' while in England, suggesting instead that Cunningham's change of heart was 'a matter of conviction rather than a calculated career move.'[56] He does not, however, argue that Cunningham was insensible to the political implications of his changed view but only that there is no evidence to suggest either that he was pressured or that he changed them for private gain.[57] Some of Cunningham's contemporaries were less forgiving. William Maclean, who served as an army medical officer in India from 1838 to 1860, attributed the former's anti-

---

[52] Bellew, *History of Cholera in India from 1862 to 1881*, 8.

[53] Ibid., 8–9.

[54] Ibid.

[55] Arnold, 'Cholera and Colonialism,' 143.

[56] Harrison, *Contagion*, 147–49.

[57] Ibid., 149.

contagionism to political self-interest.[58] Maclean knew that Cunningham was influenced by James Bryden's argument about cholera not assuming epidemic force unless introduced from an endemic area by monsoon winds.[59] However, in lectures at the Army Medical School at Netley (1861–1885), he emphasized the role played by imperial Britain's fear that if cholera was seen to follow 'the great lines of human intercourse,' foreign nations would introduce quarantine regulations 'to the detriment of Indian trade.'[60]

Questions about how quarantine would affect free trade were a staple in discussions about how transport technologies disseminated disease. However, while Maclean did not point to it, around the time that anti-contagionism gained ascendancy in India, railways *themselves* had become rather important to the colonial state. Thus, closing off railway links—even selected ones— could not but be inimical to revenues. In 1871, India had about 5,000 miles of track and British companies had invested £95 million in India's guaranteed railways between 1845 and 1875.[61] Around 1870, the colonial state had also decided to invest directly in railway construction.[62] The expansion was substantial and, by the time Cunningham left in 1885, almost 50 per cent of the approximately 12,000 miles of open track belonged to state lines.[63] Annual passenger traffic had quadrupled from 20 to 80 million between 1872 and 1885, and the 3.5 million tons of goods and minerals that railways transported in 1872 had reached almost 19 million annually by 1885.[64] Gross railway receipts in 1885 stood close to 180 million rupees, yielding net earnings of over 90 million rupees, of which two-thirds belonged to state-assisted and state-owned railways.[65] As a head of income, railway revenue and receipts stood

---

[58] William Campbell Maclean, *Diseases of Tropical Climates: Lectures Delivered at the Army Medical School* (London: Macmillan, 1886).

[59] Ibid., 229.

[60] Ibid., 231.

[61] W.J. Macpherson, 'Investment in Indian Railways, 1845–75,' in *The Economic History Review* 8, 2 ns (1955): 177–86, quote on 177; and *Statistical Abstract from 1867/8 to 1876/7*, 88.

[62] Bell, *Railway Policy in India*, 91–99.

[63] This included assisted companies and state lines and excluded guaranteed companies and lines in native states. *Statistical Abstract Relating to British India from 1876/7 to 1885/6* (London: HMSO 1887), 175–76.

[64] *Statistical Abstract from 1867/8 to 1876/7*, 90, 91; *Statistical Abstract from 1876/7 to 1885/6*, 178, 179.

[65] *Statistical Abstract from 1876/7 to 1885/6*. Gross receipts = 17.9 million in tens of rupees (180); net earnings = 9.1 million in tens of rupees (182).

at 119 million rupees in 1884–85, tabulated second only to the 218 million rupees brought in as land revenue.[66]

Those who believed in anti-contagionism did not suggest that no measures be taken: 'Cunningham and his associates declared themselves to be as much in favour of good sanitation and clean drinking-water as their contagionist opponents.'[67] However, anti-contagionism did affect the broad understanding of how cholera could and should be dealt with and 'the continuing uncertainty over the nature of cholera and the mode of its transmission' became a 'substantial obstacle to state interventionism.'[68] Given the demographics of cholera mortality in colonial India, the public impact of this burden fell disproportionately on the country's poor, especially the rural poor; further, while there was no axiomatic relationship between cholera and famine, epidemic cholera's mortality 'was doubled, even trebled,' when it coincided with famine.[69]

By the time Maclean's lectures were published, however, an emphasis on preventive intervention with cholera was on the ascendant and, at least for this purpose, railway travel was being correlated again with the spread of cholera epidemics. Railway travel to the 1892 Kumbh in Hardwar was banned. Anxiety had returned that railways would not only intensify crowd density at the *mela* but also facilitate the widespread diffusion of contagion outward from the centre if an epidemic broke out. It would not be long after this that sanitary, medical, and railway authorities would become occupied with another epidemic, this time of bubonic plague. From October 1896, increased control over railways as points of exit and entry became central to the feverish attempt to contain the plague epidemic without introducing general land quarantine.[70]

Barricaded against Plague

As plague spread out from Bombay in 1896, M.E. Couchman's account showed it travelling 'along the lines of railway and traffic in the interior of the Presidency,' with each of these localities themselves becoming 'fresh centres'

---

[66] Land Revenue = 21.8 million in tens of rupees; railways = 11.9 million in tens of rupees. The next was opium at 88 million (8.8 million in tens of rupees). *Statistical Abstract from 1876/7 to 1885/6*, 71.

[67] Arnold, 'Cholera and Colonialism,' 145.

[68] Ibid., 143.

[69] Ibid., 124–25.

[70] In 1896, mileage stood at over 20,000. *Statistical Abstract from 1894–95 to 1903–04*, 138.

of dispersion.[71] People used railways to flee the epidemic. Ill and infected passengers were found in railway carriages and at railway stations, cases coming by rail from 'even as far as Calcutta.'[72] At first glance, railways seemed an unlikely carrier given that bubonic plague was transmitted by the rat flea (unlike in its pneumonic form, when it spread from person to person through droplet infection). However, humans served as carriers, transporting *X. cheopis* across the country 'in their clothing or baggage,' while the large grain trade transported infected fleas and rats.[73] Ira Klein has emphasized that health authorities did not fully understand plague transmission until World War I. Nevertheless, railways carried many possible transmitters identified at that time: infected humans and animals; articles and merchandise contaminated with infected secretions; and infected rats in grain, straw, or skeleton crates.

Loath to interrupt the grain trade, the colonial state described general land quarantine as an 'impolitic' move that would encourage European powers to urge 'greater restrictions on Indian trade.'[74] Limited quarantine was instituted when outbreaks were restricted to 'a small place, the inhabitants of which can be easily and surely isolated,' as happened in Khandraoni in Gwalior state.[75] More generally, the Bombay government decided to focus its attention on ensuring that no contaminated grain was exported.[76] Meanwhile, the Government of India decided to not stop third-class railway traffic out from infected areas as had been suggested, arguing that this would not contain the infection since passengers travelling first and second class could still be carriers.[77] More importantly, it reasoned that *continuing* railway travel was necessary to

---

[71] W.J. Simpson, *A Treatise on Plague, dealing with the Historical, Epidemiological, Clinical, Therapeutic and Preventive Aspects of the Disease* (Cambridge: Cambridge University Press, 1905), 70. He notes slow diffusion as 'one of the most constant characteristics.' (70).

[72] Ibid., 200.

[73] Klein, 'Plague, Policy, and Popular Unrest,' 737–40.

[74] Telegram from Secretary, Govt. of India (Home) to Secretary, Bombay (General Dept.), 12 March 1897, in *Plague in India, 1896, 1897*, compiled by R. Nathan (Simla: Government Central Printing Office, 1898), Vol. III, appendix viii, no. 5, 38–39.

[75] Secretary, Govt. of India (Home) to Secretary, Govt. of Bombay (General Dept.), 29 March 1897, in *Plague in India*, Vol. III, appendix viii, no. 17, 46–47.

[76] Telegrams from Secretary, Govt. of India (Home) to Secretary, Govt. of Bombay (General) and to Chief Secretary, NWP and Oudh, India (Home), 15 March 1897, in *Plague in India*, Vol. III, appendix X, nos. 8–9, 423.

[77] Telegram from Secretary, Govt. of India (Home) to Secretary, Bombay (General Dept.), 12 March 1897.

contain the epidemic: if they were prevented from travelling by rail, people would simply 'scatter over the country-side, and find an egress by ways which would render inspection and control difficult or impossible.'[78] Controlling ingress and egress at railway nodes through medical inspection thus became vital to containing plague; this was seen as an especially important measure because of the increasing concern with people fleeing infected areas, some estimates suggesting that 200,000 people—'fully one quarter of the population of Bombay'—fled in the fall of 1896.[79] Thus, railway stations became a vital locus for preventing an exodus from infected areas and an influx into sterile ones.

Barrier 1: the surveillance system

From October 1896 onwards, passengers leaving Bombay in specific 'through' trains on the Bombay, Baroda, and Central Indian Railway began to be medically examined at Grant Road station, while those travelling on the Great Indian Peninsular were examined at Victoria terminus.[80] The Home department recognized that medical inspection of railway passengers would not isolate all cases of bubonic fever; however, officials argued that the process would likely 'arrest some' and thus help contain the spread.[81] Initially, medical examination was conducted under sections 47(d) and 71 of the 1890 Railways Act, bubonic plague having been now added to the list of infectious and contagious diseases regulated under these sections.[82] The normative assumptions in such inspection were apparent, medical officers being urged to identify anyone who seemed suspicious either by reason of symptoms and appearance or because of 'the dirty condition of his clothes or effects.'[83] The

---

[78] *The Plague in India, 1896, 1897*, compiled by R. Nathan (Simla: Government Central Printing Office, 1898), Vol. I, 293.

[79] Myron J. Echenberg, *Plague Ports: The Global Urban Impact of Bubonic Plague, 1894–1901* (New York: New York University Press, 2007), 64.

[80] J.K. Condon, *The Bombay Plague, Being a History of the Progress of Plague in the Bombay Presidency from September 1896 to June 1899, Compiled Under the Orders of the Government of India* (Bombay: Education Society, 1900), 141.

[81] J. Woodburn (Home Dept.), 10 October 1896, in Home: Sanitary (Plague), November 1896, nos. 174–208, NAI.

[82] Section 117 specified the penalties for any contravention of these regulations, whether by a contagious passenger or a railway servant. Russell and Bayley, *The Indian Railways Act IX of 1890*, 126, 174, 237; Nathan, *Plague in India*, Vol. I, 130.

[83] Nathan, *Plague in India*, Vol. I, 293–94; Telegram from Secretary, Govt. of India (Home) to Secretary, Bombay (General Dept.), 12 March 1897; General Regulations

personal effects of those deemed likely to carry infection were to be fumigated with sulphur, while carbolic acid or corrosive sublimate was reserved for disinfecting 'specially dirty or suspicious' articles.[84] Particularly keen scrutiny was advocated for some groups: labourers and emigrants who were to be scrutinized because they were mobile; people who 'travel[led] in bodies;' and anyone who seemed to be itinerant—'that class of persons, who when they enter a town can neither be traced nor depended on to give information of plague.'[85]

As plague spread, a more extensive, coordinated, and intrusive system of medical inspection on railways was suggested. By February 1897 passengers began to be examined under special provisions in the Epidemic Diseases Act (III of 1897).[86] Beginning with Bombay, every presidency and province drew up a list of inspection stations at which passengers would be examined. In Bombay, this growing list included Kalyan, Palghar, Ahmedabad, Bhusawal, Hotgi, Londa, Dhond, and Rajevadi. Bengal's largest inspection stations were at Khana and Katihar, while the major inspections in the NWP included Manikpur, Jhansi, Saharanpur, and Ghaziabad (for a detailed list, see Table 5.1).

Trains had their carriage doors locked between inspection stations, where all passengers disembarked to be inspected on the platform or line. They could continue on their journey only after the appropriate medical officer had certified in writing that all aboard were free of plague symptoms.[87] Bengal's sanitary commissioner recorded the involved process at Khana, a junction on the main line between Bombay and Calcutta.[88] Thirteen officials attended every train: a European station-master and European police sergeant, two head constables, and nine constables.[89] As railway *khalasis* unlocked carriages, three constables on the up-platform ensured that no one got out on the wrong side.

Women were examined separate from men. On the platform, women were

---

Issued before Passing of Epidemic Diseases Act, in *The Plague in India, 1896, 1897*, compiled by R. Nathan (Simla: Government Central Printing Office, 1898), Vol. II, appendix iv, 193–94.

[84] Ibid.

[85] Ibid.

[86] Plague Resolutions of the Govt. of Bombay; Nathan, *Plague in India*, Vol. I, 291–92. This extended to British India; for the entire Act, see *Plague in India*, Vol. II, appendix IV, 137–41; for enactments in Native States, ibid., appendix IV, 142–44.

[87] Nathan, *Plague in India*, Vol. I, 316, 319; Regulations issued by the Govt. of the North-Western Provinces and Oudh, in *Plague in India*, Vol. II, appendix IV, 225–26.

[88] Nathan, *Plague in India*, Vol. I, 324; also Vol. III, 118–26.

[89] Ibid.

Table 5.1. Railway Inspection Stations, 1896–97.

MADRAS							
Perambur	SIR	Tuticorin	SIR	**Guntakal**	MR	**Kondapalli**	Bezwada Extn
Podanur	MR		MR	**Arkonam**	MR		
BOMBAY							
Kalyan	GIPR	Khandala	GIPR	Poona	GIPR	Grant Road	BBCI
Bhusawal	GIPR	Sholapur Barsi	GIPR	Ahmedabad	BBCI	Palghar	BBCI
Manmad	GIPR	Sholapur-Mohol	GIPR	Anand	BBCI	Broach	BBCI
Hotgi	GIPR	Kurla	GIPR	Surat	BBCI	Hubli	BBCI
Byculla	GIPR	Thana	GIPR	Santa Cruz	BBCI	Londa	SMR
Dhond	GIPR	Mana	GIPR	Bandra	BBCI	Rajiwadi	SMR
SIND							
Karachi City	NWR	**Dadu**	NWR	**Kotri**	NWR	Shikarpur	HSR
Karachi Cantonement	NWR	**Ruk**	NWR	**Sukkur**	NWR	Hyderabad	HSR
BENGAL							
Kathiar	EBSR	**Khana**	EIR	**Damukdia**	EBSR	**Khudra Road**	ECR
NWP and OUDH							
Agra	EIR	Cawnpore	O&RR	Rudauli	O&RR	Hathras Jn.	RMR
Allahabad	EIR	Chandausi	O&RR	Ramnagar	O&RR	Muttra	RMR
Aligarh	EIR	Daryabad	O&RR	Rampur	O&RR	Ganeshpur	RMR
Etawah	EIR	Fyzabad	O&RR	**Saharanpur**	O&RR	Haldwani	R&K
Fatehpur	EIR	Hardoi	O&RR	Shahjahanpur	O&RR	Kathgodam	R&K

Contd.

Contd.

Ghaziabad	EIR	Hardwar	O&RR	Unao	O&RR	Lakhimpur	R&K
Tundla	EIR	Jaunpur	O&RR	Meerut	NWR	Pilibhit	R&K
Moghal Sarai	EIR	Kotdwara	O&RR	Muzaffarnagar	NWR	Sitapur	R&K
Mirzapur	EIR	Lucknow	O&RR	Banda	IMR	Ghazipur	BNWR
Ajodhya	O&RR	Lhaskar	O&RR	**Jhansi**	IMR	Bahraich	BNWR
Akbarpur	O&RR	Malipur	O&RR	Lalitpur	IMR	Gonda	BNWR
Benaras	O&RR	Moradabad	O&RR	Orai	IMR	Goprakhpur	BNWR
Bareilly	O&RR	Rae Bareli	O&RR	Farukhabad	RMR		
Bara Banki	O&RR	Roorkee	O&RR	Hathras City	RMR		

CENTRAL PROVINCES

Nagpur	GIPR	Burhanpur	GIPR	Bilaspur	BNR	Jubbulpore	EIR
Harda	GIPR	Sohagpur	GIPR	Raipur	BNR	**Itarsi**	BIR
Sioni (Malwa)	GIPR	Narasinghpur	GIPR	Bina	IMR	Khandwa	RMR
	GIPR	Wardha	GIPR				

PUNJAB

Sadikabad	NWR	Chichwatni	NWR	Amritsar	NWR	Gurdaspur	NWR
Rahim Yarkhan	NWR	Montgomery	NWR	Meean Meer East	NWR	**Pathankot**	NWR
Kotsamaba	NWR	**Raewind**	NWR	Lahore	NWR	Sialkot	NWR
Khanpur	NWR	Meean Meer West	NWR	Gujranwala	NWR	Ranbirsinghpura	NWR
Feroza	NWR	Ghazi Ghat	NWR	**Warizabad**	NWR	Tawi (Jummoo)	NWR
Chuadri	NWR	Muzaffargarh	NWR	Gujrat	NWR	Hissar	RFR

Contd.

Contd.

Chanigoth	NWR	Darya Khan	NWR	**Jhelum**	NWR	**Bhatinda**	RFR
Ahmadpur	NWR	Kundian	NWR	Rawalpindi	NWR	**Ferozepore Cant.**	RFR
Mubarakpur	NWR	Khushab	NWR	Khushalgarh	NWR	Ferozepur City	RFR
Kulanchwala	NWR	Jagadhri	NWR	Hasan Abdal	NWR	Rewari	RMR
Samasata	NWR	UmballaCant.	NWR	Attock Bridge	NWR	Gurgaon	RMR
Bhawalpur	NWR	Umballa City	NWR	NowsheraCant.	NWR	Delhi	D-U-K
Sher Shah	NWR	Ludhiana	NWR	Peshawar City	NWR	Karnal	D-U-K
Mooltan Cantonement	NWR	Jullundar Cant.	NWR	Peshawar Cant.	NWR	Thanesar	D-U-K
Mooltan City	NWR	Jullundar City	NWR	Batala	NWR	**Kalka**	D-U-K
CENTRAL INDIA							
Rutlam	RMR	**Ujjain**	RMR	Indore	RMR	**Sutna**	EIR
RAJPUTANA							
Ajmere	RMR	Nusseerabad	RMR	Pindwara	RMR	Chittor	SIR
Bandikui	RMR	Bhilwara	RMR	Baewar	RMR	Dholpur	IMR
Bhurtpore	RMR	Nadbai	RMR	Jeypore	RMR	Bickaneer	JBR
Ulwar	RMR	Abu Road	RMR	Phulera	RMR	Merta Road	JBR
Khairthal	RMR	Nana	RMR	Rajgarh	RMR	Jodhpur	JBR
Kherli	RMR						
BALUCHISTAN							
Bostan	NWR	Hirok	NWR	Sibi	NWR	Kiki Abdullah	NWR
Chaman	NWR	Harnai	NWR	Quetta	NWR	**Sharigh**	NRW
		Mach	NWR				

Contd.

Contd.

				MYSORE			
Bangalore Cantt.	SMR	Harihar	SMR	Yasvantpur	SMR		
				HYDERABAD			
Gulbarga	GIPR	Raichur	GIPR	Vikarabad	NGSR		
Wadi	GIPR			Hyderabad	NGSR		
				BERAR			
Malkapur	GIPR	Akola	GIPR	Bandera	GIPR	Amraoti	AR
Shegaon	GIPR	Murtizapur	GIPR	Chandur	GIPR		
				Nandura	GIPR	Khamgaon	KR

Sections in charge of a commissioned Medical Officer are in bold

Key: AR: Amroti Railway; **BBCI:** Bombay, Baroda, and Central Indian Railway; **BIR:** Bhopal–Itarsi Railway; **BNR:** Bengal–Nagpur Railway; **BNWR:** Bengal and North-Western Railway; **D-U-K:** Delhi-Umballa-Kalka Railway; **EBSR:** Eastern Bengal State Railway; **ECR:** East Coast Railway; **EIR:** East Indian Railway; **GIPR:** Great Indian Peninsular Railway; **HSR:** Hyderabad–Shadipalli Railway; **IMR:** Indian Midland Railway; **JBR:** Jodhpur–Bickaneer Railway; **KR:** Khamgaon Railways; **MR:** Madras Railway; **NGSR:** Nizam's Guaranteed State Railway; **NWR:** North-Western Railway; **O&RR:** Oudh & Rohilkund Railway; **R&K:** Rohilkund & Kumaon Railway; **RFR:** Rewari–Ferozepore Railway; **RMR:** Rajputana–Malwa Railway; **SIR:** South Indian Railway; **SMR:** Southern Mahratta Railway

Source: Tabulated from data in Nathan, *Plague in India, 1896, 1897,* Vol. iii, 96–100

either lined up with their backs turned towards men or were shielded by screens – 'between purdahs or kanats, so as to shield them altogether from the public gaze.'[90] Care was to be taken 'to avoid wounding their feelings in any way,' and the police were 'not allowed to handle them at all.'[91] Male medical officers and women doctors examined men and women respectively, focusing on the parotid glands near the ear, as well as on the axillae, femoral, and inguinal regions. Suspicious cases had their temperature taken. (Subsequently, the parotid glands were examined only if the passenger had symptoms of fever.) When the examination was complete, passengers in the first carriage were allowed to re-enter it, women first, before passengers in the second carriage de-trained for inspection.[92]

The sheer medical intrusiveness of the general scrutiny during this epidemic has been recorded, as has the fact that large numbers of Indians 'feared, detested and tried to circumvent' many of the government's interventions.[93] The medical examination of railway passengers was thus part of a larger grid of official measures that included 'mandatory hospitalization of victims, segregation of contact, disinfection of plague-ridden houses [and] evacuation of epidemic locales,' many of which engendered confrontation, sometimes violent ones.[94] Obviously, railway passengers disliked the scrutiny, especially given the public nature of the medical examination on a station platform, *purdah*s and *kanat*s notwithstanding. However, objections got passengers labelled as 'contumacious': should any passenger decline to be so examined, no time was to be wasted in conversation but:

> [H]e is locked in and the carriage is cut off, and put into a siding, he being liable to the railway company for any loss or inconvenience they may sustain on this account.[95]

At major inspection stations—or at minor ones in which medical officers could be found roaming around, checking symptoms—any person suspected of being infected or infectious was detained. A medical officer then decided

---

[90] Ibid.
[91] Ibid.
[92] Nathan, *Plague in India*, Vol. I, 325.
[93] Klein, 'Plague, Policy, and Popular Unrest,' 739.
[94] Ibid.
[95] Nathan, *Plague in India*, Vol. I, 324–25; also Vol. III, 118–26.

whether those detained were sent to a hospital or temporary plague camp, or else discharged.[96] Major inspection stations had temporary hospital and observation sheds in their vicinity, each accommodating four patients, each of them given 600 cubic feet of space.[97] The accommodation was racially segregated though 'certain natives' were given similar privileges. Thus, the Bombay government ordered that 'Natives of a class' whom the chief medical officer deemed could not be 'properly accommodated' at Palghar or Kalyan were to be sent back to Bombay by train. Europeans were to be sent to St. George's hospital and Indians to the plague hospital at Parel 'or any other convenient hospital.'[98] Khana junction's plague camp accommodated 40 patients in two structures, with six rooms for their families and eight rooms for hospital attendants. Its contact camp housed passengers from the same carriage as a plague case, and its 'suspicious camp' accommodated those who seemed ill but remained undiagnosed. European patients were housed in a separate hut. Quarantine lasted for seven days.[99]

Detained passengers were required to have their luggage disinfected, except when the medical officer thought it fit to declare such disinfection unnecessary, the clause intended to allow lenient treatment of first- and second-class passengers.[100] Thus, it was usually third-class passengers whose belongings were scrutinized and subject to disinfection. Even more carefully scrutinized were people deemed 'suspicious' or 'dirty' and medical officers were to be given the 'widest discretion' in identifying and detaining such persons.[101] Any 'suspicious' articles were boiled in a carbolic acid solution (1:40) for 10 minutes, while articles made with leather, wood, and glue were either soaked

---

[96] Regulations issued by the Govt. of the NWP, in *Plague in India*, Vol. II, appendix IV, 225–26; Bombay Govt., Rules for Minor Inspection Stations, notification 883-351-P, 17 February 1897 and Regulations Issued by the Govt. of Madras, 5 February 1897, in *Plague in India*, Vol. II, appendix IV, 187-8-3.

[97] Nathan, *Plague in India*, Vol. I, 323; Bombay Govt. Resolution no. 996-471-P., dated 24 February 1897, in *Plague in India*, Vol. II, appendix IV, 173–74.

[98] Ibid.

[99] Nathan, *Plague in India*, Vol. I, 323–24.

[100] Telegram from Secretary, Govt. of India (Home) to Secretary, Govt. of Bombay (General Dept.), 28 February 1897, *Plague in India*, Vol. III, appendix viii, 36–40; J P. Hewett, Secretary, Govt. of India (Home) to Secretary, Govt. of Bombay (General Dept.), 6 March 1897 and 27 April 1897 both in *Plague in India*, Vol. III, appendix viii, pp. 136–40; Orders to Local Governments, in *Plague in India*, Vol. III, appendix viii, 140–42.

[101] *Plague in India*, Vol. III, 14, 39–43, 52–53, 75–76.

in a mercury perchloride solution or washed with the carbolic acid and soft soap solution that was also used for metallic articles. These objects were then dried in the sun for an hour (artificially during the rains). Anything that could not be thus disinfected was burnt.

Railway stations outside epidemic areas instituted 'medical surveillance' to track passengers arriving from infected districts through the estimated incubation period.[102] The stations included on this list were constantly updated, the list itself circulated to station-masters. Unregulated mobility or itinerant behaviour was actively discouraged: passengers coming from stations on such lists had to provide designated authorities, whether railway staff, police, or medical officers, with detailed information about themselves, their whereabouts, and their movements. In addition to names and addresses, they were to explain their reasons for travelling and their intentions regarding future movement.[103] Local authorities—ranging from *mamlatdars*, town or village headmen, and secretaries of municipalities to civil surgeons, district superintendents of police, and local police stations—were responsible for tracking whether these passengers showed any symptoms of plague.[104] This 'surveillance system' became more widespread by late 1898 as the epidemic continued; simultaneously, however, detention began to be criticized for 'practically clos[ing] the channels of business.'[105]

Large numbers of Indians, whether infected or not, experienced the epidemic through the process of medical inspection instituted at railway stations. In 1896 itself, railways carried upwards of 150.5 million passengers, of which about 34 million travelled on the GIPR and the BBCI, not only two of the five largest lines but also the ones most affected by plague regulations.[106] Both lines transported fewer passengers in the subsequent years, the figures for each dropping from 17 million in 1896 to 14 million in 1897 and 1898.[107] By

---

[102] The order of 6 March was preceded by telegrams and correspondence between the Govt. of India and local governments. *Plague in India*, Vol. III, appendix viii, 126–30. For the formal order, see Vol. III, appendix viii, 131–32. The February instruction of 'inspections of parade of passengers' is mentioned in a telegram from Secretary, Govt. of NWP and Oudh (Judicial) to Secretary, Govt. of India (Home), 10 February 1897, Vol. III, appendix viii, 126.

[103] Nathan, *Plague in India*, Vol. 1, 331–32.

[104] Ibid.

[105] Plague Resolutions of the Govt. of Bombay.

[106] *Statistical Abstract from 1894–95 to 1903–04*, 141.

[107] Ibid.

1898, their passenger figures had crawled back to 16 million each, back to over 17 million in 1900. Portions of the EIR were also affected, traffic dropping from 19 million in 1895 to 18 million in 1896 and in 1897, returning to 19 million in 1898.[108]

Barrier 2: disinfecting vehicles

The Railways Act of 1890 already prescribed procedures for disinfecting railway carriages used by infected passengers: an infected carriage was to be washed with boiling water and carbolic acid and to be fumigated with sulphur.[109] In March 1897, supplementary orders were issued requiring railways to sprinkle carbolic acid on the floors and seats of contaminated carriages and to wash interior woodwork with a mercury perchloride solution. Disinfected carriages were to remain unused for 10 days.[110] Further orders were issued in April 1897 when it was discovered that the BBCI was skimping on procedures by disinfecting only those carriages whose floors or seats had been contaminated by 'the evacuations, etc., of the infected person,' and also immediately re-using such inadequately disinfected carriages.[111]

The new orders were more specific, insisting that every carriage in which a suspected or declared case of plague had been found had to be detached from the train at that station (or the nearest medical inspection station).[112] It was to be left saturated in soft soap and lime-water for a few hours and the interior and exterior were to be disinfected with solution, with particular attention being paid to any crevices and *jhilmi*s built into the carriage.[113] Thereafter, the carriage was to be left in the open for 48 hours.[114] Trains from infected areas

---

[108] Ibid.

[109] Rules for the Conveyance by Rail of Persons Suffering from a Contagious Disease, 23.

[110] Orders issued under Act no. III of 1897 (G.O. no. 136/XVI-404-D-104), 8 March 1897, quoted in letter from Chief Secretary, Govt. of North-Western Provinces and Oudh, to Secretary, Govt. of India (Home), 17 March 1897, in *Plague in India*, Vol. III, appendix viii, 165.

[111] Letter 349 R.T. from G.A. Anderson, Undersecretary, Govt. of India (Public Works) to local governments, 21 April 1897, in *Plague in India*, Vol. III, appendix viii, 165–68.

[112] Letter 349 R.T. from G.A. Anderson to local governments, 21 April 1897.

[113] Three gallons of water: three *oz* of corrosive sublimate: one *oz* of hydrochloric acid.

[114] The new order (Letter 349-R.T. of 21 April 1897) decreased the time specified for disuse from 10 days to 48 hours. When the discrepancy was pointed out, the 48-hour rule was allowed to stand. Secretary, Govt. of North-West Provinces and Oudh, (Judicial) to Secretary, Govt. of India (Home), 30 April 1897, in *Plague in India*, Vol. III,

had to be disinfected even if no cases of plague were detected in them. While the government preferred these being disinfected at the medical inspection station closest to the boundary, pressure from the GIPR eventually led it to concede that these could be disinfected at the end of the journey. Special attention was given to third- or intermediate-class carriages, goods vehicles carrying passengers, and luggage vans, which had to be washed with mercury perchloride (1:1,000) or carbolic acid (wineglassful to a gallon) solution. If contaminated, upholstered first- and second-class carriages had to have their cushions burnt, the woodwork disinfected, and the interior repainted. If a 'suspicious case' had travelled in it, the carriage was to be sprayed with disinfecting solution. The GIPR objected strenuously to burning upholstery or repainting the interior and held off implementing the regulations issued in April 1897 while the governments of Bombay and India were considering its objections, a process that continued till early June.[115]

When it was pointed out that plague had spread despite inspection and disinfection regulations being in force for over two years, officials contended that the medical examination of railway passengers had ensured that the dissemination was gradual, stating that 'there can be little doubt that it [plague] has been largely checked by this measure.'[116] Railway passengers had not been as accommodating as the authorities wanted and official reports recorded how passengers had attempted to evade this intrusion: some by 'alighting before arrival at, and walking past inspection-stations' and others by booking to intermediate 'non-infected stations.'[117] However, officials believed that, generally speaking, the system served as a powerful deterrent against travelling with symptoms of plague. Of the thousands of passengers examined, 'only an infinitesimal number' were found infected with plague, and of the thousands detained for observation, 'a comparatively small number developed plague.'[118]

---

appendix viii, 167–68; Secretary, Govt. of India (Home), to Secretary to the Govt. of the NWP and Oudh (Judicial), 3 May 1897, in *Plague in India*, Vol. III, appendix viii, 167–68.

[115] Secretary, Govt. of Bombay (Public Works: Railways), to Secretary, Govt. of India (Public Works), 22 May 1897, in *Plague in India*, Vol. III, appendix viii, 168–72; Telegram from Works, Simla, 5 June 1897, in *Plague in India*, Vol. III, appendix viii, 168–72; Govt. of India (Public Works) to Secretary, Govt. of Bombay (Public Works: Railways), 7 June 1897, in *Plague in India*, Vol. III, appendix viii, 168–72.

[116] Plague Resolutions of the Govt. of Bombay.

[117] Ibid.

[118] Ibid.

Pilgrim Contagion

In the early twentieth century, continuing plague and a resurgence of cholera heightened anxiety about contagion. Consequently, the role of railways in spreading infectious diseases was strongly emphasized by the provincial pilgrim committees appointed in 1912 in Bihar and Orissa, the United Provinces, Madras, and Bombay.[119] These refocused attention on the insanitary condition in which railway passengers travelled, especially when on pilgrimage, with large numbers being relegated to goods wagons meant for carrying merchandise or to open carriages reserved for livestock. Such transport, argued the provincial committees, was not only even more insanitary than overcrowded third-class passenger carriages, but also further exacerbated the potential for infectious contact.

The pilgrim's progress

While railway companies often blamed goods wagons on the excessive rush around large festivals like the *maha* Kumbh, the phenomenon was more widespread. Passengers continued to be transported in 'pilgrim specials' and 'mela rakes' even when visiting places of pilgrimage that attracted people all year round and during annual festivals or else agricultural and commercial *mela*s (often both, simultaneously) that attracted roughly similar numbers each year.[120] The use of goods wagons for passengers stemmed from shortages in rolling-stock, initially the result of a severe underestimation of the potential of passenger traffic in India (Chapter 1). However, even when burgeoning numbers of 'pilgrim-passengers' became a statistical norm, railway companies remained loath to invest in additional passenger stock. They were equally loath to lose the revenue that such 'pilgrim-passengers' provided. Thus, even as they complained about inadequate stock, railway companies actively courted such passengers: whether by urging Calcutta's orthodox Brahmins to specify that devotees could use railways without losing religious merit or by making special provisions for the *kanwar*s of pilgrims travelling to Hardwar.[121] The Railway

---

[119] Office note by W.W. Clemesha, Sanitary Commissioner, Govt. of India, 7 March 1916, in RT: A, no. 655-T-16/6-34, November 1917, NAI.

[120] W.W. Clemesha, Sanitary Commissioner, Govt. of India to Secretary, Dept. of Education, 27 September 1916, in RT: A, no. 655-T-16/6-34, November 1917, NAI.

[121] George Smith, 'John Clark Marshman, 1794–1877: Historian and Journalist,' *Twelve Indian Statesmen* (London: John Murray, 1897); Proceedings of Railway Conference, O&RR, Lucknow, 1–3 December 1903, in PWD: RT A: June 1904, 74–75, NAI.

Board itself advertised pilgrim 'destinations' and broadcast propaganda about the facilities that different railways offered 'to assist the erring one to achieve speedy absolution.'[122]

Railway companies insisted that railway travel had improved the conditions under which pilgrims travelled and had made their journeys more sanitary. To mark the contrast, they described pre-railway pilgrimages as being conducted without proper food, water, and sanitation, with pilgrims suffering 'all the horrible and loathsome diseases to which flesh is heir.'[123] Despite such assertions, travelling in goods wagons was far from ideal and the practice faced continued criticism.[124] The most comprehensive critique, however, came from the provincial pilgrim committees appointed in 1912, explicitly concerned with the 'question of the transport of pilgrims by rail.'[125] Every committee included the province's sanitary commissioner, a civil servant, an 'unofficial Indian gentleman,' and a railway representative.

Focusing particularly on how goods wagons spread the 'dejecta' of infected passengers, the committees explained how these were more likely to transmit

---

[122] *The Travellers' Companion: Containing a Brief Description of the Places of Pilgrimage and Important Towns in India*, compiled by Abdul Rasheed (Calcutta: Superintendent of Government Printing, 1910), preface; John Mitchell, *Wheels of Ind* (London: Thornton Butterworth, 1934), 263, 268–89.

[123] Mitchell, *Wheels of India*, 264, 269–70.

[124] *Urdu Dehli Gazette* (Agra), 24 April 1875, in NNR: NWP, Oudh, Punjab, and CP. The correspondent was writing about pilgrims travelling by the EIR from Benaras and Allahabad on the occasion of the solar eclipse. Similarly, the *Rohilkhand Akhbar*'s correspondent highlighted the overcrowding that he had witnessed when travelling from Moradabad to Rajghat on the O&RR on the occasion of the *Somwatíamáwas* in July 1874 (15 July 1874), in NNR: NWP, Oudh, Punjab, and CP. Also W.H.L. Impey, Secretary, Govt. of NWP & Oudh, (PWD: Railway), to Secretary, Govt. of India (Home), 8 May 1894, in Home: Public B, December 1894, nos. 137–38, NAI; Babu Brijnandan Pershad (Rais, Moradabad), Summary of Proposals, Prog. of Railway Conference, O&RR, December 1903; Memorial by Secretary, Indian Association, to Secretary, Govt. of India (PWD), 4 October 1901, PWD: RT: A, May 1902, nos. 60–64, India Prog., IOR.P/6378, BL; Question by Sachidananda Sinha, Imperial Legislative Council, 18 September 1911, in RT: A, October 1911, no. 104, NAI. Discussing travel by members of the Bihar and Orissa committees, Ahuja describes the range of complaints that they received from the public. *Pathways of Empire*, 265–66.

[125] *Report of Pilgrim Committee: Bihar and Orissa*, 31, 34; *Report of Pilgrim Committee: Bombay* (Simla: Government Monotype Press, 1916), in Railway Board: Traffic A, October 1916, no. 895-T.-16/1, NAI. Also, W.W. Clemesha, Sanitary Commissioner to Govt. of India, Office Note, 7 March 1916.

contagion than regular passenger carriages. Lacking partitions and seats like regular passenger carriages did, crowded wagons put people in even closer proximity to each other. Any ill passenger sitting on the wagon floor would foul it with his or her dejecta as well as contaminate the clothes of other passengers sitting nearby on the same wagon floor.[126] In a regular passenger carriage this dejecta would have passed to the floor 'and the passengers would naturally betake themselves to the seat to avoid pollution.'[127] Further, the extreme temperatures in iron wagons could excite or revive 'old and chronic dysenteries and diarrhœas' in passengers, the situation made worse by the fact that goods wagons obviously lacked lavatories.[128] Halts provided little relief, since the height and structure of a goods wagon made it very difficult for passengers to enter and exit it. Goods wagons were equally unhygienic for being unventilated, being so constructed to protect their cargo from engine-sparks and the threat of fire and theft. Long bogies were often completely unventilated, while those that were ventilated usually only had small *jhilmil*-patterned openings covered inside with fine-meshed wire gauze or else manhole-like openings at either end of the wagon near floor level.[129] Most wagons were dirty and passengers often found themselves seated on floors coated in coal dust, sharp *kankar*, or sticky *gur*, as well as in wagons that had recently transported bone and hide.[130]

What is to be done? The fortunes of the pilgrim

Reiterating how goods wagons endangered health and promoted infectious contact, the reports suggested that passenger stock be increased and improved.[131] However, they also anticipated that railway companies would complain about financial constraints. Consequently, they were fairly cautious in their recommendations. The Bombay report censured class I wagons that were constructed of steel and completely unventilated but did not censure class II wagons, 'designed for goods, horses and pilgrims.'[132] Railway companies argued

---

[126] *Report of Pilgrim Committee: Bihar and Orissa*, 35.

[127] Ibid.

[128] Ibid., 34.

[129] Ibid.

[130] The Bihar and Orissa report from which the description is taken was considered to be 'especially comprehensive' and was the one selected to be sent to the various railways. Notes in Railway Dept., January 1917, RT: A, November 1917, no. 655-T-16/6-34, NAI.

[131] *Report of Pilgrim Committee, Bihar and Orissa*, 39; *Report of Pilgrim Committee, Bombay*.

[132] *Report of Pilgrim Committee, Bombay*.

that it was financially infeasible to increase passenger stock and administratively unviable to borrow stock from other lines, especially with existing differences in gauge.[133] Instead, they contended that eliminating wagons would prevent pilgrims—as many as three-fourths—from going on pilgrimages, and blamed the need for wagons on the haste of passengers rushing home after a festival.[134]

Perhaps anticipating such responses, most practical suggestions made by the pilgrim committees focused on making wagons more sanitary and comfortable: if railways stopped using long, unventilated bogie wagons, and those carrying bones and hides; if they used wooden ones, or boarded the floors of iron wagons; if they located man-hole or flap-shutter ventilators where these could generate a draft; and if they ensured that wagons were cleaned properly before being used for passengers.[135] In principle these differed little from previous suggestions, whether those made in 1892 or in 1903.[136] Neither did the pilgrim reports substantively address how in the absence of seats or benches passengers could be protected from infected dejecta that fouled the floor of goods wagons, nor did they raise the 1903 suggestion that benches be put in wagons used for passengers.[137] While some railways agreed to wooden floors and improved lavatory halts, responses were not encouraging.[138] The NWR argued that there was as much danger of infection in a passenger carriage as in a wagon, while the EIR insisted that seats would increase the discomfort of passengers and that wooden wagons were harder to disinfect and thus more

---

[133] Agent O&RR to Secretary, Railway Board, 27 July 1917, in RT: A, no. 393-T-16/23-26, November 1917, India Prog., IOR.P/10198, BL.

[134] Proceedings of Railway Conference, O&RR, December 1903. Later, the government stated that goods wagons were used 'so as not to disappoint those anxious to make the pilgrimage.' T.R. Wynne, Reply to Sachidanand Sinha, Imperial Legislative Council, 18 September 1911, RT: A, October 1911, no. 104, NAI. Agent, BNWR, to Secretary, Railway Board, 8/11 August 1916.

[135] *Report of Pilgrim Committee, Bihar and Orissa,* 35–36. W.W. Clemesha, Sanitary Commissioner to Secretary, Dept. of Education, 27 September 1916.

[136] W.H.L. Impey, Secretary, Govt. of NWP & Oudh, (PWD: Railway), to Secretary, Govt. of India (Home), 8 May 1894, in Home: Public B, December 1894, nos. 137–38, NAI.

[137] *Report of Pilgrim Committee, Bihar and Orissa,* 35–36. W.W. Clemesha, Sanitary Commissioner to Secretary, Dept. of Education, 27 September 1916; Proceedings of Railway Conference, O&RR.

[138] Internal Note: Abstract of replies to Railway Board's letter of 27 June 1916 in connection with Recommendations made by Pilgrim Committee, Bihar & Orissa, RT: A, no. 655-T-16/6-34, November 1917, NAI.

likely to carry disease.[139] Perhaps oblivious to his tautological reasoning, its agent argued that wagons could not be fitted for passengers since they were 'intended for goods.'[140]

Consequently, railways continued using goods wagons: even in 1917, the EIR was using *mela* rakes thought to be 'not quite fit' for passengers.[141] The Bengal–Nagpur (BNR) had stated in 1916 that it used goods wagons when 'it becomes impossible to clear the congestion' and the BBCI that it was using goods wagons on its metre gauge lines.[142] The NWR, Madras and Southern Mahratta (MSMR), and Oudh and Rohilkund (O&RR) all continued using wagons 'for ordinary annual festivals,' the last suggesting instead that wagons be *formally* converted into pilgrim stock.[143] The South Indian Railway (SIR) seemed to be the only line conveying pilgrims in passenger stock, 'albeit with a certain amount of overcrowding.'[144]

Who will foot the bill: the passenger as pilgrim

Effective medical containment of infected or contagious passengers was a major concern for the pilgrim committees. The method followed by some railways like the EIR and BNR of occasionally appointing medical staff to roam around at *mela* stations was seen to be inadequate. As proof, the Bihar report pointed out that in 1912, 25 per cent of the sick were dead before they were discovered in BNR trains or waiting sheds.[145] Insisting that 'the better and quicker the railway communications become, the faster and further will infectious diseases spread,' the reports suggested that medical staff be posted at *mela* stations and important junctions during festivals to scrutinize all

---

[139] Agent, EIR to Secretary, Railway Board, 26 March 1917, in RT: A, no. 393-T/16/23-26, November 1917, India Prog., IOR.P/10198, BL; Agent, NWR to Secretary, Railway Board, 25 October 1916, in RT: A, no. 655-T-16/6-34, November 1917, NAI.

[140] Agent, EIR to Secretary, Railway Board, 26 March 1917.

[141] Ibid.

[142] Agent, BNR to Secretary, Railway Board, 17 July 1916; and General Traffic Manager, Bombay, to Agent, BBCI, 26 September 1916, both in RT: A, no. 655-T-16/6-34, November 1917, NAI.

[143] Agent, O&RR to Secretary, Railway Board, 30 September 1916; Agent, NWR to Secretary, Railway Board, 25 October 1916; Agent, MSMR to Secretary, Railway Board, all in RT: A, no. 655-T-16/6-34, November 1917, NAI.

[144] W.W. Clemesha, Sanitary Commissioner, to Secretary, Dept. of Education, 27 September 1916.

[145] *Report of Pilgrim Committee: Bihar and Orissa*, 49, and appendix VI.

passengers.[146] They had in mind a permanent form of the medical regimen that had become common at minor plague inspection stations in 1896–97: surgeons would meet all trains, watch passengers, mill amongst them on platforms, in *sarais* and in waiting sheds, and look in carriages and wagons for anyone who seemed sick or showed suspicious symptoms.[147] They could question passengers instead of physically examining them but adequate medical staff and hand-ambulances were to be ready to convey any sick passenger to hospital. Further, the carriage/wagon, *sarai*/shed, or privy where the patient had been lying had to be disinfected thoroughly, and a competent medical officer was to ensure disinfection of all who had travelled in a carriage or wagon with an infected patient.[148] Railway companies resisted such suggestions, denying that such regular medical inspection of passengers was their responsibility; they believed that local civic, sanitary, and medical establishments should bear the administrative and financial costs of any such regimen.

The suggestion that drew most ire was that improved sanitation at gathering places be funded by a surcharge added to the railway tickets of passengers who travelled to and from these. Proponents of the surcharge argued that 'the very poor' continued to come by road so pilgrims who possessed 'the money to travel by rail' could afford the surcharge.[149] A surcharge had been profitable earlier at Hardwar and Benaras, where one *anna* had been added to the price of railway tickets issued from beyond a certain radius. However, unlike in Hardwar and Benaras where passengers paid a surcharge coming into the city, the report suggested that this new tax be levied on passengers coming in *and* going out of the city. This would not only double the proceeds but also ensure that 'the payer is usually quite unaware that he is being taxed.'[150]

While they were cognizant of the fact that a surcharge on tickets conflated all railway passengers with pilgrims, the committee believed this to be only fair, given that all railway passengers, irrespective of whether they were pilgrims or not, ran the risk of contracting disease. The suggestion was seen as fair and not inimical to commerce because traffic within a 30-mile radius was exempted— thus, suburban passengers visiting the pilgrimage centre 'in the ordinary course of business' would not be penalized. Railway administrations pointed out that the surcharge only taxed pilgrims who used the rail, burdening them

---

[146] Ibid. 48–49.
[147] Ibid., 49–50.
[148] Ibid., 50.
[149] Ibid., 84.
[150] Ibid.

with the entire cost of sanitary improvements. Further, it upset the carefully calibrated mean at which ticket prices were calculated to attract passengers while maximizing profits. The committee retaliated by arguing that 'railways have revolutionized pilgrim traffic and …disease is spread by them.'[151]

While the tax was being discussed, the 1918 Kumbh *mela* loomed ahead.[152] By now wagons were critical for transporting coal, earlier moved by sea. Between 2.5 and 3 million people were estimated to attend the Kumbh in January–February 1918, which were the two best months for raising coal. The sacrifice of (an anticipated) 900 goods wagons, combined with the blocking of the line for passenger specials, seemed catastrophic.[153] To resolve the problem, the Railway Board prohibited railways from issuing tickets between 3 January and 26 February 1918 for Allahabad (and about 95 other stations). Railway authorities suggested that the ban be issued under section 2 of the Epidemic Diseases Act (III of 1897); however, the order was issued eventually under a new clause in section 3 of the Defence of India Act (1915).[154]

Disease, Epidemics, and Mobility

The correlation between medicine and railway technology in colonial India thus demonstrates how knowledge about epidemiology was routed through technologies of mobility, governance, and control. As railways themselves became central to proving contradictory arguments about transfer through contagious contact, medical conclusions about epidemics became linked with anticipating the effect of quarantine on trade, commerce, and the colonial state's burgeoning investment in railway infrastructure. Even as international medical

---

[151] Ibid., 86.

[152] W.W. Clemesha, to Secretary, Dept. of Education (Govt. of India), 27 September 1916; W.W. Clemesha, Sanitary Commissioner, (Govt. of India), to E.D. Maclagan, Secretary, Govt. of India (Dept. of Education), 1 February 1917, Pro. no. 7 of office notes for RT: A, no. 655-T-16/6-34, November 1917, NAI; E.D. Maclagan, Secretary, Govt. of India to Secretaries to Governments of Madras, Bombay, United Provinces, and Bihar & Orissa (Municipal Depts), 15 February 1917, in RT: A, no. 655-T-16/6-34, November 1917, NAI.

[153] Notes in the Railway Board, RT: A, no. 544-T-17/12-16, April 1918, NAI; R.W. Gillian, President, Railway Board to James Meston, Lieutenant-Governor of United Provinces, 8 November 1917, in Home: Political 'Deposit', July 1918, no. 3, in RT: A, no. 544-T-17/12-16, April 1918, NAI.

[154] Secretary, Railway Board, to Railways, 19 December 1917, in RT: A, no. 544-T-17/12-16, April 1918, NAI.

consensus held that railways were potent vehicles for the epidemic transfer of cholera, yet in India railways were deployed to support a non-contagionist view of the disease. At the same time, however, medical inspection at railway stations was seen as the most efficient way to contain a growing plague epidemic without introducing general land quarantine deemed to be commercially and financially unviable. Given the number of railway stations included in the *cordon sanitaire* that spread outward from Bombay Presidency after 1896, thousands of railway passengers found themselves being medically examined: possibly detained or quarantined, their belongings inspected, and either cleaned or destroyed. Many tried to evade this intrusion, which was purposely geared to be harshest towards third-class passengers, as well as those deemed either poor or itinerant; however, officials claimed that the system served as a powerful deterrent against travelling with symptoms of plague. Perhaps it was this success that spurred official suggestions that railways be made fiscally responsible for instituting a permanent regimen of medical examination at all railway stations that served centres of pilgrimage, deemed to be potent cauldrons of contagion. While railway companies contended that such responsibilities lay with local civic, sanitary, and medical establishments, they were challenged with the argument that spreading railway communications could be directly correlated with the spread of infectious diseases.

Designing Rule
Power, Efficiency, and Anxiety

In 1942, a press communiqué titled 'National Importance of Travelling Less'
asked the Indian public to help the war effort by eschewing train travel. At
the same time, a 'Travel Less' broadcast at Bombay's Regal cinema threw up
a drawing of Shivaji on horseback, followed by the exhortation: 'Shivaji rode
a horse: why travel by train.'[1] An advertising consultant to the Railway Board
explained that this publicity was meant to ensure that railways would not be
'cluttered up with unimportant passenger traffic' during wartime.[2] The ensuing
'Discourage Travel' campaign reminded people of how Shivaji's horse and
Shah Jehan's elephant used to be 'good enough' means of travel.[3] However,
as the campaign spread, some in the Railway Board became concerned about
the political implications of such images—whether of the Maratha leader or
of the Mughal emperor—as well as the dangers of creating 'an anti-railway

---

[1] Press Communiqué, 30 April 1942, and letter to the editor, 12 May 1942, both
enclosures in Railway Board: TX: B, August 1943, no. 9060-TX-1/1-35, NAI.

[2] Advertising consultant to the Railway Board, 27 January 1942, Railway Board:
TX: B, August 1943, no. 9060-TX-1/1-35, NAI.

[3] Along with Noah's ark and Julius Caesar's chariot. 'Discourage Travel' was
the title of the film prepared by the Information and Broadcasting Department.
Railway Board: TX: B, August 1943, no. 9060-TX-1/1-35, NAI.

sense' and suggested that passenger traffic be discouraged only until 'normal' conditions returned.[4]

Almost a century before the 'Discourage Travel' campaign, the newly minted prospectus of the (provisionally registered) Great Bombay, Baroda, Cawnpore, and Lucknow railway company had emphasized the 'incalculable' military importance of railways lines to the imperial state.[5] Like other firms hoping to attract official support for their commercial plans to construct railways in British India—including governmental guarantee on investment—they were quick to highlight the potential of railways to swiftly convey troops as well as luggage, stores, artillery, and other 'cumbrous materials' that attended a march, enable the government to distribute its forces strategically, and facilitate rapid concentration of troops.[6]

No state, imperial or not, was oblivious to the strategic value of railways. Thus, while commercial concerns were important, military ones remained critical in planning and building. L.C.A. Knowles highlights the strategic concerns that informed the planning of French and German railways, also pointing out that some lines, such as those of Prussia with the Russian frontier, 'would never have been built if the motive had been purely financial.'[7] England was described as anomalous in this respect but, generally speaking, railways were seen to have 'a significant impact on military strategy in the middle of the nineteenth century,' especially in relation to the Franco-Austrian War (1859), the American Civil War (1861–65), and the Austro-Prussian War (1866).[8]

---

[4] Note no. 22, 4 June 1942, Railway Board: TX: B, August 1943, no. 9060-TX-1/1-35, NAI.

[5] Prospectus of the Intended Great Bombay, Baroda, Cawnpore, and Lucknow Direct Railway Company, Enclosure to letter no. 123 of 1 November 1847 to Directors of East India Company. Railways: Home Correspondence, IOR.31478, L/PWD/2/43 (1845–48), BL.

[6] Note no. 22, 4 June 1942, Railway Board: TX: B, August 1943, no. 9060-TX-1/1-35, NAI.

[7] L.C.A. Knowles, *The Industrial & Commercial Revolutions in Great Britain during the Nineteenth Century* (London: George Routledge, 1921) 253–54; Brian Bond discusses its specific importance in Prussia in 'War and Peace: Mechanized Warfare and the Growth of Pacifism,' in Asa Briggs, ed., *The Nineteenth Century: The Contradictions of Progress* (London: Thames and Hudson, 1970), 209–10. See also Richards and MacKenzie, *The Railway Station*, 125–26.

[8] Stephen Badsey, 'The Impact of Communications and the Media on the Art of War since 1815,' in Geoffrey Jensen and Andrew Wiest, eds., *War in the Age of Technology:*

Highlighting the change, Brian Bond argues that 'without railways the huge conscript armies of the later 19th century could not have been moved and fed;' he recounts the British military strategist J.C.F. Fuller's 'pardonable hyperbole' that it was George Stephenson who was the father of the 'nation in arms.'[9] Robert G. Angevine examines not only the military use of railroads in the American Civil War but also how army engineers influenced railway planning and construction in north America; discussing China's relatively late entry into railroad building, Bruce Elleman, Elisabeth Koll, and Y. Tak Matsusaka describe the military applications of rail technology as 'the first and foremost component' of 'railway power' of the kind that took root in China in the late 1890s, especially after the Sino-Japanese War (1894–95).[10]

Within this matrix, a host of *specific* considerations underpinned the imperial state's strategic reliance on railways in colonial India. Most critical was how speed would qualitatively change the nature of British control over India: some army men emphasized how, compared with Britain, the ordinary dispersion of troops in India was 'nearly in the Ratio of 1,000 miles compared to 100 miles.'[11] The situation was exacerbated by the fact that in a colonial context, troops were required as much for internal control as for military needs at frontiers. The

---

Myriad Faces of Modern Armed Conflict (New York: New York University Press, 2001), 70; L.C.A. Knowles, *Economic Development in the Nineteenth Century: France, Germany, Russia and the United States* (Abingdon and New York: Routledge, 2006 [1932]), 228. In J.N. Westwood, *Railways at War* (San Diego: Howell-North, 1980) and Haywood, *Russia Enters the Railway Age* (525–29), one finds discussions about the military use of the St. Petersburg-Moscow railway during 1852–56 and arguments about how a railway to the Black Sea would have been even more useful during the Crimean War.

[9] Bond, *War, and Peace*, 209–10. He was referring to J.F.C. Fuller's analysis in *The Conduct of War, 1789–1961: A Study of the Impact of the French, Industrial, and Russian Revolutions on War and Its Conduct* (London: Eyre and Spottiswoode, 1961).

[10] Robert G. Angevine, *The Railroad and the State: War, Politics, and Technology in Nineteenth Century America* (Stanford: Stanford University Press, 2004). Also, William G. Thomas, *The Iron Way: Railroads, the Civil War, and the Making of Modern America* (Stanford: Stanford University Press, 2011); Bruce Ellman and Stephen Kotkin, eds., *Manchurian Railways and the Opening of China: An International History* (Armonk: M.E. Sharpe), 3–4.

[11] Major J.P. Kennedy, Memorandum upon Indian Railways, 14 September 1852, Enclosure to Despatch no. 51 of 22 September 1852, Railway Letters from Home Govt., 1852–61, NAI. Also in Indian Council of Historical Research (henceforth ICHR), *Railway Construction in India*, edited by S. Settar, Bhubanes Misra, M.P. Kanth, and A.G. Lal (New Delhi: ICHR, 1999), Vol. 1, doc. 161.

speed of railways, it was argued, would counter the limitations engendered by a limited British presence in India as well as the susceptibility of European troops to 'tropical' illnesses during long marches.[12] Imperial functionaries argued that railways would overcome not only the travails of distance and disease but also of seasonality, allowing for a considerable expansion of the marching season. These arguments made railways a far more effective means of military transport than both road and water: roads were frequently in a state of disrepair, while the usability of waterways was affected both by summer and the monsoons. Thus, while troop mobility and concentration had been always a staple concern of the colonial state (as its building of military highways attested to) railways offered a panacea for several intractable problems of movement and supply.

The *extent* to which strategic concerns influenced early railway policy in colonial India is more striking given how British manufacturing and trade dominated the initial conversation about building railways in India. Appalled to discover that Brazil took 10 times as much British goods per capita as did India, it was English and Scottish mercantile houses that had pushed for Britain's 'greatest colony' to be covered with a railway network.[13] This fact, combined with the lucrative contracts secured by railway companies, turned much of the scholarly spotlight on contractual and financial negotiations, at least in relation to the initial decade of railway planning in India.[14]

This does not mean that scholars are oblivious to strategic discussions about railways: in fact, in his study of 'Private Enterprise at Public Risk' Daniel Thorner quotes 'the most extreme statement of the day on the governmental function of railroads.'[15] However, comparatively speaking, analyses of the period before 1857 are dominated by concerns about the political economy of colonialism—Thorner's larger project, after all, is on 'investment in empire.' Even among those who emphasize the presence of strategic interests in the early decades, especially the political import of Dalhousie's 1853 plan for railway expansion, the 1857 Rebellion is seen as the critical moment in strategic planning: Kerr notes how 'the Mutiny reinforced the determination of government to push ahead with trunk line construction,' while Laura Bear

---

[12] Rajit K. Mazumder, *The Indian Army and the Making of Punjab* (Delhi: Permanent Black, 2003), 1; T.A. Heathcoate, *The Indian Army: The Garrison of British Imperial India, 1822–1922* (London: David & Charles, 1974), 155.

[13] Thorner, 'Capital Movement and Transportation,' 389.

[14] The most important is Thorner's *Investment in Empire*. Manu Goswami discusses the political economy of colonial (state) space in *Producing India*, 46–49.

[15] Cameron's minute of 1846 is quoted in Thorner, *Investment in Empire*, 86–87.

describes economist Hyde Clarke's 1857 pamphlet titled *Colonisation, Defence, and Railways in our Indian Empire* as 'the first clear statement of the potential importance of railways to the security of [European] populations in India.'[16]

Focusing on military concerns not only before 1857 but also before Dalhousie's celebrated 1853 minute, this chapter instead highlights the pre-1853 consensus about the strategic role of railways among military men, railway promoters, and the commercial firms encouraging railway construction in India. All argued that railways were *qualitatively* different from other means of transport where military efficiency was concerned; such arguments translated into calculations of how the military savings engendered by railways would offset the financial demands of railway companies that the state was loath to acquiesce to. Given this prehistory, 1857 might be better understood as the event that sloughed off the rhetoric of colonial improvement through which railways had been publicly explicated before that. It was because 1857 made so *public* the strategic core of railways that, after the Rebellion, the imperial government had to actively reintroduce the language of public convenience when discussing railway planning. This shift was especially visible in discussions pertaining to railway stations: even as the state became increasingly preoccupied with making railway stations defensible, it began, on paper, to elevate passenger convenience above an unequivocal commitment to defence. However, defence had not become unimportant. Instead, stressing the public and commercial benefits of making stations secure allowed the state to recover the argument that railways were a technology for public consumption while shifting many of the costs of defensive constructions on to railway companies.

The state's anxiety about railway links and infrastructure generated increasing preventive and punitive legislation against any interference with these. However, this same anxiety, including reliance on collective responsibility, itself created space for people to settle local conflicts and negotiate tense community relationships. Throughout the nineteenth century, 'interference' with railway property—involving acts ranging from people throwing stones at moving trains to removing rails or placing objects upon the

---

[16] Bear, *Lines of the Nation*, 22, 26; also see Kerr, *Building the Railways of the Raj*, 35–37. The Rebellion itself was seen as an important moment of rupture, succeeded by extensive political, administrative, and military reorganization. Mazumder, *Indian Army*, especially 54–58; Peter Duckers, *The British Indian Army, 1860–1914* (Princes Risborough: Shire Publications, 2003); Thomas Metcalf, *Ideologies of the Raj*, Vol. 3:4 of the *New Cambridge History of India* (Cambridge: Cambridge University Press, 1997).

line—were everyday acts through which people tried to draw administrative attention to their immediate needs and complaints as well as to settle local jealousies and conflicts, hoping their individual—often petty—forays would gain the attention of an anxious state. Towards the close of the century, the visibility of railways as military instruments intensified as radical anti-colonial activity began focusing on sabotage, derailment, and robbery. However, even as radical nationalists deployed railway sabotage to challenge imperial might, they relied, much like the state itself did, on the smooth and uninterrupted functioning of railways: train journeys became a staple part of the travel undertaken in the planning and execution of railway sabotage.

Imperial Lines of Control

Given the limited numbers of European troops present and the distances to be traversed across a challenging topography, the logistics of troop mobility and concentration were a constant preoccupation for the imperial state in India. Many had always seen the British element of the army as indispensable, both because of the racial order of command and the belief that these men were fighting for their 'country's empire.'[17] Concerns about numbers, distance, and topography were compounded by the susceptibility of European forces to 'tropical' diseases, the list ranging from sunstroke to malaria and cholera; concerns of health limited where such troops could be stationed, compounding concerns about mobility.[18] Severe cholera outbreaks occurred in the early to mid-1840s, precisely when the strategic import of railways was being discussed. The 1845 epidemic in Karachi afflicted 410 of the 1,091 men in the 86th foot, leaving 238 dead, while the Bombay Fusiliers lost 221 of their 790 men.[19] Given the truism about an army's efficiency being inversely proportionate to the time required to concentrate troops, the distances to be traversed across difficult terrain in a limited marching season (while keeping troops generally

---

[17] Whether directly employed by the EIC or belonging to the British army and temporarily stationed in India. Heathcote, *Indian Army*, 155.

[18] A detailed account was authored by a Royal Navy surgeon, who claimed 'fifteen years of observation and experience, in a vast variety of climates.' James Johnson, *The Influence of Tropical Climates, More Especially the Climate of India, on European Constitutions; the Principal Effects and Diseases Thereby Induced, Their Prevention or Removal, and The Means of Preserving Health in Hot Climates, Rendered Obvious to Europeans of Every Capacity: An Essay* (London: J. Callow, 1815), 16.

[19] Heathcoate, *Indian Army*, 158.

stationed in sanitized locations), made the state especially attuned to the strategic potential of railways in India.

The pre-1853 consensus

This was true well before Dalhousie's celebrated minute of February 1853, which promoted a grid of trunk railways as crucial to increasing military efficiency 'while diminishing the numbers and cost.' The minute has attracted its fair share of attention, Laura Bear identifying it as *the* moment in which railways morphed into 'a grand project of reconstructing the technology of rule in India.'[20] Given Dalhousie's position as governor-general, the minute was both important and influential. However, it was not novel: Dalhousie's plan echoed a decade worth of discussion—and agreement—on the subject.

This pre-1853 consensus included not only military men and government officials but also astute railway promoters and commercial and mercantile firms. Irrespective of whether they themselves were invested in the military importance of railways, they were careful to stress its importance to the colonial state, with whom lay the decision to accept or reject the financial guarantees being demanded by railway companies. Thus, one of the earliest proponents of a scheme for railways in India, Rowland Macdonald Stephenson, ascertained the views of mercantile firms in India *after* he had soused their importance 'in a military point of view.'[21] In his opening letter to the principal mercantile houses in Bengal and the Bengal Chamber of Commerce in August 1844, he mentioned 'several' communications on the strategic value of railways.[22] Likewise, even though commercial firms in Bengal were asked to assess the commercial profitability of proposed links 'between the out ports and the markets of consumption for English manufacture,' they felt the need to confirm how from a 'military point of view there is no question of the advantages that would attend a railroad,' insisting that government would 'of course reap the chief benefit.'[23]

---

[20] Bear, *Lines of the Nation*, 23. Minute by Lord Dalhousie to Court of Directors, 20 April 1853, *PP*. Mf. Reel no. 60, Correspondence regarding Railway Communication in India, NAI (also ICHR, *Railway Construction in India*, Vol. 2, doc. 174).

[21] Later, the founder and managing director of the EIR. George D. Bearce, *British Attitudes towards India: 1784–1858* (London: Oxford University Press, 1961), 217; also ICHR, *Railway Construction in India*, Vol. 1, doc. 12.

[22] R.M. Stephenson to principal mercantile houses and Bengal Chamber of Commerce, 15 August 1844, in IOR.31478 L/PWD/2/43, BL (also ICHR, *Railway Construction*, Vol. 1, doc. 17).

[23] Messrs Colvin, Anislie, Cowie, and Company to R.M. Stephenson, 24 August 1844, in IOR.31478 L/PWD/2/43 (also ICHR, *Railway Construction*, Vol. 1, doc. 18);

Even as commercial firms endorsed the strategic import of railways in general terms, military men expounded its specific advantages.[24] A decade before Dalhousie's minute, Colonel George Warren, the town major of Fort William, detailed how railways were *the* panacea for the specific military constraints that India imposed, enumerating the same list of benefits that the governor-general's minute would contain: how they would transport troops and stores and transmit instructions and intelligence in 'as many hours as at present it requires days, and even weeks, to accomplish;' how this would offset the limitations of a limited European presence and allow troops to be garrisoned at 'healthier stations,' thus saving 'much loss of life from sickness;' how it would mean that stores would not have to be stored in large quantities at the various depots 'and [that] the destruction incidental to the climate, which now obtains, would also be avoided.'[25]

Others explained that railways would significantly increase the army's restricted active season in India. Lieutenant Charles Handfield described how, without railways, it took his detachment over two weeks (from 20 November to 8 January) to cover the distance from Chinsurah (about 30 miles from Calcutta) to Allahabad. Further, he had found it hard to convey troops even on the strategically important Grand Trunk Road during the rainy season when 'parts of the road were broken up' owing to insufficient provision for carrying off water.[26] The disrepair of many roads, including vital military links, in this period seems widespread. Thus, Anand Yang describes how '[i]ts strategic importance notwithstanding' the Grand Trunk Road in colonial Bihar was in poor condition; Nitin Sinha recounts how the New Military Road in the same area had begun to deteriorate by the late 1830s; and Ravi Ahuja has pointed out that in colonial Orissa 'important military roads—not to speak of minor thoroughfares—were rarely kept in

---

Messrs Livingston, Syers, and Company to R. M. Stephenson, 28 August 1844, in IOR.31478 L/PWD/2/43, BL (also ICHR, *Railway Construction*, Vol. 1, doc. 22).

[24] Captain Goodwyn, Garrison Engineer, Civil Architect and Superintendent of Suspension Bridges and Iron Rooping, Reply to R. M. Stephenson, 12 August 1844, in IOR.31478 L/PWD/2/43, BL (also ICHR, *Railway Construction*, Vol. 1, doc. 16). Colonel George Warren, Town Major of Fort William, Reply to R.M. Stephenson, 17 September 1844, in IOR.31478 L/PWD/2/43, BL (also ICHR, *Railway Construction*, Vol. 1, doc. 37).

[25] Colonel George Warren's reply to R.M. Stephenson, 17 September 1844.

[26] Lieutenant Charles Handfield, reply to R.M. Stephenson, 9 September 1844, in IOR.31478 L/PWD/2/43, BL (also ICHR, *Railway Construction*, Vol. 1, doc. 33).

regular repair by the colonial administration but were rather brought into a passable condition when actually required.'[27]

If monsoons posed a problem, so did summer. Major J. P Kennedy pointed out that it was impossible to campaign in summer without 'a fearful expense of life and health to our Troops,' such restrictions limiting the active season to less than six months.[28] He estimated, however, that a line of railway would allow for the 1,446 miles between Calcutta to Peshawar to be covered in 70 to 100 hours. The military implications of this difference were compounded by Kennedy's calculation that ordinary dispersion of troops in India was 'nearly in the Ratio of 1,000 miles compared to 100 miles at home.' The strategic lag imposed by this fact was further exacerbated by the fact of simultaneous conflicts occurring at locations that he estimated to be almost 2,000 miles apart. Thus, Kennedy was adamant that railways had a strategic value in India *much higher* than 'if our consideration had reference to Europe.'[29]

He detailed this difference using the example of the Anglo-Sikh conflict in 1845–46. It took six days to congregate the nearest troops to meet the Sikh army after it had crossed the Sutlej on 15 December 1845; until then the small imperial force at Ferozepore remained exposed. Making Ferozepore defensible, however, meant that the adjacent stations of Ludhiana, Ambala, and Meerut (from where troops were commandeered) were left unprotected. After 'utmost exertions and forced marches,' less than 13,000 men could be congregated in the week between 11 and 18 December. Three days later, the number had increased only to 17,000 men (facing an army of 60,000).[30] Pointing out that such strategic 'peril' represented compulsions intrinsic to the 'very nature of our empire in India,' Kennedy explained that the strategic use of railways in India would increase imperial security while decreasing cost: if it became possible to concentrate a field force of 50,000 or 60,000 men (with stores and provisions) in 20–60 hours instead of the existing mean period of three or four months, then troops could be reduced by as much as one-third without compromising security.

[27] Yang, *Bazaar India*, 34; Sinha, *Communication and Colonialism*, 165–66, Ahuja, *Pathways of Empire*, 161. Further, that 'the extended scope for river transport during the monsoon months could only partly compensate for the impassability of most roads and the inaccessibility of most ports in that season' (152).

[28] Kennedy, Memorandum upon Indian Railways, 14 September 1852.

[29] Ibid.

[30] Ibid.

Though it is a later example, yet Kennedy's calculation is one of the more detailed expositions of how railways would effect such military efficiency as would allow for substantial financial savings, thus offsetting the financial guarantees being demanded by railway companies. While willing to provide free land to railway companies, official opinion was less amenable to the demand—increasingly prominent after 1845—for minimum guaranteed return on capital invested.[31] The Court of Directors and the governor-general's council refused to sanction such a guarantee even for an experimental line, the latter stating clearly that free land was all that 'the Government can afford'[32] Such opposition led some to argue that the financial savings resulting from increased military efficiency would allow government to afford the guarantee; others stressed how the strategic value of railways nullified any concern about the expense of guarantee. Unlike his council, Hardinge had supported the guarantee in 1846, explaining the benefits to the state that would accrue from railways.[33] Like Kennedy would do later, he actualized the value of increased military efficiency, which he pegged at '50,000/- a year on the lowest scale.' The argument gained teeth as railway companies increasingly stressed how the entire project hinged on the issue of guarantee.[34] When the Board of Control continued to oppose the proposal, the East Indian Railway Company launched a public campaign in London, explaining to the Court of Directors how this opposition jeopardized the possibility of connecting Calcutta with

---

[31] R.M. Stephenson to F.J. Halliday, Secretary to the Govt. of Bengal, 15 July 1844, in IOR.31478 L/PWD/2/43, BL (also ICHR, *Railway Construction*, Vol. 1, doc. 12); R.M. Stephenson to Secretary, East India Company, 13 December 1844, in IOR.31478 L/PWD/2/43, BL (also ICHR, *Railway Construction*, Vol. 1, doc. 42).

[32] Court of Directors to Govt. of India, despatch of 7 May 1845, in *PP*. Mf. Reel No. 44, East India, NAI (also ICHR, *Railway Construction*, Vol. 1, doc. 48); Minute by Thomas H. Maddock, President in the Council of Governor-General, 1 May 1846, *PP*, Mf. Reel no. 46, Rlys. in India, Rly Reports from India, 21–22, NAI (also ICHR, *Railway Construction*, Vol. 1, doc. 56); Governor-General of India in Council (T. H. Maddock, President, C.H. Cameron, T. Millett) to Court of Directors, 9 May 1846, in *PP*, Mf. Reel no. 46, Rlys in India, Rly Reports from India, 13, NAI (also ICHR, *Railway Construction*, Vol. 1, doc. 59).

[33] Hardinge's Minute of 28 July 1846, *PP*, Mf. Reel no. 46, Rlys in India, Rly Reports from India, 23–24, NAI (also ICHR, *Railway Construction*, Vol. 1, doc. 61).

[34] George Larpent, Chairman of the East Indian Railway Company, to Court of Directors, 3 February 1847, IOLR.31478 L/PWD/2/43 (also ICHR, *Railway Construction*, Vol. 1, doc. 70). For a detailed discussion of the financial negotiations between 1846 and 1849, see Thorner, *Investment in Empire*, Chapter 6.

the North-West Provinces.[35] By August 1847, the Court had agreed not only to a 5 per cent return (instead of the 4 per cent requested originally), but also to the demand that this guarantee be extended to 25 years, instead of the original 15.[36] The agreement was nearly scuttled in 1848 by a continental revolution, economic distress, and questions about whether the promised guarantee pertained to interest or dividend; however, it was saved by some last minute lobbying in London.[37]

By 1849, the contracts were in place but the 'struggle for guarantee' had turned cost into the foremost issue pertaining to railway construction. It was in this context that one can read Kennedy's minute: in 1851–52, he was trying to explain how a governmental guarantee remained viable, even 'under the worst aspect that that risk can assume.'[38] To make his case, he calculated that railways would allow for reductions in at least three-fourths of the military expenditure, or on over 69 of 93 million company's rupees spent in 1848–49. In Bengal, increased efficiency would allow the usual annual expense of 49 million to be reduced to 37 million, a saving of approximately 25 per cent. This saved 12 million Company's rupees per annum or £1,248,384 (taking the rupee at 2s). If invested well, this saving would yield enough to fund railway construction in Bengal on government account or else offer a guarantee 'without increasing the public charges of Bengal' even if the government was required to pay the entire guaranteed interest annually to railway companies. Major W.E. Baker, the consulting engineer for railways, agreed that the power of concentrating troops by railway would compensate for the numerical strength of the army 'in a ratio perhaps as high as that assumed by Major Kennedy.'[39] He cautioned against

[35] Thorner, *Investment in Empire*, 120–25; Larpent, Chairman of the East Indian Railway Company, to Court of Directors, 3 February 1847.

[36] Directors of East Indian Railway Company, to Court of Directors, 18 August 1847, IOLR.31478 L/PWD/ 2/43 (also ICHR, *Railway Construction*, Vol. 1, doc. 84). The same terms were offered to the GIPR on 29 September 1847. Larpent, Chairman, East Indian Railway Company, to Court of Directors, 3 February 1847.

[37] Thorner, *Investment in Empire*, 129–60.

[38] Kennedy, Memorandum upon Indian Railways, 14 September 1852. The import of Kennedy's detailed analysis was heightened by the correspondence between military and railway men: Kennedy also served as the consulting engineer to the Government of India for railway construction, later becoming consulting engineer to the Bombay and Baroda Railway Company.

[39] Memorandum from Major W.E. Baker, Consulting Engineer, Government of India (Railways) to Court of Directors, 1 February 1853, *PP*. Mf. Reel no. 60, Correspondence Regarding Railway Communication in India, 138–51, NAI. Also in ICHR, *Railway Construction in India*, Vol. 2 (New Delhi: ICHR, 1999), doc. 169.

assuming that savings on military establishments would single-handedly provide enough to fund railway communication, given that railways would be 'in the hands of the people' and 'efficient only by their sufferance.' However, he believed that the strategic advantages made it unnecessary to calculate or justify the military potential of railways in pecuniary terms.

The routes

The two experimental lines sanctioned after contracts had been signed in 1849 were explicitly commercial: the first ran from Howrah towards Raniganj and the Burdwan coal fields, and the second east from Bombay to Kalyan, towards the Deccan cotton fields.[40] However, this should not obscure the importance given to strategically valuable lines when specific routes were being planned. In this context, Dalhousie's 1853 minute becomes valuable not merely for its discussion of 'trunk' railways but also for its vigorous commitment to strategic rather than commercial routes even *after* government had committed itself to a guaranteed return on railway investment.

Two proposed routes demonstrate this point. Considered highest in 'importance and value' was the railway from Calcutta to the North-West Provinces, which Dalhousie viewed '*first*, with especial reference to the powers of the state [emphasis added].' Intended to link 'every important military station from Calcutta to the Sutlej,' this would connect all military depots with the arsenal in Fort William, so as to 'infinitely' diminish risks entailed in extending the frontier '1,500 miles from the capital.' Dalhousie was equally sensible to its value in effecting speedy concentration of men and materials, whether the attack came from Kabul or Nepal, two prominent eventualities identified by him. Further, it would enhance the 'consciousness of our [imperial] power,' thus deterring any 'combined attacks' planned by native states.

In taking the line through the Ganges valley, Dalhousie had argued that the strategically viable option coincided with 'the interests of trade.' However, when the two did not coincide so fortuitously, as when examining the route westward from Agra, he argued that the military advantages of the line on the right bank of the Jumna gave it 'such preponderance over the line by the Doab as to outweigh the somewhat superior commercial promise of the latter.'[41]

---

[40] Kerr, *Building the Railways of the Raj*, 27.
[41] Dalhousie, quoted and endorsed in Home Govt., Financial (Railway) Dept., Railway Letters from the Home Govt., 17 June 1856, Despatch no. 19 of 1856, Register of Letters, 1852–61, NAI.

Ironically, the commercially viable line was built eventually, but for military reasons. In 1858, the governor-general and PWD explained how the earlier decision in favour of a line crossing the Yamuna at Agra —'in the face of the admitted fact that the Doab line was of superior Commercial promise'—had been based on pre-1857 military calculations, including the 'capital importance' of Delhi as a point on the main line. However, the post-Rebellion need to marginalize Delhi as a political and military arsenal was effected by selecting the Doab route.[42]

Similarly, when linking Agra and Bombay, two routes were suggested: the first, seen to be superior 'on political grounds' ran from Surat to Agra by way of Baroda and Neemuch, while the more commercially advantageous one would run 'up the valley of the Nerbudda' to join the Bengal railway somewhere near Mirzapur. Dalhousie believed that both were necessary, yet if only one was possible then he favoured the Baroda to Neemuch link. Linking Agra and Bombay would annihilate that vast distance that deprived the two armies of 'the advantages of mutual co-operation' and obviate the risks borne by relief regiments that either landed at Calcutta and encountered India's weather 'where its character is worst' or else faced the seasonal limitations on landing at Karachi.

Dalhousie was certainly keen to emphasize how commercially viable many of these strategic lines were: he stressed how the Ganges line ran 'in great measure along or in close contact with the main lines of existing traffic & trade throughout the Presidency.'[43] However, commercial interests had the edge over strategic ones in lines internal to the presidencies. Thus, when selecting which route in Bombay Presidency would help make the previously sanctioned Callian line profitable, Dalhousie finally supported the one in the direction of Khandesh rather than Poona, though the latter had 'considerable political value.' (He did suggest that both be undertaken simultaneously.) However, he refused his support for the link between Calcutta and Diamond Harbour even when the Court emphasized it as one that would 'materially

---

[42] Note by Offg. Secretary (PWD: Railway), Calcutta, 21 December 1857, in PWD: Railway A, 19 July 1858, no. 34, NAI. Minute by the Governor General, Allahabad, 14 July 1858, in PWD: Railway A, 19 July 1858, no. 34, NAI.

[43] The public would be saved the 'the heavy tax' that carriage of troops through the area necessitated. Dalhousie being quoted in Home Government, Financial (Railway) Dept., Railway Letters from the Home Govt., 17 June 1856, Despatch no. 19 of 1856.

promote' shipping and mercantile interests. Finding that it offered 'no benefit whatsoever' to government, he suggested that shipping and mercantile interests fund the line themselves.

Going public

Given this official prehistory, 1857 did not as much demonstrate the strategic value of railways as make it *public*, removing the rhetorical skin of 'improvement' through which railways had been publicly explicated. During the Rebellion, even the limited 274 miles of railway open—65 in Madras, 88 in Bombay, and 121 in Bengal—was deployed in imperial defence, despite not even being in areas at the heart of the conflict.[44] Some letters to the editor publicly suggested that railways rather than steamers should be used to hasten the deployment of troops arriving from England; others emphasized the necessity of protecting railway lines, some even suggesting that guns mounted on temporary carriages be placed in large railway trucks to be placed at stations or at appropriate places on the line.[45] The state's military appropriation of railways was further highlighted when, in May 1858, railway staff at Calcutta were placed in custody because they grew tired of holding up a train for some Madras Fusiliers who were running late.[46] The urgent need for more railways was emphasized in public statements about the 'all-important' ability to transport 'compact and highly trained bodies of European troops from one point of India,' and the dangers of allowing a colonized population to believe that 'on any point, whether ten miles or at 1,000 miles away, the authority of England can be overthrown for a day by Asiatics of any race or creed.'[47]

The military instrumentality of railways also became explicit in suggestions that the 'expensive English system' be replaced with single lines 'through the jungle and the wilderness' that required 'one-tenth' of the time and expense

---

[44] Estimated for year ending 30 June. *Statistical Abstract from 1840 to 1865*, 58.

[45] From Behrampore they would march to Bogwangolah, or the nearest *ghat* on the Ganges, at which place the steamers should await to take them to the Upper Provinces. Alpha, Letter to the Editor, *The Englishman and Military Chronicle*, 21 August 1857; *The Friend of India*, 10 September 1857.

[46] 'The Progress of the Revolt,' *The Friend of India*, 28 May 1858. Procedurally prescribed in G.O.G.G. no. 1209 dated 23 May 1855: see Letter no. 52 of 30 October 1857, Railway General Letters: From Public Works Dept. (Railway) to Court of Directors, 1852–61, NAI.

[47] *Times* (London), 27 June 1857; *The Englishman and Military Chronicle*, 30 June 1857.

and would allow imperial control to be secured with a relatively small army.[48] Such public anxiety encouraged speculative ventures, like the proposal for a 'Portable Railway' by William H. Villers Sankey, who described his model as the 'speediest and surest method' of re-establishing British rule.[49] Since such a railway comprised nothing more than a series of overlapping timber frames placed continuously end to end, so work could begin immediately wherever wood could be obtained.[50] The fate of Sankey's proposal remains unclear but it demonstrates how public the state's strategic reliance on railways had become, an anxiety that entrepreneurs like him tried to tap into—as Sankey explained, the portable railroad would help his straitened financial circumstances.[51]

This strategic appropriation was recognized by a colonized population: from as early as July 1857 there were incidents of rails being 'torn up by the mutineers' to prevent conveyance of troops and supplies between Allahabad and Kanpur.[52] Those who tried to repair this track faced resistance, first from a group of 150 men and then a second group of 50, in which 'many were recognised to be sepoys of the late 6th N. I.' Fourteen were hanged for the crime. While not overwhelming in 1857–58, these attacks became part of a pattern of responses, as attested to by 'A Constant Railway Traveller' who documented such attempts, while demanding stringent vigilance by railway authorities.[53]

---

[48] *Times* (London), 27 June 1857.

[49] W.H.V. Sankey to Lord Shelburne (from Turin), 21 October 1857, enclosure to Commissioners for the Affairs of India to James C. Melville, letter no. 1049 of 9 November 1857, Railway Home Correspondence: IOR.31478 L/PWD/2/59, BL; W.H.V. Sankey to Board of Commissioners for Affairs of India (from Turin), n.d., Enclosure to Letter from Commissioners for Affairs of India to J.C. Melville, no. 1139[?], 9 December 1857, in Railways: Home Correspondence, IOR.31478 L/PWD/2/59 (1857), BL.

[50] After the line was determined, a small layer of ballast was to be laid along the whole line and frames laid down, e i t h e r staked to the piles or firmly bedded in the ballast, after which bands of iron were to be fastened vertically to the inside of the frames with bolts.

[51] The Earl of Clarendon forwarded it to the Commissioners for the Affairs of India, who in turn sent it to the Court of Directors. Lord Shelburne, Earl of Clarendon, to Commissioners for the Affairs of India, 4 November 1857; Foreign Office to Sir George Clerk, 17 November 1857; Commissioners for the Affairs of India to J.C. Melville, 9 December 1857, in Railways: Home Correspondence, IOR.31478 L/PWD/2/59 (1857), BL; Despatch no. 18, 18 May 1858; Railway Letters from the Home Government: 1852–61: Financial (Railway) Dept.: (Home) PWD: Railway, NAI.

[52] *The Friend of India*, 16 July 1857.

[53] A Constant Railway Traveller (Calcutta), Letter to the Editor, 27 August 1857, in *The Englishman and Military Chronicle*, 31 August 1857.

Rhetoric and reality

As Ian Kerr has noted, 1857 created an almost obsessive focus with the protection of railway lines.[54] It also generated discussion about protecting railway infrastructure: rolling stock, works, bridges, tunnels, and stations. Officials stressed that tracks could be rebuilt but if rolling stock was rendered unfit for traffic or engineering stocks were destroyed, then the railway became 'completely useless.'[55] Protecting railway stations became important not only because these were repositories for such property but also because they were increasingly seen as spaces of refuge for Europeans in India.[56] As such, local governments were instructed to assess how these could be made defensible and capable of holding off 'the attack of any Native force.'[57]

It was obvious that each station required individual attention. Thus, one situated within musket shot of the walls and houses of Delhi required more extensive defensive works than another at Allahabad, where an enemy approach could be seen from a distance.[58] Nevertheless, general defensive aspects were invoked, the most prominent including suggestions to build elevated water tanks or towers, while ensuring that these were secure from being occupied by any attacking party. It was also suggested that stations could be surrounded with a wall and a ditch, compelling assailants to approach by one of the regular entrances 'all of which should be commanded from some point of control.'[59] C.B. Thornhill of the 4th Division was in favour of constructing Martello towers at large stations, one at each end of the main line of station buildings and alongside station wells, being armed with two iron 12 pounders, 25 Enfield rifles, a 'suitable' supply of ammunition, a guard of European infantry, and some artillery men.[60] Captain J.F. Glover, executive engineer at Nainital,

---

[54] Kerr, *Building the Railways of the Raj*, 35–37.

[55] Secretary, Govt. of India (PWD), 6 December 1864.

[56] Bear, *Lines of the Nation*.

[57] Referred to in C.B. Thornhill, Offg. Commissioner, 4th Division, to Offg. Secretary to Govt. of NWP, 14 March 1859, NWP Prog., PWD (Railway), August 1859, nos. 6–11, IOR.P/237/26, BL.

[58] Lt-Col. A. Cunningham, Chief Engineer, NWP, to G.E.W. Couper, Secretary, Govt. of NWP (Allahabad), 7 June 1859, North Western Provinces Prog., PWD (Railway), August 1859, nos. 6–11, IOR.P/237/26, BL; C.B. Thornhill, to Secretary to Govt. of NWP, 14 March 1859, North Western Provinces Prog., PWD (Railway), August 1859, nos 6–11, IOR.P/237/26, BL.

[59] C.B. Thornhill to Offg. Secretary to Govt. of NWP, 14 March 1859.

[60] Like on England's south coast in the Napoleonic era, intended to withstand sieges. Sheila Sutcliffe, *Martello Towers* (Fairleigh: Dickinson, 1973), 15–16. For smaller

suggested that four to six towers placed at commanding positions were required at large stations, with each tower being armed by one or two pieces of heavy ordnance.[61] Fortified with a ditch with a masonry escarp, these would make the station defensible irrespective of whether it was suddenly attacked by a body of armed men or by 'incendiaries or single men' intent on damage. Station buildings were to be arranged so as to mutually flank one another and railway staff were to be trained to work guns and muskets. Such heavily fortified and armed stations were to be located near a cantonment of European troops and away from 'a Native City.'

In the midst of such discussions, the governor-general stipulated—rather surprisingly—that railway stations should be designed 'primarily for the convenience of traffic;' he suggested that buildings could be arranged so as to be 'mutually protective' as far as this coincided with the convenience of traffic.[62] Given the heightened military anxiety of the moment, this statement arouses curiosity. Laura Bear has suggested that it represents the competing claims of rendering the railway station simultaneously a 'military command and neutral public sphere.'[63] While railway stations were certainly growing into public spheres, yet in 1858 there were only 332 miles of track open to traffic.[64] Thus, at this point, 'public convenience' seems more of a discursive tool designed to make railway companies bear the costs of defensive construction and modifications rather than evidence of the state's commitment to an expanding public sphere.

The expense of railway stations had been a concern even before 1857: commenting on the newly signed deeds of 1849, the Court had warned the Government of India about the 'large sums of money' that railway companies in Europe had 'most unnecessarily and extravagantly expended

---

stations, he suggested a single tower two stories high, adjoining the station well, with the lower storey serving as a guard house and weapons store. Lt-Col. A. Cunnigham to G.E.W. Couper, Secretary, Govt. of NWP (Allahabad), 7 June 1859.

[61] Abstract of Opinion on the Proposal for Making Railway Stations in India Defensible, North Western Provinces Prog., PWD (Railway), August 1859, nos. 6–11, IOR.P/237/26, BL.

[62] Extract from Prog. of Governor-General, in R. Baird Smith, Offg. Secretary, Govt. of India (PWD) to Govt. of Bengal, 7 October 1859, in Bengal Prog (PWD: Railway), 27 October 1859, no. 101, IOR.P/16/36 (July–October 1859), BL.

[63] Bear, *Lines of the Nation*, 38.

[64] *Statistical Abstract from 1840 to 1865*, 58.

in ornamental works, especially those connected with the stations and offices.'[65] Pronouncements about passenger convenience notwithstanding, defence remained crucial: the governor-general suggested using 'such simple and inexpensive facilities for defence as will at once suggest themselves to any intelligent Engineer, Civil or Military.'[66] The fact that stations were assessed and designed on a case-by-case basis allowed for much practical latitude in emphasizing defence. Thus, in a January 1860 discussion on the railway through Delhi, the argument that stopping thoroughfares from the King's Garden towards the Kashmere Gate was 'somewhat inconvenient to the public' was shot down; it was countered by emphasizing how this would 'greatly facilitate the defence of the European portion of the city against attack from the Native side.'[67] While the proposal to locate Lucknow station (on the Kanpur and Lucknow Railway) at or near the Charbagh had found favour with the governor-general, the local government was instructed to pay attention

> …to the importance of placing it where it shall be within command of troops, and of arranging the buildings in as compact a manner as is practicable, and having regard to the eventual possibility of forming a defensive position in connexion with them, by the help of a few towers or other strong points to be supplemented by earthen parapets, &c., as occasion may hereafter require.[68]

While reiterating that it did not desire to prejudge any of these issues, the Government of India stressed how convenient it would be for the commissariat depot to be placed in the station, thus allowing all buildings to be brought within a single set of defences. It suggested that the possible advantage of

---

[65] Despatch from Court of Directors to Govt. of India, 14 November 1849, *PP*: Mf. Reel no. 54, Rly. Communication in India, 1–8, NAI. (Also ICHR, *Railway Construction*, Vol. 1, doc. 122, quote on I-406). See also Robbins, *The Railway Age*, 50–52. Richards and MacKenzie discuss the costs of 'imposing terminal[s]' in other European cities: reportedly £690,000 on Dresden station, £1,300,000 on Cologne station, and £1,700,000 on Frankfurt station: *The Railway Station*, 23–24.

[66] Extract from Prog. of Governor-General, in R. Baird Smith, Offg. Secretary, Govt. of India (PWD) to Govt. of Bengal, 7 October 1859.

[67] Major Greathede, Secretary, Govt. of NWP (Railway Dept.), to Lt.-Col H. Yule, Secretary, Govt. of India (PWD), n.d., United Provinces Prog. (NWP: Railway Dept.) 16 January 1860, no. 55, IOR.P/237/28 (January–March 1860), BL.

[68] Colonel R. Strachey, Secretary, Govt. of India (PWD), to Chief Commissioner of Oudh, 30 March 1864, PWD: Railway A, March 1864, nos. 33–34, NAI.

bringing the military stores into the neighbourhood of the station should be considered when fixing the site for railway stations; further that in the case of stations on newly projected lines at places where troops were cantoned, arrangements should be made 'as far as is practicable with regard to the protection of the Railway Stations,' that plans should be submitted for the sanction of the Government of India before work could begin, and that a commanding officer and military engineer be included on the planning committee.[69] These instructions were sent to local governments as a guide 'in dealing with stations on new lines of railway.'[70]

Local governments that were not particularly amenable to these suggestions were nudged to reconsider. Thus, when the Bombay government emphasized limitations engendered by the fact that all railway stations had already been fixed in the presidency, they were instructed to revisit the subject. They were advised that it was still possible to 'make the main stations sites defensible at a small expense' and given specific suggestions about loop-holed enclosure walls, with strong gates so arranged as to be readily shut, and small towers at the angles to flank the enclosures. This would 'enable the Railway authorities to secure much valuable property, and save many lives in the events of a tumult or sudden insurrection.'[71] The emphasis on securing 'valuable property' suggested the government's vested interests: as long as 'public convenience' was specified as primary and defence as secondary, the expenditure would be viewed as legitimately belonging to the railway company.

This conclusion is borne out in a terse exchange between London and Calcutta. As Secretary of State, Charles Wood had endorsed a government circular suggesting that sites for stations should be selected and station buildings arranged in a manner that 'might assist in making the station defensible in case such a measure became necessary.'[72] However, he had supported this

---

[69] In forwarding this communication to the Government of Bombay, 'European troops' was specified instead of just 'troops.' PWD: Railway A, March 1864, nos. 33–34, NAI.

[70] Strachey to Chief Commissioner of Oudh, 30 March 1864.

[71] Lieut. Col. H. Rivers, Secretary, Govt. of Bombay (Railway Dept.), to Secretary, Govt. of India (PWD), 21 May 1864, PWD: Railway A, June 1864, nos. 127–28, NAI; Colonel R. Strachey, Secretary, Govt. of India (PWD), to Secretary, Govt. of Bombay (Railway Dept.), 29 June 1864, PWD: Railway A, June 1864, nos. 127–28, NAI.

[72] Secretary of State to Govt. of India, 22 February 1866, PWD: Railway: A, 18 June 1866, nos. 109–11, NAI.

suggestion based on the impression that 'no material extra expense would be imposed upon the Railway Companies thereby' and was unhappy to learn not only that the government was contemplating 'extra works' but also that 'under the 4th Clause of their Contracts, the cost of such works ought to devolve on [railway] Companies.' This, the Secretary of State disagreed with. He insisted that 'operations of an armed force' lay beyond the scope of contracts and that government could only ask railway companies to improve station defences *if* the new arrangements or alterations did not involve any material expense.[73] In this situation, it could only be astute for government to adopt a formula in which the defensive capability of stations was described not only as necessary for railway companies but also a concern that be integrated with the 'primary' needs of public convenience. This allowed the Government of India to inform local governments that while defensive works had to be limited to what railway companies were 'willing to do,' yet they believed that it was clearly in the interests of railway companies that 'the chief stations should be capable of defence in the manner already explained.'[74]

Anxiety, Protest, Crime, and Sabotage

It was precisely such anxiety about securing railway infrastructure that created space for people to gain the state's attention by committing 'crimes' against railways. Even though some incidents during 1857–58 had demonstrated railway sabotage as an explicitly political activity, it would be some decades before these would become a systematic component of anti-colonial nationalism. Throughout the nineteenth century, however, everyday 'interference' with railway property preoccupied an anxious state. While many such acts were specifically geared to draw administrative attention to immediate grievances or to settle local conflicts, the colonial state read them through the lens of criminal sabotage. As Lisa Mitchell has argued when discussing the pulling of train alarms as a political practice through which ordinary people sought to communicate with the state, the state itself continued to view society 'through the prism of public order,' designating protest and resistance as

---

[73] Ibid.

[74] Circular 9R, of 1866: Lieut-Col. C.H. Dickens, Secretary, Govt. of India (PWD), to local govts., 18 June 1866, and Govt. of India to Secretary of State, n.d., PWD: Railway A, both in PWD: Railway: A, 18 June 1866, nos. 109–11, NAI; Secretary, Govt. of India (PWD) to Secretary, Govt. of Bombay (Military Dept.), 6 December 1864, PWD (Railway), United Provinces (NWP) Prog., IOR.P/217/38, BL.

criminal activities.[75] Arguably, this was not peculiar to colonial India for states generally remained vigilant about railways, both as forms of property and as means of communication. Thus, the 1861 Malicious Damage Act in England prescribed fairly severe penalties (including penal servitude) for damage to railway property, its punitive power combined with the Offences Against Persons Act which punished any action that endangered any person on railway property.[76] However, even as 'malicious damage' to railways was criminalized in many places, its political implications were different in a colonial setting where interference with railways was designated as treasonous.

It was thus that in 1895 the Commander-in-Chief, George White, suggested the death penalty as the only adequate response to 'train-wrecking,' irrespective of whether the perpetrators 'compassed the death of any person or not.'[77] In fact, the Indian Railways Act (of 1890, based substantially on an 1879 Act) already prescribed penalties for any attempt to wreck a train, including transportation for life or imprisonment for 10 years.[78] Section 126 prescribed such penalties not only for a slew of specific actions—attempts to remove rails and sleepers, tamper with any signal or light, throw objects across any railway line, or turn, lock, or divert any points or machinery—but also more generally for *anything* that 'does or causes to be done or attempts to do any other act or thing in relation to any railway.' Sections 127 and 128 separately penalized 'malicious' attempts to hurt anyone travelling by railway or endanger their safety by 'wilful act or omission.' However, this seemed inadequate to White, who also suggested that the death penalty be in effect at all times (though he was willing to accept that, in practice, it would be rendered effective only during periods of 'large concentration of troops'). As the matter went up for discussion in the

---

[75] Mitchell, 'To Stop Train, Pull Chain,' 457. Speaking to a similar distinction, Sandra Frietag discusses the anxiety generated among colonial officials about 'events that had been organized over large distances, involving large numbers of participants' that made it difficult or impossible for them 'to maintain the state's ultimate authority to maintain order.' See her 'Collective Crime and Authority in North India,' in Anand Yang, ed., *Crime and Criminality in British India* (Tuczon: University of Arizona Press, 1985), especially 140–41.

[76] Jack Simmons, 'Malicious Damage,' in Simmons and Biddle, *British Railway History*, 305–6.

[77] Military Dept. Notes, 29 June 1895 and 1 July 1895, apropos letter from Quartermaster General in India, 26 June 1895, in Home: Judicial, May 1896, nos. 187–90, NAI.

[78] Trevor, *Law Relating to Railways*, 300–1; Bell, *Railway Policy in India*, appendix B.

public works' and home departments, the military department emphasized the dangers that would accrue from any 'dislocation' of the railway system.[79] Some in the PWD pointed out the futility of escalating the punishment, arguing that this would make it more difficult to secure convictions.[80] This seeming equivocation was quashed as the military department reiterated how train-wrecking jeopardized the empire's security.[81]

1850s–90s: deploying the anxiety of the state?

Practices classified under the category of 'train-wrecking' were not new to the 1890s when this discussion proliferated. In discussions of the Santal rebellion, railway infrastructure was 'among the very first and most frequently destroyed objects' mentioned in the reports.[82] Describing the term 'train-wrecking' itself as one of 'official invention,' Dipesh Chakrabarty saw it as encompassing a host of 'crimes:' from the 'childish mischief' of a youngster 'pelting a single stone at a running railway engine' to more deliberate and malicious attempts either 'by people unconnected with railways' or—most important to him—attempts by railway servants 'usually of the very low rank.'[83] Looking at the early decades, Chakrabarty thus identifies a case of damage linked with 'social tensions'—people in Bhagalpur in 1866 (a famine year) trying to derail trains to protest the high cost of food that they 'attribute[d] to the exportation of grain from the District.'[84] Most frequently, however, he sees it being used by 'low-rank railway coolies, gangmen, and other menials,' offering two examples from 1875 and 1876, the latter a more explicit and planned instance, possibly linked with 'three public works *mistrys* who had been lately discharged.'[85]

---

[79] Military Dept. Notes, 4 July 1895, in Home: Judicial, May 1896, nos. 187–90, NAI.

[80] PWD notes by A.C. Trevor and W.S.S Bissett, 10 July 1895, Home: Judicial, May 1896, nos. 187–90, NAI.

[81] Military Dept notes by P.J. Maitland, 3 August 1895, Home: Judicial, May 1896, nos. 187–90, NAI.

[82] Ranajit Guha's *Elementary Aspects of Peasant Insurgency* (1983, 142–43), quoted in Mitchell, 'To Stop Train, Pull Chain,' 477–78.

[83] Dipesh Chakrabarty, 'Early Railwaymen in India: "Dacoity" and "Train-Wrecking" (c. 1860–1900),' in *Essays in Honour of Professor S.C. Sarkar* (Delhi: People's Publishing House, 1976), 529–31.

[84] Ibid., 530.

[85] Ibid., 531–33.

In that it was used to ventilate grievances, usually immediate ones, Chakrabarty identifies such incidents as having 'protest value' without being a 'clear-cut protest-form' when examined from the point of view of concerted industrial action.[86] Relevant here would be Ian Kerr's argument about how segments of the railway workforce used collective action during the nineteenth century to protest arrears and reductions in wages, demand higher wages, dispute supervisory practices, and complain about working conditions.[87] Even though he sees the last decade of the nineteenth century as the period 'when the pace of protest quickened and Indian railwaymen became extensively involved in labour protests,' one of the incidents that he describes is in fact from 1859, among those working on the Bhore Ghat incline. While the attack there was on Europeans and not on railway infrastructure, which was still under construction, the workers did exploit 'the fear of delays in the completion of a vital segment of the growing railway network.'[88]

Whether or not they fitted under the rubric of working-class protest or collective action, such practices demonstrate how people, in their everyday lives, were able to exploit the state's anxiety about railways to draw attention to their immediate grievances. The list of people using this method—from Jammon Seth, a discharged gateman from northern Bengal, the various permanent-way men identified by the director-general of railways, or the dismissed gangmen who were identified by the Bombay government—shows how low-level employees, often with access to tools, could use railway infrastructure to make visible their immediate needs and complaints, as well as to negotiate jealousies and vendettas, relying on the state to come down with a heavy hand on those seen as responsible for such damage.[89]

By the mid-1890s, train-wrecking had proliferated enough to call for large, formal assessments of numbers and motives. In one such assessment, figures secured from 15 railway companies led to 91 incidents being classified as 'train-wrecking' in just a three-year period between 1892 and 1895.[90] Most of the interference involved people placing 'obstructions' on the line, ranging from rails, trollies, wooden sleepers, and beams to stone ballast, coping stones, boulders, bricks, gate wings, and chairs, as well as other objects like sleepers, fish-plates, stones, fencing posts, logs of wood, tree branches, and telegraph

---

[86] Ibid., 534–35.

[87] Kerr, 'Working Class Protest in 19th Century India,' quote on 35.

[88] Ibid., 35–37.

[89] The examples are cited in Chakrabarty, 'Early Railwaymen,' 534–35.

[90] Statement Showing Cases of Train-wrecking on Indian railways, K.W. no. III, Home: Judicial, May 1896, nos. 187–90, NAI.

poles. In rare instances, iron washers were jammed between rail joints, timber was placed in an upright position between rails, fish bolts and keys were removed from the rails, or the rail itself was removed from the track.

While most of the offenders remained unknown, yet in about one-fourth of cases, the motive was listed as 'mischief,' 'maliciousness,' or 'wilfulness.' In some cases where offenders were known, the damage was being used to settle local scores among railway employees. In two of the three cases on the Rajputana–Malwa railway where the motive had been ascertained, the sabotage was attributed to railway employees, one hoping to 'bring his mucaddam or gangmen into trouble,' and the other to 'get neighbouring villagers into trouble.'[91] Their actions involved rails being placed across the line: two rails were placed at mile 4-12 between Palan and Delhi on 3 January 1893, a railway employee placed an iron rail at mile 4-4 across the line between Agra Cantonment and Bichpur on 12 February 1895, and another placed a rail at mile 604/10=11 between Mursan and Raya on 25 April 1895. In the last case, the three accused were sentenced to transportation for life. The perpetrators of such 'mischief' relied on the state's anxiety about railway links, hoping to bring down heavy punishment on those who would be held responsible eventually. Perhaps recognizing the link, some officers challenged White's idea about introducing the death penalty by arguing that it would only draw attention to railways as a target: 'suggest[ing] to those disposed to injure us more weak points than it could protect.'[92]

White's suggestions, however, were part of a larger push for systematic military protection of railways and coincided with the formation of a Railway Defence Committee. This assessed the comparative strategic importance of various lines in India, discussed how armoured patrol trains could be used to protect railways, and planned the permanent defence of over a thousand railway bridges and tunnels, 'the destruction of any one of which would involve a long interruption of the traffic on the line on which it is situated.'[93] Railway lines, or sections within them, were classified based on their strategic import, including whether alternative routes existed or not, as well as the length

---

[91] Statement Showing Cases of Train-wrecking on Indian Railways.

[92] PWD notes by A.C. Trevor and W.S.S Bissett, 10 July 1895; Home Dept. notes by C.H.A. Hill, 16 August 1895 and Home Dept. notes by A. Mackenzie, 18 August 1895, both in Home: Judicial, May 1896, nos. 187–90, NAI.

[93] Report of the Railway Defence Committee, 1899, enclosure to Military Dept. memorandum, 20 March 1901, in PWD: RT: A, April 1901, no. 9, India Prog., IOR.P/6148, BL.

of detour involved; crucial lines in which mobilization might require the simultaneous use of two alternative routes were classified as class I in terms of imperial strategic value (Table 6.1).[94]

Table 6.1. Classification of Strategic Railways

	Railway	*Section*
Class I	North-Western	Umballa to Pershawar
		Lahore to Chamman
		Ruk to Karachi
		Golra to Khushalgarh
		Sialkot to Wazirabad
Class II	Oudh and Rohilkund	Saharanpore to Moghal Serai
	Southern Punjab	Delhi to Samasata
	North Western	Raewind (via Ferozepore and Bhatinda) to Rajpura
	East Indian	Umballa to Moghal Serai
Class III	Indian Midland	Itarsi to Tundla
	North-Western	Sind-Sagar and Mrai Attock branches
	Great Indian Peninsular	Bombay to Itarsi
Class IV	Bombay, Baroda, and Central Indian with Rajputana Malwa	Bombay to Bhatinda, Delhi, and Agra, Marwar to Kotri
	Great Indian Peninsular	Itarsi to Allahabad
		Bombay to Raichur
	East Indian	Moghal Serai to Calcutta
	Madras	Raichur to Madras
	Nizam's	Hyderabad to Wadi
Class V	Southern Mahratta	Poona, Hubli, Guntakal, Bangalore
	Bengal–Nagpur and Great Indian Peninsular	Calcutta to Bhusawal
	Madras	Madras to Calicut
	East Coast	
Class VI	Bengal and North-Western	Cawnpore to Parbatipore (with loops)
	Eastern Bengal State	Calcutta to Darjeeling
	Burma	
	North-Western	Wazirabad to Khanewal, Branches: Jhansi to Cawnpore, Bhilaspur to Khatni, Khatni to Bina

Source: Tabulated from information in Report of the Railway Defence Committee, 1899, enclosure to Military Dept. Memorandum, 20 March 1901, in PWD: RT: A, April 1901, no. 9, India Prog., IOR.P/6148, BL.

---

[94] Ibid.

By 1902 the colonial state was also armed with the Indian Railways (Emergency) and the Indian Railways Property Protection Acts.[95] The first ensured that through a notification in the *Gazette*, the governor-general could take over direct government control over all railways in India, 'together with the plant and staff,' including railways owned by private companies. In notified areas, ordinary law would be suspended for purposes of protecting railway property and special officers would mediate between railway administrations and military authorities, informing railways about mobilization orders and timetables and commandeering necessary engine power and staff.

In its reliance on collective responsibility as a general strategy to secure railway property, the Railways Property Protection Acts made railway 'sabotage' an everyday reality for many, including those who may not have actually taken part in any such acts. According to the Act, subsequent to a public notification by the district collector, the area's inhabitants became 'jointly and severally responsible' for the security of any and all railway property. They were to be held accountable for any damage unless they could specifically prove that they had exercised 'reasonable care and diligence' in actively protecting such property.[96] Liability would not be confined to those villages through which the line ran, but would extend to all those in the area that the district magistrate thought necessary, a requirement explained as being necessary to prevent a 'strong troublesome village' removed from the line from toying with sabotage.[97] District magistrates could also deploy the Code of Criminal

---

[95] Military Dept. memorandum, 18 January 1901 and Order in Council (199/1L), 18 January 1901, in PWD: RT: A, January 1901, no. 119, India Prog., IOR.P/6148, BL; Govt. of India (Military Dept.) to George Hamilton, Secretary of State, 7 March 1901, encl. to Military Dept. memorandum, 20 March 1901; Secretary of State to Govt. of India, 19 December 1902, RT: A, February 1903, no. 18 (confidential), India Prog., IOR.P/6611, BL; and RT: A, September 1905, nos. 78–79, India Prog., IOR.P/7087, BL.

[96] Military Dept. memorandum, 18 January 1901. It drew upon suggestions made earlier in the North-Western Provinces and Oudh as well as in Delhi division. Chief Secretary, Govt. of NWP and Oudh, to Secretary, Govt. of India (Home Dept.), 21 August 1897 and Commissioner & Superintendent, Delhi Div. to Junior Secretary, Govt. of Punjab, 23 November 1898, both encl. to Military Dept. memorandum, 20 March 1901. The Military Dept. was keen on anticipatory legislation that it believed would not be passed in the Legislative Council in ordinary times, 'unless after prolonged and possible acrimonious discussion.' Govt. of India (Military Dept.), to George Hamilton, Secretary of State, 7 March 1901.

[97] Govt. of India (Military Dept.) to George Hamilton, Secretary of State, 7 March 1901.

Procedure; the ensuing fines were to compensate railways for injury to railway property or for expenses incurred in prosecuting offenders. Thus, even those unconnected with or unaffected by railways in other ways were now liable for any damage to railways in their area. Subsequently, if the offender remained unidentified, the population of multiple towns and villages had to bear the cost of special patrols billeted to protect railway property.

Railway sabotage: 1907–15

The state was well armed with a swathe of powers by the early twentieth century, when 'politico-criminal' sabotage began to include increasing incidents of derailment: bombs that were either placed on railway tracks or else thrown at railway carriages with the specific objective of assassinating imperial functionaries and train robberies intended to fund revolutionary action. Officials linked these with the activities of *samitis*, increasingly radicalized subsequent to the 1905 partition of Bengal and the official repression of protest.[98]

Though they remained unsuccessful, in 1907 repeated attempts were made to derail trains carrying Andrew Fraser, the lieutenant-governor of Bengal. In the first attempt, Ullash Kumar Dutt was disturbed while laying a dynamite mine on Fraser's Calcutta to Ranchi route. The few dynamite cartridges that he did manage to lay exploded under the train without doing any damage. Subsequently, Barinrda Kumar Ghose, Profulla Kumar Chaki, and Bibhuti Bhushan Sarkar tried to blow up the lieutenant-governor's special train near Chandranagore railway station while he was returning to Calcutta. They failed since the train did not come that way on the appointed night.[99] In the third attempt, Barindra laid a mine comprising six pounds of dynamite with a fuse and detonator near Kharagpur, hoping to blow up the lieutenant-governor's train when he was returning from Cuttack. He himself returned to Calcutta 'by the last train,' leaving Profulla and Bibhuti to place the fuse at 2.30 a.m.[100]

---

[98] Preface by C.R. Cleveland (25 October 1917) to the confidential report by James Campbell Ker, personal assistant to the Director of Criminal Intelligence, titled *Political Trouble in India: 1907–1917* (Calcutta: Superintendent of Government Printing, 1917), reproduced by Oriental Publishers, 1973. For *samitis*, see Sumit Sarkar's *Swadeshi Movement in Bengal, 1903–08* (New Delhi: People's Publishing House, 1973), 4.

[99] Confession of Barindra Kumar Ghose before R.S. Mukherjee, DSP-CID, Bengal, 3 May 1908, Appendix 1, in Home: Political: A, May 1908, nos. 112–50, NAI.

[100] Memorandum on Discoveries made in Calcutta Concerning the Anarchist Society of Barindra Kumar Ghose, in Home: Political A, May 1908, nos. 112–50, NAI.

The attempt was 'nearly successful' for the ensuing explosion blew a hole in the permanent way that was five feet in diameter and bent one of the rails.[101] However, the train did not derail. Those involved in the attempt—includng Barindra Kumar Ghose, Bibhuti Bhushan Sarkar, and Ullash Kumar Dutt—were arrested, ostensibly in relation to some other activities.[102]

Even if nothing more than 'conspiracy' could be pinned on them in terms of the first two attempts on Fraser's train, yet it was posited that, in the third attempt, as the mine had been laid and had exploded, they could be indicted for an attempt to murder based on their confessions.[103] The state retaliated with the Explosive Substances Act of June 1908, which introduced severe punishment not only for anyone who used (or attempted to use) explosives but also for those who had explosives in their possession or were linked with their manufacture.[104] The arrests of May 1908 and the legislation passed in June 1908 did not end the strategy of train-wrecking using bombs. However, it had an effect on the components of the incendiary devices that were being deployed in train-wrecking. A May 1908 raid at the premises of Barindra's society had yielded 'a regular factory for bomb-making' and destructive 'infernal machines,' varying in size from 'small assassination bombs to large shells.'[105] However, the bomb thrown at a train that had left Shamnagar at 7.13 p.m. on 12 August 1908 had a coconut casing and was charged with metal spikes and explosives, while those that exploded near the distant signal at Chandranagore comprised bullets and marbles cased in coconut shells.[106] Some, like the one thrown at

---

[101] Ker, *Political Trouble in India*, 323.

[102] Occurring on the morning of 2 May 1908. *The Administration of Bengal under Sir Andrew Fraser, K.C.S.I, 1903–08* (Calcutta: Bengal Superintendent Book Depot, 1908), 21.

[103] Notes in Criminal Intelligence Dept., 8 May 1908 (H.A. Stuart) and 9 May 1908 (H.A. Adamson), in Home: Political A, May 1908, nos. 112–50, NAI.

[104] *Administration of Bengal under Sir Andrew Fraser*, 22.

[105] Ibid., 21. Further memorandum on Anarchist Society of Birendra Kumar Ghose, in Home: Political A, May 1908, nos. 112–50, NAI; Memorandum on Discoveries made in Calcutta.

[106] In the first incident the bomb fell short of the train, while in the second case the man closest to the explosion was injured. Fragments of the bombs were taken for examination and official communiques flew back and forth but no offenders were identified or apprehended. Appendices to Notes in File: Extract from Indian News Agency Telegram, 13 August 1908; and Chief Secretary, Govt. of Bengal to Secretary, Govt. of India (Home Dept.), Telegram (Poll.), 14 August 1908, both in Home: Political: A, December 1908, nos. 28–32, NAI. *The Empire* (Calcutta), 26 November 1908.

an Eastern Bengal State Railway (EBSR) up-passenger train near Agarpara on 24 November 1908 had jute wrapping encasing the shell.[107] In addition to metal spikes and some explosives, the later bombs were packed with a range of ad hoc materials: marbles, rifle and revolver bullets, air gun pellets, darts, and shards of glass, as well as nails (such as that in the bomb that exploded under the third-class carriage of a passenger train standing at Akole station on the Great Indian Peninsular Railway or GIPR).[108]

When the offenders remained unidentified in many of these cases, the Railways Property Protection Act was used to effect punishment. The 1908 'bomb outrages' on the EBSR led to a punitive patrol being imposed on the line for six months, even though it was clear that in cases of lines running through a series of towns and villages, the vast majority of those being penalized could do little to stop the sabotage.[109] A force comprising three sub-inspectors, eight head constables, and 110 constables, under an assistant superintendent of police, was to patrol the line from a point one mile south of Dum Dum junction to Barrackpore station for six months, from sunset to 1 a.m.[110] Barring one, 'outrages' on Europeans travelling on suburban trains to Barrackpore had occurred within these limits of time and place. The inhabitants of the country within two miles of the line on each side bore the levy, estimated at Rs. 37,500.[111]

Notwithstanding heightened legislation and punishment, such assassination attempts did not cease; between 1910 and 1914 there were extensive discussions about protecting the viceroy when travelling by rail.[112] At the same time, there

---

[107] F.W. Duke, Offg. Chief Secretary, Govt. of Bengal, to Secretary, Govt. of India (Home Dept.), 3 December 1908, in Home: Political B, December 1908, nos. 48–49, NAI.

[108] Ibid.; Telegram from Chief Commissioner, Central Provinces, to Secretary, Govt. of India (Home Dept.), 20 July 1908, Home: Political A, January 1909, nos. 5–6, NAI.

[109] F.W. Duke, Offg. Chief Secretary, Govt. of Bengal, to Secretary, Govt. of India (Home Dept.) Calcutta, 4 February 1909, Home: Political A, May 1909, nos. 153–57, NAI.

[110] F.W. Duke to Secretary, Govt. of India (Home Dept.) Calcutta, 27 April 1909, Home: Political A, May 1909, nos. 153-157, NAI.

[111] This levy excluded Europeans and Eurasians, those in military and civil employ of Government, and 'menials and dependents living on their premises.' It also excluded people residing on EBSR premises, managing agents of mill companies, and proprietors of mills not resident within the area.

[112] RT: B, February 1910, nos. 4–5; RT: A, March 1911; RT: A, February 1914, nos. 70–135 (Confidential). These references are available in the Railway indexes in IOLR (BL) but the confidential ones have not been printed

were also cases of train robberies explicitly intended to fund 'anarchist' plots.[113] One of the incidents that generated much official concern and discussion involved a theft committed on 11 October 1910, when a private consignment was being sent from Naraingang to Kaoraid on the EBSR. At Dacca, seven or eight youths 'of Bhadralog class' entered the next compartment and after the train had left Rajendrapur, climbed over the partition and attacked the four men escorting the treasure.[114] They stabbed one of the escorts in the carriage, another while he was attempting to escape through the window, and stabbed and shot a third, throwing his body from the train. They threw the bags of treasure out of the train (Rs. 8,000 of the original Rs. 23,000 was recovered from the line). The train *dacoity* was attributed to the same intersections that had spurred the attempts at assassinations on trains: it was suggested as 'extremely probable' that Suresh Chandra Das Gupta who had been named in the robbery was a member of the Madhyapara Gyan Bikashini Samitia, a branch of the Anushilan Samiti.[115]

---

[113] This is different from both the category of 'cooly-dacoits' that Dipesh Chakrabarty writes of, linking it with 'low rank employees' like coolies, maintenance workers, and platelayers (Chakrabarty, 'Early Railwaymen in India,' 524–29) and the broader category of railway dacoits, train thieves, and railway thugs. Ravi Ahuja alludes to railways being appropriated as 'vehicles of crime,' which enabled dacoits to operate in an even more extensive geographic area (*Pathways of Empire*, 286). It is of this that William Crooke was complaining of when he wrote of how '[T]he extension of railway travelling has, by providing facilities for escape, greatly assisted this class of crime ["thugee"].' William Crooke, *Things Indian: Being Discursive Notes on Various Subjects Connected with India* (London: Charles Scribner, 1906), 476–77. In his critical introduction to a reprint of M. Pauparao Naidu's *The History of Railway Thieves: with Illustrations & Hints on Detection* (1915), Vinay Lal writes of how the book speaks to histories of policing, along with 'development and uses of fingerprinting, the colonial systems of classification, the colonial apparatus and machinery of "law and order," notions of criminality, the advent of photography, and the development of the railways.' M. Pauparao Naidu, *The History of Railway Thieves*, fourth edition (1915), reprinted and edited with a critical introduction by Vinay Lal (Gurgaon: Vintage, 1995).

[114] Express Telegram (Home: Political) from Viceroy (Simla) to Secretary of State for India (London), 19 October 1909, in Home: Political B, June 1910, nos. 108–24, NAI.

[115] Chief Secretary, Govt. of Eastern Bengal and Assam, to Chief Secretary, Govt. of India (Home Dept.), 20 October 1909; Deposition of Rash Mohan Dutt, signed before S. E. Stinton, 12 October 1909, both in Home: Political B, June 1910, nos. 108–24, NAI.

During the wars

By 1915, railway sabotage—in the specific combination of assassination and *dacoity* linked with *samiti* activities—lost the intensity demonstrated between 1907 and 1914, not least due to the repressive power of the Defence of India Act. However, the security of railways continued to be critical to the imperial state, which appropriated them during the wars. The military potential of railways had been explored in detail in an 1877 report that considered how to adapt Indian railways for military transport.[116] The report assessed how much of the present rolling stock was suitable for military traffic, the adequacy of every class of stock on each railway for military purposes, and how passenger carriages and goods wagons could be altered to make them compatible with the needs of military transport. When World War I broke out, the Railway Board created within itself a special War Branch, which absorbed the previously created munitions branch and began dealing with the manufacture of munitions, the construction of military railways, and the supply of 'materials and personnel to Military Railways in East Africa, Mesopotamia, and on the Frontier.'[117] In World War I, India supplied practically the entire railway transport employed in Mesopotamia, while the 'construction and working of military railways in the East' remained almost exclusively dependent on the Indian railway system for staff and materials.[118] Figures compiled for 1917–18 indicated that about 1,800 miles of track, 13,000 feet of bridging, 200 engines, and more than 6,000 vehicles were sent out of the country.[119] In addition to the extensive strategic use of railways to convey troops and essential military supplies like coal, strategic lines were swiftly constructed within British India.[120] The 300-mile-long Nushki extension through Baluchistan up to the Persian boundary near Mirjawa was constructed in less than a year of actual

---

[116] *Adaptation of Railways for Military Transport* (Simla: Government of India Press, 1877), BL.

[117] Note by President, Railway Dept. (Railway Board), 28 February 1917, Railway Board: Establishment B, May 1917, no. 501E-17/1-3, NAI.

[118] Rushbrook Williams, *Moral and Material Progress of India: In the Years 1917–18* (Calcutta: Superintendent Govt. Printing, 1918), 1–3, 23–24, 93–96.

[119] Ibid.

[120] Local Government and Railway Administrations Asked to Discourage Passenger Traffic on the Occasion of Religious Melas and Festivals, RT: A, May 1917, no. 222 T.-17/1-4, India Prog., IOR.P/10197, BL; Abstract of replies to Railway Board, RT: A: June 1917, 1-T.-17/1-2, in RT: A, December 1917, nos. 3–45, NAI.

work. Extending railways to the Persian frontier, this line—running through 'the most inhospitable country'—was considered necessary to counter the possibility of Germany 'stirring up trouble through the avenues of Russian Turkistan and Persia.'[121]

Railways having been monopolized for war purposes, ordinary railway traffic was 'discouraged.' This was also true later, during World War II, when shortages in coast-wide shipping required that railways be used extensively to transport coal. Over one million tonnes of coal were transported by railways from the Bihar and Bengal coal-fields alone. At the same time, war conditions demanded that special trains be run to convey both troops and prisoners of war. It was estimated that almost 2,000 such 'specials' were run in nine months.[122] Thus, to prevent a breakdown of 'essential rail Transport,' passenger services had to be reduced to skeletal proportions. As the advertising consultant to the Railway Board cautioned in 1942, in times of war, railways could hardly be 'cluttered up with unimportant passenger traffic.'[123]

'Atmosphere of Gunpowder'

From when they were initially conceptualized to the end of imperial domination, railways remained critical to the empire's military and political control over India. Discussions in the 1840s and 1850s had focused on how railways would be able to counter many of the existing limitations on troop mobility, whether stemming from limited numbers of Europeans, their susceptibility to 'tropical' illnesses, and the ensuing need to house them in specific climates and sanitized locations, or from the fact that road and river transport not only took much longer than railways would but also were vulnerable to poor maintenance and the vicissitudes of weather. The military instrumentality of railways became so stark in 1857–58—even though only about 300-odd miles of track was functional then—that the language of 'public convenience' had to be actively reintroduced thereafter. Notwithstanding such language, strategic concerns remained central, both in the legislation to protect railways links and in the defensive arrangements suggested for railway stations. Details about the expenditure on military and strategic railways constructed between 1885 and 1910 elicited the recalcitrant claim that many of these '*are now* of commercial

---

[121] Williams, *Moral and Material Progress: 1917–18*, 1–3, 23–24, 93–96.
[122] Press Notes, Railway Board: TX: B, August 1943, no. 9060-TX-1/1-35, NAI.
[123] Advertising consultant to the Railway Board, 27 January 1942.

value also' (emphasis added).[124] Pointing out that railways were to the British what roads had been to the Romans, the British jurist and historian James Bryce stated in 1914 that in India railways were 'primarily strategic lines, as were the Roman roads,' concluding that:

> The traveller from peaceful England feels himself, except perhaps in Bombay, surrounded by an *atmosphere of gunpowder* all the time he stays in India [emphasis added].[125]

However, if railways had become central to sustaining and embodying the militaristic undergirding of state and empire, they also became central to people's ability to protest both. The serious vigilance elicited by communication infrastructure certainly allowed the state to penalize village boys mischievously throwing stones at passing trains; however, the same hyper-vigilance also allowed ordinary people to use 'train-wrecking' as a mechanism to draw the state's attention to their needs and grievances as well as to exploit it as a way to settle local issues. When apprehended, the perpetrators faced severe penalties, especially since in a colonial context such 'crimes' could be read as treasonous rather than malicious. However, this also left the state constantly anxious as well as enmeshed in a spiral of escalating legislation. Neither could it eliminate 'sabotage' as one of the mechanisms through which militant nationalism challenged the imperial state, especially in the opening decade of the twentieth century.

Even as 'anarchists' attacked colonial officials during railway travel, the smooth and uninterrupted functioning of trains had become important to the planning and execution of their opposition. This is best exemplified, in the third—almost successful—attempt on the lieutenant-governor's train in December 1907. Barindra, Profulla, and Bibhuti had taken the morning train from Howrah to Kharagpur, where they waited the whole day in the railway waiting shed. From Kharagpur, they took an afternoon train (3 p.m.) to Narayangarh, where they alighted about an hour later, walking back towards

---

[124] Outlay to end of 1884–85: Rs 2,29,99,445; Outlay to end of 1909–10: Rs. 18,79,14,665; Difference in outlay from 1 April 1885 to 31 March 1910: Rs. 16,49,15,220, in Question and answer in the Imperial Legislative Council, 22 September 1911, Railway Statistics: A, November 1911, no. 4, NAI.

[125] James Bryce, *The Ancient Roman Empire and the British Empire in India; The Diffusion of Roman and English Law throughout the World: Two Historical Studies* (London and New York: H. Milford and Oxford University Press, 1914), 1, 13–14.

Kharagpur by the road running alongside the railway tracks. They laid the mine at about 10 p.m., after which Barindra took the 11 p.m. train from Narayangarh, being back in Howrah the following morning.[126] The strange conjunction of railway trains being used to plan and execute attempts to derail railway trains was compounded by the fact that the intended target, Fraser, had recently intervened personally to effect a railway link to Ranchi—he had been appalled to find that it was 70 miles distant from a line of railway.[127]

---

[126] Confession of Barindra Kumar Ghose. This was not an isolated case. In their attempt to assassinate the mayor of Chandranagore, members of Barindra's society used trains, travelling separately to Howrah Bridge, and then from the Howrah railway station to Mankundu station, from where they walked to Chandranagore. On their return, they used a boat and a train, and then walked back to Maniktolla house. Indu Bhushan Roy, Confession before R.S. Mukherjee, DSP, CID (Bengal), 3 May 1908, Appendix 1, in Home: Political A, May 1908, nos. 112–50, NAI.

[127] *Administration of Bengal under Sir Andrew Fraser*, 132–33.

Marking Citizen from Denizen
Dissent, 'Rogues,' and Rupture

Some years before he would begin amassing hundreds of miles of rail travel across India, M. K. Gandhi postulated that railways, along with lawyers and doctors, were ruining the country.[1] This statement became staple fodder for those who saw in Gandhi's condemnation of railways the heart of his apparently obscurantist views about technology. Others deemed it a sign of bad faith, seeing that Gandhi's extensive journeying across India on railway trains was integral to how he discovered the country, and the country discovered him: it was not only the image of Gandhi striding stick in hand that became a staple of nationalist iconography but also that of him at the door of a railway carriage, the station platform crowded with people demanding '*darshan*.' However, even as *darshan* 'occupies a prominent place in descriptions of Gandhi's tours,' Shahid Amin has demonstrated how popular appropriation of Gandhi in Gorakhpur in 1921–22 not only varied from the formats prescribed by the local Congress-Khilafat leadership but also 'clashed with the basic tenets of Gandhism itself.'[2]

---

[1] M.K. Gandhi, *Hind Swaraj or Indian Home Rule* (Ahmedabad: Navjivan, 1938 [1908/9]).

[2] Shahid Amin, 'Gandhi as Mahatma: Gorakhpur District, Eastern UP, 1921–22,' in Ranjit Guha, ed., *Selected Subaltern Studies* (Delhi: Oxford University Press, 1988), 288–348, 290, 342 (first published in *Subaltern Studies*, Vol. III, 1984).

This disjunction offers an important lens to examine the ways in which railways became central to the language and practice of dissent in colonial India. At the level of discursive nationalism, railways were central to conversations about what precisely constituted India's ruin (or progress); in more corporeal ways, they were vital to how nationalist elites physically transported themselves and the dictates of *satygraha* into India's interiors. Thus, railway lines, which had been imagined as conduits that allowed India's rulers to travel to hill stations to recuperate and replicate a sense of home, instead became the means through which the message of *satyagraha* was transmitted. Similarly, railway stations, which were seen to be armoured and defensible spaces where imperial populations could seek refuge if threatened, became vital spaces for anti-imperial mass agitations.[3]

However, even as the crowded train doorway, the politically tense platform, or burnt signal room embodied the nation reclaiming railways from imperial control, these spaces also marked disjunctions between elite and popular politics. On the one hand, railways were the means through which large numbers of people came into contact with nationalist leaders; however, crowds at railway stations who insistently demanded *darshan* also inverted conventional relationships between leaders and masses. Thus, railway stations were contingent spaces, as amenable to national collections as to the making of 'rogues,' as less obedient *satyagrahis* found themselves being described in the lexicon of authorized nationalism. Even as an oppositional *hartal* spirit travelled along railway lines, popular action in railway spaces challenged the dictates of formal nationalism, while frequently invoking the authority of nationalist elites. Leaders like Gandhi, whose name was often associated with practices ranging from ticketless travel to the pulling of train alarms to dislocate traffic, insisted that such acts had no official sanction. However, mass radicalism ignored many such dictates; meanwhile, elite authority sought to re-establish control by excluding such acts from the pale of *satyagraha*, ousting those who sabotaged railway infrastructure from the bounds of *swaraj* itself. Thus, even as railways and railway spaces were critical to the historical tissue of formal nationalist dissent, *how* one deployed railways became central to distinguishing citizen from denizen, the process acutely exacerbated in 1947–48, when railway trains physically became the vehicle through which unknown numbers of people experienced Partition.

---

[3] Both Laura Bear and Dane Kennedy discuss the importance of railways to imperial recuperation. Bear, *Lines of the Nation*; Kennedy, *The Magic Mountains*.

Conversations with the National Mind

Even if once chooses to read his critique of railways as obscurantism or bad faith, Gandhi's *Hind Swaraj* ruptured the isomorphism between imperial ideologies of domination and early anti-colonial critiques of such domination. In suggesting that railways were vehicles of national ruin rather than progress, it dissociated technological modernization from being a measure of civilization. Conscious of being charged with 'social conservatism,' many Indian nationalists had been emphatic that they did not doubt the progressive potential of railways but instead only opposed 'their actual mode of operation in India at that particular point of time.'[4] This critique focused on the political economy of colonialism, which had engendered a railway system whose costs were borne by the Indian exchequer, while its benefits were reaped by foreign business interests.[5] Even as many of the early nationalists vehemently disagreed with the British claim that railways had been catalytic in India's progress, they remained acutely sensible to its potential, which included a hefty list dominated by:

> ...the provision of cheap and quick transport, promotion of national cohesion and solidarity, opening of new markets, creation of new employment opportunities encouragement to internal and foreign trade, prevention of famines, stimulation of agricultural production, 'demonstration' effect on the process of industrialisation, direct encouragement to engineering industries and workshops, and enlargement of the sphere of enterprise in general.[6]

Gandhi was not necessarily the first or the only one to challenge this set of structural correlations. Discussing 'counter narratives' to the modernizing potential claimed for railways, Marian Aguiar locates Gandhi as one among four 'spiritual nationalists'—the others being Swami Vivekananda, Aurobindo Ghose, and Rabindranath Tagore—who challenged 'on moral grounds, the theoretical framework of the Enlightenment, especially its devotion to science.'[7]

---

[4] Bipan Chandra, *The Rise and Growth of Economic Nationalism in India: Economic Policies of the Indian National Leadership, 1880–1905* (Delhi: PPP, 1966), 189–90. Those whose views Chandra surveys include: G.V. Joshi, G.S. Iyer, Lajpat Rai, Surendranath Banerjea, N.G. Chandavarkar, Ambalal Sakerlal Desai, R.C. Dutt, G.K. Gokhale, Madan Mohan Malviya, V.N. Mandlik, Pherozeshah Mehta, Bipin Chandra Pal, M.G. Ranade, and D.E. Wacha.

[5] Ibid., 189–90.

[6] Ibid., 179.

[7] Aguiar, *Tracking Modernity*, xix. 48–49.

However, *Hind Swaraj* remains one of the most substantive and systematic explications of the argument that railways were responsible for a rather wide range of corrupt practices and moral 'evils.' Its critique is even more relevant here because railways would become central both to how Gandhi disseminated *satyagraha* as well as to how his 'followers' developed their own explications of what *satyagraha* meant in terms of everyday politics.

In his critique, Gandhi focused on disease and deprivation to stress the link between railways and moral collapse. He argued that railways spread plague by carrying germs, allowing people to move indiscriminately, and violating such 'natural segregation' of contagion as had been earlier enforced by distance. He also suggested that railways increased the frequency of famines by facilitating the transport of grain 'to the dearest markets' and heightened the pressure of famine by making people 'careless' and, presumably, unprepared.[8] Gandhi himself asserted these critiques, rather than explicating or substantiating them. However, some of the correlations that he suggested were corroborated, ironically enough, in contemporary official discussions as well as in later scholarly analyses.[9]

---

[8] Gandhi, 'The Condition of India (continued): Railways' in *Hind Swaraj*.

[9] Reports submitted by the official pilgrim committees stressed how railways spread disease (Chapter 5). The relationship between railways and famine was more vexed. The imperial government argued that railways improved distribution and decreased famines but other—contemporary commentators—pointed out how railways 'may possibly have increased the risk of famine, since they induce the producer to export the grain which was formally stored up in good years to meet the scarcity of bad years.' The 'comparative quickness' with which railways carried food into famine-stricken areas did not compensate for the loss of such 'domestic reserves.' Bryce, *Ancient Roman Empire and the British Empire in India*, 20–21.

Critical scholarship emphasizes that famines 'occurred more frequently, and were probably of greater intensity and covered larger parts of India in the colonial period than in earlier ages'. Ajit K. Dasgupta, *History of Indian Economic Thought* (London: Routledge, 1993), Chapter 5, also 57 (table 5.1). Dasgupta cites M. Alamgir's *Famine in South Asia: Political Economy of Mass Starvation* (Cambridge: Oelgschlager, Gunn and Hain, 1980) and Lucille F. Newman, ed., *Hunger in History* (Oxford: Blackwell, 1990), as also Ira Klein for 'a contrary view.' I. Klein, 'When the Rains Failed, Famine, Relief and Mortality in British India,' *Indian Economic and Social History Review* 21, 2 (1984): 185–214. In his *Poverty and Famines: An Essay on Entitlement and Deprivation* (Delhi: Oxford University Press, 1984), Amartya Sen argues that not only did World War II make food supply a low priority for India's British rulers, but also that the hysteria was exploited by Indian traders who hoarded food.

Even if such suggested links were not corroborated, Gandhi would most likely have stuck with the charges since they spoke to his more substantive point: that railway technology served to 'accentuate the evil nature of man' by allowing evildoers to fulfil 'their evil designs with greater rapidity.' Asserting that while any propensity for good travelled at a snail's pace, Gandhi insisted that evil 'had wings' and thus that railways could be 'a distributing agency for the evil one only.' His immediate example was the changing demographic in India's pilgrimage centres. Before there were railways, he argued, only devotees had traversed the hard path to holy places, undaunted by the 'very great difficulty' involved in the pilgrimage.[10] Now, railways having made travel easy, these pilgrimage centres were filled with rogues who spread trickery and cheating.[11]

Although Gandhi himself did not cite them, precisely the same had been suggested by others, both in different forums, and much earlier. Almost three decades before Gandhi, Bharatendu Harishchandra had suggested something similar in the satirical play 'Prem Jogini' (1874–75).[12] Delineating *Kasi ke chhayachitra arthat Kasi ke do bhale bure fotograpf* (Reflections of Kasi or a couple of good and bad photographs), the play's agenda of reform was articulated through a discussion of public spaces in the city, including the temple of Govindrayji, the *gaibi*, the Mughal Sarai railway station, and the quarters of a *pandit*. Significantly, the section dealing with the Mughal Sarai railway station—where trains for Banaras halted before the bridge into the city was constructed—was titled *'Pratichhavi vārāṇasī'* or the counter-image of Varanasi. It was here that a group of agents always loitered, waiting 'to snare the unwary pilgrim' as soon as the latter alighted from a train.[13] While his satirical

---

[10] Gandhi, 'The Condition of India (continued): Railways.'

[11] Ibid. To counter the imperial claim that it was railway links that made India a coherent nation-state, Gandhi argued that the fact that these pilgrimage centres were along India's extremities—Shvetbindu (Rameshwar) in the south, Jagannath in the southeast, and Hardwar in the north—suggested that India always had been 'one undivided land so made by nature.' He clarified that he was not contending that there were no differences among Indians. Chandra, *Rise and Growth of Economic Nationalism*, 179.

[12] From *Harishchandrachandrika*, the literary supplement of *Kavivachandsudha*. Vasudha Dalmia, *The Nationalization of Hindu Tradition: Bharatendu Harischandra and Nineteenth-Century Banaras* (Delhi: Oxford University Press, 1997), 302–7. Dalmia offers a vital account of how Hindu traditions, late nineteenth-century social reform, and processes of nationalization coalesced.

[13] Dalmia, *Nationalization of Hindu Traditions*, 306–7.

essays in the journal *Kavivachansudha* were directed at a host of culprits, in Prem Jogini Harischandra remained focused on how Indians themselves were 'responsible for their plight.'[14]

A similar critique was articulated in public accounts that described the 'un-holiness' in pilgrimage centres by recounting how many pilgrims alighting from trains were subjected to fraud and extortion. An account in Lucknow's *Roznamcha* that was roughly contemporaneous with Prem Jogini severely censored the avaricious *pragwals* who inundated railway stations, 'pouncing' upon those coming to the Magh *mela*, and extorting goods and money from travellers.[15] Neither were such practices geographically or temporally restricted: three decades after Prem Jogini, a series of provincial pilgrim committee reports described the 'touts' who flocked to every pilgrim train, complained about priests and their 'agents,' and described *panda*s as a class 'distinguished chiefly by their rapacity.'[16]

While not insignificant in its details, the centrality of Gandhi's intervention lies not as much in the specifics that he chose to comment on—whether plague, famine, or immorality in holy places—but rather in his assertion that railways vitiated rather than improved the moral (and material) condition of India. This diagnosis, rather than a simple militaristic view of the situation, populated Gandhi's claim that 'but for the railways, the English could not have such a hold on India as they have.' His critique is far from unassailable, not least because the moral economy that he accused railways of disrupting had been embroiled in its own logic of domination and subordination.[17] However, its substantive import lies in how it related the festishization of railway technology to the structure of colonial domination, simultaneously denying that railways were either a catalyst for, or arbiter of, progress.

Neither to be fetishized nor discarded, railways— like technology broadly— were to be used as and when necessary. Over a decade after he wrote *Hind Swaraj*, and with hundreds of miles of railway travel under his belt, Gandhi explained that he did not expect that railways would fall into disuse in India once *swaraj* had been achieved. However, reiterating his earlier assertion that

---

[14] Mohan Lal, ed., *Encyclopaedia of Indian Literature* (Delhi: Sahitya Akademi, 1992), 3844.

[15] *Roznamcha* (Lucknow), 9 January 1873, in NNR: Punjab, NWP, Oudh, and CP.

[16] *Report of the Pilgrim Committee, Bihar and Orissa, 1913* (Part IV).

[17] See E.P. Thompson's 'The Moral Economy of the English Crowd in the Eighteenth Century,' reproduced in his *Customs in Common: Studies in Traditional Popular Culture* (New York: The New Press, 1993), 185–258, especially, 186–88.

progress was a gradual rather than speedy process, he advised the nation 'to make a limited use of these agencies and not to be feverishly anxious to connect seven hundred fifty thousand villages of India by telegraph and railways.'[18] Some years later, he explained in *Navajivan* that while it may seem impossible to function without railways, yet it was possible to restrict their use if people realized that these 'have not been on the whole a blessing to the country.'[19]

Rather than being a sign of hypocrisy or bad faith, the effectiveness with which Gandhi continued to use railways demonstrates how effectively he subordinated railway technology to his needs. He was never insensible of the role that railways played in effecting his transition to the popular leader of a mass nationalist movement.[20] In a letter to Sonja Schlesin in June 1918 he highlighted the extent to which 'constant railway travelling' was integral to his work.[21] It was not only how he physically reached millions of Indians; Gandhi believed that railway travel provided him 'an opportunity of contact with the national mind *which nothing else does*' (emphasis added).[22] Believing that third-class travel facilitated an incomparable experiential affinity between people and those claiming to represent them, he described it rather dramatically 'as the most precious among my experiences,' concluding that: 'Had I never travelled 3rd class, I would never have felt like the poor and [been] one of them.'[23] Even when he himself stopped using the third-class for reasons of health, he did not give up advocating third-class railway travel for all Congressmen and

[18] M.K. Gandhi, 'Notes: Railways and Telegraphs,' *Young India*, 17 November 1921, *CWMG*, Vol. xxi (Ahmedabad: Publications Division, Ministry of Information and Broadcasting, 1966), 437–49.

[19] M.K. Gandhi, 'Bullock v. Car,' *Navajivan*, 8 August 1926, *CWMG*, Vol. xxxi (Ahmedabad: Publications Division, Ministry of Information and Broadcasting, 1969), 276–77. As David Arnold has pointed out, he was critical of technology when it replaced the right to work. David Arnold, 'The Idea of Gandhi,' in his *Gandhi: Profiles in Power* (Harlow: Pearson, 2001), 1–14.

[20] M.K. Gandhi to Saraladevi Chaudhrani, Bezwada, 23 August 1920, *CWMG*, Vol. xviii (Ahmedabad: Publications Division, Ministry of Information and Broadcasting, 1965), 191–20.

[21] M.K. Gandhi to Sonja Schlesin, Nadiad, 23 June 1918, *CWMG*, Vol. xiv, 447–48.

[22] M.K. Gandhi, 'Notes: Carping Criticism,' *Young India*, 11 May 1921, *CWMG*, Vol. xx (Ahmedabad: Publications Division, Ministry of Information and Broadcasting, 1966), 86–89.

[23] M.K. Gandhi, 'Bengal Notes,' 7 May 1925, *Young India*, 14 May 1925, *CWMG*, Vol. xxvii (Ahmedabad: Publications Division, Ministry of Information and Broadcasting, 1968), 54–60.

volunteers.[24] When a Faridpur committee arranged a first-class saloon carriage for him during a 1925 tour in Bengal, Gandhi described the episode as a '1st-Class Scandal,' explaining how journeying in a 'luxuriously fitted 1st-class compartment,' rendered him as unapproachable to millions of Indians as the viceroy ensconced in Simla.[25]

Use and Misuse: The Railway Station

As railway travel became central to aligning the nationalist leadership with the everyday reality of millions of Indians, the railway station became a space where mass nationalism expressed itself, though its political practices not infrequently challenged the authority of formal nationalism. In the 1920s and 1930s, the railway station was integral to familiarizing Indians with the ethics and politics of *swaraj* and *satyagraha*: it was where nationalist leaders often encountered and addressed large numbers of people and where nationalist funds were collected. Thus, in the midst of Non-Cooperation, those coming to station platforms were advised to 'bring money with them' to help effect nationalists tasks.[26] Accounts of railway journeys described how villagers 'attended the stations in their hundreds and, at several places, in their thousands and … paid their pice.'[27] On some slow trains, like one that Gandhi took on a branch line between Serajgunj to Ishurdi, such stations could come up 'every ten minutes.'[28] Noting that he was able to alight at all stations, pass through crowds, make the collection, and return to his compartment in time, Gandhi commended how Bengal's youth had so efficiently organized the 'collection from thousands at wayside stations within a few minutes.'[29]

Crowds: a mind of their own

However much it contributed to (or was appropriated by) formal nationalism, popular action at railway stations refused to be contained within its parameters.

---

[24] Gandhi, 'Notes: Carping Criticism,' *Young India*, 11 May 1921.

[25] Gandhi, 'Bengal Notes,' 7 May 1925, *Young India*, 14 May 1925.

[26] M.K. Gandhi, Speech at Railway Station, 21 May 1921, *Navajivan*, 9 June 1921, *CWMG*, Vol. xx, 112–13.

[27] M.K. Gandhi, 'Notes: Silent Workers,' *Young India*, 16 July 1925 *CWMG*, Vol. xxvii (Ahmedabad: Publications Division, Ministry of Information and Broadcasting, 1968), 381-82.

[28] Ibid.

[29] Ibid.

In this it resembled popular radicalism more generally, both in how it appropriated elite programmes to negotiate causes and conflicts not specified in them as well as for its radicalism, which often included a frisson of coercion, if not violence.[30] Gandhi quickly became vexed with the demands of crowds at railway stations—that 'obstinate quest for his darshan' which Jacques Pouchepadass recorded earlier in Champaran.[31] The unsanctioned nature of such 'quests' is repeatedly attested to in Gandhi's own words: he complained of nights in trains being 'always disturbed by crowds,' and described how the demands of *darshan* embarrassed him as well as consumed valuable time: 'It puts an undue strain upon my nerves and deprives me of the peace I need for writing during the odd moments I get during my travels.'[32] Such complaints came in from different parts of the country: Pouchepadass records it in Champaran, Amin records it in Gorakhpur, and Ranajit Guha alludes to such instances stretching from Kasganj to Kanpur, Lahore to Bhiwani, Jalarpet, Bhiwani, and Karachi.[33]

The force of popular demands at railway stations in fact compelled the mahatma to undertake some rather un-mahatma-like actions. Not knowing how to avoid 'embarrassingly attentive' crowds, which he described as 'vast, noisy and pressing,' Gandhi occasionally sought to escape them.[34] In a 1924 piece titled 'Forgive Me Please!' he apologized for disappointing the 'many brothers and sisters of Ahmedabad' who had gathered at the railway station to

---

[30] Ranajit Guha describes how Gandhi opposed social boycott during the Non-Co-operation movement on both moral and political grounds. *Dominance Without Hegemony: History and Power in Colonial India* (Harvard: Harvard University Press, 1997), especially 122–31. Anand Yang discusses it in the context of the markets and *haath*s of colonial Bihar in his *Bazaar India*, especially 168–70, 186–92, 216–18.

[31] Jacques Pouchepadass, 'Local Leaders and the Intelligentsia in the Champaran Satyagraha (1917): A Study in Peasant Mobilization,' *Contributions to Indian Sociology* NS 8, 1 (1974): 67–87, see especially, 82–83.

[32] M.K. Gandhi to Saraladevi Chaudhrani, Bezwada, 23 August 1920; M.K. Gandhi, 'Notes,' *Young India*, 11 August 1921, *CWMG*, Vol. xx, 486–93.

[33] Pouchepadass, 'Local Leaders and the Intelligentsia,' 82–85; Amin, 'Gandhi as Mahatma,' 306–7; Guha, *Discipline and Mobilize*, 138–39.

[34] M.K. Gandhi, Punjab Letter, 3 November 1919, *CWMG*, Vol. xvi (Ahmedabad: Publications Division, Ministry of Information and Broadcasting, 1965), 282–86; M.K. Gandhi, Notes, *Young India*, 11 August 1921; M.K. Gandhi, 'Illuminating Documents,' 30 April 1925, *CWMG*, Vol. xxvi (Ahmedabad: Publications Division, Ministry of Information and Broadcasting, 1968), 574–78.

meet him. Anxious about possibly unbridled eagerness, he had been persuaded by Vallabhbhai Patel (who was travelling with him) to stop the train before it reached the station and instead head to the ashram.[35]

Notwithstanding occasional attempts to escape popular attention, the nationalist leadership was fully cognizant of the fact that large swathes of popular, everyday, politics occurred at railway stations. Neither were they unaware of the fact that their control over such popular action was, at best, tenuous. In fact, half of the 20 instructions for controlling crowd action devised in the early months of the Non-Cooperation movement pertained explicitly to popular behaviour at railway stations. In an essay titled 'Democracy versus Mobocracy' that was published in September 1920, Gandhi suggested rules for avoiding what he described as the pitfalls of the 'mob-law stage.' Though speaking of irresponsible crowd behaviour in general, he chose to exemplify this substantially through examples of popular action at railway stations, which he had been 'ashamed to witness.'[36] In particular, he condemned the 'unwitting destruction' of passengers' luggage by demonstrators who even 'trampled upon one another' and made 'unmusical and harsh noises;' Gandhi argued that there was 'as much [nationalist] honour in staying out as in entering the station,' and insisted that large crowds 'should never enter the station' since they would inconvenience traffic.[37] Further, 10 of the 20 instructions (nos. 3 through 14) intended to rein in such 'mobocracy'—a term that Guha describes as 'a sign of craving for control and its frustration'—pertained *specifically* to crowd discipline in railway spaces.[38]

The instructions specified that volunteers were to remain posted at various points within the crowd, their first duty being to ensure that demonstrators did not trample upon passengers' luggage. Large crowds were told never to enter a station since they would invariably 'inconvenience traffic.' Gandhi urged people to stay outside the station till close to when a train was scheduled to arrive; once inside, they were to leave 'a clear passage' in front of the train for passengers and another one—mid way through the crowd—for the national

---

[35] M.K. Gandhi, 'Forgive Me Please!' *Navajivan*, 1 June 1924, *CWMG*, Vol. xxiv (Ahmedabad: Publications Division, Ministry of Information and Broadcasting, 1967), 173.

[36] M.K. Gandhi, 'Democracy versus Mobocracy,' *Young India*, 8 September 1920, *CWMG*, Vol. xviii (Ahmedabad: Publications Division, Ministry of Information and Broadcasting, 1965), 240–44.

[37] Ibid.

[38] Guha, *Discipline and Mobilize*, 139; Gandhi, 'Democracy versus Mobocracy.'

leaders who disembarked. They were urged not to form chains, not to move till the 'heroes' reached their coach, and only to raise national cries 'on the arrival of the train, on the heroes reaching the coach and on the route at fair intervals.'

Such instructions show both the continuing autonomy of popular politics as well as attempts to establish elite control over it: a vexed Gandhi continued to complain of crowd indiscipline at railway stations. Chastising shouting crowds, he insisted that demonstrations at railway stations had become 'a menace to the comfort of the travelling public' and were best avoided altogether.[39] Again, his remonstrations were in vain: in August 1921, he was livid at the intensity and insistence of the crowds that he continued to encounter.[40] The crowds that came to Agra and Tundla stations in August 1921 refused to hear what was being said to them, choosing to 'only shou[t]…louder' when asked to keep quiet. Finding it impossible to make his way through them, Gandhi found himself being pushed into the dining room, surrounded by a crowd that 'hovered about it and in its eagerness to have a peep…broke the panes of the door.'[41]

Contingency at the railway station

Untamed effusiveness for national leaders was hardly the most extreme form of unauthorized popular behaviour at stations. As the 'Delhi Tragedy' demonstrated, railway stations could be incendiary spaces. Their public location, when combined with how busy specific stations were, could facilitate a quick groundswell of large crowds here. They were also politically charged: large crowds collected here frequently for meetings and demonstrations, as well as while going to or returning from these. As the Congress Disorders Report suggested in 1920, the 'hartal spirit' frequently travelled along railway lines.[42] Crowds at railway stations thus seemed particularly amenable to being transformed into 'mobs,' the official appellation used to describe the events that occurred at Delhi station on 30 March 1919.[43]

---

[39] M.K. Gandhi, 'Notes: Discipline,' *Young India*, 18 May 1921, *CWMG*, Vol. xx, 104–8.

[40] M.K. Gandhi, *Young India*, 11 August 1921.

[41] Ibid.

[42] *Report of Commissioners Appointed by the Punjab Sub-Committee of the Indian National Congress* (Lahore: K. Santanam, Secretary to the Commission of Enquiry, 1920), Vol I: Report (hereafter *Congress Disorders Report*), Vol. II: Evidence. The authors of the *Congress Disorders Report* included M.K. Gandhi, C.R. Das, Abbas S. Tayabji, and M.R. Jayakar.

[43] Govt. of India (Home Dept.) to Edwin Montagu, Secretary of State for India, Simla, 3 May 1920, in *Report of Disorders Enquiry Committee, 1919–1920* (Calcutta: Superintendent of Government Printing, 1920) document no. 2, xi-xliii.

The Rowlatt Satyagraha in Delhi had begun 'quietly' on the morning of Sunday, 30 March.[44] Some *satyagrahis*, however, hoped that they could coerce sweetmeat sellers at Delhi station who had ignored the call for *hartal* into closing up their shops. The latter complained, the railway police took two members of the group into custody, news of the incident spread, and 'the crowd at the station grew apace.' In about two hours, railway officials, police, a magistrate, and 'regular English troops' had arrived there. The leaders of the crowd demanded that those arrested be released, the officials denied arresting anyone and, in Donald Ferrell's analysis of the incident, the crowd transformed itself into a mob that threw brickbats at police and officials. The initial crowd of people at the station had been 'somewhat rowdy but not inclined to violence.' However, they were now transformed into a 'mob' that was simultaneously more coherent and more amenable to violence, throwing brickbats at the police and at officials.[45] According to the official account, the sheer accuracy of the attack, combined with 'general hysteria,' led one of the officials to order the troops to open fire. Seven people collapsed as others—terrified—tried to disperse.[46]

Gandhi was extremely critical of the violence unleashed on the crowd at the station and wrote a letter criticizing the palpably excessive actions taken by local authorities. However, he simultaneously pointed out how the crowd's actions, if official accounts were correct, had violated the tenets of *satyagraha*. He specifically pointed to four aspects of crowd behaviour: coercing sweetmeat-sellers into closing their stalls, preventing people from boarding tram-cars and other vehicles, throwing brickbats, and demanding the release of the men arrested for coercing sweetmeat sellers.[47] Being coercive, such actions

---

[44] Donald Ferrell, drawing on George Rudé's definitions in *The Crowd in History: A Study of Popular Disturbances in France and England, 1730–1848* (1964). Donald W. Ferrell, 'The Rowlatt Satyagraha in Delhi,' in Ravinder Kumar, ed., *Essays on Gandhian Politics* (Oxford: Clarendon Press, 1971), 189–90.

[45] Ferrell, 'The Rowlatt Satyagraha in Delhi,' 189–90. Ferrell defined a crowd as a collection of people 'that has a focus of interest, but usually has little cohesion, and has no proclivity to violence.' He defined mobs as a collection of people 'that had a focus of interest, coheres, and will follow a spontaneous leadership. It usually proceeds to activities of a violent nature.'

[46] Ferrell, 'The Rowlatt Satyagraha in Delhi.'

[47] M.K. Gandhi, Letter to the Press on the Delhi Tragedy, Letter to the Editor, *Bombay Chronicle*, 3 April 1919, *CWMG*, Vol. xv (Ahmedabad: Publications Division, Ministry of Information and Broadcasting, 1965), 174–76. The letter was released through the Associated Press of India and published also in *New India*, 4 April 1919 and *Amrita Bazar Patrika*, 5 April 1919.

violated—even before any violence erupted—the kernel of *satyagraha*, which insisted on persuasion in the form of 'suggestions and advice.'[48]

Leaders and followers?

Whether expressed as popular 'hostility' to European travellers, 'intimidation of railway staff,' or travelling without tickets, crowd action at railway stations continued. Even more poignantly, Gandhi remained central to those undertaking such actions: several such non-civil actions were attributed to non-cooperators returning from meetings held by Gandhi, while many explicitly invoked Gandhi's name while undertaking actions that clearly transgressed his exhortations. Gandhi's express disapproval failed to stem the tide. The manager of the Ferozepore branch of the Alliance Bank of Simla described those he encountered at Ludhiana station at 5 a.m. one morning in March 1920 (when he and his wife were changing trains there) as crowds of 'the most menacing and hostile Indians.'[49] Hutchinson wrote that the crowd first jeered at his wife and then tried 'to get into our compartment, sometimes from both sides, all the while shouting *Mahatma Gandhi ki jai.*' At Ludhiana station, a policeman on duty helped him keep the crowd out of his compartment. However, at each successive station, 'the crowd got down from their carriages' and repeated the behaviour exhibited at Ludhiana. Hutchinson concluded that:

> The crowd was practically in possession of the train, none had a ticket, and they all entered whichever compartment they pleased, only being kept out of mine by force.

Imperial officials continued to implicate Gandhi when explaining the agitated nature of nationalist crowds at railway stations. In one such enquiry in the House of Lords, it was explained that the crowd in question had 'just been attending one of Mr. Gandhi's great demonstrations.'[50] Further, that, 'as so often happens in India now, it took possession of the train, and travelled without taking any ticket.'[51] This was almost identical to a statement by Michael

---

[48] M.K. Gandhi, Letter to the Press on the Delhi Tragedy, 3 April 1919.

[49] J.L. Hutchinson, Manager, Alliance Bank of Simla, Ferozepore Branch, to Mr. G. Wall, Indian Police, Superintendent of Police, Ferozepore, 9 March 1921, in Home: Political, May 1921, no. 111, NAI.

[50] Parliamentary Debate, House of Lords, 4 May 1921, Home: Political, May 1921, no. 111, NAI.

[51] Extract from Debate of the House of Lords, 4 May 1921, in Home: Political, May 1921, no. 111, NAI.

O'Dwyer about another group of people that '*as usual* on those occasions, invaded the railway station, intimated the staff, took possession of the train, and travelled without tickets' (emphasis added).[52] Similarly, the Commissioner of Jullunder reported how in Ferozepore district a crowd returning from a meeting in March 1921 refused to present their tickets to the station-master when they alighted from the train at Moga. Instead, they kept shouting '*Mahatma Gandhi ki jai, ticket nahin hai*' (Hail Mahatma Gandhi, we have no ticket).[53] Responding to this, the station-master opened the platform gate, reportedly saying '*Phatak khula hai*' (the gate is open).

The extent of such incidents remains disputed. A 1921 enquiry in the House of Lords suggested that such intimidation, combined with ticketless travel, was fairly common.[54] However, officials in the Home department in India were more equivocal. Many preferred to attribute such incidents to unbridled enthusiasm, often of students, and to caution against the harm that would be done by stressing 'isolated incidents as though they give a true picture of the state of affairs in India.'[55] The Punjab government echoed this anxiety. Thus, in the case of the bank manager Rawlinson travelling with his wife to Simla, it was suggested that those trying to enter his carriage were passengers with first- and second-class tickets who were agitated by the fact that they could not find seats in first- and second-class compartments.[56]

On the other hand, internal reports documented a series of incidents through the winter and spring of 1920–21—occurring in multiple locations ranging from Lahore to Nankana Sahib, Shahpur, and Attock—in which crowds pushed past station barriers, took possession of trains, and travelled without tickets, especially to and from political meetings.[57] A crowd of men coming

---

[52] Enclosure to demi-official letter from F.W. Duke, India Office, to the Hon'ble Sir William Vincent, Kt., K.C.S.I., 5 May 1921, in Home: Political, May 1921, no. 111, NAI.

[53] Reported in superintendent of police's diary for the week ending 12 March 1921. G.F. Montmorency, Chief Secretary, Govt. of Punjab, to H.D. Craik, Offg. Secretary, Govt. of India (Home Dept.), Simla, 12 July 1921, in Home: Political, May 1921, no. 111, NAI.

[54] Parliamentary Debate, House of Lords, 4 May 1921.

[55] Notes in the Home Dept., in Home: Political, May 1921, no. 111, NAI.

[56] G.F. Montmorency, Chief Secretary, Govt. of Punjab, to H.D. Craik, Offg. Secretary, Govt. of India (Home Dept.), Simla, 12 July 1921.

[57] Ibid.

from the Serai Kala fair who were travelling without tickets were alleged to have assaulted such members of the station staff who challenged them; five of the ticketless travellers were arrested and sent up for trial. The fact that non-cooperation meetings had been banned under the Seditious Meetings Act kept some areas relatively quiet. However, it could not prevent railway stations being appropriated by popular politics. Thus, 'crowds' that had gone by train to Ghaziabad to attend non-cooperation meetings banned in Delhi (where the Seditious Meetings Act was in force) were described as practically having taking possession of Delhi main station.[58] Non-cooperators were said to have 'brushed aside' station staff and railway police, with many of them travelling both ways without paying for their tickets.[59]

The empire strikes back

The imperial state retaliated. During periods of heightened conflict, many railway stations began resembling military posts 'with soldiers and guns scattered all over.'[60] Having come in on the Calcutta mail from Kanpur, Lala Girdhari Lal penned a vivid description of Amritsar station on the morning of 11 April: several groups of policemen watched over the railway lines from the canal bridge, while at the foot-bridge, a 'guard of some European soldiers' searched all passengers and their belongings, taking sticks away from everyone. No one was permitted to go over the carriage-bridge.[61] A similar show of might underlay the so-called parade at Kasur where—after the Jallianwala Bagh massacre (13 April) and after Martial Law had been proclaimed (16 April)—the whole town was required on 1 May to gather at the railway station, ostensibly for purposes of identification.[62] There they sat, 'bareheaded in the hot sun till 2 o'clock, without water or food,' in an exercise undertaken 'to strike terror.'[63]

In an attempt to reclaim the station from popular nationalism, the state amended the previous Railway General Rules of 1906 and established more stringent orders by September 1921. Existing regulations (rule 42) already

---

[58] C.A. Barron, Chief Commissioner, Delhi, to H.D. Craik, Secretary, Govt. of India (Home Dept.), Delhi, 3 June 1921, in Home: Political, May 1921, no. 111, NAI.

[59] Ibid.

[60] Statement by Lala Girdhari Lal, Deputy Chairman, Punjab Chamber of Commerce, (Statement 1, 1–2) before the Congress Disorders Committee, quoted in *Congress Disorders Report*, Chapter V, part II.

[61] Statement by Lala Girdhari Lal.

[62] 'Kasur,' *Congress Disorders Report*, Chapter V, part II.

[63] Ibid.

authorized railway administrations to exclude from railway premises any person who was not a bona fide passenger, nor had any business there.[64] However, the demonstrations of 1920–21 at stations led officials to stress that the legislation did not provide for the removal of passengers who arrived by train but then refused to leave the premises. The Railway Board expanded the purview of rule 42 to allow railway administrations to remove anyone who had arrived at the station but 'having no business connected with the railway refuses to leave the premises when required to do so.'[65]

More punitive legislation was considered as soon as the call for Civil Disobedience was given. The Railway Board immediately sought to assess whether there was an increase in 'this evil' of ticketless travel and, if so, whether it could be attributed to official Congress activity.[66] By the 1930s, this was combined with the practice of alarm-chain pulling that, as Lisa Mitchell shows, had begun to be used 'to address wider nationalist agendas within the larger anti-colonial programme by halting trains and causing general inconvenience to the railways and therefore to the state.'[67] In a confidential letter, the agent of the Great Indian Peninsular Railway (GIPR) informed the chief commissioner of railways that he had garnered information that the Allahabad Congress Committee had decided to advance Civil Disobedience 'by encouraging the public not to purchase tickets when travelling by any Government concern, meaning, I take it, Railways.'[68] At that juncture, however, the offense of travelling without a valid ticket was a non-cognizable one. Consequently, it was suggested that fresh legislation be initiated that would make ticketless travelling a cognizable, non-bailable, offence, with any offenders being subject

---

[64] RT: A, December 1921, no. 494.T.-21/ nos. 1–8, India Prog., IOR.P/11065, BL.

[65] Ibid.

[66] Communication from Railway Dept. to H.W. Emerson, Secretary, Home Dept., 6 August 1930, in Home: Political, 1930, no. 257, NAI.

[67] It had begun as a mechanism to combat overcrowding. Mitchell, 'To Stop Train, Pull Chain,' 478, 483–84. She points out that on 10 August 1942, 'in the wake of the passage of the Quit India Resolution at the Bombay session of the All India Congress Committee on 8 August and the arrest of Gandhi and the rest of the Congress' national leadership the following day,' discussions among the Railway Board elicited the suggestion to disable alarm chains in trains. However, this was not to be applied universally but was to be restricted to lower-class carriages: 'The appended proposal suggested that alarm chains might be rendered inoperative either "on all 3rd and Inter carriages," or, alternately, "On all 3rd and inter carriages which do not include a women's compartment"' (486–87).

[68] Agent, GIPR, to Guthrie Russell, Chief Commissioner of Railways, Railway Board, 31 July 1930, in Home: Political, 1930, no. 257, NAI.

to imprisonment for three months; it was also suggested that railway officials be given immediate powers to eject anyone travelling without tickets from trains as well as to arrest them (subsequently handing them over to a police officer).[69]

Similar to how he had railed against people either stopping trains or forcibly entering them without tickets during Non-Cooperation, so in 1931 Gandhi insisted that Congress had not launched any campaign of ticketless travel.[70] Speaking to representatives of the Allahabad Boatmen's Association and some Congressmen in February 1931, he explicitly criticized a recent incident in which villagers had travelled without tickets to attend a public meeting at Allahabad, explaining that even when *swaraj* was attained, some fare would have to be charged for railway service.[71] (In this case the situation had been resolved by Jawaharlal Nehru paying railway authorities to secure the release of all those arrested.[72]) This decision held till the end of the end of the decade, Gandhi explaining to Nagpur Congress workers at Wardha in December 1939 that ticketless travel was not an officially sanctioned form of civil disobedience.[73]

Violence and Non-Violence: A Lexicon of Authority

Equally vexing to authorized norms of *satyagraha* was the recrudescence of sabotage as part of oppositional politics. This had been a particularly potent

---

[69] Notes in the Home Dept., 11 August 1930, in Home: Political, 1930, no. 257, NAI. Statement by K.J. McNeill, Superintendent, Watch and Ward Dept., GIPR, in Home: Political, 1930, no. 257, NAI.

[70] M.K. Gandhi, 'Instructions to UP Peasants,' *Young India*, 9 March 1921, *CWMG*, Vol. xix, 419–20.; Communication from Railway Dept. to H.W. Emerson, Secretary, Home Dept., 6 August 1930, in Home: Political, 1930, no. 257, NAI; M.K. Gandhi, Speech to Boatmen's Association, Allahabad, *The Hindu*, 4 February 1931, *CWMG*, Vol. xlv (Ahmedabad: Publications Division, Ministry of Information and Broadcasting, 1971), 150.

[71] Gandhi, Speech to Boatmen's Association, Allahabad, *The Hindu*, 4 February 1931.

[72] Editor's note, Gandhi's speech to Boatmen's Association (Allahabad), 4 February 1931.

[73] Discussion with Nagpur Congress Workers, which took place at Wardha on 27 December 1939, appeared in the *Harijan* of 6 January 1940 and in *The Hindu* of 28 December 1939. *CWMG*, Vol. lxxi (Ahmedabad: Publications Division, Ministry of Information and Broadcasting, 1978), 62-64. However, Mahadev Desai's summary, from which the discussion is reproduced in *CWMG* appeared with the note: 'Gandhiji's talks to the Congressmen who came to Wardha from surrounding places were not meant for publication. But as incomplete and inaccurate paragraphs have crept into the Press, it has been thought advisable to give the foregoing summary.'

weapon of anti-colonial action in the late 1890s and early 1900s (Chapter 6) but had been muzzled to some extent by the legislative onslaught unleashed during World War I. However, it resurfaced, at least as far as 'railway sabotage' was concerned, once the Rowlatt agitations began. Its presence is evidenced by the fact that the Hunter Report devoted a whole chapter (viii) to documenting 'the persistent and widespread attacks on the railway and telegraph systems,' focusing on how this prevented the arrival of fresh troops and made calls for assistance 'impossible.'[74] In this period, the Punjab government cited the risk of a general breakdown of communication as one of its 'gravest anxieties;' across many areas incidents of train-wrecking were listed as the 'chief incident,' ranging from the attempt in Nadiad on a train conveying British troops to Ahmedabad to the derailment of a train at Malakwal on 17 April.[75] In a two-day period between 11 and 12 April a railway workshop was attacked and an armoured train derailed in Lahore district, with railway stations being burnt at Wagah and Kasur, the latter combined with attacks on Europeans travelling in three trains that had been held up at the station. A 'riotous mob' at Wazirabad set fire to railway bridges and attacked a mail train, while 'persistent and determined attacks' on railway stations and against railway employees were reported from Chuharkhana, Sheikhupura, and Sangla. In fact, it was the substantial damage to railway (and telegraph) communication in Gujranwala that was officially cited as the reason for it being bombed aerially.

The nationalism of 'rogues'

Those who facilitated or participated in such 'sabotage' were deemed *rogue* elements—neither *satyagrahis*, nor nationalists, nor citizens. Both in the Congress Disorders Report as well as in Gandhi's testimony resides a narrative in which such 'rogue' elements played a catalytic role in generating and sustaining violence, inflaming contingent situations into ensuing acts of sabotage, whether derailment, tearing down of railway tracks, or burning of railway stations. This schema is explicit in Gandhi's comments on the derailment of a troop train near Nadiad on 11 April; he expressed his 'deliberate opinion' that the people of Nadiad were not in league with those who went there to derail the train but had instead 'exercised all the powers at their disposal'

---

[74] Govt. of India (Home Dept.) to Edwin Montagu, Secretary of State for India, 3 May 1920; *Report of the Disorders Enquiry Committee, 1919–20*, Majority Report, Chapter VIII, 89–91.

[75] Ibid. Majority Report, Chapter VIII, 90.

to restrain any such violent activity.[76] He offered a similar conclusion when speaking of incidents attributed to the people of Barejadi and Kaira. In the case of Kaira, Gandhi stated that those who derailed a train comprised 'a definite party of people some of whom were really *drunkards*' (emphasis added).[77] He did not know whether they went to the railway station with any intent of violence or not, but concluded that having reached the station they said: 'Let us do this thing.' He dismissed the suggestion that the inhabitants of the town were involved in the derailment, insisting that had they known of any such plan they would almost certainly 'have gone and turned these men away.' For Gandhi, far from being the perpetrators of railway sabotage, true *satyagrahi*s acted as a check, 'ever so light,' upon what he described as 'previously existing lawless elements.' It was with this sentiment in mind that he railed against the punitive action against Nadiad and Baredji, whose *patidar*s and *bania*s paid for the additional police levied there.[78] While the collector, Mr. Robertson, tried to prove that the derailment 'was undoubtedly caused by Nadiad people,' being the 'direct outcome of the persistent agitation against Government which has been going on among the people of Nadiad for some years,' Gandhi asked:

> Should the patidars, banias, and landowners be punished because a few *ruffians* in a fit of *madness* go to the station and pull down the rails? [emphases added][79]

The official Congress report offered a similar narrative to explain how events unfolded at Kasur railway station, which was set on fire and where European passengers came under attack. While accepting that the news of Gandhi's arrest as well as of the deportation of local leaders like Dr. Satyapal and Dr. Kitchlew had inflamed the situation there, the report emphasized that this had resulted only in a *hartal* for part of the day, leading to a public meeting with 'unexceptionable' speeches.[80] This changed on 12 April, when

---

[76] M.K. Gandhi, Evidence before Disorders Inquiry Committee (Ahmedabad), 9 January 1920, *CWMG*, Vol. xvi (Ahmedabad: Publications Division, Ministry of Information and Broadcasting, 1965), 378–460.

[77] Ibid.

[78] M.K. Gandhi, 'Audi Alteram Partem,' *Young India*, 30 August 1919, *CWMG*, Vol. xvi, 75–78.

[79] Quoted in M.K. Gandhi, 'Fine on Nadiad and Barejadi,' *Navajivan*, 7 September 1919, *CWMG*, Vol. xvi, 98–102; Gandhi, 'Audi Alteram Partem,' *Young India*, 30 August 1919.

[80] 'Kasur,' in *Congress Disorders Report*, Chapter V, part II.

a complete *hartal* took place—the Congress report attributed the heightened frisson of tension to travellers who had come in from Amritsar, some of whom 'had given an exaggerated picture of the events there and inflamed the minds of the *gullible* or the *disreputable* element in Kasur' (emphases added). The crowd that proceeded to the railway station and sought to set fire to it was described as a combination of '*idlers*' and middle-class people; however, the report stressed how the fire that was started in the lamp-room was hurriedly put out by some responsible leaders who tried to thwart the violent intentions of the crowd. It was this same crowd that proceeded to the signal station, where a train had just arrived, emptied the water compartment of its contents and, seeing some Europeans, 'made a disgraceful attack on them.' However, they were foiled again, this time by 'the timely appearance' of Mr. Ghulam Mohiyuddin, a pleader of Kasur, and his friends. When the train proceeded, however, two English soldiers in it got out and fired on 'the howling mob'. The 'mob' then clubbed them to death.[81]

The burning of the railway station at Gujranwala on 14 April elicited the same explanation. The crowd that had gathered at a railway bridge near the station owing to a rumour that a dead calf had been hung up there was aggravated by descriptions of Jallianwala transmitted by passengers on a train from Wazirabad passing through Gujranwala station.[82] The Congress report concluded that the situation exploded because—owing to 13 April and after being holidays for *baisakhi*—Gujranwala had attracted a large crowd of *holiday-makers* 'who are at no time averse to having a drink, and were least so on this occasion.' To quote the report, on the 14th, in Gujranwala, were present those elements

> ...that go to make a crowd unruly, viz., the holiday mood of 'do as you please,' the drink, the resentment over the Government doings, the knowledge of mob excesses elsewhere, and idleness.[83]

It was this combination of drunk, unruly, and idle people that were 'evidently bent upon stopping the train' and in the process threw stones at it as well as tried to set fire to the Gurukul bridge. The fire was put out by some railway staff and some 'Indian gentlemen;' foiled in their attempt, the crowd headed to the Kachi bridge on the other side of the station. The local superintendent

---

[81] *Congress Disorders Report*, Chapter V, part II.
[82] 'Gujranwala,' in *Congress Disorders Report*, Chapter V, part II.
[83] Ibid.

of police Mr. Herron fired, killing several people and wounding some others. Some of the wounded were then brought to a meeting organized in the town, and a crowd 'bent upon seeking vengeance' proceeded to the railway station and burnt it.[84]

In the lexicon of *satyagraha*, railway sabotage was defined as 'tragic,' being instigated or committed by—as the Congress report described them—holiday makers, drunkards, idlers, ruffians, and disreputable or gullible elements.[85] Gandhi not only deemed such actions as 'terrible and shameful,' to quote his description of the removal of the railway track near Nadiad on the night of 11 April,[86] but also as 'cowardly,' which was his appellation for the actions of those who tore down the railway tracks in Kaira, 'thus endangering the lives of soldiers who were proceeding to restore peace and order.'[87] Such acts were not only placed outside the purview of *satyagraha* methods but also deemed an illegitimate form of anti-imperial or national movements: the nation that countenanced such lawless action *lost* its right to protest against injustice.[88]

The 'roguery' of nationalism

Though railway sabotage was cast as being outside the pale of *satyagraha* and its perpetrators deemed ineligible for *swaraj*, yet it persisted. One of the more dramatic cases was a 1929 attempt on the viceregal special train: on 23 December, a fairly sophisticated bomb connected to a battery exploded on the Nizamuddin–Delhi section of the North-Western Railway (NWR), having been buried between the rails near mile 952/6. It severely damaged the coaches next to the one in which the viceroy was travelling, missing his by a hair's breadth.[89] Comparing this strike with sabotage attempts dominant between

---

[84] Including governor of the gurukul, Lala Rallya Ram, Mr. Labh Singh, Bar-at-law, Mr. Din Muhammad, pleader, and others. Ibid.

[85] M.K. Gandhi, The Duty of Satyagrahis, Speech at Nadiad, 6 July 1919, *CWMG*, Vol. xv, 434–39.

[86] Gandhi, Evidence before Disorders Inquiry Committee (Ahmedabad), 9 January 1920; G.K. Gillion, 'Gujarat in 1919,' in Kumar, *Essays in Gandhian Politics*, 142–43.

[87] M.K. Gandhi, The Duty of Satyagrahis, Speech at Nadiad, 6 July 1919, *Young India*, 9 July 1919, *CWMG*, Vol. xv, 434–39.

[88] M.K. Gandhi, 'The Congress,' in *Navjivan*, 11 January 1920, *CWMG*, Vol. xvi, 462–68.

[89] The coaches which were damaged severely were (if counting from the engine), the third and fourth, with the latter being more affected. The viceroy's coaches were, in the same order, fifth and sixth. Office of Senior Superintendent of Police, Delhi, to Chief Commissioner, Delhi, 24 December 1929; and E.B. Robey, Senior Govt. Inspector of

1907 and 1915, the senior superintendent of police at Delhi concluded that the perpetrators were 'two known absconders from the Lahore conspiracy case.'[90] Arguing that 'Indian public opinion' had expressed 'unreserved condemnation' of sabotage, the imperial state *also* cast railway saboteurs outside of genuine oppositional politics. However, this time Congress elites were included among those so excluded: the Home department stated that the only 'conspicuous exception' to the condemnation of violence was in ranks of the Indian National Congress.[91] It was the Congress, it argued, that was disposed to 'encourage those who follow methods of violence.'

The relationship between railway sabotage and mass action under the rubric of Gandhian *satyagraha* became most vexed during Quit India. Though large numbers of Congress leaders had been arrested by 9 August 1942, official reports ascribed to their dictates the ensuing 'orgy of destruction of communications,' arguing that such plans for sabotage has been sketched out before the arrests.[92] The damage to railway communication was quite significant: from 11 August onwards block instruments and control rooms in railway stations were said to have been 'singled out for destruction' and large parts of the East Indian Railway and almost the entire Bengal and North-Western Railway systems were 'put out of action.'[93] For a 'considerable period' Bengal was almost cut-off from northern India, while communication with Madras suffered from damage to railways in Guntur district and around Bezwada. The sabotage was described as carefully strategic, paralyzing 'all transport, trade and industry' in coal and focusing on the parts 'most obviously exposed to enemy attacks.' These targets, stated official accounts, could not have been better selected if the object was 'to dislocate the communications of the defending forces on the east coast.'[94]

Railways, Circle no. 4, Lahore to Secretary, Railway Board, Lahore, 18 January 1930, both in Home: Political, 1930, no. 4/13/1930, NAI.

[90] Confidential Report from Senior Superintendent of Police, Delhi, to Chief Commissioner, Delhi; Deputy Commissioner, Delhi, to Superintendent of Police, CID, Delhi, 27 December 1929, Home: Political, 1930, no. 4/13/1930, NAI.

[91] Home Dept., Govt. of India (signed by Lord Irwin, W.R. Birdwood, B.N. Mitra, Muhammed Habibullah, G. Rainy, J., Crerar, G.E. Schuster, B.L. Mitter), to Wedgewood Benn, Secretary of State for India, 9 January 1930, Home: Political, 1930, no. 4/13/1930, NAI.

[92] Govt. of India (Home Dept.), *Congress Responsibility for the Disturbances, 1942–43*, (Delhi: Govt. of India Press, 1943), 22.

[93] *Congress Responsibility for the Disturbances*, 22.

[94] Ibid.

Refusing to entertain the suggestion that Quit India was 'a spontaneous outburst on the part of the public precipitated by the action of Government against the popular leaders,' the official report blamed Congress workers and provincial committees. Secret instructions advocating derailment were alleged to have been sent from Bombay to the Kerala Provincial Congress Committee (KPCC) and 'prominent Congress workers' in Akola were accused of urging millworkers to sabotage communications (13 August). It was alleged that the vice-president of the Mandla District Congress Committee had asked a crowd of about 1,500 to destroy government records, railway lines, and bridges (15 August), that the secretary of a local *tehsil* Congress in Bijnor had helped organize a 'mass attack' on a railway station, and that a local Congress 'dictator,' along with nine other members of district Congress committees had been 'prominent' in the attack on a railway station in Barabanki district.[95] The attack on Tenali railway station in Guntur district (12 April) was linked to two persons who had returned the previous day from the All-India Congress Committee (AICC) meeting in Bombay, while C. Krishnan Nair, a Congress worker from Delhi (and a member of the Narela Gandhi ashram) was imprisoned for two years, allegedly for setting fire to a railway station on 12 November. In the west Godavari district of Madras, it was alleged that there were several well-known Congressmen among those arrested on the night of 24 December while they were preparing to remove bolts from railway lines and organizing an attempt to blow up a railway bridge.

Official reports argued that Gandhi specifically encouraged railway sabotage through pamphlets that had been written and distributed in the name of the Congress and had thus been accepted by local Congressmen 'as genuine accounts of his last message,' prior to his arrest.[96] Though its provenance remained unknown, a two-part pamphlet titled 'Six Commandments of Gandhi Baba' alleged to be circulating in the Central Provinces was central to the charges levied against him. In direct contravention of the instructions to remain within the limits of non-violence that were prescribed in the first part of the pamphlet, the second part included instructions to destroy tram, motor, and rail services.[97] The *Harijan*, especially in issues published soon after

---

[95] Ibid., 27–28, 30–31.

[96] Ibid., 36.

[97] Along with compelling closure of factories, mills, colleges, schools, and bazaars; destroying telephone and telegraph wires; advising the police not to obey government orders and to violate all prohibitory orders of government. Ibid., 36–37.

Congress leaders were arrested, was charged with promoting sabotage and an extract from 23 August 1942 was cited as describing as 'permissible within the bounds of non-violence' the following acts: cutting telegraph wires, uprooting railway tracks, destroying bridges, and burning petrol tanks. Responding to a question on what was permissible for "'disorganizing Government" within the limits of non-violence,' K.G. Mashruwala, one of its editors, had stated that dislocating traffic communications was permissible *if* it was executed non-violently and without endangering life. He argued that cutting wires, removing rails, and destroying small bridges could not be objected to in a struggle like this as long as it was accompanied by ample precautions 'to safeguard life.'[98] Though Mashruwala had clarified that he was voicing his personal belief, the report concluded that his statements must have Gandhi's explicit approval, arguing that the editors of *Harijan* would not dare to depart radically from Gandhi's ideas.[99]

The broader Congress organization was similarly charged, a slew of pamphlets of unknown provenance being attributed to them.[100] One titled Inquilab bulletin no. 1 contained instructions to '[c]ompletely paralyse communications and transport' including cutting railways, while another attributed to the Bombay Congress (17 August 1942) made it the 'legitimate' duty of a people to 'deny the use of communication to troop movement and troop supplies.' Bulletin no. 6, titled 'War of Independence,' included instructions to stop 'all trains carrying troops and war materials.' A conspiracy was suggested when, in addition to a letter instructing people to prevent the running of railways (which had been recovered from Kesho Deo Malaviya), handbills were distributed warning people not to travel by train on October 15th 'or else his life shall be in danger.'[101] The letter itself had stated that getting vital communications suspended or preventing the functioning of railway stations was not tantamount to violence, clarifying that 'as far as possible' it was imperative to ensure that no lives were lost in the process. After Malviya's arrest, acharya Jugal Kishore was alleged to have issued a programme, based on 'receipt of instructions' from the AICC, which specified that dislocating communication and transport so as to make it impossible for 'these oppressors' to use them remained within the purview of non-violence.[102] As part of the

---

[98] Ibid., appendix XIV.

[99] Ibid., 37.

[100] Ibid., appendix XV.

[101] Ibid., 27.

[102] Ibid., 37.

evidence was included a set of (undated) instructions attributed to the AICC: commenting on the spread of 'our revolution' from urban areas to rural ones, this emphasized how:

> The war on communications (railroads, telegraphs and motor cars) prevented the enemy from concentrating his military might and distances became the strongest weapon of the revolution.[103]

The alleged instructions also offered plans for future action, stating that since March 1943 and the months around it would 'almost decide the fate of the Indian Revolution,' so obstructing rent and revenue collection required that 'roads and telegraphs and railways...[be] put out of action and destroyed throughout the country.'

During all this time, Gandhi continued to disagree vehemently with the official diagnosis that railway sabotage was part of sanctioned Congress *satyagraha*.[104] In a letter written in late 1939, he had been vexed by rumours that—as part of the 'great ferment and preparation for civil disobedience' in the United Provinces—anonymous placards were being circulated asking people to 'cut wires and tear up rails.'[105] Putting paid to any such suggestions at an AICC meeting in Bombay in 1940, he was adamant that anyone who indulged in railway sabotage would be considered to be an *impediment* to *satyagraha*.[106] Later, in the case of the many circulars included in the appendices to the Disorders Report, Gandhi pointed out that the 'governing clause' had insisted on non-violence, while stressing that the authenticity of many of these documents was questionable.[107] He did not defend the paragraph attributed

---

[103] Ibid., appendix VI.

[104] M.K. Gandhi to Additional Secretary Govt. of India: Home (Detention Camp), 15 July 1943, *CWMG*, Vol. lxxvii (Ahmedabad: Publications Division, Ministry of Information and Broadcasting, 1979), 105-99.

[105] M.K. Gandhi to Jawaharlal Nehru (Railway Station, Delhi), 4 November 1939, *CWMG*, Vol. lxx (Ahmedabad: Publications Division, Ministry of Information and Broadcasting, 1977), 328.

[106] M.K. Gandhi, Speech at AICC meeting, Bombay-1, 15 September 1940, in *Harijan Sevak*, 21 September 1940, *CWMG*, Vol. lxxiii (Ahmedabad: Publications Division, Ministry of Information and Broadcasting, 1978), 4-13.

[107] Thus, a circular of 29 July 1942 attributed to the Andhra Pradesh Congress Committee, opened with the statement that 'The whole movement is based on non-violence. No act which contravenes this instruction should ever be undertaken.' *Congress Responsibility for the Disturbances*, appendix IV.

to Mashruwala but deemed it 'an error of judgment' likely to occur when the applicability of a 'novel' subject was being considered; it was possible, he stated, that Mashrulwala had heard him recently debating the question whether any interference with bridges, rails, and the like could be classified as non-violent. He defended himself from charges of sanctioning railway sabotage by drawing a fundamental distinction between man and machine—he 'would destroy a harmful machine without compunction, never the man.'[108]

The Barrier of a Railway Journey

If mass nationalism had appropriated railways in its anti-colonial struggle, then in the violence that pervaded railway platforms and railway trains during Partition, a retreating British state not only sought validation of various imperial tropes about its Indian colony but also tried to resurrect grandiloquent ideas of empire. 'Indian Massacres Grow: Every Station is Site for New Battle' was *Daily Mail* correspondent Ralph Izzard's headline for 27 August 1947,[109] while the *New Statesman*'s special correspondent described how a train from west Punjab 'arrived with 25 dead bodies on board and more than 100 passengers with stabbing wounds of varying degrees of seriousness' to prove his claim that there had been a complete breakdown of civil administration in the absence of a supposedly restraining imperial hand.[110]

This structure is sharply visible in a narrative by Derek Gordon Harington Hawes, who recounted two railway journeys—one of them aborted—in a piece that was acerbically titled 'Four Days of Freedom.'[111] Hawes, who had served in the Indian Army and been a member of the Indian Political Service since 1934 was stationed at Lahore in 1947. On 14 August, he escorted two servants of his superior officer (Colonel W) from the Civil Lines to the Lahore railway station, so they could leave for Simla. Hawes writes that news of 'a fresh massacre of Muslims in Amritsar' about 30 miles away had 'led to a

---

[108] M.K. Gandhi to Additional Secretary Govt. of India (Home Dept.), Detention Camp, 15 July 1943.

[109] Ralph Izzard, 'Indian Massacres Grow: Every Station is Site for New Battle,' *Daily Mail*, 27 August 1947.

[110] Special correspondent (Punjab), 'Muslims Butchered by Armed Mobs of Sikhs: Breakdown of Civil Administration,' *New Statesman and Nation* (Jullundar), 24 August 1947.

[111] Papers of Derek Gordon Harington Hawes, Mss.Eur.D1225/20 (1947–48), BL. The article was published in *Blackwood Magazine* in February 1948.

retaliatory attack on Sikhs who were trying to leave Lahore by train.' When he reached the station, he had found the station yard not only 'crowded with a mass of men, women, and children, and cluttered with all the impedimenta of Indian travel' but also with 'two grey corpses just inside the entrance porch.' The platform was empty, as was the train, and 'there were half a dozen more corpses strewn about the platform.' Returning home, the group travelled to Simla by road instead.

If Lahore station had demonstrated for Hawes an inexorable descent into mayhem ensuing from a mere 'four days of freedom,' his next train journey fuelled an allied narrative of the necessity of an imperial hand. Aboard the night train that left Kalka at 10.30 p.m. on 18 August, he described the impromptu halts at wayside stations caused by rumours of violence at stations up the line. The train reached Ludhiana at about 7 p.m.; the next day at noon, Hawes boarded the Calcutta–Lahore mail. At about 2 p.m. the train stopped at Moga, where it was 'derailed and attacked' by Sikh 'mobs' that Major Rob—on his way to Kashmir with his wife and daughter— described as advancing and retiring in military formation. The *New Statesman* suggested premeditation, reporting that all the Sikh passengers had been tipped off at a previous station and had left the train. However, the mobs surrounding the train were driven off by shots fired by British passengers, a few others with arms, and by the train's armed escort, 'which consisted of two Muslim Sepoys, two Hindus, and one Sikh.' The Major and Mr. Hawes decided to spend the night not in the derailed train, which was surrounded by long grass that could be 'easily set on fire,' but at a deserted station up the line. About 150 passengers, 'all Muslims,' followed them to the station. Mobs approached but were driven off when a 'Sikh Sepoy' killed one of them; during the night a military patrol arrived and left with one section of the stranded passengers. Analyzing the event, the newspaper emphasized the 'valiant and successful defence [that] was organized by two British passengers,' explaining that those who had insisted on staying behind with the train were killed during the night.

To the populations affected by Partition, such narrative renderings of imperial heroics were not of much import; the railway train, however, was. Whether explicating the potential of mass nationalism to dismember or bond, whether suggesting the possibility of safety or a foreboding of death, the train became the historical mediator of Partition for unknown numbers of people. In the immediate aftermath of Partition, searing images of terror and brutality saturated stories of railways trains with only corpses as passengers, whether Krishan Chander's, 'Peshawar Express,' Bhisham Sahni's, 'The Train has

Reached Amritsar,' or F.A. Karaka's description of a train laden with people sitting close to each other and resting their shoulders on each other, not because they were tired or sleeping but because they were dead.[112] More recently, the voices of those who experienced this terror have begun to be recorded.[113] One such account is that by Damyanti Sahgal who, at the time of Partition, lived in Kotra, 30 miles from Lahore, 'near Raiwind station on the road to Multan.'[114] Her father refused to leave but her uncle, a commissioner in Lahore division, urged Damayanti to flee: 'At the most he [her father] will be killed,' her uncle stated, 'but you, you will be gutted.' She came to Lahore, with a servant (a small boy) and some money given her by her father; she was told to go to Kulu Manali. When she reached Amritsar, however, she discovered that 'they had started stopping trains, killing people in them.' The panic increased. She recalls:

> Train. train. Everyone was full of fear ... they kept saying put your windows up, put your windows up, Amritsar is coming and they're cutting people down there. We put our windows up. God knows what they were doing outside, we were too frightened even to look, we kept praying our train would not stop at the station.

She had no doubt that 'we were lucky:' '... from there our train passed straight through.'[115]

However, even as it became a vehicle of death, the train also offered the possibility of escape: accounts of Partition offer descriptions of station platforms

---

[112] D.F. Karaka, *Then Came Hazrat Ali: Autobiography* (Bombay: Popular Press, 1972), in the chapter titled 'The Train that Dripped Blood,' 253–63, quotations on 258–60. In her *Tracking Modernity*, Marian Aguiar examines such narratives in a chapter titled 'Partition and the Death Train,' 73–99.

[113] See Urvashi Butalia, *The Other Side of Silence: Voices from the Partition of India* (New Delhi: Viking, 1998), 87–88. Also Gyanendra Pandey, *Remembering Partition: Violence, Nationalism and History in India* (Cambridge: Cambridge University Press, 2001).

[114] Damyanti Sahgal's narrative, in Butalia, *Other Side of Silence*, 87–88.

[115] Ibid., Her narrative of course also points us to further questions about 'tension in the meaning of individual citizenship,' as David Gilmartin terms it in his discussion of the relationship between state, community and everyday life as well as questions of representation. 'Partition, Pakistan, and South Asian History: In Search of a Narrative,' *The Journal of Asian Studies* 57, 4 (November, 1998): 1068–95, quote on 1090, n. 26. The issue is further complicated by questions about 'recovering' women after Partition. See especially Urvashi Butalia, 'Community, State and Gender: On Women's Agency during Partition,' *Economic and Political Weekly* 28, 17 (1993): WS13–24.

on either side of the border packed with people waiting for a train that would take them across. If the sundered inner world of a railway compartment became the metonym for Partition, then it was also the same compartment that offered the possibility of a moment of community—even if fleeting—as the protagonist of S.H. Vatsayan 'Ajneya's' paradoxically titled 'Getting Even' demonstrates. However, even for the 'lucky ones' who survived the train journeys and managed to escape violence, the train became the tangible barrier between past and present, journeys without a possibility of return.

Even as they physically created insuperable barriers between the past and future of millions, railway lines had themselves become etched into South Asia's landscape as a new system of links, with villages, towns, and cities both located and stratified in terms of their proximity to or distance from a railway line and the presence or absence of a railway station. Lahore, 'the first city in the Punjab,' had become:

> ...a big Railway Junction for Peshawar, Calcutta, Karachi and Bombay. The distance between Lahore and Delhi is 298 miles.[116]

The slightly smaller Kasur was:

> ...an important town in the Lahore District, about 40 miles from Lahore. It is an important railway station on the main line, and a fairly important trade centre, with a population of 24,000.[117]

And the significantly smaller Patti and Khemkarn were identified simply as:

> ...two small railway stations, a few miles from Kasur.[118]

After 1947, of course, these were railway stations separated by an international boundary line.

---

[116] *Congress Disorders Report*, 74.
[117] Ibid., 97.
[118] Ibid., 104.

Conclusion

Transport technology has changed significantly since passenger railways first began running in the mid-nineteenth century. Domestic and international airline travel is a booming industry, automobiles and buses increasingly choke urban traffic, and metro rail systems are proliferating as a mass transit necessity in many cities. However, railway transport remains central to India's public. In 2012–13, railways in India carried an astounding eight billion passengers.[1] The significance of this figure is even more dramatic when contrasted with the number of people using other forms of transport: in 2012-13, the number of airline passengers, both domestic and international, was somewhere between 60 and 75 million, while the total number of registered motor vehicles in 2012—including taxis, two-wheelers, buses, and goods vehicles—stood at 159.49 million.[2] It is not only numbers, however, that speak to the continuing

---

[1] No. of passengers carried 8,420,713,000. Table 19.1 (Railway Statistics—Summary), in Government of India, Ministry of Statistics, *Statistical Yearbook, India, 2015.* (New Delhi: Central Statistics Office, 2015; available at: http://mospi.nic.in). All websites referred to in this chapter were last accessed on 06 January 2015.

[2] For airline passengers, Government of India lists 57,647,000 as the number of passengers carried domestically in 2012–13 and 11,783,000 as the number of passengers carried in international services. See Table 23.1 (Civil Aviation—Indian Scheduled Operations), Government of India, Ministry of Statistics, *Statistical Yearbook, India, 2015.* World Bank data for airline passengers offers the figure of 75,322,747 under the country heading 'India' in 2013 (available at data.worldbank.org). The figures for motor vehicles

relevance of railways in India. This book has suggested some of the important ways in which, from the mid- to late nineteenth century onwards, Indians felt the ever-increasing presence of railways in their lives, being compelled to negotiate the wide range of transformations being wrought by railway travel, technology, and infrastructure. Many of these remain true even today. To highlight both the enduring impact of railway technology in the lives of Indians as well as how the historical meaning of new technology is materialized through everyday use, this conclusion will briefly juxtapose two transport 'revolutions' separated by more than a century.

If the mid- to late nineteenth century was characterized by the railway 'revolution,' then in the last decade or so a more recent 'transportation revolution' has occupied a fair share of public conversation in India. The Delhi metro, a rapid mass transit system, has garnered national and international attention for its technological sophistication: including the engineering gymnastics required to build 'in, above and beneath some of the most densely populated square miles on earth,' the regenerative braking system that allowed it to save 1,12,500 megawatt hours of power generation between 2004 and 2007, and its being built to resist earthquakes up to 7.5 on the Richter scale.[3] Among these many 'firsts,' however, one cannot but be struck by how often the impact of the metro has been assessed in relation to railways. This is not

---

can be found in Table 20.1 (Number of Motor Vehicles Registered in India, Taxed and Tax Exempted, as of 31 March 2012), Government of India, Ministry of Statistics, *Statistical Yearbook, India, 2015*.

[3] While Calcutta's metro system as well as Bombay's suburban rail system precede Delhi's, the latter has garnered unparalleled attention for its technological sophistication. Other attributes highlighted in the press include underground mobile telephone coverage, an automatic fare collection and ticketing system, and the introduction of a single journey contact less token. Neha Lalchandani, 'Delhi Metro Scores a World First with Carbon Credits,' Times News Network, 19 January 2011; David Rohde, 'Clean, Modern Subway, Efficiently Built. In India?' *New York Times*, 29 January 2003; 'Delhi's Metro Rail Sets World-Class Standards,' Indo-Asian News Service, 18 December 2004; Zia Haq, 'One Helluva Ride Ahead,' *Hindustan Times*, 1 January 2005; Bryan Pearson, 'Tens of Thousands Go for Joy Ride on Delhi's New Underground Line,' Agence France-Presse, 3 July 2005; 'Decade of Being a Metro, '*Hindustan Times*, 4 February 2013.

In 1998, the year that the metro began to be constructed, Delhi had over three million registered motor vehicles (personal and commercial) travelling its over 26,000 km of road. Government of NCT of Delhi, *Statistical Abstract of Delhi, 2012*, (Delhi: Directorate of Economics and Statistics, 2012), 65–66, tables 5.5 and 5.6 (available at: http://delhi.gov.in/DoIT/DES/Publication/abstract/SA2012.pdf).

only because the metro, being a light-rail system, has immediate structural and technological affinities with rail transport. Instead, in the popular press, India's railways have become central to explicating Delhi's new metro, the latter's public identity shaped by its purported distance from the former.

As dramatic foil to the metro's heroic narrative of a 'new India' one finds the *Financial Times'* Edward Luce referencing the 'traditional infrastructure' of India's railways.[4] Juxtaposing the metro hub at Connaught Circus—still under construction when he was writing—with the New Delhi railway station about two miles away, Luce complained that the latter boasted no 'smart tickets' like the metro did and that its platforms were not cool and clean like those of new metro stations but instead crowded with hawkers, 'coolies,' and passengers, some of them 'waiting hours.'[5] Luce was not alone in such juxtaposition; the *New York Times* offered an equally detailed contrast:

> Within the calm, air-conditioned, marble-lined [metro] station [at Kashmere Gate], there is none of the chaotic squalor of hawkers and beggars that characterizes mainline railroads in India, nor do desperate travelers hang from the sides of the trains.[6]

Similarly, the *Australian Magazine* described the metro's near perfect punctuality as 'a small miracle in a land where trains are notoriously unpunctual and prone to whims of timetabling.'[7] It then lauded the metro's 'spruce Customer Service Staff' as being

> a long remove from the classic Indian railway station with its ticket-sellers mired in triplicate forms and Dickensian ledgers, and 'Delayed Passengers' rooms the size of town halls.[8]

If such press be believed, the only ostensible link between Delhi's metro and India's railways is a sentimental one: metro stations were supposed to have

---

[4] Edward Luce, 'Clean, Efficient, On Time ... Welcome to the New India,' *Financial Times*, 30 October 2004.

[5] Ibid.

[6] Amelia Gentleman, 'Delhi Delighted with its New Metro,' *New York Times*, 12 March 2005.

[7] Susan Kurosawa, 'No More Delhi-Dallying,' *Australian Magazine*, 26 April 2003. Quoting the *Hindustan Times*, Kurosawa stated that: 'For Indian Railways, a train is punctual if it arrives or departs within ten minutes of its scheduled time.'

[8] Kurosawa, 'No More Delhi-Dallying.'

digital clocks but its (then) managing director E. Sreedharan, who is a former Konkan Railway official, insisted that metro clocks 'should be like those on railway stations.'[9]

While these specific discussions juxtapose India's railways and Delhi's metro as antipodal, yet by suggesting how railways inform public understanding of more recent transport systems, they also create space for a more detailed assessment of the relationship between the two. As a caveat, differences of scale are important, speaking as they do to the question of how and by whom the systems are used: in 2011-12, Indian railways had about 64,399 km of running track open to traffic while Delhi's metro, even when completed in 2021, will be about 428 km long; further, while the number of daily riders on the approximately 190 km of Delhi's metro has increased from 0.92 million in August 2009 to 2.5 million in August 2013, this figure pales in comparison to the daily passenger traffic for railways.[10] However, without minimizing important differences in time, context, use, and technology, substantive assessments of the metro bear striking resemblance to how the impact of railways was being assessed more than a century ago.

Although the press does not pursue it, most important here are the analogies in how the historical impact of new technology is both realized and understood through its being implicated in everyday use. These analogies are not restricted to the immediate or obvious, such as the fact that Sreedharan, popularly considered the architect of the metro, himself worked for Indian railways for more than three decades or that his initial handpicked team for the Delhi metro was drawn from railway personnel.[11] Not even that the metro, like railways when these were first introduced, was hailed for how much travel time it saved Delhi's commuters.[12] Or that metro links, again like railways, simultaneously expand and contract the city: integrating remote areas into the city whilst making them accessible to more and more people, effectively

---

[9] 'Decade of being a Metro,' *Hindustan Times*, 4 February 2013.

[10] Metro Records Highest Ridership, *Times of India*, 6 August 2009; 'Delhi Metro Sets Ridership Record with Over 25 Lakh Commuters,' *Economic Times*, 10 August 2013; Ministry of Urban Development, 'Phase-III of Delhi Metro Rail Project Approved,' Press Information Bureau, Government of India (available at: http://pib.nic.in/newsite/erelease.aspx?relid=74442, 7 October 2013); Table 19.1 (Railway Statistics—Summary), in Government of India, Ministry of Statistics, *Statistical Yearbook, India, 2015*.

[11] 'A Conversation with E. Sreedharan,' by Heather Timmons and Pamposh Raina, *New York Times*, 5 October 2011.

[12] A 2007 study pegged it at a precise 66 minutes on average every day. 'Metro Makes Major Impact in Delhi,' *The Hindu*, 6 June 2007.

reducing Delhi's 'overwhelming vastness, to a friendlier size.'[13] Instead, the analogies are more embedded, stressing as they do the creative and combative relationship between large-scale technological change and the everyday life of the people that it affects. In innumerable assessments of the Delhi metro and of how it affects both the city and the lives of those who live in it, one hears more than an echo of similar conversations from more than 150 years ago.

Expectation and surprise

Instantly apparent is the set of shared expectations about how transport technology will galvanize the society in which it is introduced. In the context of colonial India, railways were deemed as historical catalysts that would literally drag supposedly laggard colonial spaces into History Proper, to a (future) time and space in which colonial masters were already ensconced (Chapter 4). Expectations about the Delhi metro are no different: in the words of the *Washington Post*'s Rama Lakshmi, the metro is 'New Delhi's Ticket to the Future.'[14] In a changing global economy, both the direction and content of this future have changed. Described as being 'a century ahead of most of the creaking lines of the London Underground,' Delhi's metro is not meant to catch up with nineteenth-century imperial capitals.[15] Instead, it aspires towards 'the ranks of swank Asian cities such as Tokyo, Singapore and Taipei.'[16] The direction of the future may indeed have changed but the expectations remain analogous. In 1853, it was railways that would make us modern; in 2002, the task has devolved on to the metro.

Equally, international surprise about Delhi's millions being willing and able to use the metro remind one of the disbelief engendered by the soaring popularity of railway travel in colonial India. Since colonial officials had deemed Indians an inherently somnolent population, so exponentially increasing passenger numbers thwarted imperial expectations. However ahistorical they were, such expectations nonetheless played a vital role in railway planning, especially in heightening the emphasis on freight rather than passenger traffic. Hence, many of the chronic problems of third-class

---

[13] Priyanka Kotamraju, 'Life in a Metro,' *Indian Express*, 20 January 2013.

[14] Rama Lakshmi (*The Washington Post*), 'Subway is New Delhi's Ticket to Future,' *Seattle Times*, 26 December 2002.

[15] Luce, 'Clean, Efficient, On Time.'

[16] Lakshmi, 'Subway is New Delhi's Ticket to Future.'

railway travel in colonial India—from persistent overcrowding to the fact that paying passengers found themselves being transported in wagons means for either goods or livestock—arose because of how unprepared colonial officials and railway companies were for the quantity of passenger traffic that actually materialized (Chapter 1).

Albeit in reconfigured form, the enduring power of such narration remains visible in contemporary discussions of how alien to Delhi—and India—Delhi's metro is. Soon after the metro's maiden run, a lengthy piece in the *New York Times* asked in disbelief: 'Clean, Modern Subway, Efficiently Built. In India?' The *Australian Magazine's* piece titled 'No More Delhi-Dallying' echoed the surprise, describing the metro's slogan of 'Quick, Effective, Modern' as being 'surrealistic' in a city like Delhi.[17] Almost a decade later, the surprise has not waned: in a 2010 piece, the *New York Times'* Lydia Polgreen describes the success of the Delhi metro as 'a feat bordering on miraculous.'[18] If colonial India's imperial administration had been shocked by the fact that Indians chose to use railways, the Delhi metro apparently demonstrates that 'elaborate high-tech development projects can be planned and executed effortlessly in the developing world.'[19] As millions use the Delhi metro, one is reminded of how, even as colonial officials agonized about whether or not Indians with their 'peculiar' sense of time could be made to comprehend standardized railway timetables, soaring passenger figures showed that millions had figured out how to catch a train, with the more vocal in fact asking railways to tailor timings to their convenience (Chapter 4).

Democratization and stratification

Like railways, Delhi's metro is implicated simultaneously in conversations about social democratization and social stratification. Thus, Manu Joseph's recent analysis of the metro's impact is titled: 'Delhi Metro Reaches across Class Lines.'[20] Pointing out that almost two million passengers use the metro on

---

[17] Kurosawa, 'No More Delhi-Dallying.'

[18] Lydia Polgreen, 'In India, Hitching Hopes on a Subway,' *New York Times*, 13 May 2010.

[19] Delhi's Metro Rail Sets World-Class Standards, Indo-Asian News Service, 18 December 2004.

[20] Manu Joseph, 'Delhi Metro Reaches across Class Lines,' *New York Times*, 17 July 2013 (and on 18 July 2013, and simultaneously in the *International Herald Tribune*). Joseph is editor of the Indian newsweekly *Open* and author of the novel *The Illicit Happiness of Other People.*

weekdays, Joseph highlights how it has democratized Delhi's stratified society by compelling its elites and masses to travel together, 'once again.' Sketching an image of '[a] man reading on his iPad sitting next to a housemaid,' Joseph describes the metro as a space where 'the otherwise unbridgeable classes' are in such physical proximity as would be unimaginable in a middle-class home in Delhi.[21] Joseph's depiction is concerned with contemporary Delhi and with questions of class (rather than caste) but the imagery is not new. Behold the shock of the colonial official Edward Davidson when he saw that 'a sacred Brahmin now sits in a third-class [railway] carriage with a Dome.'[22] (And not all commentators have shifted this way. *The Guardian's* Jason Burke writes of how 'social barriers imposed by class or caste—the tenacious ancient hierarchy determining an individual's status—are eroded in the packed carriages of the metro's overcrowded trains.'[23])

Of course, the historical context of Joseph's analysis is distinct. Thus, the inequalities he discusses are specific to late twentieth-century urban India and focus on the effects of economic liberalization and the ensuing consumption spree that has encouraged the urban affluent to explicitly distinguish themselves, not least by secluding themselves in private automobiles. For Joseph, this was when public transport became 'almost entirely the carrier of the poor, who stared from its windows and open doors at private automobiles as if they were the enemy.' Despite the difference in historical context, Joseph's analysis of the long-term democratizing role of the metro is, again, reminiscent of earlier prognoses for the railways. According to a colonial official writing in 1868, in 'advancing eastwards' the railway 'was overturning prejudices, uprooting habits, and changing customs as tenaciously held and dearly loved almost as life itself.'[24] According to Karl Marx writing in the *New York Daily Tribune* in 1853, railways would spur industrialization and, by consequently allowing India to mature, would help dissolve caste.[25] For Joseph, writing in

---

[21] Joseph, 'Delhi Metro Reaches across Class Lines.'

[22] Edward Davidson, *The Railways of India with an Account of their Rise, Progress, and Construction: Written with the Aid of the Records of the India Office* (London: E. & F.N. Spon, 1868), 3. Davidson's monograph was one of the earliest book-length treatments of railways in India.

[23] Jason Burke, 'Delhi Metro Calls for "Decorum" as Videos of Passenger "Intimacy" Surface,' theguardian.com, 24 July 2013.

[24] Davidson, *Railways of India*, 3.

[25] Karl Marx, 'The Future Results of British Rule in India,' *New York Daily Tribune*, 8 August 1853.

the *New York Times* in 2013, it is the metro that is such a catalyst: he suggests that by erasing social distinction in its carriages, and thus 'by raising the bar for the vacant gaping eyes,' the metro engenders those processes through which 'cities mature.'[26]

By offering a speedy and relatively comfortable way to avoid Delhi's traffic glut, the metro has indeed attracted many who earlier preferred less public modes of transport. The press offers various stories of those who now eschew the private automobile for the public metro, whether Hitesh Arora, the college student who now travels from the satellite town of Gurgaon to a college in Delhi University's north campus or V.K. Sinha, 'a senior police officer' who stopped driving from his Kaka Nagar residence in New Delhi to Gurgaon and instead travelled in the metro.[27] In Sinha's words:

> [The] [m]etro is more convenient and I stay fresh and reach office on time....I leave home at 8.30 am, take a bus or an auto to the Jor Bagh Metro station and reach office by 9.30 am.[28]

At the same time, much of Delhi's 'upper-crust' continue to eschew the metro, being 'still beholden to the chauffeur-driven car.' They are worried, they say, about congestion and 'the many odours of others' bodies.'[29] Thus, even as the Delhi metro's carriages flatten hierarchies of class, some among Delhi's elites hope that it will formally institute spatial hierarchies. Not too long ago the *Hindustan Times* reported that an executive working in one of Delhi's multi-national corporations wrote the newspaper 'demanding "premium coaches" in Delhi Metro' as a way to 'attract the non-cattle class to Metro.'[30] Such coaches, he argued, would attract those who currently 'avoid the service because of the subaltern crowd.'[31]

Shorter commutes and its different function obviously distinguishes the metro from colonial railways, as does the fact that railways already offer separate classes of travel based on fare. Despite such differences, the simultaneous

---

[26] Joseph, 'Delhi Metro Reaches across Class Lines.'

[27] 'Decade of being a Metro.'

[28] Ibid.

[29] Joseph, 'Delhi Metro Reaches across Class Lines.'

[30] Shivani Singh, 'Infrastructure Alone Can't Cure Delhi's Sclerosis,' *Hindustan Times*, 30 January 2012.

[31] It remains unclear whether people would pay a higher fare for such premium coaches, should they be provided. Singh, 'Infrastructure Alone Can't Cure Delhi's Sclerosis.'

discussion of social homogenization and stratification generated by the metro bears comparison with those made in the late nineteenth century, when railways first began running in India. While railway space had encouraged some social democratization by compelling—to return to Davidson's description—the *baboo* and the *dome* to sit together in the same third-class carriage, yet shared physical space and proximity in railway spaces had also generated fractious conversations about separation and stratification (Chapter 2). Many who could not afford a first- or second-class carriage objected to travelling in undifferentiated third-class carriages, seated next to those they deemed their social inferiors. Neither was such anxiety restricted to the taboos of religion or caste. Though they were far from being a cohesive group in any sense of the term, colonial elites combined entitlements based on wealth, rank, and 'breeding' to demand separate space, often combining these with concerns of hygiene and sanitation. This was how some ended up arguing—much like the depiction of Delhi's 'upper crust' in Joseph's 2013 piece—that separate carriages were necessary to forestall contact of sanitary bodies with people they deemed as 'not clean enough' (Chapter 2).

The metro's administration has 'steadfastly refused to fuel class divides.'[32] The resolution is not dissimilar to that of nineteenth-century imperial officials who rejected demands for third-class railway carriages or compartments to be segregated on the basis of caste or religion (or 'rank'). Despite this surface similarity, there are important differences in how the question was both understood and dealt with in a colonial economy versus in a post-colonial democracy. While some colonial officials had decried such segregation as being inimical to the very 'social improvement' that railways were intended to foster, most rejected such demands as being inimical to railway revenue. The instrumentality of an imperial state was visible in the fact that railways continued to reserve compartments, carriages, and retiring rooms for Europeans and Anglo-Indians, explaining these as a response to 'native' demands for segregated space. The Delhi metro obviously cites democratic principle rather than financial instrumentality when rejecting the idea of premium coaches. And it is possible that such refusal may mean that, at least in its coaches, social homogenization may become more enduring than stratification. As Joseph has suggested, Delhi's elites may eventually convert to the metro, drawn by its convenience and reach, even more so as Delhi's roads become more congested and chauffeurs cease to be either 'cheap or servile.'

---

[32] Ibid.

The one segregated space that the Delhi metro does provide is for women passengers, for whom it reserves the first car of every metro train. When the metro first opened, four seats in each car were reserved for women; however, from October 2010 onwards, the first coach in every train became a 'Ladies special.'[33] Journalists have pointed out that the decision to provide such exclusive space was made in the late 1980s, with Delhi's transport corporation deciding to introduce 'L-Special' buses in the early 1990s.[34] This is true but only if one limits oneself to the history of post-Independence India. Several railway companies in colonial India had provided 'females-only' carriages from as early as 1854; after 1890, females'-only compartments in the lowest class on every passenger train—often termed 'zenana' compartments—became de rigueur, mandated through the Railways Act. These *zenana* compartments on colonial railways were similar to facilities provided on railways in many other parts of the world; in contrast, India is one of two metro networks in the world to provide a separate women's compartment (Dubai is the other.)[35]

In important ways, the metro's reserved space for women is quite different from its colonial counterpart. For one, the former was introduced in response to popular demands, including a Delhi government survey which revealed that 'nearly half the women traveling in metro did not feel safe using the public transport.'[36] This issue was heightened by estimates that nearly a quarter of all metro passengers were women. In contrast, the decision to introduce special female accommodation on colonial railways was driven by colonial officials stressing the extent to which Indian women—coalesced under the category of 'Oriental' women—needed secluded accommodation if they were to use railways (Chapter 2). Such colonial views sought and found support from among elite groups of Indian men, who insisted that during railway travel women must remain within the protective ambit of male family members while being secluded from all strangers, men and women alike. While railway companies briefly experimented with providing such special secluded accommodation, it remained available only to the very wealthy who could afford to reserve an entire carriage. Most other women continued to travel in females'-only

---

[33] 'Decade of being a Metro.'

[34] Ibid.

[35] 'Women's Reserved Coach in Delhi Metro from Saturday,' *Hindustan Times*, 1 October 2010.

[36] Ibid.; 'Special Coach Only for Women in Delhi Metro,' CNN-IBN, 27 September 2010 (available at: http://ibnlive.in.com/news/special-coach-only-for-women-in-delhi-metro/131770-3.html).

railway carriages mandated in the third-class. However, even as they were used by millions, such females'-only carriages continued to carry a patina of reproach, being seen as inadequate to maintaining respectability. The patina of reproach was conjoined with more than a frisson of danger, with female passengers being systematically seen as prey, vulnerable to theft, unwanted attention, and sexual assault. From the late nineteenth century onwards, such threats were seen increasingly in racial terms, with the public and press emphasizing how the security of Indian women passengers was compromised by the judicial leniency afforded to European and Eurasian railway employees who dishonoured, raped, or abducted them (Chapter 2).

In contrast, the metro is perceived to be a public space where women are safer than in most other public spaces in Delhi. In the last decade, female commuters have repeatedly stressed how the metro saves them from the groping and pawing that occurs in overcrowded buses or else from the threat of being abducted by taxi or auto-rickshaw drivers.[37] Women had found the well-policed metro safe even before special women's coaches were introduced on it; public testimonials continue to attest to this sense of security.[38] Commenting on the fatal rape of a female commuter on a chartered bus in December 2012, metro commuters stressed the contrast with the metro, whose stations are manned by members of the central national guard and outfitted with close-circuit cameras, metal detectors, and X-ray machines. Women can hit an emergency button to call for help, leading one commuter to state unequivocally: 'You can't rape anybody in the Metro.'[39]

While these significant differences distinguish the females'-only carriages on colonial railways from the women's reserved spaces in Delhi's metro, some aspects of the public discussion surrounding this space remain similar, particularly those that link expanding public transport to female empowerment. In the mid-nineteenth century, colonial officials had stressed the great social benefits that would ensue if Indian women were encouraged to use railways. Penning one of the most influential documents on the subject, Sir William Muir, lieutenant-governor of the North-West Provinces between 1868 and 1874, argued that nothing else would contribute more to 'the eventual

---

[37] 'Delhi Women Find Metro Rail Safe,' Indo-Asian News Service, 16 October 2004; 'Delhi Metro Liberates Female Commuters,' Agence France-Presse, 21 March 2006; Luce, 'Clean, Efficient, On Time;' Joseph, 'Delhi Metro Reaches across Class Lines.'

[38] Ibid.

[39] Anjani Trivedi, 'Are Delhi's Buses Safe for Women?' *New York Times*, 17 December 2012.

introduction of a more civilized and rational treatment of the female sex in India' (Chapter 2). More recently—and even when expressed less dramatically than the Agence France-Presse's declaration 'Delhi Metro Liberates Female Commuters'[40]—public analyses document how the metro effects mobility for Delhi's women, allowing them to travel without a male escort. For some, like 17 year-old Anukriti Sinha, this means an unaccompanied trip to a distant shopping mall;[41] for others, it is as fundamental as having a career. Thus, 21-year old Megha Kumari, living in Sitaram Bazar, could not use her professional computer certificate as her parents worried about her safety while travelling to and from work—until the metro convinced them otherwise.[42]

Shaping public behaviour

As the metro becomes more and more integrated into the fabric of Delhi's everyday life, there are increasing questions about how its spaces affect public behaviour. For some, the answer is quite unequivocal: the metro 'has not only changed the way we travel and calculate distance but also how we behave in public space.'[43] Interest in how people's use of mass transit systems 'both reflects changing values and behaviour in India's vast cities and contributes to that change' is reflected in a recent press release that asked rather directly: 'If citizens change their way of travelling, do they change their way of living?'[44]

The idea that public travel is a preceptor in an imagined ascent from savagery to civilization is an enduring one; equally enduring is the idea that educating the masses into becoming good passengers makes them into better citizens. In a 1929 piece titled 'Educating the Third Class Passenger' journalist H. Sutherland Stark had explained that the difficult conditions of third-class railway travel stemmed from the fact that Indian passengers were 'insufficiently taught how to travel like sane human beings,' and hence created the debilitating conditions of which they complained (Chapter 1). Stark suggested procedures for educating passengers: providing railway staff with training courses and manuals to help passengers 'behave,' introducing 'railway literature' in the curriculum of village schools, developing stories that would tell the masses how

[40] 'Delhi Metro Liberates Female Commuters.'
[41] Ibid.
[42] 'Decade of being a Metro.'
[43] Ibid.
[44] Burke, 'Delhi Metro Calls for "Decorum"'; 'Delhi Metro Train—New Era Begins,' 5 October 2011, PRLog—Global Press Release Distribution.

journeys could be made comfortable, publishing books designed to instruct people, and offering lectures at small stations. Neither was Stark alone; a decade earlier, M.K. Gandhi had stressed how railway travel offered a chance to create a civic body of citizens, arguing that educating railway passengers provided an opportunity for 'a splendid education to millions in orderliness, sanitation, decent composite life, and cultivation of simple and clean tastes' (Chapter 1).

One can see clear analogies with how the Delhi metro is seen to 'educate' its passengers and, consequently, shape the public behaviour of Delhi's masses. Some see the metro as an enclave where people behave better than they do in the world outside, their improved behaviour regulated by the deterrence of a punitive fine. Describing the punctual arrival of metro trains and the absence of spitting in metro spaces, Manu Joseph stressed how 'everything about the Delhi Metro and how people behaved inside it was the opposite of the nation outside.'[45] Others see the shift as an enduring one and suggest that 'Delhi'ites have acquired a new habit, thanks to Metro—patience at public places.'[46] By way of illustration, Zia Haq describes a scenario:

> At the ticket counter, the queue forms almost instantly. There's nobody herding commuters into lines. The walls aren't paan-stained; people respect its sanctity. Smokers resist any urge to light up. The lowest denomination ticket is for Rs 6 *but discipline comes free* [emphasis added].[47]

Using announcements on the public address system and 'admonitory posters' on the walls, the metro administration is actively trying to shape passenger behaviour.[48] Stick-figure illustrations accompany written text pertaining to 'the four big no-nos. No smoking. No littering. No spitting. No food or drink.'[49] Some of those interviewed are critical of such instructions: Sophea Lerner, an Australian sonic media artist and researcher who has lived in Delhi for several years believes that announcements telling commuters not to befriend 'any unknown person' encourage 'withdrawal from the shared social space.'[50] However, others argue that these same instructions, whether

---

[45] Joseph, 'Delhi Metro Reaches across Class Lines.'
[46] Haq, 'One Helluva Ride Ahead.'
[47] Ibid.
[48] Kotamraju, 'Life in a Metro.'
[49] *Christian Science Monitor* (Boston), 11 April 2006.
[50] 'Delhi Metro Train—New Era Begins.'

telling people to wait for those coming out of the train before walking in, or advising them not to talk to strangers or play loud music, has 'maybe even civilised us a bit.'[51]

Space, sight, land, and air

Even as the metro is evaluated as an agent of social change—whether through democratizing Delhi society, empowering its female commuters, or 'civilizing' the behaviour of it population—it's most tangible impact has been on Delhi's physical environment, both visible and invisible. As Rashmi Sadana notes, it will soon be difficult to remember what Delhi was like before the metro.[52] Just as a growing network of railway tracks, stations, embankments, bridges, signals, and crossings permanently altered the landscape of colonial India, so in Delhi metro stations are new landmarks and 'metro pillars' offer a new address. Ajit Singh and Rakesh Kumar, the proprietors of a recently opened eatery, wanted an 'easy address,' and ended up using the metro pillar as one: '55/2, Opposite Pillar No. 191, South Patel Nagar Market.'[53] Meanwhile, the elevated parts of the metro have changed the city's skyline: the metro line passing near the Qutub Minar had to be re-routed because it threatened to obstruct people's view of the iconic monument that is inextricable from the city's history.[54]

Even more direct has been the impact on those whose land was required and acquired for the metro. Land for the Delhi metro has been acquired—as land for railways was—by invoking the state's right to acquire property for public purposes. In fact, land for the metro was acquired under regulations prescribed in the Land Acquisition Act of 1894, which—though it has been amended over the previous century—is the same one that systematized land acquisition rules for railways (Chapter 3).[55] Further, like with railways, the metro itself does not purchase the land directly. In colonial India, land for railways was purchased by government and handed over, free of charge for

---

[51] Kotamraju, 'Life in a Metro.'

[52] Rashmi Sadana, 'On the Delhi Metro: An Ethnographic View,' *Economic and Political Weekly* Xlv, 46 (November 2010): 77-83.

[53] 'Decade of being a Metro.'

[54] Sadana, 'On the Delhi Metro.'

[55] Succeeding the Land Acquisition Acts X of 1870 and VI of 1857. The 1857 legislation decreed that conflict was subject to arbitration, a principle that held till the Land Acquisition Act X (1870) required disputed cases to be referred to civil courts. A new Land Acquisition Act is scheduled for 2014.

99 years, to railway companies. In the case of the metro, land that belongs already to Delhi government agencies is leased to the Delhi Metro Rail Corporation (DMRC), while private land is acquired by the Delhi government through its land acquisition collector. The substantive difference, of course, is that the Delhi metro has to *pay* for the land thus acquired. In contrast, the British companies that owned railways in India in the decades before the state intervened directly received land free of charge from the imperial government, a measure guaranteed to decrease the infrastructure costs of railway companies and increase their expectation of profit.

Like with railway land, valuation of and compensation for metro land has generated anxiety and conflict. Aside from the financial compensation provided, the government has instituted a programme to relocate and rehabilitate those affected by the metro's construction—'Project affected persons' as they are called in legalese.[56] Opinions vary on the fairness of the compensation. Some—like the owners of 38 shops that were demolished to construct Hauz Khas station—have complained that they were not fairly compensated; in the same set of interviews, however, 'more than a dozen businessmen interviewed around the construction all praised the project.'[57] Others insist that the project 'ran roughshod' over 'land-rights issues.'[58] In several cases, the conflicts have ended up in civil court and in some cases the compensation awarded has had to be significantly increased (in one case by 1.26 crore or 12.6 million rupees).[59] Much of this is congruent with the confusion, anxiety, and contests generated by railway construction in colonial India: complaints about government collectors and railway commissioners undervaluing land or compensating the wrong party, complaints against careless surveyors and railway officers empowered to enter people's property; complaints about the process of arbitration that withheld compensation until all claims were sorted.

In some instances, the question is not about valuation or compensation but about heritage, especially when digging underground lines. Railway construction had to contend in several cases with questions about archaeological

---

[56] T.C. Nakh, Additional Secretary, Land and Building Department, Government of NCT of Delhi, Circular no. F.1/23/01/L&B/WC/11554-581, dated 25 October 2006 (available at: http://www.delhimetrorail.com/projectsupdate/RelocationPAPs.pdf).

[57] Rohde, 'Clean, Modern Subway, Efficiently Built. In India?'

[58] Polgreen, 'In India, Hitching Hopes on a Subway.'

[59] 'Centre, Delhi Metro Told to Pay More for Land Acquired for Barakhamba Station,' *Indian Express*, 30 July 2012.

remains or—more important in the 1860s and 1870s, immediately after the 1857 Rebellion—religious buildings that literally came in their way. Heritage monuments rather than religious buildings per se have been at the focus of the metro's construction (although in July 2012 some controversy was generated when excavations for the metro unearthed a structure that some claimed was the Akbarabadi mosque built under Shahjahan).[60] On the whole, however, it is not religious shrines (perhaps because the metro is being careful) but historical buildings that have elicited concern. Ironically, much anxiety has been generated by the metro's 'Heritage line,' which is intended to make Delhi's historical monuments accessible.[61] It took the National Monuments' Authority (NMA) two years to sign off on several segments of the Heritage metro and that too with the caveat that the Archaeological Survey of India (ASI) continuously and carefully monitor its impact on neighbouring heritage structures.[62]

It might take a little more time to grasp some of the more substantive physical effects of metro construction, especially those generated by practices like underground tunnelling. Some of these potential effects may be averted if the metro follows such precautionary measures as have been legally mandated. Mass transit systems are expected to affect topography—thus, in the colonial context it was understood that the construction of massive railway embankments would affect drainage patterns in the areas in which they were built, usually low-lying or deltaic ones that experienced heavy seasonal rainfall or seasonable floods. The damage (as opposed to change) that ensued in many of these areas was not necessarily from the construction of the embankment per se but because railway companies ignored the precautionary and compensatory measures prescribed. Thus, while railway embankments changed drainage patterns, the actual damage occurred because railway companies failed to build adequate drainage in these embankments, despite being contractually obliged to do so (Chapter 3).

---

[60] 'To Keep the Past Alive,' *Hindustan Times*, 21 April 2007. Unauthorized construction of a new mosque began at the disputed site, the ASI issued a public notice seeking that the 'illegal construction' be removed, and on 20 July 2012, a court order banned all construction activity on the site.

[61] Priyanka Sharma, 'Heritage Metro Hits Hurdle,' *Indian Express*, 8 January 2013.

[62] 'NMA Green Signal to Metro Heritage Line,' *Times of India*, 18 January 2013 (Times News Network). The heritage line is an extension of the Central Secretariat line to Kashmere Gate that links some important heritage structures in Delhi including Red Fort, Jama Masjid, and Kashmere Gate.

At the same time that the construction of the metro has caused its share of dust and diversion, there have been simultaneous attempts to minimize this. Some of this is facilitated by technology: the German-built mechanical worm, which is 'nearly eight times the length of a city bus and six times as powerful' has—invisible to the public—tunnelled under Delhi's surface.[63] There have also been active measures to minimize both structural damage and visible inconvenience: in the construction near Hauz Khaz station, people noticed the 'steel girders erected to steady the walls of nearby buildings and monitors that measure vibrations' as well as the fact that 'dump trucks haul dirt only at night and crews wash down the streets before morning.'[64]

Public opinion has served as somewhat of a watchdog. Thus, traders at Sarojini Nagar market threatened protests if authorities did not take cognizance of the fact that the metro station—while eventually boosting business—would nevertheless block one side of the market during the construction phase.[65] While it is hard to tell which specific issue prompted the decision, the DMRC did adopt a new, less intrusive, technology for its third and current phase of construction, one that allows it to build underground subways on busy roads without disrupting traffic. This 'Box Pushing' technology negates the need for vertical excavation or large-scale digging; instead six reinforced cement concrete (RCC) boxes are pushed with the help of hydraulic jacks to create the 48-metre long subway tunnel.[66] Similarly, recent reports that metro construction had generated vibrations in houses in Janakpuri led the metro's chief Mangu Singh to replace the Vibring Cisco method being used there with the new Pile Foundation method.[67]

Like with railways, some of the metro's impact will take longer to assess, even if the effects are immediate. Both railways and the metro have affected tree cover, both requiring that large numbers of trees be felled. Obviously, the scale of deforestation generated by railways was much higher, both because of the length of railway tracks across India, as well as the use of valuable wood for railway sleepers (Chapter 3). However, people have expressed concern about

---

[63] Atul Mathur, 'Tunnel to Tomorrow,' *Hindustan Times*, 13 October 2009.

[64] Rohde, 'Clean, Modern Subway, Efficiently Built. In India?'

[65] Suhash Munshi, 'Market versus Metro: Sarojini Nagar Traders Threaten Protests over Planned Station,' *MailOnlineIndia*, 15 November 2012.

[66] 'DMRC Adopts New Tech to Avoid Traffic Disruptions during Metro Station Construction,' *Indian Express,* 16 August 2013.

[67] Pragya Singh, 'DMRC Aces Green Test for Giant Leap in Network,' *The Pioneer*, 28 July 2013.

the extent of trees felled on land acquired by the metro. The construction of three metro corridors (Central Secretariat to Kashmere Gate, Yamuna Vihar to Mukundpur, and Janakpuri to Botanical Garden) will result in 16,000 trees being felled. To compensate, DMRC will have to pay Rs. 28,000 per tree or else plant trees equal to the number axed.[68] The metro has offered a plan for 'compensatory afforestation' (on 32 hectares of land at Garhi Mandu).[69] Such measures are part of a new initiative to assess and limit how the metro will affect people and their environment, from disposal of soil and loss of trees to noise, vibration, and disruption of utilities and facilities.[70]

The situation is different, however, in relation to environmental concerns like air quality. Though the smoke emitted from a steam engine was palpably visible to everyone, 'pollution' as a concept was still being developed in the nineteenth century, and it took time and an increasing density of rail traffic before the effect of such carbon monoxide emission on people's health began to be studied. Especially given the plague and cholera epidemics that ravaged India in the late nineteenth and early twentieth centuries, links between railway travel and health focused almost exclusively on how this technology encouraged the spread of contagious diseases (Chapter 5). Contemporary accounts recognized the speed with and distance to which railways could disperse contagion, as well as their role in effecting dangerous concentrations of people. Thus, formal legislation focused on restricting infectious contact in railway carriages as well as on preventing the dispersion of contagious diseases through railway passengers.

In contrast, the metro is seen to have a positive effect on the health of Delhi's population, earning plaudits for helping reduce both congestion and pollution on Delhi's roads.[71] A survey conducted by the Central Road Research Institute (CRRI) some years after the metro was inaugurated revealed that it had prevented the creation of over 2,275 tonnes of poisonous gases and helped save 33,000 tonnes of fuel; more important to the health of

---

[68] Singh, 'DMRC Aces Green Test for Giant Leap in Network.'

[69] Ibid.

[70] Delhi Metro Rail Corporation, 'EIA for Phase III Corridors of Delhi Metro, August 2011' (http://www.delhimetrorail.com/projectsupdate/delhimasseia.pdf).

[71] In initial analyses, it was estimated that the metro would decrease pollution levels by at least 25 per cent ('and reduce fuel consumption by Rs. 6 to 7 billion every year'). 'Metro Goes Underground, Bowls over Manmohan,' Indo-Asian News Service, 19 December 2004.

the ordinary resident of Delhi was the fact that it helped reduce consumption of fuel containing hydrocarbons and decreased two important vehicular pollutants, namely, nitrogen dioxide and carbon monoxide.[72] In contrast, railways remain under severe scrutiny, both because of the air pollution that they generate as well as for their role as bulk carriers for several pollution intensive commodities like coal, iron ore, cement, fertilizers, and petroleum.[73] While railways are experimenting with measures like regenerative braking and liquefied natural gas instead of diesel, commentators argue that for substantive impact, these changes need to be introduced on a much larger scale than they have so far.[74]

I began the conclusion by pointing out how I was struck by the ways in which the popular press explicated the Delhi metro by juxtaposing it against India's railway system. The distinctions posed suggested a need to understand the import of new technology in relation to preceding technologies, even if through narratives of disjunction. At the same time, the conversation indicated another way to explore the impact of railways—by exploring analogies between two transport 'revolutions' more than a century apart. The attempt proved fruitful, especially in highlighting how the historical meaning of new technology is materialized through everyday use. Even an impressionistic series of comparisons between the 'traditional infrastructure' of railways—to return to Edward Luce's depiction—and the 'Tunnel to Tomorrow'—as the *Hindustan Times* recently described the Delhi metro—suggests the resilience of certain questions: about how people navigate and inhabit the abstract systems, spaces, and technologies that grid our overwhelmingly urban-industrial society;

---

[72] 'Metro Makes Major Impact in Delhi,' *The Hindu*, 6 June 2007; Deepti Goel and Sonam Gupta, The Effect of Metro Rail on Air Pollution in Delhi, Working Paper no. 229. Centre for Development Economics, Department of Economics, Delhi School of Economics (http://www.cdedse.org/pdf/work229.pdf)

[73] 'Environment Management in Indian Railways,' Report no. 21 of 2012–13 of Comptroller and Auditor General of India, Performance audit of environment management in Indian railways, 1 December 2012, especially 10–23. Attachment linked at: http://www.indiaenvironmentportal.org.in/content/368977/performance-audit-of-environment-management-in-indian-railways.

[74] Rail Mantralay, Govt. of India, 'Indian Railways: Annual Reports and Accounts, 2010–11,' http://www.indianrailways.gov.in/railwayboard/uploads/directorate/stat_econ/Annualreport10-11/Annual_report_10-11_eng.pdf; Anil Sinha, Rail Stations Suffer from Air and Noise Pollution: CAG,' *Deccan Herald*, 21 December 2012; S.N. Mathur, 'Modernise Indian Railways,' *Indian Express*, 21 October 2012.

about how everyday life is a historical space for a symmetrical and reciprocal dialogue between technology and society; and about how popular processes of adapting to, contesting, and accommodating technological change determine the historical impact of such change. These are precisely the issues that the entire book has been concerned with.

Bibliography

Archives

National Archives of India (Delhi)

Correspondence and Circulars

- Railway General Letters, 1852–61.
- Railway Letters from Court of Directors, 1852–61.
- Railway Letters from the Home Government, 1852–61.
- *Railway Circulars of 1883*

Proceedings

- Home: Railway; Home: Railway A
- Home: Judicial
- Home: Political; Home: Political A; Home: Political B; Home: Political Deposit
- Home: Public B
- Home: Sanitary (Plague); Home: Sanitary (Plague) B
- PWD: Railway; PWD: Railway A
- PWD: Railway Traffic; PWD: Railway Traffic A; PWD: Railway Traffic B
- Railway Board: TX B; Railway Board: Establishment B
- Railway Statistics A

India Office Records, British Library (London)

Correspondence

- Railways: Home Correspondence

Proceedings

- India Proceedings: PWD: Railway Traffic; PWD: Railway Traffic A
- India Proceedings: Railway Traffic; Railway Traffic A
- Bengal Proceedings: PWD: Railway
- Bengal Public Works Proceedings: Railway
- Bihar and Orissa Proceedings: PWD: Railway A
- Economic and Overseas Department Proceedings
- Oudh Proceedings and United Provinces Proceedings: PWD: Railway
- United Provinces and North-West Provinces Proceedings: PWD: Railway

Papers

- Papers of Derek Gordon Harington Hawes, Mss/Eur/D1225/20 (1947–48).
- Papers of the Marquess Curzon of Kedleston, Viceroy of India 1898–1905; Lord Privy Seal 1915–19; Foreign Secretary 1919–24.
- Papers of John Pitt Kennedy, Consulting engineer to Government of India for railways 1850–52 and Director of Bombay, Baroda and Central India Railway.
- Papers and correspondence of John Chapman (1801–54), railway promoter.
- Indian Railways Collection of Michael G. Satow, correspondence, papers and articles relating to Indian Railways, together with locomotive diagrams and photographs.
- Miscellaneous papers of Alexander Izat (1844–1920), Public Works Dept, Government of India 1863–89; Agent and Chief Engineer, Bengal and North Western Railway, 1883–1904, 1886–1913.

Reports (in chronological order)

- *Adaptation of Railways for Military Transport* (Simla: Government of India Press, 1877).
- *Report on Sanitary Measures in India in 1875–76: with Miscellaneous Information up to June 1877*, Vol. ix (London: Eyre and Spottiswoode, 1877).
- 'Some Passenger Statistics,' *Indian Railway Gazette: A Monthly Journal Devoted to Railways, Engineering and Matters of General Interest* 2(6) (1 June 1908).
- *Report of the Pilgrim Committee, Bihar and Orissa, 1913* (Simla: Government Central Branch Press, 1915).

- *Report of the Pilgrim Committee: Bombay* (Simla: Government Monotype Press, 1916).
- East India Railway Committee (1920–21). *Report of the Committee appointed by the Secretary of State for India to Enquire into the Administration and Working of Indian Railways*: Vol I: Report; Vol. II: Evidence taken in London; Vol. III: Evidence taken in India; Vol. IV: Written Statements.

Nehru Memorial Museum and Library (Delhi)

Native Newspaper Reports

- Agra and Oudh Native Newspaper Reports
- Bengal Native Newspaper Reports
- Madras Native Newspaper Reports
- Punjab, North-West Provinces, Oudh, and Central Provinces Native Newspaper Reports
- United Provinces Native Newspaper Reports

Newspapers

- *Bombay Times and Journal of Commerce, The*
- *Delhi Gazette*
- *Englishman and Military Chronicle, The* (Calcutta)
- *Friend of India, The* (Serampore)
- *Hindoo Patriot, The* (Calcutta)
- *Lahore Chronicle, The*
- *New Statesman and Nation, The* (Jullundar).
- *Searchlight* (Patna)
- *Statesman, The* (Calcutta)

Rail Museum Archive (Delhi)

Reports

- Railway Board Annual Reports

Magazines and Publicity Material

- *Bombay, Baroda, and Central Indian Railway Magazine*
- *East Indian Railway Supplement*
- *Indian State Railways Magazine*

- *Indian State Railway Tourist Pamphlets*
- *South Indian Railway Illustrated Guide* (Madras: Higginbotham & Co., 1900)
- *Traveller's Guide: South India* (Trinchinopology: Chief Commercial Superintendent, South Indian Railway, n.d.).

Digitally Accessed Reports (in chronological order)

- *Medical Press and Circular: A Weekly Journal of Medicine and Medical Affairs: From June to December 1869* (London: Medical Press and Circular Office, 1869). Last accessed at <https://archive.org> on 06 January 2015.
- 'Question XV: The Twenty Four Hour Day,' Proceedings of the fifth session, London, June–July 1895, in *Bulletin of the International Railway Congress Association*, Vol. xi (1897) (Brussels: P. Weissenbruch and London: P.N. King and Son, 1897). Last accessed at <books.google.com> on 06 January 2015.
- 'Fuel on Indian Railways: Native *versus* British Coal,' *The Railway News*, London, 27 October 1900, reprinted in *The London News: Finance and Joint-Stock Companies Journal*, LXXIV, July–December 1900 (London: Railway News' Offices, 1900): 615. Last accessed at <books.google.com> on 06 January 2015.
- Government of India, Ministry of Statistics. 2015. *Statistical Yearbook, India, 2015*. New Delhi: Central Statistics Office. Last accessed at <http://mospi.nic.in> on 06 January 2015.
- Delhi Metro Rail Corporation. 2011 (August). EIA for phase III Corridors of Delhi Metro. Last accessed at <http://www.delhimetrorail.com/projectsupdate/delhimasseia.pdf> on 06 January 2015.
- Environment Management in Indian Railways: No. 21 of 2012–13 Performance Audit of Environment Management in Indian Railways by the Comptroller and Auditor General of India, 1 December 2012. Last accessed at <http://www.environmental-auditing.org/Portals/0/AuditFiles/Environment%20Management%20in%20Indian%20Railways.pdf> on 06 January 2015.
- Deepti Goel and Sonam Gupta, The Effect of Metro Rail on Air Pollution in Delhi, Working Paper No. 229, Centre for Development Economics, Department of Economics, Delhi School of Economics. Last accessed at <http://www.cdedse.org/pdf/work229.pdf> on 06 January 2015.

Newspapers

- *Australian Magazine*
- *Christian Science Monitor*
- *Financial Times*
- *Hindu, The*

- *Hindustan Times, The*
- *Indian Express, The*
- *International Herald Tribune*
- *Mail Online India*
- *New York Times, The*
- *Pioneer, The*
- *Times, The*
- *Times of India, The*
- *Washington Post, The*

Published

Adam-Smith, Patsy. 1980. *Romance of Victorian Railways*. New York, NY: Rigby.

Aguiar, Marian. 2007. 'Railway Space in Partition Literature.' In *27 Down: New Departures in Indian Railway Studies*, edited by Ian Kerr, 39–67. Hyderabad: Orient Longman.

———. 2008. 'Making Modernity: Inside the Technological Space of the Railway.' *Cultural Critique* 68 (1): 66–85.

———. 2011. *Tracking Modernity: India, Trains, and the Culture of Mobility*. Minneapolis, MN: University of Minnesota Press.

Ahuja, Ravi. 2003. '"The Bridge-Builders": Some Notes on Railways, Pilgrimage and the British "Civilising Mission" in Colonial India.' In *Colonialism as Civilizing Mission: The Case of British India*, edited by Harald Fischer-Tiné and Michael Mann, 195–216. London: Anthem Press.

———. 2009. *Pathways of Empire: Circulation, Public Works and Social Space in Colonial Orissa, c. 1780–1914*. Hyderabad: Orient BlackSwan.

Alamgir, M. 1980. *Famine in South Asia: Political Economy of Mass Starvation*. Cambridge, MA: Oelgschlager, Gunn, and Hain.

Allen, Francis R. 1957. *Technology and Social Change*. New York, NY: Appleton-Century-Crofts.

Ambedkar, B.R. 1968 (1935). *Annihilation of Caste, with a Reply to Mahatma Gandhi, and Castes in India, their Mechanism, Genesis and Development*. Jullundur City: Bheem Patrika Publications.

———. 1989 (n.d.). 'Waiting for a Visa.' Unpublished Writings, in *Dr. Babasaheb Ambedkar: Writings and Speeches*, Vol. 12. Mumbai: Government of Maharashtra.

Amin, Shahid. 1988 (1984). 'Gandhi as Mahatma: Gorakhpur District, Eastern UP, 1921–2.' In *Selected Subaltern Studies*, edited by Ranajit Guha, 288–350. Delhi: Oxford University Press.

———. 1995. *Event, Metaphor, Memory: Chauri Chaura 1922–1992*. Delhi: Oxford University Press.

Anand , Mulk Raj. 2004 (1936). *Coolie.* In *Mulk Raj Omnibus,* edited by Saros Cowasjee, 129–401. Delhi: Penguin.

Anderson, D.Y. 1929. 'Communications-Railways.' *Annals of the American Academy of Political and Social Science* 145 (2): 59–67.

Andrews, W.P. 1848 (1846). *Indian Railways and Their Probable Results with Maps and an Appendix Containing Statistics of Internal and External Commerce of India.* London: T.C. Newby.

Angevine, Robert G. 2004. *The Railroad and the State: War, Politics, and Technology in Nineteenth Century America.* Stanford, CA: Stanford University Press.

Anstey, Vera. 1977 (1949). *The Economic Development of India.* New York, NY: Arno Press.

Appadurai, Arjun. 1996. *Modernity at Large: Cultural Dimensions of Modernity.* Minneapolis, MN: University of Minnesota Press.

Arnold, David. 1980. 'Industrial Violence in Colonial India.' *Comparative Studies in History and Society* 22 (2): 234–55.

———. 1986. 'Cholera and Colonialism in British India.' *Past & Present* 113 (1): 118–51.

———. 1991. 'Bodies of Knowledge/Highways of Steel: Science and Technology in Modern India.' *South Asia Newsletter* (Centre of South Asian Studies, School of Oriental and African Studies, University of London) 17: 9–11.

———. 1993. *Colonizing the Body: State Medicine and Epidemic Disease in Nineteenth-century India.* Berkeley, CA: University of California Press.

———. 2000. *Science, Technology, and Medicine in Colonial India, The New Cambridge History of India.* Cambridge: Cambridge University Press.

———. 2001. *Gandhi: Profiles in Power.* Harlow: Pearson Educational.

———. 2013. *Everyday Technology: Machines and the Making of India's Modernity.* Chicago, IL: University of Chicago Press.

Arnold, David, and Erich deWald. 2012. 'Everyday Technology in South and Southeast Asia: An Introduction.' *Modern Asian Studies* 40 (1): 1–17.

Avineri, Shlomo, ed. 1968. *Karl Marx on Colonialism and Modernization: His Despatches and Other Writings on China, India, Mexico, The Middle East and North Africa.* New York, NY: Doubleday & Co.

Badsey, Stephen. 2001. 'The Impact of Communications and the Media on the Art of War since 1815.' In *War in The Age of Technology: Myriad Faces of Modern Armed Conflict,* edited by Geoffrey Jensen and Andrew Wiest, 66–102. New York, NY: New York University Press.

Bagchi, Amiya Kumar. 2000 (1972). *Private Investment in India, 1900–1939.* London and New York, NY: Routledge & Kegan Paul.

Banerjee, Prathma. 2006. *Politics of Time: 'Primitives' and History-writing in a Colonial Society.* Delhi: Oxford University Press.

Bartky, Ian. 1989. 'The Adoption of Standard Time.' *Technology and Culture* 30 (1): 25–56.

Baudrillard, Jean. 1981. *For a Critique of the Political Economy of the Sign*, translated and with an introduction by Charles Levin. St. Louis, MO: Telos Press.

Bayly, C.A. 1996. *Empire and Information: Intelligence Gathering and Social Communication in India, 1780–1870.* Cambridge: Cambridge University Press.

Bear, Laura. 1994. 'Miscegenations of Modernity: Constructing European Respectability and Race in the Indian Railway Colony, 1857–1931.' *Women's History Review* 3 (4): 112–31.

———. 2007. *Lines of the Nation: Indian Railway Workers, Bureaucracy, and the Intimate Historical Self.* New York, NY: Columbia University Press.

Bearce, George D. 1961. *British Attitudes towards India: 1784–1858.* London: Oxford University Press.

Beaumont, Michael and Michael Freeman, eds. 2007. *The Railway and Modernity: Time, Space and the Machine Ensemble.* Oxford: Peter Lang.

Bell, Horace. 1894. *Railway Policy in India.* London: Rivington, Percival & Co.

Bellew, Henry Walter. 1885. *The History of Cholera in India from 1862 to 1881: A Descriptive and Statistical Account of the Disease as Derived from the Official Published Reports of Several Provincial Governments.* London: Trubner and Co.

Benjamin, Walter. 1996 (1915). 'The Life of Students.' In *Walter Benjamin, Selected Writings*, Volume 1, 1913–1926, translated by Rodney Livingstone, 37–46. Cambridge, MA: Belknap Press of Harvard University Press.

———. 2007 (1936). 'The Work of Art in the Age of Mechanical Reproduction.' In *Illuminations*, edited and with an introduction by Hannah Arendt. New York, NY: Random House.

Berghaus, Erwin. 1964 (German, 1960). *The History of Railways.* London: Barrie and Rockliffe.

Bergstrom, Janet, ed. 1999. *Endless Night: Cinema and Psychoanalysis, Parallel Histories.* Berkeley, CA: University of California Press.

Bhalla, Alok, ed. 1994. *Stories About the Partition of India.* Delhi: Harper Collins.

———. 2006. *Partition Dialogues: Memories of a Lost Home.* Delhi: Oxford University Press.

Bhattachary, Amitrasudan. 1994. 'A Biographical Sketch.' In *Bankimchandra Chatterjee: Essays in Perspective*, edited by Bhabatosh Chatterjee, 557–62. New Delhi: Sahitya Akademi.

Bhattacharya, Nandini. 2011. 'The Logic of Location: Malaria Research in Colonial India, Darjeeling and Duars, 1900–30.' *Medical History* 55: 183–202.

Biddle, Gordon. 2003. 'Railways, Their Builders, and the Environment.' In *Impact of Railways on Society in Britain: Essays in Honour of Jack Simmons*, edited by A.K.B. Evans and John Gough, 117–28. Burlington: Ashgate.

Bourdieu, Pierre. 1977. *Outline of a Theory of Practice.* Cambridge: Cambridge University Press.

Briggs, Asa. 1970. *The Nineteenth Century: The Contradictions of Progress*. New York, NY: McGraw-Hill.

Bryce, James. 1914. *The Ancient Roman Empire and the British Empire in India; The Diffusion of Roman and English Law throughout the World: Two Historical Studies*. London and New York, NY: H. Milford and Oxford University Press.

Buchanan, R. A. 1986. 'The Diaspora of British Engineering.' *Technology and Culture* 27 (3): 501–24.

Buck-Morss, Susan. 1999 (1989). *The Dialectics of Seeing: Walter Benjamin and the Arcades Project*. Cambridge, MA: MIT Press,

Burton, Antoinette. 2003. *Dwelling in the Archive: Women Writing House, Home, and History in Late Colonial India*. Oxford and New York, NY: Oxford University Press.

Bury, Harriet. 2007. 'Novel Spaces, Transitional Moments: Negotiating Text and Territory in Nineteenth-Century Hindi Travel Accounts.' In *27 Down: New Departures in Indian Railway Studies*, edited by Ian Kerr, 39–67. Hyderabad: Orient Longman.

Butalia, Urvashi. 1993. 'Community, State and Gender: On Women's Agency during Partition.' *Economic and Political Weekly* 28 (17): WS 13–24.

———. 1998. *The Other Side of Silence: Voices from the Partition of India*. New Delhi: Viking.

Carter, Ian. 2001. *Railways and Culture in Britain: The Epitome of Modernity*. Manchester: Manchester University Press.

Ceserani, Remo. 1999. 'The Impact of the Train on Modern Literary Imagination.' *Stanford Humanities Review* 7 (1): 127–35.

Chakrabarty, Dipesh. 1974. 'The Colonial Context of the Bengal Renaissance: Early Railway Thinking in Bengal.' *Indian Economic Social History Review* 11: 192–206.

———. 1976. 'Early Railwaymen in India: "Dacoity" and "Train-Wrecking" (c. 1860–1900).' In *Essays in Honour of Professor S.C. Sarkar*, 523–50. Delhi: People's Publishing House.

———. 2000. *Provincializing Europe: Postcolonial Thought and Historical Difference*. Princeton, NJ: Princeton University Press.

———. 2000. 'Witness to Suffering: Domestic Cruelty and the Birth of the Modern Subject in Bengal.' In *Questions of Modernity* (Contradictions of Modernity, vol. 11), edited by Timothy Mitchell, 49–86. Minneapolis, MN: University of Minnesota Press.

———. 2002. *Habitations of Modernity: Essays in the Wake of Subaltern Studies*. Chicago, IL: University of Chicago Press.

Chandra, Bipan. 1966. *The Rise and Growth of Economic Nationalism in India: Economic Policies of the Indian National Leadership, 1880–1905*. Delhi: People's Publishing House.

———. 1988. *Indian National Movement: The Long-Term Dynamics*. Delhi: Vikas Publishing House.

Chatterjee, Kumkum. 1999. 'Discovering India: Travel, History and Identity in Late-Nineteenth and Early Twentieth Century India.' In *Invoking the Past: The Uses of History in South Asia*, edited by Daud Ali, 192–227. Delhi: Oxford University Press.

Chatterjee, Partha. 1993. *Nation and Its Fragments: Colonial and Postcolonial Histories*. Princeton, NJ: Princeton University Press.

———. 1997. *Our Modernity* (author's translation of Srinjan Halder Memorial Lecture, 1994). (Rotterdam and Dakar: SEPHIS and CODESRIA).

———. 1998 (1996). *Nationalist Thought in the Colonial World: A Derivative Discourse?* Minneapolis, MN: University of Minnesota Press.

———. 2004. *The Politics of the Governed: Reflections on Popular Politics in Most of the World*. New York, NY: Columbia University Press.

Chattopadhyay, Bankimchandra. 2005 (1873). *Indira*. In *The Bankimchandra Omnibus*, Vol. 1, translated by Marian Maddern, 253–338. New Delhi: Penguin.

———. 1986 (18??). 'Bengal's Peasants.' ('Bangerdesher Krishak') In *Sociological Essays: Utilitarianism and Positivism in Bengal*, translated by S. N. Mukherjee and Marian Maddern, 113–58. Calcutta: Rddhi.

Clarke, Hyde. 1857. *Colonization, Defence and Railways in Our Indian Empire*. London: John Weale.

———. 1881. 'The English Stations in the Hill Regions of India: Their Value and Importance, with Some Statistics of their Products and Trade.' *Journal of Statistical Society of London* 44 (3): 528–73.

Cohn, Bernard. 1996. *Colonialism and Its Forms of Knowledge*. Princeton, NJ: Princeton University Press.

Condon, J.K. 1900. *The Bombay Plague, Being a History of the Progress of Plague in the Bombay Presidency from September 1896 to June 1899, Compiled Under the Orders of the Government of India*. Bombay: Education Society.

Cornish, W.R. 1870. *Report on Cholera in Southern India for the Year 1869*. Madras: Government Gazette Press.

Crook, J. Mordaunt. 2003. 'Ruskin and the Railway.' In *The Impact of the Railways on Society in Britain*, edited by A.K.B. Evans and J.V. Gough, 129-34. Farnham: Ashgate.

Crooke, William. 1906. *Things Indian: Being Discursive Notes on Various Subjects Connected with India*. London: Charles Scribner.

Cunningham, J.M. 1873. *Cholera Epidemic of 1872 in Northern India*: Calcutta: Office of the Superintendent of Government Printing.

Dalmia, Vasudha. 1997. *The Nationalization of Hindu Tradition: Bharatendu Harischandra and Nineteenth-Century Banaras*. Delhi: Oxford University Press.

Danvers, Julian. 1860. *Report to the Secretary of State for India on Railways to the End of the Year 1859*. London: Her Majesty's Stationary Office.

Dasgupta, Ajit K. 1993. *History of Indian Economic Thought*. London: Routledge.

Datta, V. N., ed. 1975. *New Light on the Punjab Disturbances: Volumes VI and VII of Disorders Enquiry Committee Evidence*, with an introduction by V.N. Datta. Simla: Indian Institute of Advanced Study.

Davidson, Edward. 1868. *The Railways of India with an Account of their Rise, Progress, and Construction: Written with the Aid of the Records of the India Office.* London: E. & F. N. Spon.

Day, J.A.S. 1848. *A Practical Treatise on the Construction and Formation of Railways.* London: John Weale.

De Certeau, Michel. 1988 (1984). *The Practice of Everyday Life.* Berkeley, CA: University of California Press.

Den Otter, A. A. 1997. *Philosophy of Railways: The Transcontinental Railway Idea in British North America.* Toronto: University of Toronto Press.

Derbyshire, Ian D. 1987. 'Economic Change and the Railways in North India.' *Modern Asian Studies* 21 (3): 521–45.

———. 1995. 'The Building of India's Railways: The Application of Western Technology in the Colonial Periphery, 1850–1920.' In *Technology and the Raj,* edited by Roy MacLeod and Deepak Kumar. New Delhi: Sage Publications.

Desai, A. R. 2005 (1946?). *The Social Background of Indian Nationalism.* Delhi: Popular Prakashan.

Dirks, Nicholas B. 2001. *Castes of Mind: Colonialism and the Making of Modern India.* Princeton, NJ: Princeton University Press.

Donovon, D.G. 2011. 'Forests at the Edge of Empire: The Case of Nepal.' In *The British Empire and the Natural World: Environmental Encounters in South Asia,* edited by Deepak Kumar, Vinita Damodaran, and Rohan D'Souza. Delhi: Oxford University Press.

D'Souza, Rohan. 2006. *Drowned and Damned: Colonial Capitalism and Flood Control in Eastern India.* Delhi: Oxford University Press.

Duckers, Peter. 2003. *The British Indian Army, 1860–1914.* Princes Risborough: Shire Publications.

Dudley, Clyde B. and Morris D Morris. 1975. 'Selected Railway Statistics for the Indian Subcontinent, 1853–1946–47.' *Artha Vijana* 18 (3): 1-150.

Dutt, R.C. 1901–1903. *Economic History of India,* 2 vols. London.

Dutt, R.C. 1985 (1904). *India in the Victorian Age: An Economic History of the People.* Delhi: Daya Publishing House.

East India (Progress and Condition). 1861. *Statement Exhibiting the Moral and Material Progress of India during the Year 1859–60.* London: Her Majesty's Stationery Office.

———. 1867. *Statement Exhibiting the Moral and Material Progress of India during the Year 1865–66.* London: Her Majesty's Stationery Office.

———. 1894. *Statement Exhibiting the Moral and Material Progress of India during the Year 1891–92.* London: Her Majesty's Stationery Office

———. 1903. *Statement Exhibiting the Moral and Material Progress of India during the Year 1901–02.* London: His Majesty's Stationery Office.

———. 1906. *Statement Exhibiting the Moral and Material Progress of India during the Year 1904–05*. London: His Majesty's Stationery Office.

———. 1913. *Statement Exhibiting the Moral and Material Progress of India during the Year 1911–12*. London: His Majesty's Stationery Office.

East India (Statistical Abstracts). 1867. *Statistical Abstract Relating to British India, from 1840 to 1865* (First number). London: Her Majesty's Stationary Office.

———. 1870. *Statistical Abstract Relating to British India, from 1860 to 1869* (Fourth number). London: Her Majesty's Stationary Office.

———. 1878. *Statistical Abstract Relating to British India, from 1867/8 to 1876/7* (Twelfth number). London: Her Majesty's Stationary Office.

———. 1887. *Statistical Abstract Relating to British India, from 1876/7 to 1885/6.* (Twenty-first number). London: Her Majesty's Stationary Office.

———. 1896. *Statistical Abstract Relating to British India, from 1885–86 to 1894–95* (Thirtieth number). London: Her Majesty's Stationary Office.

———. 1905. *Statistical Abstract Relating to British India, from 1894–95 to 1903–1904* (Thirty-ninth number). London: His Majesty's Stationary Office.

———. 1915. *Statistical Abstract Relating to British India, from 1903–04 to 1912–13* (Forty-eighth number). London: His Majesty's Stationary Office.

———. 1922. *Statistical Abstract Telating to British India, from 1910–11 to 1919–20* (Fifty-fifth number). London: His Majesty's Stationary Office.

Echenberg, Myron J. 2007. *Plague Ports: The Global Urban Impact of Bubonic Plague, 1894–1901*. New York, NY: New York University Press.

Edwardes, S. M. 1909. *Gazetteer of Bombay City and Island*, Vol. 1. Bombay: Times Press.

Elleman, Bruce and Stephen Kotkin, eds. 2009. *Manchurian Railways and the Opening of China: An International History*. Armonk, NY: M.E. Sharpe.

Esty, Joshua. 2012. *Unseasonable Youth: Modernism, Colonialism, and the Fiction of Development*. New York, NY: Oxford University Press.

Evans, A. K. B and J. V. Gough, eds. 1993. *The Impact of the Railway on Society in Britain: Essays in Honour of Jack Simmons*. Aldershot: Ashgate.

Everdell, William R. 1997. *The First Moderns*. Berkeley, CA: University of California Press.

Fabian, Johannes. 2000 (1983). *Time and the Other: How Anthropology Makes its Object*. New York, NY: Columbia University Press.

Faith, Nicholas. 1990. *The World the Railways Made*. London: The Bodley Head.

Ferrell, Donald W. 1971. 'The Rowlatt Satyagraha in Delhi.' In *Essays on Gandhian Politics*, edited by Ravinder Kumar, 189-235. Oxford: Clarendon Press.

Field, Charles Dickinson. 1870. *Chronological Table of, and Index to, the Indian Statute-Book Year 1834*. London: Butterworth.

Findlay, George. 1894. *The Working and Management of an English Railway*. London: Whittaker and Co.

Fischer-Tiné, Harald. 2009. *Low and Licentious Europeans: Race, Class and 'White Subalternity' in Colonial India*. New Delhi: Orient Blackswan.

Foucault, Michel. 1972 (1971). *The Archaeology of Knowledge and the Discourse on Language*, translated by A. M. Sheridan Smith. New York: Pantheon Books.

Frietag, Sandra. 1985. 'Collective Crime and Authority in North India.' In *Crime and Criminality in British India*, edited by Anand Yang, 140-63. Tucson, AZ: The University of Arizona Press.

Fuller, C.J., and John Harris. 2000. 'For an Anthropology of the Modern Indian State.' In *The Everyday State and Society in Modern India*, edited by C.J. Fuller and Véronique Bénéï, 1–30. New Delhi: Social Science Press.

Fuller, J. F. C. 1961. *The Conduct of War, 1789–1961: A Study of the Impact of the French, Industrial, and Russian Revolutions on War and Its Conduct*. London: Eyre and Spottiswoode.

Gadgil, Madhav and Ramachandra Guha. 1993. *This Fissured Land: An Ecological History of India*. Berkeley, CA: University of California Press.

Gait, E.A. 1913. *Census of India, 1911*. Volume I: India, part I: Report. Calcutta: Superintendent, Government Publishing.

Gandhi, M. K. 1917. *Third Class on Indian Railways*. Lahore: Gandhi Publications League.

———. 1938 (1908/9). *Hind Swaraj or Indian Home Rule*. Ahmedabad: Navjivan.

———. 1962 (1919). 'Jagannath's Case.' In *Law and the Lawyers*, compiled and edited by S. B. Kher, 170–74. Ahmedabad: Navjivan (first published in *Young India*, 30 July 1919)

———. 1983 (1927–29). *Autobiography: The Story of My Experiments with Truth*, translated by Mahadev Desai. Dover: New York.

Gao, James Zheng. 1997. *Meeting Technology's Advance: Social Change in China and Zimbabwe in the Railway Age*. Westport, CT: Greenwood.

Gardner, James B. 1983. *Ordinary People and Everyday Life: Perspectives on the New Social History*. Nashville, TN: American Association for State and Local History.

Ghosh, P.C. 1948. *A Comprehensive Treatise on North Bihar Flood Problems: Being a Description of the River System and Their Behaviours and Tendencies with Suggestions for Flood Mitigation*. Patna: Superintendent, Government Printing.

Ghosh, Suresh Chandra. 1978. 'The Utilitarianism of Dalhousie and the Material Improvement of India.' *Modern Asian Studies* 12 (1): 97–110.

Giddens, Anthony. 1990. *The Consequences of Modernity*. Stanford, CA: Stanford University Press.

Gilmartin, David. 1998. 'Partition, Pakistan, and South Asian History: In Search of a Narrative.' *Journal of Asian Studies* 57 (4): 1069–95.

Gordon, Charles Alexander. 1877. *Notes on the Hygiene of Cholera*. London and Madras: Bailliere, Tindall, and Cox and Gantz Brothers.

Goswami, Manu. 2004. *Producing India: From Colonial Economy to National Space*. Chicago, IL: University of Chicago Press.

Government of India (Sanitary). 1869. *Report on Measures Adopted for Sanitary Improvements in India during the Year 1868 and up to the Month of June 1869 Together with Abstracts of Sanitary Reports for 1867 forwarded from Bengal, Madras, and Bombay.* London: Eyre and Spottiswoode.

Government of India (Punjab). 1870. *Punjab Record or Reference Book for Civil Officers*, Vol. 5. W.E. Ball, Manager.

Government of India (North-West Provinces). 1872. *Selections of the Records of the North-Western Provinces* (second series). Allahabad: Government Press.

Government of India (Sanitary Commissioner). 1873. *Abstract of Proceedings of the Sanitary Commissioner with the Government of India during the year 1872.* Calcutta: Office of the Superintendent of Government Printing.

Government of India (Railway Board). 1906. *Summary of the Administration of Indian Railways during the Viceroyalty of Lord Curzon of Kedleston*, Vol. I: January 1899–April 1904 and Vol. II: December 1904–November 1905. Calcutta: Office of the Superintendent of Government Printing.

Government of India (Bengal). 1908. *The Administration of Bengal under Sir Andrew Fraser, K.C.S.I, 1903–08.* Calcutta: Bengal Superintendent Book Depot.

Government of India (Punjab). 1911. *Punjab Mutiny Records: Reports*, Vol. VIII, parts 1 and. 2. Lahore: Punjab Government Press.

Government of India. 1928. *Studies in Malaria as it Affects Indian Railways.* Calcutta: Central Publication Branch.

Government of India (Home Department). 1943. *Congress Responsibility for the Disturbances, 1942–43*, Vol. I: Report, Vol. II: Evidence. Delhi: Government of India Press.

Government of India (Ministry of Information and Broadcasting). 1966. *Our Railways.* Delhi: Publications Division, Ministry of Information & Broadcasting.

Grübler, Arnulf. 1998. *Technology and Global Change.* Cambridge and New York, NY: Cambridge University Press.

Guha, Ranajit. 1983. *Elementary Aspects of Peasant Insurgency in Colonial India.* Delhi: Oxford University Press.

———. 1997. *Dominance Without Hegemony: History and Power in Colonial India* (Harvard, MA: Harvard University Press).

Gumprez, Ellen McDonald. 1974. 'City-Hinterland Relations and the Development of a Regional Elite in Nineteenth Century Bombay.' *Journal of Asian Studies* 33 (4): 581-601.

Gupta, Akhil and James Ferguson, eds. 1997. *Culture, Power, and Place, Explorations in Critical Anthropology.* Durham, NC: Duke University Press.

Habermas, Jürgen. 2000 (1985). *The Philosophical Discourses of Modernity: Twelve Lectures.* Translated by Frederick Lawrence. Cambridge, MA: The MIT Press.

Hamilton, Adelbert. 1884. 'Discrimination in Railway Facilities.' *The American Law Register* 32 (7): 417-34.

Harrington, Ralph. 2001. 'The Railway Accident: Trains, Trauma and Technological Crisis in Nineteenth-Century Britain.' In *Traumatic Pasts: History, Psychiatry and Trauma in the Modern Age, 1870-1930*, edited by Mark S. Micale and Paul Lerner, 31-57. Cambridge: Cambridge University Press.

Harrison, Mark. 1994. *Public Health in British India: Anglo-Indian Preventive Medicine 1859–1914*. Cambridge: Cambridge University Press.

———. 2012. *Contagion: How Commerce has Spread Disease*. New Haven, CT: Yale University Press.

Harvey, David. 2001. *Spaces of Capital: Towards a Critical Geography*. New York, NY: Routledge.

Hawes, Christopher J. 2013 (1996). *Poor Relations: The Making of a Eurasian Community in British India, 1773–1833*. Abingdon: Routledge

Haywood, Richard M. 1998. *Russia Enters the Railway Age, 1842–55*. Boulder, CO: East European Monographs.

Heathcoate, T. A. 1974. *The Indian Army: The Garrison of British Imperial India, 1822–1922*. London: David & Charles.

Highmore, Ben. 2002. *Everyday Life and Cultural Theory*. London: Routledge.

Howse, Derek. 1980. *Greenwich Time and the Discovery of Longitude*. Oxford: Oxford University Press.

Hughes, Hugh, compiler. 1976. *Steam in India*. 4 vols. Truro: Barton.

———. 1990–1996. *Indian Locomotives: Part 1 – Broad Gauge, 1851–1940; Part 2 – Metre Gauge, 1872–1940*; Part 3 – Narrow Gauge, 1863–1940; *Part 4 – 1941–1990*. Harrow: Continental Circle.

Huddlestone, G. 1906. *History of the East Indian Railway*. Calcutta: Thacker, Spink & Co.

Hunter, William. 1920. *Report of the Disorders Inquiry Committee, 1919-20 Appointed by the Government of India to Investigate Disturbances in Punjab, Delhi and Bombay*. Reprint, Delhi: Deep Publications.

Hurd, John M. 1983. 'Railways.' In *Cambridge Economic History of India, vol. 2*: c. 1757– c. 1970, edited by Dharma Kumar. Cambridge: Cambridge University Press.

Hurd, John, and Ian Kerr. 2012. *India's Railway History: A Research Handbook*. Leiden: Brill.

Husain, Intizar. 2006 (1954). 'Kataa Hua Dabba.' In *The Colour of Nothingness: Modern Urdu Short Stories*, translated by Muhammad Umar Menon. Delhi: Oxford University Press.

Inden, Ronald. 1990. *Imagining India*. Bloomington, IN: Indiana University Press.

Indian Council of Historical Research (ICHR). 1999. *Railway Construction in India: Selected Documents*, Vols I–III. New Delhi: ICHR.

Indian National Congress (Punjab Subcommittee). 1920. *Report of the Commissioners Appointed by the Punjab Sub-Committee of the Indian National Congress*. Lahore: K. Santanam (Secretary to the Commission of Enquiry), Vol I: Report.

Jackson, Alan. A. 2003. 'The London Railway Suburb.' In *Impact of Railways on Society in Britain: Essays in Honour of Jack Simmons*, edited by A.K.B. Evans and John Gough, 169–79. Burlington: Ashgate.

Jameson, Fredric. 1981. *The Political Unconscious: Narrative as a Socially Symbolic Act*. Ithaca, NY: Cornell University Press.

Jarrett, Michael. 2001. 'Train Tracks: How the Railroad Rerouted Our Ears.' *Strategies: A Journal of Theory, Culture, and Politics* 14 (1): 27–45.

Jayal, Niraja Gopal. 2013. *Citizenship and Its Discontents: An Indian History*. Boston, MA: Harvard University Press.

Jefferson, Mark. 1928. 'The Civilizing Rails.' *Economic Geography* 4 (3): 217-31.

Johnson, Emory R. 1909. 'Characteristics of American Railway Traffic: A Study in Geography.' *Bulletin of the American Geographical Society* 41 (10): 610-21.

Johnson, James. 1815. *The Influence of Tropical Climates, More Especially the Climate of India, on European Constitutions; the Principal Effects and Diseases Thereby Induced, Their Prevention or Removal, and The Means of Preserving Health in Hot Climates, Rendered Obvious to Europeans of Every Capacity: An Essay*. London: J. Callow.

Kapur, Mohan Lal. 1968. *Romance of Hockey*. Ambala Cantt.: Indian Hockey Federation.

Karaka, D. F. 1972. *Then Came Hazrat Ali: Autobiography*. Bombay: Popular Press.

Kellett, John R. 1969. *The Impact of Railways on Victorian Cities*. London: Routledge & K. Paul.

Kennedy, Dane. 1996. *The Magic Mountains: Hill Stations and the British Raj*. Berkeley, CA: University of California Press.

Ker, James Campbell. 1917. *Political Trouble in India: 1907–1917*. Calcutta: Superintendent, Government Printing (reproduced by Oriental Publishers, 1973).

Kern, Stephen. 1983. *The Culture of Time and Space 1880–1918*. Cambridge, MA: Harvard University Press.

Kerr, Ian J. 1985. 'Working Class Protest in 19th Century India: Example of Railway Workers.' *Economic and Political Weekly* 20 (4): PE34–40.

———. 1995. *Building the Railways of the Raj*. Delhi: Oxford University Press.

———. 2003. 'Representations and Representations of the Railways of Colonial and Post-Colonial South Asia.' *Modern Asian Studies* 37 (2): 287–326.

———. 2005. 'Reworking a Popular Religious Practice: The Effects of Railways on Pilgrimage in 19th and 20th South Asia.' In *Railways in Modern India*, edited by Ian J. Kerr, 304-27. Delhi: Oxford University Press.

———. 2007. *Engines of India: The Railways that Made India*. Westport, CT: Praeger.

Klein, Ira. 1973. 'Death in India.' *Journal of Asian Studies* 32 (4): 639–59.

———. 1984. 'When the Rains Failed, Famine, Relief and Mortality in British India.' *Indian Economic and Social History Review* 21 (2): 185–214

———. 1988. 'Plague, Policy and Popular Unrest in British India.' *Modern Asian Studies* 22 (4): 723–55.

Knowles, L.C.A. 1921. *The Industrial & Commercial Revolutions in Great Britain during the Nineteenth Century.* London: George Routledge.

———. 2006 (1932). *Economic Development in the Nineteenth Century: France, Germany, Russia and the United States.* London: Routledge.

Kolsky, Elizabeth. 2010. *Colonial Justice in British India: White Violence and the Rule of Law.* New York, NY: Cambridge University Press.

Kostal, R.W. 1994. *Law and English Railway Capitalism, 1825–75.* Oxford: Oxford University Press.

Kumar, Deepak, Vinita Damodaran, and Rohan D'Souza, eds. 2011. *The British Empire and the Natural World: Environmental Encounters in South Asia.* Delhi: Oxford University Press.

Kwashira, Vimbai C. 2009. *Green Colonialism in Zimbabwe, 1890–1980.* Amherst, MA: Cambria Press.

Lal, Mohan, ed. 1992. *Encyclopaedia of Indian Literature.* Delhi: Sahitya Akademi.

Lambert, Anthony J., ed. 1984. *Nineteenth-Century Railway History through the Illustrated London News.* London: David & Charles.

Landes, David S. 1983. *Revolution in Time: Clocks and the Making of the Modern World.* Cambridge, MA: Harvard University Press.

Lardner, Dionysius. 1850. *Railway Economy: A Treatise on the New Art of Transport.* London: Taylor, Walton, and Mayberly.

Larkin, Brian. 2008. *Signal and Noise: Media, Infrastructure, and Urban Culture in Nigeria.* Durham, NC: Duke University Press

Larson, John Lauritz. 1984. *Bonds of Enterprise: John Murray Forbes and Western Development in America' Railway Age.* Cambridge, MA: Harvard University Press.

Lee, C.E. 1940. *The Centenary of Bradshaw.* London: Railway Gazette.

———. 1946. *Passenger Class Distinctions.* London: Railway Gazette.

Lefebvre, Henri. 1991. *The Production of Space.* Translated by Donald Nicholson-Smith. Oxford: Blackwell.

———. 2003. *The Urban Revolution.* Translated by Robert Bononno and with a foreword by Neil Smith. Minneapolis, MN: University of Minnesota Press.

———. 2004. *Rhythmanalysis: Space, Time and Everyday Life.* Translated by Stuart Elden and Gerald Moore. New York, NY: Continuum.

Le Goff, Jacques. 1980. *Time, Work, and Culture in the Middle Ages.* Chicago, IL: University of Chicago Press.

Lehmann, Fritz. 1965. 'Great Britain and the Supply of Railway Locomotives of India: A Case Study of "Economic Imperialism."' *Indian Economic and Social History Review* II (4).

Lewin, Henry Grote. 1968 (1936). *Railway Mania and Its Aftermath 1845–1852.* Newton Abbot: David & Charles.

Löwy, Michael. 2005. *Fire Alarm: Reading Walter Benjamin's On the Concept of History*. Translated by Chris Turner. New York, NY: Verso.

Ludtke, Alf, ed. 1995. *The History of Everyday Life: Reconstructing Historical Experiences and Ways of Life*. Translated by William Templer. Princeton, NJ: Princeton University Press.

Lyon, Andrew. 1873. *The Law of India*, Vol. II: *The Miscellaneous Laws*: Calcutta and London: Thacker, Spink, & Co and W. Thacker & Co.

Mack, Kenneth W. 1999. 'Law, Society, Identity, and the Making of the Jim Crow South: Travel and Segregation on Tennessee Railroads, 1875–1905.' *Law & Social Inquiry* 24 (2): 377–409.

Maclean, Kama. 2008. *Pilgrimage and Power: The Kumbh Mela in Allahabad, 1765-1954*. New York, NY: Oxford University Press.

Maclean, William Campbell. 1886. *Diseases of Tropical Climates: Lectures Delivered at the Army Medical School*. London: Macmillan.

Macpherson, W. J. 1955. 'Investment in Indian Railways, 1845–1875.' *The Economic History Review* 8 (2) NS: 177–86.

———. 1972. 'Economic Development in India under the British Crown, 1858–1947.' In *Economic Development in the Long Run*, edited by. J. A. Youngson, 126-91. London: George Allen and Unwin Ltd.

Major, Susan. 2012. 'The Millions Go Forth': Early Railway Excursion Crowds, 1840-1860. D.Phil dissertation, University of York.

Malleson, G. B. and J.M. Cunningham. 1868. *Report on the Cholera Epidemic of 1867 in Northern India*. Calcutta: Superintendent of Government. Printing.

Manto, Saadat Hasan. 1985 (194?). 'The Black Shalwar.' In *Another Lonely Voice: The Life and Works of Saadat Hassan Manto*, translated by Leslie A. Flemming and Tahira Naqvi, 206–19. Lahore: Vanguard.

Markovitz, Claude, Jacques Pouchepadass, and Sanjay Subrahmanyam, eds. 2003. *Society and Circulation: Mobile People and Itinerant Cultures in South Asia, 1750-1950*. Delhi: Permanent Black.

Marshall, Peter, ed. 1970. *The British Discovery of Hinduism in the Eighteenth Century*. Cambridge: Cambridge University Press.

Marx, Karl. 1853 (25 June). 'The British Rule in India,' *New York Daily Tribune*, 25 June 1853. Reproduced in *Karl Marx on Colonialism and Modernization: His Despatches and Other Writings*, edited by Shlomo Avineri. New York: Doubleday, 1968.

———. 1853 (8 August). 'The Future Results of British Rule in India,' *New York Daily Tribune*. Reproduced in *Karl Marx on Colonialism and Modernization: His Despatches and Other Writings*, edited by Shlomo Avineri. New York: Doubleday, 1968.

Masselos, Jim. 2000. 'Bombay Time.' In *Intersections: Socio-Cultural Trends in Maharashtra*, edited by Meera Kosambi, 161-86. New Delhi: Orient Longman.

Mazumder, Rajit K. 2003. *The Indian Army and the Making of Punjab*. Delhi: Permanent Black.

McLeod, Roy and Deepak Kumar, eds. 1995. *Technology and the Raj: Western Technology and Technical Transfer to India 1700–1947*. New Delhi: Sage.

Metcalf, Thomas R. 1990. *The Aftermath of Revolt: India: 1857–70*. New Delhi: Manohar.

———. 1997. *Ideologies of the Raj*. 1997. Cambridge: Cambridge University Press.

Mishra, Dinesh Kumar. 'The Bihar Flood Story.' *Economic and Political Weekly* 32 (35): 2206–17.

Mitchell, John. 1934. *Wheels of Ind*. London: Thornton Butterworth.

Mitchell, Lisa. 2011. '"To Stop Train Pull Chain": Writing Histories of Contemporary Political Practice.' *Indian Economic and Social History Review* 48 (4): 469–95.

Mituzani, Satoshi. 2011. *The Meaning of White: Race, Class, and the 'Domiciled Community' in British India, 1858–1930*. New York, NY: Oxford University Press.

Modak, V. V. 1947. *Railway Travel in India*. Bombay: V.V. Modak.

Monson, Jamie. 2009. *Africa's Freedom Railway: How a Chinese Development Project Changed Lives and Livelihoods in Tanzania*. Bloomington, IN: Indiana University Press.

Morinis, Alan E. 1984. *Pilgrimage in the Hindu Tradition: A Case Study of West Bengal*. Delhi: Oxford University Press.

Mrázek, Rudolf. 2002. *Engineers of Happy Land: Technology and Nationalism in a Colony*. Princeton, NJ: Princeton University Press.

Mufti, Aamir R. 2007. 'Saadat Hasan Manto: A Greater Story-Writer than God.' In *Enlightenment in the Colony: The Jewish Question and the Crisis of Postcolonial Culture*, 177-209. Princeton, NJ: Princeton University Press.

Mukherjee, Meenakshi. 1985. *Realism and Reality: The Novel and Society in India*. Delhi: Oxford University Press.

Mukherjee, Mukul. 1980. 'Railways and Their Impact on Bengal's Economy, 1870–1920.' *Indian Economic and Social History Review* 17 (2): 191–209.

n.a. 1883 (12 October). 'Standard Railway Time.' *Science* 2 (36): 494-96.

Naidu, M. Pauparao. 1995 (1915). *The History of Railway Thieves, with Illustrations and Hints on Detection*, 4th edition. Reprinted and edited with a critical introduction by Vinay Lal. Gurgaon, Haryana: Vintage Press.

Nair, Janaki. 1990. 'Uncovering the Zenana: Visions of Indian Womanhood in Englishwomen's Writings, 1813–1940.' *Journal of Women's History* 2 (1): 8–34.

Nandy, Ashis. 1983. *The Intimate Enemy: Loss and Recovery of Self under Colonialism*. Delhi: Oxford University Press.

Naoroji, Dadabhai. 1901. *Poverty and UnBritish Rule in India*. London: S. Sonnenschein.

Nathan, R. 1896–89. *The Plague in India*, Vols. 1–3. Simla: Government Central Printing Office.

Negi, S.S. 2000. *Himalayan Forests and Forestry.* New Delhi: Indus Publishing.

Newman, Lucille F., ed. 1990. *Hunger in History.* Oxford: Blackwell.

Newton, David E. 1999. *Social Issues in Science and Technology: An Encyclopedia.* Santa Barbara, CA: ABC-CLIO

Odden, Karen Marie. 2001. 'Broken Trains of Thought: The Railway Crash, Trauma and Narrative in British Fiction, 1848–1910.' *Social Sciences* 62 (3).

O'Malley, L.S.S. 1907. *The Gazetteer of Darbhanga District: Bengal District Gazetteers.* Calcutta: Bengal Secretariat Book Depot.

———. 1926. *The Gazetteer of Monghyr District* (revised edition). Patna: Superintendent of Government Printing, Bihar and Orissa.

———. 2007 (1926). *Bengal and Orissa District Gazetteers: Monghyr.* New Delhi: Logos.

Pandey, Gyandendra. 1990. *The Construction of Communalism in Colonial North India.* Delhi: Oxford University Press.

———. 1992. 'In Defence of the Fragment: Writing about Hindu-Muslim Riots in India Today.' *Representations* 37: 27–55.

———. 2001. *Remembering Partition: Violence, Nationalism and History in India.* Cambridge: Cambridge University Press.

Parmar, Prabhjot 2007. 'Trains of Death: Representation of Railways in Films on the Partition of India.' In *27 Down: New Departures in Indian Railway Studies,* edited by Ian J. Kerr, 39–67. Hyderabad: Orient Longman.

Pati, Biswamoy and Mark Harrison, eds. 2009. *The Social History of Health and Medicine in Colonial India:* London & New York, NY: Routledge.

Perkins, H. 1970 (1962). *Age of the Railway.* Newton Abbot: David & and Charles.

Pollock, Sheldon, ed. 2003. *Literary Cultures in History: Reconstructions from South Asia.* Berkeley, CA: University of California Press.

Porter, Ted. 1995. *Truth in Numbers: The Pursuit of Objectivity in Science and Public Life.* Princeton, NJ. Princeton University Press.

Pouchepadass, Jacques. 1974. 'Local Leaders and the Intelligentsia in the Champaran Satyagraha (1917): A Study in Peasant Mobilization.' *Contributions to Indian Sociology* NS 8 (1): 67–87.

Prakash, Gyan. 1999. *Another Reason: Science and the Imagination of Modern India.* Princeton, NJ: Princeton University Press.

Prakash, Gyan, and Kevin Kruse. 2008. *The Spaces of the Modern City: Imaginary Politics and Everyday Life.* Princeton, NJ: Princeton University Press.

Prasad, Ritika. 2012. 'Smoke and Mirrors: Women and Railway Travel in Colonial South Asia.' *South Asian History and Culture* 3 (1): 33–46.

———. 2013. '"Time-Sense": Railways and Temporality in Colonial India.' *Modern Asian Studies* 47 (4): 1252–82.

Presner, Todd S. 2007. *Mobile Modernity: Germans, Jews, Trains.* New York, NY: Columbia University Press, 2007.

Randall, Don. 2003. 'Autumn 1857: The Making of the Indian "Mutiny."' *Victorian Literature and Culture* 31(1): 3–17.

Rasheed, Abdul, compiler. 1910. *The Travellers' Companion: Containing a Brief Description of the Places of Pilgrimage and Important Towns in India*. Calcutta: Superintendent of Government Printing.

Redfield, Isaac F. 1867. *The Law of Railways: Embracing Corporations, Eminent Domain, Contracts, Common Carriers of Goods and Passengers, Constitutional Law*. Boston, MA: Little Brown.

Reynolds, Nelson Scott. 1999. *Iron Confederacies : Southern Railways, Klan Violence, and Reconstruction*. Chapel Hill, NC : University of North Carolina Press.

Richards, Jeffrey and John M. MacKenzie. 1986. *The Railway Station: A Social History*. Oxford and New York, NY: Oxford University Press.

Richardson, R. C. 2003. 'The "Broad Gauge" and the "Narrow Gauge": Railways and Religion in Victorian England.' In *The Impact of the Railways on Society in Britain*, edited by A.K.B. Evans and J.V. Gough, 101-16. Farnham: Ashgate.

Richter, Amy G. 2005. *Home on the Rails: Women, the Railroad, and the Rise of Public Domesticity*. Chapel Hill, NC: University of North Carolina Press.

Robbins, M. 1962. *The Railway Age*. London: Routledge and Paul.

Robertson, Thomas. 1903. *Report on the Administration and Working of Indian Railways, 1903*. Calcutta: Superintendent of Government Printing.

Roy, Tirthankar. 2000. *The Economic History of India: 1857–1947*. Delhi: Oxford University Press.

Ruskin, John. 1989 (1880). *The Seven Lamps of Architecture*. Mineola, NY: Dover.

Russell, Louis Pitman and Vernon B. F. Bayley. 1903. *The Indian Railways Act IX of 1890 (as Amended by Act IX of 1896) with References to the Corresponding Sections in the Acts relating to Railways in England and India and Notes on the Principal Cases decided thereon, and an Appendix*. Bombay and London: Thacker and Co. and Steven and Haynes.

Sadana, Rashmi. 2010. 'On the Delhi Metro: An Ethnographic View.' *Economic and Political Weekly* xlv (46): 77-83.

Saha, Meghnad. 1922. 'The Great Flood in Northern Bengal.' *The Modern Review: A Monthly Review and Miscellany*, edited by Ramachadra Chatterjee, xxxii (5): 605-32.

Salomons, David. 1847. *Railways in England and in France: Being Reflections Suggested by Mr. Morrison's Pamphlet and by the Report Drawn up by Him for the Railways Acts Committee*. London: Pelham Richardson.

Sangari, Kumkum and Suresh Vaid, eds. 1999 (1989). *Recasting Women: Essays in Indian Colonial History*. New Brunswick, NJ: Rutgers University Press.

Sanyal, N. 1930. *The Development of Indian Railways*. Calcutta: University of Calcutta Press.

Sarkar, Smritikumar. 2010. 'Land Acquisition for the Railways in Bengal, 1850–62: Probing a Contemporary Problem.' *Studies in History* 26 (2): 103–42.

Sarkar, Sumit. 1973. *The Swadeshi Movement in Bengal, 1903–1908.* New Delhi: People's Publishing House.

———. 1983. *Modern India, 1885–1947:* Delhi: Macmillan.

———. 1997. *Writing Social History.* Delhi: Oxford University Press.

———. 2000. *Beyond Nationalist Frames: Postmodernism, Hindu Fundamentalism, History.* Bloomington, IN: Indiana University Press.

Schivelbusch, Wolfgang. 1986 (1977). *The Industrialization of Time and Space in the 19ᵗʰCentury.* Berkeley, CA: University of California Press.

Schroeder, Ralph. 2007. *Rethinking Science, Technology, and Social Change.* Stanford, CA: Stanford University Press.

Scott, David. 2004. *Conscripts of Modernity: The Tragedy of Colonial Enlightenment.* Durham, NC: Duke University Press.

Scott, James C. and Benedict J. Kerkvliet, eds. 1986. *Everyday Forms of Peasant Resistance in South-East Asia.* London: Frank Cass.

Sen Amartya. 1984. *Poverty and Famines: An Essay on Entitlement and Deprivation.* Delhi: Oxford University Press.

Shepherd, A.B. 1871–72. 'Cholera,' in 'Report on Practical Medicine.' In *A Biennial Retrospect of Medicine, Surgery and their Allied Sciences for 1873–74,* vol. LXV edited by Mr. H. Power, Dr. Shepherd, Mr. Warren Tay, Mr. R.B. Carter, Mr. C.H. Carter, and Dr. T. Stevenson, 67-83. London: New Sydenham Society.

Sheringham, Michael. 2006. *Everyday Life: Theories and Practices from Surrealism to the Present.* Oxford: Oxford University Press.

Sidney, Samuel. 1851. *Rides on Railways Leading to the Lake & Mountain Districts of Cumberland &.c &.c.* London: William S. Orr.

Sikangia, Ahmad Akawad. 2002. *'City of Steel and Fire:' A Social History of Atbara, Sudan's Railway Town, 1906–1984.* Porstsmouth, NH: Heinemann.

Simmel, Georg. 1950 (1903). 'Metropolis and Mental Life.' In *The Sociology of Georg Simmel,* edited by Kurt Wolff, 409-24. Glencoe, IL: Free Press.

———. 1950 (1908). 'The Stranger.' In *The Sociology of Georg Simmel,* edited by Kurt Wolff, 402-8. Glencoe, IL: Free Press.

Simmons, Jack. 1986. *The Railway in Town and Country, 1830–1914.* North Pomfret: David & Charles.

Simmons, Jack and Gordon Biddle, eds. 1997. *The Oxford Companion to British Railway History: From the 1660s to the 1990s.* Oxford: Oxford University Press.

Simpson, W. J. 1905. *A Treatise on Plague, dealing with the Historical, Epidemiological, Clinical, Therapeutic and Preventive Aspects of the Disease.* Cambridge: Cambridge University Press.

Singh, Khushwant. 1981(1956). *Train to Pakistan.* New York, NY: Grove Press.

Singh, Praveen. 2008. 'The Colonial State, Zamindars and the Politics of Flood Control in North Bihar (1850–1945).' *Indian Economic* and *Social History Review* 45 (2): 239–59.

Sinha, Mrinalini. 1995. *Colonial Masculinity: The 'Manly Englishman' and the 'Effeminate Bengali' in the Late Nineteenth Century*. Manchester: Manchester University Press.

Sinha, Nitin. 2008. 'Mobility, Control and Criminality in Early Colonial India, 1760s–1850s,' *Indian Economic* and *Social History Review* 45: 1–33.

———. 2012. 'Entering the Black Hole: Between "Mini-England" and "Smell-like Rotten Potato", the Railway-Workshop Town of Jamalpur, 1860s–1940s.' *South Asian History and Culture* 3 (3): 317–47.

———. 2012. *Communication and Colonialism in Eastern India, Bihar: 1760s–1880s*. London and New York, NY: Anthem Press.

Skempton, A.W. 1996. 'Embankments and Cuttings on the Early Railways.' *Construction History* 11: 33–49.

Smith, David Norman. 1988. *The Railway and Its Passengers: A Social History*. Newton Abbot: David & Charles.

Smith, George. 1897. 'John Clark Marshman, 1794–1877: Historian and Journalist.' In *Twelve Indian Statesmen*, 224-44. London: John Murray.

Smith, Neil. 1984. *Uneven Development: Nature, Capital and the Production of Space*. New York, NY: Blackwell.

Srinath, C. N. 1990. 'The Writer as Historical Witness: Khushwant Singh's *Train to Pakistan* and Chaman Nahal's *Azadi*.' *The Literary Criterion* 25 (2): 58–66.

Srinivas, M.N. 1952. *Religion and Society Amongst the Coorgs of South India*. Oxford: Clarendon Press.

Stephenson, R. M. 1845. *Report Upon the Practicability and Advantages of the Introduction of Railways Into British India*. London: Kelly and Co.

Stokes, Eric. 1989 (1959). *The English Utilitarians in India*. Delhi: Oxford University Press.

Stoler, Ann and Frederick Cooper. 1997. 'Between Metropole and Colony: Rethinking a Research Agenda.' In *Tensions of Empire: Colonial Cultures in a Bourgeois World*, edited by Ann Stoler and Frederick Cooper, 1-58. Berkeley, CA: University of California Press.

Strong, F. W. 1912. *Eastern Bengal District Gazetteers: Dinajpur*. Allahabad: Pioneer Press.

Tarlo, Emma. 1996. *Clothing Matters: Dress and Identity in India*. Chicago, IL: University of Chicago Press.

Teruvenkatachariar, M. 1901. *High Court Decisions of Indian Railway Cases with an Appendix Containing All the Indian Railway Acts, the Carriers' Act and Act XIII of 1855 Together with Index*. Trichinopoly: St. Joseph's College Press.

Thapar, Romila. 1996. *Time as a Metaphor of History: Early India*. Delhi: Oxford University Press.

Thomas, William G. 2011. *The Iron Way: Railroads, the Civil War, and the Making of Modern America*. Stanford, CA: Stanford University Press.

Thompson, E.P. 1967. 'Time, Work-Discipline, and Industrial Capitalism.' *Past and Present* 38: 59–97.

———. 1993 (1971). 'The Moral Economy of the English Crowd in the Eighteenth Century,' reproduced in *Customs in Common: Studies in Traditional Popular Culture*, 185-258. New York, NY: The New Press.

Thorner, Daniel. 1950. *Investment in Empire: British Railway and Steam Shipping Enterprise in India 1825–1849*. Philadelphia, PA: University of Pennsylvania Press.

———. 1951. 'Capital Movement and Transportation: Great Britain and the Development of India's Railways.' *Journal of Economic History* 11 (4): 389–402.

———. 1995. 'The Pattern of Railway Development in India.' *Far Eastern Quarterly* XIV: 201-6.

Thorsheim, Peter. 2009. *Inventing Pollution: Coal, Smoke, and Culture in Britain since 1800*. Athens, OH: Ohio University Press.

Tomlinson, B. R. 1978. 'Foreign Private Investment in India 1920–1950.' *Modern Asian Studies* 12 (4): 655–77.

Trevor, Henry Edward. 1891. *The Law Relating to Railways in British India: Including the Indian Railways Act 1890 and the Relevant Portions of Contracts between Government and the Companies*. London: Reeves and Taylor.

Tucker, Richard P. 1993. 'Forests of the Western Himalaya and the British Colonial System (1815–1914).' In *Indian Forestry, a Perspective*, edited by Ajay Singh Rawat, 163-92. New Delhi: Indus Publishing.

Urry, John. *Sociology Beyond Societies: Mobilities for the Twenty-First Century*. London: Routledge, 2000.

Vakil, C.N. 1944 'Railways and Roads in India.' *Annals of the American Academy of Political and Social Science* 233 (India Speaking): 187–192.

Varady, Robert Gabriel. 1981. Rail and Road Transport in Nineteenth Century Awadh: Competition in a North Indian Province. Ph.D dissertation. University of Arizona, Tucson, AZ.

———. 1989. 'Land Use and Environmental Change in the Gangetic Plain.' In *Culture and Power in Banaras: Community, Performance, and Environment, 1800– 1980*, edited by Sandra B. Frietag, 229-45. Berkeley, CA: University of California Press.

Waterfield, Henry. 1875. *Memorandum on the Census of British India 1871–72*. London: Eyre and Spottiswoode.

Watts, Sheldon. 1999. 'British Development Policies and Malaria in India 1897–c.1929.' *Past & Present* 165 (1): 141–81.

Weitering, Dennis. 2007. 'Sharing the Burden: Licensed Porters of Dadar Railway Station, Mumbai, and Their Search for Work, Income and Social Security.' In *27 Down: New Departures in Indian Railway Studies*, edited by Ian J. Kerr. Hyderabad: Orient Longman.

Welke, Barbara. 2001. *Recasting American Liberty: Gender, Race, Law, and the Railroad Revolution, 1865–1920*. Cambridge and New York, NY: Cambridge University Press.

Westwood, J. N. 1980. *Railways at War*. San Diego, CA: Howell-North.

Whitcombe, Elizabeth. 1972. *Agrarian Conditions in Northern India: The United Provinces under British Rule, 1860–1900*. Berkeley, CA: University of California Press.

White, John H. Jr. 1973. 'The Railway Museum: Past, Present and Future.' *Technology and Culture* 14 (4): 599-613.

Wierling, Dorothee. 1995. 'The History of Everyday Life and Gender Relations: On Historical and Historiographical Relationships.' In *The History of Everyday: Reconstructing Historical Experiences*, edited by Alf Ludtke and translated by William Templer, 149-68. Princeton, NJ: Princeton University Press.

Wittfogel, Karl A. 1957. *Oriental Despotism: A Comparative Study of Total Power*. New Haven, CT: Yale University Press.

Yang, Anand. 1999. *Bazaar India: Markets, Society, and the Colonial State in Bihar.* Berkeley, CA: University of California Press.

———., ed. 1985. *Crime and Criminality in British India*. Tucson, AZ: University of Arizona Press.

Yearley, Steven. 1988. *Science, Technology, and Social Change*. Boston, MA: Unwin Hyman.

Zerubavel, Eviatar. 1982. 'The Standardization of Time: A Socio-historical Perspective.' *American Journal of Sociology* 88 (1): 1–23.

Index

About the Author

Ritika Prasad teaches at the Department of History at the University of North Carolina at Charlotte. Her research interests include South Asian history; history of technology; technology and society; colonial and imperial history, nationalism and decolonization; subaltern history; postcolonial theory. She has published in *Modern Asian Studies* and *South Asian History and Culture*.